Contemporary Canadian Marketing Cases

Contemporary Canadian Marketing Cases

SECOND EDITION

H. F. (Herb) MacKenzie
Memorial University of Newfoundland

PEARSON

Prentice
Hall

Toronto

National Library of Canada Cataloguing in Publication

Contemporary Canadian marketing cases / [compiled by] H.F. (Herb) MacKenzie — 2nd ed.

Includes bibliographical references.
ISBN 0-13-120149-2

1. Marketing—Canada—Case Studies. I. MacKenzie, H. F.

HF5415.12.C3C65 2003   658.8′00971   C2002-905499-0

ISBN 0-13-120149-2

Vice President, Editorial Director: Michael J. Young
Acquisitions Editor: Kelly Torrance
Marketing Manager: Deb Meredith
Associate Editor: Pam Voves
Production Editor: Emmet Mellow
Copy Editor: Rodney Rawlings
Production Coordinator: Andrea Falkenberg
Page Layout: Heidi Palfrey
Art Director: Mary Opper
Interior/Cover Design: Alex Li
Cover Image: Getty/PhotoDisc

1 2 3 4 5   08 07 06 05 04

Printed and bound in Canada.

Statistics Canada information is used with the permission of the Minister of Industry, as Minister responsible for Statistics Canada. Information on the availability of the wide range of data from Statistics Canada can be obtained from Statistics Canada's Regional Offices, its World Wide Web site at http://www.statcan.ca, and its toll-free access number 1-800-263-1136.

PEARSON
Prentice
Hall

Contents

Preface

Contemporary Canadian Marketing Cases, Second Canadian Edition, is a collection of 42 marketing cases by many of Canada's best case writers.

Two considerations helped focus my selection of cases. First, I believe that cases provide an excellent basis to build rapport among everyone involved in the case-learning environment; cases should provide fun for and be interesting to both students and instructors. I have tried to include cases on current marketing issues, in the context of a variety of Canadian industries. There are cases that involve tourism and hospitality, ethics, business and agricultural markets, the Internet, co-op marketing, direct marketing, entrepreneurship, laser surgery, health care, service failure and recovery, and international marketing.

Second, I believe that the best cases provide a rich environment for student learning. You will find lots of suggestions in teaching notes to help you decide a teaching strategy for these cases. Many cases can be used for in-class exercises. I have increased the number of more comprehensive cases that are ideal for written assignments or examinations, as well as class discussions. I believe you will find an improved selection of cases in the second Canadian edition, and that they will provide you with the flexibility to personalize a course that will provide enjoyment and learning for you and for your students.

—H.F. (Herb) MacKenzie
Memorial University of Newfoundland

| EXHIBIT 1 | Primary and Secondary Focus of Cases |

		Primary focus	Consumer Markets	Business Markets	Market Analysis	International Marketing	Internet Marketing	Marketing Research	Marketing Ethics	Segmentation/Targeting	Product	Price	Distribution	Promotion	Strategy/Implementation
			Secondary Focus												
1	Financial Exercises	Quantitative analysis	•	•											
2	Pantry Pride	Intro. to marketing strategy	•					•							•
3	Toronto Designers	Intro. to marketing strategy	•	•		•							•	•	•
4	Wing and a Prayer	Intro. to marketing strategy	•										•		•
5	Cott Corporation	Intro. to marketing strategy	•	•	•	•		•			•	•	•	•	•
6	Lifestyle International	Intro. to marketing strategy	•	•									•		•
7	Metropol Base-Fort	Intro. to marketing strategy	•	•	•					•					•
8	Scotian Pride	Intro. to marketing strategy	•	•	•	•					•	•			•
9	Atlantic Waterfowl	Intro. to marketing strategy	•							•				•	•
10	Dillon Controls	Market entry/research		•	•	•		•							•

| EXHIBIT 1 | Primary and Secondary Focus of Cases (continued) |

#	Case	Primary focus	Consumer Markets	Business Markets	Market Analysis	International Marketing	Internet Marketing	Marketing Research	Marketing Ethics	Segmentation/Targeting	Product	Price	Distribution	Promotion	Strategy/Implementation
															Secondary Focus
11	Marketing In-Focus	Marketing research		•				•							
12	Eyckline Farms	Buying decision process		•							•	•		•	•
13	"Greener Pastures"	Segmentation/targeting	•	•	•					•	•	•	•	•	•
14	NCA Microelectronics	Product strategy		•							•				
15	PharmHealth	Product/brand strategy		•							•				
16	Zeneca Group PLC	Brand strategy		•							•				
17	Restored Vision	Service marketing	•								•	•			•
18	Zeneca Ag Products	Service marketing		•							•	•	•	•	•
19	EJE Trans-Lite	Price strategy		•							•	•	•		
20	Atlas Chemical	Price strategy		•	•						•	•			
21	Cdn. Novelty Printing	Channel strategy	•	•									•		
22	Parker Instruments	Channel strategy		•		•							•		
23	Murray Industrial	Channel strategy		•					•				•		
24	Hannas Seeds	Channel strategy	•	•									•		
25	Toronto Door & Trim	Wholesale/retail strategy	•	•						•			•		
26	Union Station Clothing	Retail strategy	•										•		•
27	Amway–Quixtar.com	Direct marketing strategy	•	•			•						•		
28	Wilderness Nfld. Advent.	Promotion strategy	•			•								•	
29	Maritime Trading	Promotion strategy	•				•							•	
30	The Holey War	Promotion strategy	•											•	
31	Provel	Promotion strategy		•							•	•	•	•	•
32	RBC–BMO	Communications strategy	•											•	
33	Industritech	Sales management		•										•	
34	Power & Motion	Selling/sales management		•										•	
35	Sue Jones	Selling/sales management		•										•	
36	Some Ethical Dilemmas	Selling ethics		•					•					•	
37	Health Care Corp.	Selling simulation		•										•	
38	Lucas Foods	Marketing strategy	•	•	•	•									•
39	Artventure	Marketing strategy	•		•										•
40	Rocky Mtn. House	Marketing strategy	•	•	•										•
41	Steinhouse Knitting	Marketing strategy	•	•	•	•									•
42	Agri Train	Marketing strategy		•	•			•							•

Introduction for Students

LEARNING FROM CASES

One of the most valuable experiences for marketing students is the opportunity to participate in marketing case analyses and discussions. However, to benefit most from this experience, it is important to be an active rather than a passive participant. Many students, particularly if their educational experiences have been focused on readings and lectures, find it difficult to do case analyses, and even more difficult to express themselves in case discussions. This is unfortunate because case analyses and discussions can add a whole new dimension to your marketing education and to your personal growth.

While lectures may be the most efficient method of transferring knowledge, case analyses and discussions foster learning through the development of independent thought and creativity, interpersonal communication, and decision-making skills. The focus changes from simple content to both content and process. This means that students must share responsibility for their learning, while instructors must be confident in sharing power in the classroom, encouraging student views and participation. This provides a positive learning environment for everyone. Learning from case analyses and discussions should result from the initial reading of the case and individual case preparation, through small to large group discussions.

INDIVIDUAL CASE PREPARATION

Cases vary in scope. Some are comprehensive cases that require a complete analysis, including consideration of the marketing environment; buyer behaviour; segmentation, targeting, and positioning strategies; and product, price, promotion, and distribution strategies. Other cases are more narrowly focused. You should quickly read through a case, paying particular attention to the opening and closing sections, to gain some idea of what the case involves and what decisions you are required to make.

Then, you should read the case more carefully. This is when you should underline important facts and make notes in the margins concerning your thoughts as you proceed through the case. Some careful thought after this reading will help you decide how to proceed: what decisions you must make, what numerical analysis is important, what alternatives may be appropriate, and what qualitative facts you must consider before making action-related recommendations. A word of caution here is to avoid focusing on one alternative too early. This will constrain your analysis. In most situations, there are several good alternatives, and effective managers recognize that different courses of action may enable an organization to meet its objectives.

Once you have completed your analysis, it is time to think about action—what you will do. It is sometimes easy to argue that more information is needed before you should act, but the reality is that many times, managers are required to make decisions with incomplete or imperfect information. You may need to make some assumptions, and you should test the robustness of those assumptions. For example, your success may depend very much on competitive reaction to your market strategy. You may need to assume that a competitor response will be to reduce its price by 10%. What effect will this have on the success of your strategy? What if the competitor reduces its price by 15%, or even 20%? How would this affect your performance? Would these competitor price reductions require additional changes in your marketing strategy?

A final recommendation when doing individual case preparation is to stay within the context of the case. While you may have information relating to events subsequent to the writing of the case, you should try to ignore this information when doing your analysis and deciding your recommendations. Cases are written concerning problems and issues at a particular point in time, and the situations that the decision-maker faced at that time. You should analyze the case with the information that the decision-maker had as that is the information that would have determined his or her actions. After the case discussion, or at a point where the instructor requests, you may wish to contribute additional knowledge.

While you can do too little analysis on a case, you can also do too much. You need to consider what you are expected to do with your case analysis. If you are to make a formal class presentation, or to hand in a written analysis and action plan, more time and effort will be required than if you are preparing for a large group discussion. For most cases, you should spend two to four hours doing your individual analysis. Cases can, if you are not careful, take all of the time you allow them. Beyond some point, however, there is a diminishing return from working alone on a case. You need to consider participating in a small group discussion.

SMALL GROUP DISCUSSIONS

In some classes, you may be assigned to a small discussion group or you may wish to consider forming your own group. Discussing your analysis and recommendations among a small group of peers allows you to refine and test your thinking. It provides additional learning opportunities for all participants. Many students feel more comfortable presenting and defending their recommendations, and the assumptions they have used, in this environment. To be effective, groups should consist of approximately four to six members committed to doing individual case analyses before the meetings and making contributions during the meetings. The duration of these small group discussions may vary depending on the case, but you should expect to spend 20 to 30 minutes for each meeting.

LARGE GROUP DISCUSSIONS

In an effective case course, the most significant learning takes place in large group discussions. Even if your instructor has organized the course around formal group presentations, there is usually time for questions and discussions after each presentation.

To get the most from large group discussions, you should be committed to actively participating. You must be able to listen to what others are saying and follow where the discussion is going. That means you should limit, or eliminate, note-taking. It is difficult to listen to what others are saying if you are focused on taking notes. That is a strategy you use when someone is transferring knowledge to you; for example, during a lecture. During large group discussions, you should be learning from the process, not focusing simply on the content. It is important to listen to understand what is happening if you wish to make an appropriate contribution. At the end of an effective case discussion, you should be able to review what has happened and to summarize what you have learned from the experience.

Participation is essential when working with case analyses. Some students find this process exciting and challenging, while others are intimidated and fear speaking in a large group of their peers. Small group discussions prior to class often help. Another consideration is your seating position in class. Some students gravitate to the back of the class as they find this seating position less threatening. You may wish to consider moving forward. Many students find it easier to participate from the front row. From that seating position, the size of the classroom seems smaller, and the interaction with the instructor seems more personal.

Also, participation becomes easier with practice. Like most worthwhile skills, if you do not practise, you will not improve. By partaking early on in the dialogue, it is often easier to continue making contributions as the case continues. For students less confident during discussions, another good opportunity to participate is when the direction of the discussion changes. As your confidence increases, you can increase your involvement in large group discussions.

MARKETING STRATEGY

When developing marketing strategies, managers must consider both internal and external factors that may affect marketing decisions. A marketing strategy is a plan of action focused on developing, pricing, promoting, and distributing need-satisfying goods and services to target customers. The development of a marketing strategy requires the consideration of many aspects. It often helps to have an outline to guide your thinking. Organized around internal and external analysis and action, Exhibit 1 provides a framework of factors to consider during this development.

EXHIBIT 1	A Framework for Case Analysis and Action
Internal Analysis	
Objectives	Strengths/Weaknesses
Sales growth	Marketing and sales (people and knowledge)
Market share	Other personnel
Increased profit	Financial condition
Product development	Costs and revenues
Innovation	Marketing information systems
Quality (products and service)	Production capacity
Reputation and image	Distribution channels
Employee satisfaction	Reputation and image
	Quality (products and service)

EXHIBIT 1	A Framework for Case Analysis and Action (continued)

External Analysis

Customers	Competitors
Size and growth	Relative size or market share
Segments (sizable, measurable, accessible, responsive)	Market leaders or followers
Purchase criteria (quality, price, service, etc.)	Strengths and weaknesses
Roles (initiator, user, influencer, decider, buyer, gatekeeper)	Reaction profile (aggressive or passive)
Relationship needs (transactional, or long-term orientation)	
Buying conditions (limited or extended problem-solving; new task buy, straight rebuy, or modified rebuy)	
Search (extent and type)	

Opportunities/Threats	Distribution Channels/Suppliers
Competition	Relationships (power, dependence, interdependence, cooperation)
Buyer needs (unmet, changing)	Availability, development, capacity
Channels (availability, development capacity)	Technological capabilities
Resources (human, financial, material)	Financial condition
Technology	Cost
Market (size, growth, share)	
Economic conditions	
Political and legal changes	

Action

Product	Price
Quality (higher, competitive, lower)	Level (premium, competitive, low)
Service (superior, competitive, inferior)	Discounts (cumulative, noncumulative, trade, cash, seasonal)
Warranty or guarantee, and level	
Branding (generic, family vs. independent, manufacturer vs. distributor)	
Line (depth and breadth)	
Packaging	

Promotion	Distribution
Objectives (inform, persuade, remind)	Intensity (intensive, selective, exclusive)
Budget	Motivation (margin, support)
Mix (advertising, personal selling, sales promotion, publicity)	
Push vs. pull (or both)	

As you can see from this exhibit, there are many things to consider at the analysis stage, and many more to consider before deciding a course of action. A framework helps reduce confusion by providing a basis for beginning your analysis and for deciding action. Hopefully, you will find it useful, and the case process enjoyable and rewarding.

Financial Analysis Exercises

H. F. (Herb) MacKenzie

Fundamental to any marketing analysis is an analysis of the financial and economic data relevant to each situation. You must understand what the numbers are telling you: where you are. This, along with more qualitative considerations, will suggest various courses of action. You must then be able to assess the effect of implementing these actions on financial performance: where you will be.

The following exercises provide the opportunity to practise sales, markup, and breakeven analyses, and analyses related to each element of the marketing mix.

A. SALES ANALYSIS

Canada Controllers, Inc. manufactured electric motor starters and motor control centres, used in all types of industrial plants, including mines, pulp mills, and manufacturing plants. Motor starters were installed on or near individual pieces of equipment and usually operated only a single motor. They ranged in price from $50 to several thousand dollars. Motor control centres consisted of dozens or even hundreds of motor starters that were combined in a customized enclosure and were capable of starting motors in various locations of the plant from a centralized location. They ranged in price from less than $50 000 to several hundred thousand dollars.

Analyze the following sales data for Canada Controllers, Inc.

Year	Company Sales	Industry Sales
1998	$ 10 250 970	$ 74 600 000
1999	$ 11 844 888	$ 92 300 000
2000	$ 13 384 152	$ 111 700 000
2001	$ 14 722 155	$133 500 000
2002	$16 040 063	$158 900 000

Analyze the following sales data for 2002.

Product Line	Company Forecast	Company Sales	Industry Sales
Control centres	$ 2 500 000	$ 3 233 727	$ 20 250 000
Motor starters	$ 11 500 000	$ 10 406 040	$ 122 400 000
Repair parts	$ 2 000 000	$ 2 400 296	$ 16 250 000
Total	$16 000 000	$16 040 063	$158 900 000

Analyze changes in the following sales data from 2001 to 2002.

Product Line	2001		2002	
	Sales (units)	Sales ($)	Sales (units)	Sales ($)
Control centres	28	$ 1 766 740	38	$ 3 233 727
Motor starters	16 775	$ 11 041 600	18 305	$10 406 040
Repair parts	*	$ 1 913 815	*	$ 2 400 296
Total		$14 722 155		$16 040 063

*Unit volume of repair parts not monitored.

B. MARKUP ANALYSIS

1. Northgate Convenience store wishes to sell two cans of either Coke or Pepsi for $1. If the store does not sell anything at a markup lower than 25%, what is the maximum price that it can pay for a can of either brand?

2. Tom Thompson owns an apple orchard in Alberta. He was hoping to sell his apples at roadside for $0.59 per pound, and he wanted to make a 50% markup based on his total growing cost. What is the highest cost Tom can have to produce his apples and achieve his goals?

3. Harvey Hornswaggle has just left Newfoundland for a job in Cambridge, Ontario. He has decided to bring along a truck full of partridgeberry jam, and he has been busy buying it from all the people he knows who make it. He has been paying $2 per jar for 500 millilitre jars, and he hopes to sell them through grocery wholesalers around the Toronto area. According to his friend, Fred Nitney, wholesalers generally expect to make 20% markup on their cost, and retailers generally will not sell items like this unless they make 30% markup on their selling price. Harvey thinks he should make $1 per jar. What is Harvey's markup on his cost? What is Harvey's markup on his selling price? What price will Mrs. Consumer have to pay in order for all channel members to achieve their desired margins?

C. BREAKEVEN ANALYSIS

1. Geeta, Khawla, and Ann Marie were three final-year university students who decided to operate an on-campus business producing and selling novelty t-shirts that also promoted their university name. At first the university was somewhat uncooperative, but eventually it decided to allow the students to have an unused room in the student union building for a nominal charge of $800 total for the 8 months during the regular school year. Although they were allowed to use the university name, they were prevented from using the official university logo. The young women decided that they each wanted $2000 income for the year for operating the business. Advertising and promotion costs were estimated at $400 for the year. They decided that the selling price for their t-shirts would be $12, and their best estimate of required sales to break even was 1800 shirts.

   a. What was the variable cost?

   b. What was the contribution margin?

   c. What was the margin as a percentage of sales?

   d. What was the margin as a percentage of cost?

2. Moose Elbow Archery manufactures a high-quality crossbow for hunting. The company has been in business for three years, and its anticipated fixed costs for 2004 are estimated at $200 000. It sells the crossbow for $250 to retailers throughout North America. The company's variable cost to produce each crossbow is $200. Sales for 2004 are expected to be $1 250 000.

   a. What is the breakeven point in units?

   b. What is the breakeven point in dollars?

   c. What is the company's expected profit for 2004?

   The owner's daughter, a business student at a Western Canadian college, thought that the 2004 sales forecast was too optimistic. She forecasted sales of only $875 000.

   d. What would the company's expected profit be if her estimate is accurate?

   e. If the owner of the company believed that his daughter's forecast was correct, should he shut the company down?

3. Peter Rushton operated a small bakery and deli that also sold most items at wholesale as well as retail. Many of his bakery items were sold to retailers around the city, who then resold his items to their customers. Peter reviewed his sales for 2002:

	Bakery	Deli	Wholesale
Sales	$372 201	$217 544	$443 265
Cost of goods	77 413	84 566	117 022
Contribution	294 788	132 978	326 243

Peter's major problem is that he has limited space. He only has 6 tables in his deli, each with 2 seats. The backroom operations where he prepares many deli items for his catering business is also limited. Peter now has an opportunity to rent the retail space next door to his business as the current owner has left. This would increase his rent by $48 000 per year. He estimates that it would also cost approximately $30 000 to do renovations to make the new area acceptable.

How much additional business does Peter need to make to cover his increased costs?

D. EVALUATING ADVERTISING EFFECTIVENESS

You are the advertising manager for a firm that manufactures piping products for the pulp and paper, and petrochemical industries. You have been working with a national advertising firm to develop an advertisement. You have decided to place it in trade magazines targeted at purchasing agents in these industries, and to also develop it for a more targeted direct mailing to a list of 1000 purchasing professionals that work in these industries. To control advertising expenses, you will use exactly the same ads for both advertising campaigns. The results of the two campaigns follow:

- *Campaign A.* You have placed the ad in two trade magazines: *Pulp & Paper Canada* and *Canadian Oil & Chemical.* The cost to advertise in the first magazine was $4745, and to advertise in the second magazine was $4350. It was expected the ad would be read by 700 purchasing agents in the target industries. The ad generated 206 inquiries, and 105 were later qualified by telemarketers (an average of 4 calls per hour, and they were paid $16.50 per hour) as worthy of followup by a sales representative. The ad was believed responsible for 28 sales, averaging $63 344 with a 21.4% gross margin.

- *Campaign B.* A copy of the ad was mailed to 1000 purchasing professionals on a mailing list that had been purchased for $1100 from a mailing list supplier. Other costs included printing, $1285; cover letters and envelopes, $115; and postage, $990. The ad resulted in 310 inquiries, and 164 were later qualified by telemarketers (an average of 4 calls per hour, and they were paid $16.50 per hour) as worthy of followup by a sales representative. The ad was believed responsible for 44 sales, averaging $41 445 with a 22.2% gross margin.

E. EVALUATING SALESPERSON EFFECTIVENESS

You are the sales manager for a large Canadian consumer goods company, and you are evaluating three salespeople that were hired last year. Salespeople work 230 days per year, and the average across your entire sales force was 8 sales calls per day. Which of these salespeople are the most effective, and why?

Salesperson	Karen King	Bob Bishop	Anne Hand
Territory	Calgary	Toronto	New Brunswick
Calls per day	10	8	6
Direct selling costs	$72 000	$74 000	$82 000
Conversion rate (orders/calls)	22%	26.1%	29%
Average sales/call	$3666	$4123	$3255
Average gross margin	21.1%	22.7%	23.3%
Average time per sales call	32 minutes	42 minutes	36 minutes

F. EVALUATING DISTRIBUTION CHANNELS

Upper Canada Clothing Company has been selling its industrial clothing across Canada for over 20 years. It has a four-member sales force, three are in Ontario and one is in Quebec. Total sales by this sales force in 2003 were $3.9 million. Total industry sales for competing products in Ontario and Quebec was $15.8 million. The company also has four manufacturer's agents, who are paid an 8% commission on sales. Their 2003 performance follows:

Territory	No. of Agents	Sales	Market Share
British Columbia	2	$ 886 458	17.5%
Alberta	2	$ 742 458	13.4%
Saskatchewan and Manitoba	2	$ 1 244 553	19.5%
Atlantic provinces	3	$ 937 887	26.3%
Total		$3 811 356	

The agents that sell your clothing sell between three and eight other non-competing product lines. One of the agents in British Columbia has recently complained about the commission she is being paid, and has informed you that your major competitor is paying its agents a 10% commission. You have decided that it is time to reassess your channel strategy. You are wondering whether you should continue with your current strategy, or replace all manufacturer's agents with company salespeople. The direct selling costs (salaries and selling-related expenses) for each salesperson you hire would be $90 000. You would need one salesperson for each territory. After an analysis of the situation, what would you recommend?

G. EVALUATING PRODUCT LINES

As the product manager responsible for the artificial tree line of a manufacturer of Christmas-related products, with plants in three provinces, you have been instructed to review the four items manufactured at your plant to see if one or more items could be eliminated. The company has added so many items to its product mix over the past decade that the president has decided to reduce the number of items by 20 to 40%. Each product manager has been asked to do a similar analysis. What would you recommend to the president based on the following information?

Product	Suggested Retail Price*	Projected 2004 Unit Sales Volume	Estimated Average Growth Rate 2005-2009
Spruce	$ 90	31 000	10%
Blue spruce	$100	46 000	12%
Fir	$140	62 000	6%
Pine	$180	10 200	4%
Production overhead costs		$800 400	
Plant administrative expenses		$ 140 510	
Allocation of corporate overhead		$ 110 500	
Inventory turnover		2.2 times per year	
Inventory carrying costs		5.25%	

Direct variable cost as a percentage of manufacturer's selling price:

Spruce	75%
Blue spruce	73%
Fir	75%
Pine	80%

* All sales were through retailers who insisted on a markup of 50% on sales, and who expected shipments F.O.B. destination. The cost of shipping trees averaged $2.50.

The company did not have a sales force, but sold through manufacturer's agents who received a 5% commission on sales.

Pantry Pride Stores

H. F. (Herb) MacKenzie

Brenda Howley was a marketing consultant in Somewhere, Ontario. She and her husband, Cameron Porter, a prominent corporate tax lawyer, earned a combined income over $250 000 (before taxes). They had two small children, both under five years of age.

Brenda enjoyed grocery shopping as it gave her a break from her professional and family obligations. She referred to it as "mindless" work, but she prided herself on being good at it. Brenda usually alternated between two major grocery chains in her town, Pantry Pride Stores and Freshway.

Following a series of dissatisfying experiences at one of her regular grocery stores, she decided to write to the company president. Her letter follows.

EXHIBIT 1	Letter to President of Pantry Pride Stores

October 23, 1998
16 Eden Loch Road
Somewhere, ON
E9E 3Z8

President
Pantry Pride Stores
555 Garden Place
Mississauga, ON
L9Q 8Y8

Dear Sir or Madam:

I write you today because I have been a customer of Pantry Pride Stores for over 30 years, but I am increasingly disturbed by a series of experiences I have had at the Victoria Street location in our town.

Over the past year, I have been charged incorrect prices at the checkouts seven times—three times at your competitor, Freshway, and four times at Pantry Pride. I must say, I admire the response I received each time at Freshway, but I have left your store dissatisfied each time. Let me recount some of my experiences for you so that you might appreciate the difference between what I have experienced at both stores.

My first experience was at Freshway. I had purchased a 2-litre container of ice cream. When I went through the checkout, I was overcharged $0.50. The ice cream was supposed to be on sale for $2.59, but the scanner read the regular price of $3.09. I complained to the woman at the service desk, and she insisted that I accept a full refund of $3.09. I told her I would be happy to simply get my $0.50, but she insisted that it was store policy that when customers get charged the wrong price at the checkout, they get a full refund and get the item free of charge. She refunded my money, apologized for the mistake, and asked me to please return to the store for my future grocery needs. Since then, I have had two similar experiences at Freshway.

Now, I will recount four experiences at your store. My first experience was about a year ago. I was overcharged $1 on a bottle of olive oil. I took it to the service desk and advised the woman there that I had been overcharged for the item. At that point, I did not know that you had a similar policy to Freshway, and I did not care as I was perfectly willing to settle for a $1 refund. However, the woman on the service desk asked another employee standing nearby to check the price. The second woman seemed visibly displeased that someone should ask her to do a price check, and that may explain her subsequent behaviour. I watched her stop to talk to one of the cashiers on her way to the grocery aisle, and when she finally disappeared down the aisle and failed to return after about 10 minutes, I went to see if she were still there. She was having a personal conversation with another shopper, so I returned to wait at the service desk to see how long the whole process would take. During this period, I read your sign that explained store policy with respect to overcharged prices. Eventually, when the woman returned from doing her price check, she did not address me at all, but simply said to the woman at the service desk, "She's right. Give missus a buck." As you might expect, I was quite upset with the process at this point, and I took further exception to being called "missus." I immediately informed her that I recognized her as a long-time employee of Pantry Pride Stores, and that I would have expected her to know her store policy better than me. I told her I would be pleased to explain it to her if she had not had the opportunity to read it. I grudgingly got a refund on the item.

With respect to my second experience, I admit the error was partly mine. I saw a sign that advertised white onions on special, and I decided to buy one. When I got to the checkout, I was charged a higher price than the advertised special. I asked that the price be checked, and the cashier held it in the air and asked one of the male employees who was nearby to check the price. His comment was, "One onion! &$*%#!" I mentioned to the cashier that he appeared to be having a bad day and her comment was, "Oh. That's just Ken. He's always having a bad day." The result after the price check was that the price charged was correct. Apparently, I just took a

EXHIBIT 1	Letter to President of Pantry Pride Stores (continued)

large white onion from under the sign that advertised white onions, but I really had a Spanish onion (as were all of the others under the sign). I simply paid the price and left.

On the third occasion, which occurred less than two months ago, I noticed the service desk was very busy and, to save time, I remarked to the cashier that I should get an item free as it was scanned at the checkout at a price higher than advertised. She tried to tell me that as I had not paid for the item, she could simply adjust the price. When I insisted that was unacceptable as she did not catch the error, she called over a supervisor who asked the same question, "Did she pay for it yet?" When told no, she instructed the cashier to adjust the price. I objected again, and the store manager was called for a third opinion. He agreed with me that the store policy stated that the customer would receive any item free if it scanned at a price higher than advertised at the checkout, and he instructed the cashier to deduct the item from the sale. He remarked to the two women, "Remember, we talked about this last week." I left the store thinking that customer service improvements were about to be made.

Unfortunately, late one evening last week, I had my most dissatisfying experience. When overcharged by a young man at the cash register, he asked another cashier (which happened to be the same one I had my previous experience with) what he should do. She told him to give me $0.50 and to put a note in the cash register and someone would fix it in the morning. I informed her that I was more knowledgeable with respect to store policy than she was, and that she should get some additional training as we had already been through this about a month previously. Her remark, in front of a dozen customers, was "We were told by the manager not to mention this policy unless the customer mentions it first."

That was very unsettling. First, it indicates that this store grudgingly implements store policy, and only for those customers who know what it is and who insist on it. It further implies that employees at this store are willing to take advantage of less knowledgeable customers, or those customers who are less likely or unwilling to complain. In my view, this is very unethical marketing behaviour. It is also disturbing that someone in a management position in your company supports that employees will, unknowingly or, worse, knowingly, act in an unethical manner with respect to your customers. Those employees who realize that they are being asked to behave unethically may be uncomfortable doing so and, in a better economic climate, may seek employment elsewhere.

I apologize for the length of my discourse, but I want you to be aware that the problem you have at this location is not an acute one. When I talked last year to the president of one of Canada's largest hotel chains, he explained his philosophy of customer guarantees to me. I recall he commented, that for them to be effective, customers must know what the guarantees are, they must receive compensation when the company fails with respect to its promises, and employees must see that the company pays when they fail. I would suggest that you either scrap this store policy, or that you train your managers as to why it is important and why it should be implemented properly.

Sincerely,

Brenda L. Howley

Brenda L. Howley

c.c.   Manager, Pantry Pride Stores
        Somewhere, ON

When she finished writing her letter, Brenda mailed a copy to the president. She then decided to visit Pantry Pride for one of her regular shopping trips, and she took a carbon copy of the letter, intending to personally deliver it to the store manager.

Toronto Designers

H. F. (Herb) MacKenzie

Susan Abramson, founder and owner of Toronto Designers, was reviewing the company's 2001 financial performance. She recognized that many small companies had difficulties in their first years of operations, but she was quite pleased with what she had accomplished in her first year of business. Still, she was considering ways to grow her business and make it more profitable.

The concept for her company was quite simple. Toronto Designers acted as an agency for a group of decorators, designers, and architects. When clients were considering hiring people to supply one of these services, they often had difficulty finding the best service provider—one who had both the expertise and the personality to meet their needs. Toronto Designers would match the correct service provider to individual clients, and for that service, it would charge a commission to the service provider based on the value of the service they delivered to the client. Aside from promoting her business to new clients, Susan's major concern was how Toronto Designers could maintain relationships with existing clients, because, once they were matched to an appropriate service provider, the relationship that developed was then between that service provider and the client. To complicate things more, Susan was considering

This case was written by H. F. (Herb) MacKenzie, Memorial University of Newfoundland, Faculty of Business Administration, St. John's, NF A1B 3X5 as the basis for classroom discussion. It is not intended to illustrate effective or ineffective business management. © 2002 by H. F. (Herb) MacKenzie.

operating a second business as a partnership, and she was concerned there might be a conflict of interest between the two businesses if she were to do so.

SUSAN ABRAMSON

Susan Abramson grew up in Montreal, and graduated with a Bachelor of Commerce degree from Concordia University in 1985. After moving to London, England, she came to realize her real interests were in interior design and decorating, and she enrolled at the Regent Academy of Fine Arts, where she earned a degree in interior design. Ottawa followed London, and Susan began her career helping clients with interior decorating projects. When she moved to Toronto in 1997, Susan enrolled at Seneca College and earned a degree in interior decorating.

While studying for the latter, Susan held a position in the home fashion department of one of Canada's major retailers. It gave her the opportunity to gain additional experience, but it was not very satisfying. She did not have any opportunity to express her creativity. The retailer's head office would dictate what was to be on display and how the displays were to be organized. One day, one of Susan's co-workers mentioned that she had formerly had a business that might be available to Susan, and she thought it was something Susan would enjoy. It was a consulting referral service that matched clients looking for interior design and decorating services with service providers. She provided Susan with the new owner's contact name. Even though the new owner did not seem very interested in the business, Susan was unable to come to an agreement with the woman to take it over. After further discussing with her co-worker how she had operated the business, Susan decided to start her own business, as she was interested in the concept and she didn't feel the other woman would really offer much competition.

TORONTO DESIGNERS

When Toronto Designers was first in the concept stage, Susan called a number of interior designers and decorators around the Toronto area whose names she got from the Yellow Pages or the Internet. She offered to refer business to them if they agreed to pay her 10%, the commission suggested to her by her co-worker who had originally given her the idea. She quickly found four designers and decorators who were interested and she began operating Toronto Designers in earnest. The only startup costs for the business included approximately $2000 for a computer and $300 for miscellaneous office supplies. Toronto Designers was operated from Susan's home, and she appreciated the freedom this gave her to see her two young daughters each day.

Over the first year, the number of service providers who signed on grew and at one point reached 20 people, but by the end of the year, she had settled on 10 with whom she felt most comfortable. Her portfolio of service providers included:

- One architect
- One designer/architect (really a designer with some architectural skills)
- Four designers (three capable of handling both residential and commercial projects; one specializing in "atmospherics" and feng shui)

- Four decorators (one whose husband was a general contractor/cabinetmaker; one who was a very take-charge person who likes to aggressively manage her projects; two who specialize in residential projects, but are capable of handling commercial projects as well)

The concept worked because many people were unsure of their needs when they wanted help with interior decorating or design. In fact, many were not even able to tell whether they needed a decorator or a designer, or whether they might need an architect. By calling Toronto Designers, people could discuss their needs with Susan, and she would then match their needs not only on the basis of required technical skills, but also on the basis of personality.

There was no cost to clients for this service. Once a service provider was selected, they managed the whole project directly with the client, and they paid a 10% commission to Toronto Designers, based on the revenue they received from the project. If for some reason the client did not pay, Toronto Designers waived the commission on that particular project. Contracts that Susan signed with the service providers also stipulated that commissions on first referrals would also be paid to Toronto Designers. That is, if a client referred the service provider to another client, the service provider would pay a commission on the revenue earned from that referral to Toronto Designers as well. However, if the new client made an additional referral, Toronto Designers no longer expected a commission. One of the major issues faced by Susan Abramson was how to build strong relationships with clients so that referrals were made to Toronto Designers rather than directly to service providers.

The relationships between Toronto Designers and the various service providers were necessarily based on trust. For that reason, Susan determined that she would not continue to refer business to any service provider who was not committed to an honest working relationship with Toronto Designers. In the first year of business, two decorator/designers were dropped because of honesty issues. It was increasingly easy for Susan to find good service providers committed to working with Toronto Designers because there was a growing number who wished to accept referrals from the agency. Now, many new designers and decorators were actively contacting her asking to be included.

CLIENTS

Most clients who called Toronto Designers wanted decorating advice. Susan estimated that approximately 75% of her business came from interior decorating projects, 15% from interior design projects, and 10% or less from architectural projects. It was difficult to get a better breakdown because many projects overlapped in what was required.

Toronto Designers referred 127 projects in 2001, and earned revenue of $10 015. Most interior decorating projects were two-to-four-hour consultations, for which clients paid between $200 to $500. For these smaller projects, the interior decorator would simply visit the client, ask questions concerning their decorating issues and what they preferred, and make recommendations that the clients could then implement themselves. The largest individual project was referred to the decorator Susan described as her "most forceful" personality. Susan said, "She handled 15 projects for me in 2001, and I would say 8 of them were very successful. I'm learning where to recommend her and where to recommend someone else. She is very good, but she is also the type of person who likes to really manage the whole project. Clients who are willing to have someone simply 'do it' get along well with her. She paid me $2700 commission for one project in 2001, and she told me she owes me about $500 for additional work that she did on the same project in 2002."

Occasionally, there were problem clients, but these were the responsibility of the service providers and not of Toronto Designers. Susan made sure that clients understood that Toronto Designers' responsibility ended once a referral was made to the client. The most notable example was a client who contracted for a large project that included a $50 000 wall unit. The client paid a deposit of $3000 and the service provider paid Toronto Designers an initial $300 commission. However, when the job was completed, the client balked at paying for it because he was upset that he had not been given a choice of the molding that was used on the unit. The service provider eventually renegotiated her fees but was lucky to break even on the project. In this instance, Susan waived the commission payable to Toronto Designers.

GROWTH OPPORTUNITIES

Just as Susan was considering how she could grow her business, an unusual opportunity arose. A friend she met while studying at Seneca College suggested that the two of them start an interior decorating / design business together. The two women appeared to have different but very complementary skills. While Susan's background included a business degree, Rachel McGarry had earned a degree in psychology at York University, and this helped her understand how people's personal environments could impact their lives. While Susan had the communications and interpersonal skills to manage business relationships, Rachel had been inspired to pursue interior decorating because of her strong artistic talents in sewing, drawing, and painting. While both women were talented decorators, Rachel, who particularly loved children, was developing a reputation for creating fun, funky bedrooms for them.

The opportunity was attractive, because Susan, operating Toronto Designers, already had a source of potential clients. She could simply refer clients to the new business operated by herself and Rachel. Once clients were referred to the new business, either Susan or Rachel could manage the project, depending on client needs. Alternatively, they could team-manage the project and both could be involved in each project. If they decided to do this, Susan thought it would work best for projects involving a minimum of four hours of consultation. They could meet with clients, discuss their needs, make recommendations, and with Rachel's artistic skills leave each client with a package that detailed the recommendations and that illustrated the newly decorated space.

Among the other things Susan was considering was raising her commission rate. If she could raise it from 10% to 15%, that would increase her commission revenue by 50%, and it would give her more money that she could spend on promoting Toronto Designers, hence getting more contracts she could refer to her portfolio of service providers. In 2001, Susan had spent $450 for ads in the Yellow Pages, covering three areas in and around Toronto. She also spent $77 per month to advertise in *Toronto Life*, approximately $60 per year for an Internet domain name, $8 per month to host her Web site, and $250 for a sign to advertise Toronto Designers on her Honda CRV.

For 2002, Susan was considering a direct mail campaign. A friend who operated a printing business told her he could produce a three-fold quality brochure for $400 per thousand. That would make the cost of delivering a single brochure approximately $1, including postage, a cover letter, and an envelope. Susan thought she could target some of the more upscale neighbourhoods in Toronto and that she could get a quality mailing list for about $0.06 per name if she bought 10 000 names, or $0.10 per name if she bought 3000 names. An alternative to mailing the brochures was to deliver the brochures to the homes. An advantage of this was that Susan could cover very targeted neighbourhoods by simply distributing brochures to one side of the street, saving the other side for a later campaign if it was felt necessary.

Susan was sure she could come up with more ideas, but her first decision was whether to commit exclusively to Toronto Designers, to commit to the new partnership she was considering, or to try to manage both businesses. If she chose the first or third alternative, she would need to consider how to build stronger relationships between Toronto Designers and clients. Once she was clear about what business she wanted to be in, Susan could consider her marketing strategy more carefully.

Wing and a Prayer

Marvin Ryder

Stefan Bakarich had found just the right name for his mobile bungee jumping operation—"Wing and a Prayer." It was March 1994, and he had eight weeks to the May Victoria Day Weekend—the first long weekend of the summer. If he had it figured correctly, Stefan would rent a construction crane, assemble a group of friends, and tour southwestern Ontario offering bungee jumps at tourist attractions. He and his friends could earn enough money to return to university in the fall while being paid to have fun and work on their tans over the summer.

SOME HISTORY

Bungee jumping started as a ritual practised by "land divers" on Pentecost Island in the New Hebrides of the South Pacific. To cleanse themselves of wrongdoing or as acts of courage, native men constructed 30-metre towers from thin trees. Climbing to the top, they dove off with vines tied around their ankles. Their heads would just touch the ground as the vine became taut. In the 1960s, a group of Oxford University students (who called themselves the Oxford Dangerous Sports Club) brought bungee jumping to the modern world. As a commercial curiosity, the sport was born in New Zealand in 1988 where ancient vines were replaced with modern man-made fibre cords tested to withstand more than 1361 kilograms, and where bamboo pole towers were replaced with bridges spanning deep river gorges.

The sport became popular on the west coast of the United States in the late 1980s and swept across the country in the early 1990s showing phenomenal growth. In 1991, only 20 companies in the United States offered bungee jumps. In 1992, that number had grown to 200 and by 1993, more than 400 companies in the United States were in the bungee jump business. Participation in the sport had also grown. In 1992, 1.5 million Americans experienced a bungee jump, spending more than $100 million for the thrill. In 1993, 2.5 million Americans participated, spending more than $125 million.

In Canada, the first commercial bungee operation (Bungy Zone) opened south of Nanaimo on Vancouver Island on August 4, 1990. By 1993, 30 000 people had jumped at this one site. Some Bungy Zone statistics: oldest jumper 73, youngest 14; and heaviest 150 kilograms. The most paid bungee jumps by one person was 30. The typical jumper was a thrill-seeking male aged 18 to 25. Ninety-nine percent of people who paid the fee completed the jump. Ten percent of jumpers took a second jump on the same day. Participation statistics were not available for Canada but, in 1993, there were about 35 companies which arranged bungee jumps off bridges, towers, cranes, and hot air balloons. The West Edmonton Mall had introduced indoor bungee jumping. Nanaimo had even hosted bungee jumping in the nude.

Stefan had taken his first bungee jump in May 1993. He tried to describe his experience to a friend.

> I dove straight out, in my best imitation of Superman. At first, the free-fall was exhilarating. But it was also disorienting, and after a moment I panicked. I wished there were something to grab hold of. The sound of the wind was almost deafening. The ground below rushed toward me, until everything became a blur. It was hard to believe that I was feeling 3Gs—just like airforce pilots.
>
> Suddenly, the world seemed upside-down. The ground was receding, and now I was completely confused. I was up in the air again when I realized that the cord had held.
>
> I started to descend once more. This time, there was no fear, just enjoyment. I rebounded up and down four more times, with each rise becoming smaller. Finally, the bungee cord had no more bounce, and I was lowered onto the pad where my feet were untied. Friends told me I had The Look—a certain glow common to those who had just found God or had escaped the electric chair.

During the summer of 1993, Stefan took a bungee jump training course, worked for two-and-a-half months at an amusement park in the United States, and jumped 150 more times.

OPERATIONS

Stefan's experience with a crane-based company inspired him. He had taken careful notes about its operation so that he could replicate its success in Canada. For a typical jump, a patron would be taken, in a specially designed metal cage, 40 metres to the top of a crane—a ride of 60 seconds. These jump platforms were available for $500 to $1000 though Stefan thought he could design and build one over the next eight weeks. At the top, the patron would be placed in one of two harnesses and given special instructions about jumping. One harness went around a person's ankles so that he or she would fall head first. The feet were tightly bound together with a towel and tethered to the bungee cord by a nylon strap and carabiner, a common piece of mountaineering equipment. The other harness could be strapped around a person's waist so that he or she would fall feet first. Each harness was commercially available at a cost of $150 to $300. While the patron took some time to build courage, the length of the bungee cord was adjusted to that person's weight. These "top of crane" activities could take between two and four minutes. Jumping out from the cage and away from the crane, the patron would take three seconds to fall until the bungee cord became taut and caused them to bounce. Waiting for the bouncing to stop, lowering the basket, retrieving the jumper, and removing the harness from her/him would take another two minutes.

Stefan had researched potential suppliers so he had a firm estimate of costs. He would have to pay $100 per operating hour for construction crane rental which included $1 million of liability insurance, fuel to run the generator, and a driver. Given the lack of office building construction, many companies had cranes parked in their compounds. These construction companies had been quite interested in Stefan's lease proposal. A crane operator would cost an additional $40 per operating hour. He felt the cost was justified as a skilled employee operating the crane would minimize the chances of something going wrong.

He and a jump assistant would be on the jump platform helping with instructions, adjusting the bungee cord, strapping on the harness, and communicating via walkie-talkie to the crane operator. On the ground, one person would use a microphone and sound system to speak to any crowd which had gathered and encourage them to participate. Two other people would assist on the ground by getting potential patrons to sign a liability waiver form, weighing jumpers to determine the proper bungee cord, collecting the jump fee, and talking personally with patrons in the crowd. While people under 18 could jump, a parent's or guardian's signature would be required on the waiver form. Excepting the crane operator and himself, all staff would each be paid $8.00 per operating hour.

Of course, a bare crane was not very attractive so Stefan would have to invest $700 in some cloth banners which, when hung on the crane, would also be used for promotion. Some portable tables, folding chairs, walkie-talkies, and a sound system would have to be purchased for $1700. This cost also included portable "snow" fencing which would be used to limit public access to the crane, jump platform, and retrieval area. During less busy times, the sound system would play "hip hop," "dance," "house," and "rap" music to help attract and build a crowd. His major cost was an inflatable target pad that would be used to catch a jumper only if the bungee cord broke. Though pads came in many sizes, he felt it was a wise precaution to choose the largest size available at a cost of $12 000. As he thought the business would have a three-to-five-year life, the pad and other equipment could be used year after year.

He had modelled his fee schedule on the American amusement park: $65 for the first jump and $55 for a second jump on the same day. If the patron used the waist harness rather than the ankle harness, both prices were reduced by $10.

Realistically, the company would operate for the 110-day period from the Victoria Day weekend in late May to the Labour Day weekend in early September. As he did not want to be bothered with portable lighting, he would start operations no earlier than a half-hour after sunrise and cease operations no later than a half-hour before sunset. The company would never operate during a thunderstorm or in high winds and Stefan thought that the start of a week and overcast/rainy days would see less demand for the service.

SAFETY

Bungee jumping was not without its risks. In August 1992, a man was killed in Peterborough, Ontario when he jumped from a crane. That same year, two people died in the United States and one in New Zealand from accidents. The Canadian Standards Association, a nonprofit agency, had not determined any rules for bungee jumping so regulations varied by province. Some provinces had no regulations but Ontario, working with the Canadian Bungee Association, had amended the Amusement Devices Act to regulate bungee jump operations starting in the spring of 1994.

In the legislature, Ontario Consumer and Commercial Affairs Minister Marilyn Churley said, "Operators can't just take a construction crane and set it up and have people jump off. We don't think that's safe. The government is committed to establishing and enforcing safety standards to minimize the risks to Ontarians who take part in this activity. Maintaining high standards of safety may also limit bungee operators' exposure to lawsuits and reduce the high cost of liability insurance."

Bungee jump operators were required to obtain a licence and permit ($310 fee) from the ministry prior to any jumps taking place. Before a licence could be issued, the operators' equipment designs first had to be approved by ministry engineers ($400 fee) after which a thorough on-site physical inspection of the bungee operation would be completed ($200 fee). The technical dossier of designs was to include: the jump height; a description of bungee cords including manufacturer, type of cord, and weight range of jumpers; an indication if the jump is static or portable; a description of the hoisting device including name of manufacturer, year, serial number, and safe working load; depth of water or air bag; type of harnesses to be used and types of jumps offered; wind speed restrictions; and number and function of jump personnel.

A 40-page code of safe conduct for bungee jumping operations was also in place. The code had been recommended by the Task Force on Bungee Jumping, a working partnership between government and the Canadian Bungee Association. The code required a number of safety features that must be in place on bungee equipment and technical specifications for the structure, platform, bungee cords, harness, and all other equipment used in the activity. It also outlined the qualifications for bungee jump employees including certificates in first aid and cardio-pulmonary resuscitation (CPR), and training specific to bungee jumping. Another requirement was a good first aid kit with a spinal board and speed splints which would cost an operator an additional $500.

These changes were introduced to regulate careless operators and were aimed primarily at mobile bungee operations as they had less experienced staff and more failure-prone equipment as it was repeatedly set up and dismantled. Prior to the legislation, some operators had voluntarily introduced dual carabiners for ankle harnesses so there was a backup if one failed.

Stefan planned his own set of rules. No pregnant women. No people with heart conditions. No people with high blood pressure. No people who suffered from epilepsy. No people with neurological disorders. Especially no people under the influence of alcohol and drugs. He would allow no reverse jumping (anchoring and loading the bungee cord from the ground to propel the jumper upward), no sandbagging (loading excess weight with the jumper to be released at the bottom to gain more momentum) and no tandem jumping (two or more jumpers harnessed together).

A bungee cord was made from several bound strands of latex rubber, doubled back on itself thousands of times, sheathed in cotton and nylon. The cost of these cords varied from $300 to

$1000. The cord could stretch to five times its original length. For safety, most operators retired a bungee cord after 150 jumps. Prior to the popularity of jumping, these cords were used by the U.S. Air Force on aircraft carriers, and so were constructed to military specifications.

SOME DECISIONS

To start his business, Stefan needed capital to acquire bungee cords, harnesses, the landing pad, and his operating equipment. He was aware of two Ministry of Economic Development and Trade loan programs. As a returning Canadian university student, he could apply for a $3000 interest-free loan. To qualify for this loan, he had to be over 15, returning to school, and operating a business in Ontario between April 1, 1994 and September 30, 1994. Whatever loan amount he received would be payable on October 1, 1994.

He had also heard of the Youth Venture Capital Program. It provided loans of up to $7500 to help unemployed Canadian youth aged 18 to 29 start a business in Ontario. The interest rate on the loan would be prime plus 1% and he would be expected to make principal and interest payments each month. He would also be expected to contribute a minimum of one-quarter of the loan amount to the operating capital of the firm. This program was not intended to fund a summer job experience.

Neither program would provide him with all the capital he required. He approached his parents. While not completely sold on the venture, his parents thought it would be a good learning experience so they agreed to loan him $3000 interest-free though they expected to be repaid at the end of the summer.

Needing more money, Stefan shared his plan with Zach Thompson, a friend on the university water polo team and a recent bungee jumping enthusiast. Zach had also worked part-time with a bungee jump operator but he had only jumped 40 times in the last year. He would act as a jump assistant. Zach proposed a partnership and a joint application for any government loan. Profits would be split 50-50. Like Stefan, he would replace a "paid" worker on the jump crew but would not draw any hourly wages. Of all people Stefan contacted, Zach asked the most questions.

Where would they operate the business? Stefan thought they could create a base of operations in Grand Bend. When special events occurred, like the Western Fair in London, Ontario, or the Zurich Bean Festival, they could pull up stakes and move to that location for a few days.

Would they only offer bungee jumps? Zach thought they could sell some complementary products. A colourful logo could be designed for Wing and a Prayer and applied to t-shirts and baseball caps. Selling for $20 and $10 respectively, these items would have a 100% markup on cost and could add extra revenue. Zach had also thought about selling a personalized video. That would mean purchasing a camcorder ($1800), developing some stock footage for opening and closing credits, and somehow editing/processing on-site the video footage shot so the patron could quickly get her/his tape. Zach thought they could sell the videos for $25. Building on these ideas, Stefan thought about offering a colourful poster that might be especially popular among children. To produce 1000 posters would cost $800 but they could be sold for $4 to $6, generating a very healthy profit margin.

Would they make any money? That required some financial analysis, including a breakeven analysis. Zach felt they needed to assess a second scenario: the likelihood that they would make enough money to return to university in the fall. These analyses would be needed along with their marketing plan when any loans were sought.

If this was going to be their summer occupation, they needed to get started right away.

Cott Corporation

H. F. (Herb) MacKenzie

Cott Corporation is the world's largest supplier of retailer-branded, carbonated soft drinks, producing and distributing products to mass-merchandise, grocery, drugstore, and convenience store chains from its 15 beverage manufacturing facilities in Canada, the United States, and the United Kingdom. For example, Cott produces private-label brands for Wal-Mart in the United States, and President's Choice drinks for Loblaw Cos. Ltd. in Canada.

Cott began operations in Quebec in 1952, importing carbonated beverages from the United States. Eventually, the company started producing its own product in Canada. Expansion followed to Ontario, western Canada, and the Atlantic provinces, and to both the United States and Europe. Cott has differentiated itself through innovation, and by producing quality products, providing superior service, and achieving cost efficiency. Cott's growth can be largely attributed to these factors and to its strategic retail branding and category management expertise, which it customizes to meet the specific needs of each retail customer.

Because Cott manufactures branded products for its customers, its products compete with manufacturer, or national, brands for shelf space and for sales in retail stores where they are sold. Its largest competitor is the U.S.-based Coca-Cola Company, the global soft-drink industry leader. Coca-Cola has approximately 21% market share of the nonalcoholic, ready-to-drink beverage market in both Canada and the United States; however, the company and its subsidiaries sell products in nearly 200 countries around the world. Approximately 70% of volume and 80% of profit come from global markets. When Cott-produced products compete with Coca-Cola products outside Canada and the United States, special issues may arise due to changes in the market environment.

In Britain, for example, the largest supermarket chain, J. Sainsbury PLC, contracted with Cott Corporation for the supply of a retailer-branded cola. At the time, Coca-Cola had a 60% share of the £670-million cola market. The Sainsbury cola was packaged in red-and-white cans, as was Coca-Cola. Where "Coca-Cola" was written vertically down the can, Sainsbury had "Cola" written in a similar but slightly more silvery red script. The Sainsbury brand also had the word "Classic" on the can, along with "Original American Taste." Sainsbury stocked the competing products side by side, but priced its private-label brand 25% less than the "real thing." While Coca-Cola might have sued, it is questionable whether it could have won. The cola giant would have had an easier time almost anywhere else in Europe where many countries have a general concept of unfair competition, a concept missing from British law which focuses on a narrow definition of trademark.

In Japan, there exists one of the world's most competitive soft-drink markets. Approximately 500 manufacturers offer more than 7000 different soft drinks, and introduce about 1000 new ones annually. Cott Corporation does not yet operate there; however, Coca-Cola Japan manages more than 25 brands and 60 flavours. The company and its Japanese partners maintain 930 000 vending machines, as this method of distribution accounts for more than 50% of all soft drink sales there. Some years, Japan has provided as much as 20% of the company's global profit. However, the company's most popular product in Japan is not its flagship brand, but a milky sweet drink called Georgia coffee.

In the future, if Cott wishes to continue its strong growth trend, it may wish to consider entry to Japan or some other Asian market.

Lifestyle International

Joseph J. Schiele

In September 1997, Christina Blake, general manager of Vitality's Canadian operations, located in Windsor, Ontario, faced the following problem. She had just been notified that her company would be merging with Long-Life and Healthy Choice, two other direct selling companies, to form one company known as Lifestyle International. Christina was assigned the task of managing the merger between Vitality and Long-Life's Canadian operations. After reviewing the situation, Christina wondered what action she should take next.

DIRECT SELLING

Direct selling involved the sale and distribution of a company's products and services through a network of distributors. Distributors were independent contractors who purchased products directly from a company for their own use and for resale to retail consumers.

Direct selling enabled distributors to become involved on a part- or full-time basis. Companies concentrated their efforts on encouraging individuals to develop their own

Prepared by Joseph J. Schiele, Faculty of Business Administration, University of Ottawa. Revised by H. F. (Herb) MacKenzie, Faculty of Business Administration, Memorial University of Newfoundland. Support for the development of this case was provided by the Direct Selling Education Foundation of Canada. © 1999 by the Direct Selling Education Foundation of Canada. Reprinted with permission.

business, at their own pace, without the costly expense inherent in franchise operations or other startup enterprises. Direct selling gave individuals the opportunity to go into business without significant risk, yet offered them significant upside potential, albeit wholly dependent upon their own efforts.

Direct selling used word-of-mouth advertising to grow and capture market share. It was people talking to other people, sharing something that they believed in. In addition, direct selling allowed an individual to leverage his or her time, talent, and energy to earn commissions from sales to all the people that were introduced to the business.

Compensation plans developed for distributors provided several opportunities for distributors to earn money. Each distributor was required to purchase and sell products in order to earn compensation. Distributors could not simply develop a down-line sales organization or receive payment based upon the recruitment of new distributors.

The first method of earning a commission through a direct selling system was through commissions on sales volumes generated by a distributor's down-line sales organization. This organization consisted of additional distributors introduced to the company by the distributor.

A direct selling company's ability to increase sales was significantly dependent on its ability to attract, motivate, and retain distributors. A company did this by utilizing a marketing program which it believed was superior to programs offered by other direct selling companies. Programs provided financial incentives, distributor training and support, low-priced starter kits, little or no inventory requirements, and little or no monthly purchase requirements.

INDUSTRY OVERVIEW

The World Federation of Direct Selling Associations estimated that 1998 Canadian retail sales by direct selling sources would amount to $1.6 billion. The percentage of sales by major product groups was as follows: home and family care products (cleaning, cookware, and cutlery, etc.), 11%; personal care products (cosmetics, jewellery, and skin care, etc.), 30%; services and miscellaneous, 14%; wellness products (weight loss, vitamins, and nutritional supplements, etc.), 36%; and leisure items (books, toys, and games, etc.), 9%. Canadian retail sales by direct selling sources were expected to experience an average annual growth rate of 10 to 15% over the next five years.

The location of these sales, that were sold to an estimated 1.3 million distributors, reported as a percentage of sales dollars, was as follows: in the home, 75%; in the workplace, 10%; over the phone (in a followup to a face-to-face solicitation), 11%; and at temporary or other locations (fair, exhibition, shopping mall, etc.), 4%.

The sales strategies used by direct selling companies to generate sales varied considerably. These methods, as a percentage of sales dollars, were as follows: individual one-on-one selling, 65%; party-plan or group selling, 29%; and customers placing an order directly to the firm (following a face-to-face solicitation), 6%.

COMPETITION

Vitality, Long-Life, and Healthy Choice marketed and sold a variety of products including herbal remedies, vitamins, food supplements, skin and personal care items, household and commercial cleaners, and water purification systems. They competed with many other companies marketing similar products to those that they sold. They also competed directly with other direct selling companies in the recruitment of distributors.

Not all companies sold all the types of products marketed by Vitality, Long-Life, and Healthy Choice. For example, some competitors were known for and identified with sales of herbal formulations, others with household cleaning and personal care products, while others were known for and identified with sales of nutritional and dietary supplements. Some competitors also marketed products and services in addition to those that Vitality, Long-Life, and Healthy Choice sold.

Another source of competition in the sale and distribution of health and nutrition products was from direct retail establishments such as large retailers, independents, and non-category stores (e.g., drugstores). The most prominent retailer was the General Nutrition Center (GNC) which had a number of retail stores located both in the United States and in Canada.

There were also many direct selling companies with which the companies competed for distributors. Some of the largest of these were Amway, Herbalife International Inc., Rexall Sundown Inc., Market America Inc., and Relive International Inc. Vitality, Long-Life, and Healthy Choice competed for these distributors through a marketing program that included its commission structure, training and support services, and other benefits.

PROPOSED MERGER

Background

In September 1997, Christina Blake was notified that her company, Vitality, would be merging with Long-Life and Healthy Choice, two other direct selling companies, to form one company known as Lifestyle International. This merger would form one of the world's largest and most dynamic direct selling companies. With hundreds of thousands of distributors, 600 full-time employees, and 52 distributor service centres in over 33 countries around the world, Lifestyle International would be well positioned to serve the market within which it operated.

Exhibit 1 presents summary information for Healthy Choice, Long-Life, and Vitality with respect to the dates each company was founded and the countries within which they operated.

EXHIBIT 1	Summary Information for Healthy Choice, Long-Life, and Vitality		
	Healthy Choice	Long-Life	Vitality
Founded	1970	1975	1983
Market presence	Eastern Europe	Caribbean Islands	United Kingdom
	Western Europe	Asia	Ireland
	Africa	Canada	Eastern Europe
		United States	Western Europe
			Canada
			United States
			Mexico

As part of this initiative, Christina was assigned the task of managing the merger of Vitality and Long-Life's Canadian operations. The two companies were to move into one Canadian location, and conduct business as one company. The proposed merger was intended to take advantage of each company's strengths and established distributor network. Christina's task was to effect this change as efficiently as possible without anyone losing their job from either company.

LIFESTYLE INTERNATIONAL VALUES

Lifestyle International had identified a set of core values that would guide everything it did. These values included:

- *People are number one.* Lifestyle International was committed to putting people first. It believed the first step to achieving any goal was to focus on the needs of the individual.
- *Products that satisfy.* In order to create lifelong customers, Lifestyle International was committed to offering only those products that satisfied the needs and wants of consumers.
- *Complete integrity.* Lifestyle International was committed to conducting itself with complete integrity in all aspects of its business.
- *Opportunity for all.* Regardless of sex, race, age, politics, religion, education level, or culture, Lifestyle International was committed to ensuring all people would have equal access to Lifestyle International products and business opportunities.
- *Long-range thinking.* Lifestyle International was committed to taking a long-range approach to all company decisions to ensure growth and stability of the company for many years to follow.

LIFESTYLE INTERNATIONAL MISSION STATEMENT

Lifestyle International's mission was to provide ongoing opportunity for financial security and independence through the development of a successful business; to provide each person with the support needed in the development and attainment of his or her full potential; to provide a continuous supply of superior health-related products to meet the needs of people everywhere; and to cause Lifestyle International to become a household name, recognized for its products and sought after as an excellent business opportunity.

VITALITY: GENERAL COMPANY BACKGROUND

Company Structure

Vitality was a large U.S.-based company with operations throughout the world. Christina Blake was the general manager of its Canadian operations, which were a separate legal entity registered in the Province of Ontario. She reported directly to the vice-president of operations for the United States. Christina was educated at York University. She had worked in various progressive positions for several multinational companies across several industries. Christina had joined Vitality in 1990 as general manager.

Vitality's Canadian operations, which consisted of one 400 square metre office and warehouse facility located in Windsor, Ontario and approximately 139 square metres in a public warehouse facility located in western Canada, served as an independent sales, marketing, and distribution company for Vitality products in Canada.

The Windsor location was responsible for managing all aspects of the Canadian operation including inventory control, administration of the company marketing plan, accounting, distributor network management and administration, and commission cheque calculation and issuance. All transactions, inventory control, and record-keeping were managed using a sophisticated computerized system.

Management and General Workforce

Six people were employed in Canada who worked from Vitality's Windsor office. These included Christina Blake, General Manager; Sharon Newson, Operations Manager; Mary Elise, Distributor Services; Tricia Martin, Inventory Control and Purchasing; Liz Clayson, Order Entry and Communications; and Craig Barnes, Warehousing. Vitality's Western Canada location was staffed by a single individual who performed general shipping and receiving duties for the region.

Exhibit 2 gives an organizational chart for Vitality's Canadian operation.

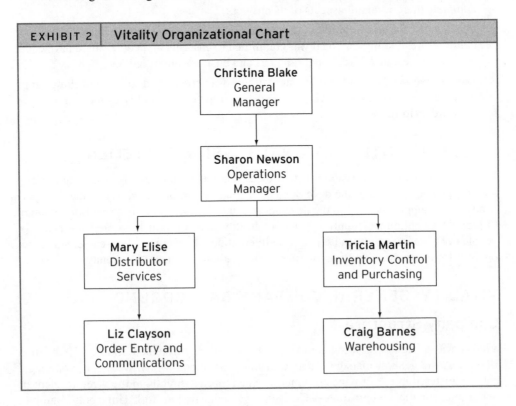

EXHIBIT 2   Vitality Organizational Chart

Corporate Culture

The people who worked for Vitality's Canadian operation conducted themselves in a highly professional manner, meeting at scheduled times, and proceeding from day to day in a very formal fashion. In addition, workers were also highly team-oriented, always working together to ensure that corporate goals and objectives were met.

Vitality management continuously challenged employees on a regular basis to ensure personal growth and advancement. Goal-setting and training contributed to the professional advancement of staff. All Vitality employees constantly looked for ways to improve upon the operation and felt a strong commitment to the work that they did.

In addition, Vitality's Canadian employees had a strong understanding of the corporate marketing plan and operation in general. Christina believed that was the result of the extent to which the Canadian operation was maintained and controlled by the Windsor head office located in Canada.

Products Sold—Description

Vitality sold and marketed a variety of health-related products across various regions in Canada, including Nova Scotia, Ontario, Manitoba, Alberta, and British Columbia. These products included herbal remedies, vitamins, food supplements, skin and personal care items, household and commercial cleaners, and a water purification system that were all sourced from a company-owned manufacturer located in the United States.

Shipments of these products were ordered and received monthly and inventory levels were determined by the Windsor head office on the basis of anticipated sales volumes.

Sales and Marketing

Distributors were supported by a marketing plan that used Vitality's reputation for offering high-quality products as a basis to promote the company. This marketing plan provided distributors with discounts on products purchased from the company that were based on the sales volumes of a distributor's personal sales and a distributor's down-line distributor network.

The number of active distributors who sold and marketed Vitality products across Canada during 1993, 1994, 1995, and 1996 was 7200, 9100, 8300, and 9200, respectively. These distributors had contributed to the steady increase in sales revenues for the same period.

Sales and Profitability

Vitality's Canadian sales and profitability had remained relatively stable over the last four years. Aside from a slight decrease in 1995, sales levels had increased steadily. Sales levels for 1993, 1994, 1995, and 1996 were $2.3, $2.7, $2.4, and $2.7 million dollars, respectively.

LONG-LIFE: GENERAL COMPANY BACKGROUND

Company Structure

Long-Life was a large U.S.-based company with operations throughout the United States and Canada. Shelly-Lynn Costa was the operations manager for Long-Life's Canadian operations. She reported directly to the vice-president of operations for the United States.

Long-Life's Canadian operation consisted of one 492 square metre office and warehouse facility, located in Windsor, Ontario that served as a distribution centre for Long-Life products in Canada. This facility's primary role was to provide Canadian distributors with product and sales support and to warehouse the products sold and marketed in Canada.

Long-Life's Canadian operations were heavily dependent upon the U.S. head office for corporate services such as inventory control, accounting, marketing, and commission cheque calculation and issuance. All general day-to-day transactions and record-keeping were managed using a manual recording process. An outdated computer terminal that linked Long-Life's Canadian operation to the United States was used to input current inventory levels from which the U.S. head office would determine how much new inventory would be sent to the Canadian operation. For the most part, computers were not used within Long-Life's Canadian operation.

Management and General Workforce

Four people were employed in Canada who worked from Long-Life's Windsor office. These included Shelly-Lynn Costa, Operations Manager; Lisa Bartow, Distributor Relations; Alice Pistone, Shipper and Receiver; and Dave Milstone, part-time Office Assistant.

Exhibit 3 shows an organizational chart for Long-Life's Canadian operation.

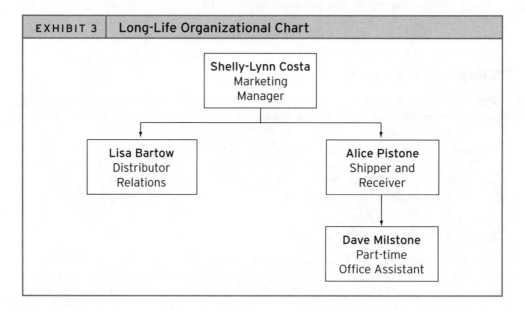

EXHIBIT 3	Long-Life Organizational Chart

These people worked collectively to provide the support necessary to Long-Life's Canadian distributors. All other Long-Life employees worked out of the U.S. head office.

Corporate Culture

The people who were employed at Long-Life's Canadian operation worked in a rather casual and relaxed environment. People often met informally and proceeded from day to day in a carefree fashion. Employees generally worked independently of each other, performing the duties that related to their specific jobs.

Employees at Long-Life did not feel very challenged by their activities from day to day. There was limited goal-setting or planning for personal development. Most of the staff were content on maintaining the roles that they had performed for the company during the last several years.

In addition, aside from senior management, Long-Life's Canadian employees had limited knowledge of the corporate marketing plan or operation in general. Christina believed that this was the result of the extent to which the Canadian operation was maintained and controlled by the head office located in the United States.

Products Sold—Description

Long-Life sold and marketed a variety of health-related products across various regions in Canada, including Nova Scotia, Quebec, Ontario, Alberta, and British Columbia. These products included herbal remedies, vitamins, food supplements, skin and personal care items, household and commercial cleaners, and a water purification system that were all sourced from the manufacturer located in the United States that Vitality owned.

Shipments of these products were ordered and received monthly and inventory levels were determined by the U.S. head office on the basis of anticipated sales volumes.

Sales and Marketing

Distributors were supported by a marketing plan that used Long-Life's reputation as an excellent business opportunity as the basis for promoting the company. This plan provided distributors with discounts on products purchased from the company that were based on the sales volumes of a distributor's personal sales and a distributor's down-line distributor network.

The number of active distributors who sold and marketed Long-Life products across Canada during 1993, 1994, 1995, and 1996 was 5100, 8200, 3300, and 1100, respectively. During 1995 and 1996, approximately 7000 distributors left Long-Life to join another direct marketing company formed by one of Long-Life's senior executives. This decrease in the number of active distributors contributed to the dramatic decline in sales revenues for the same period.

Sales and Profitability

Long-Life (Canada) sales and profitability varied over the last four years. Aside from a significant increase in sales for the 1994 period, sales and profitability had dramatically declined. Sales levels for 1993, 1994, 1995, and 1996 were $1.7, $2.5, $0.86, and $0.31 million dollars, respectively. The company had experienced a net loss for the 1995 and 1996 periods.

DECISION

Having the information that she felt relevant, Christina wondered what action she needed to take next.

Metropol Base-Fort Security Group

Stephen S. Tax and
Walter S. Good

Pat Haney, president of Metropol Base-Fort Security Group (Metropol), was sitting in his office contemplating the future direction of his company. Metropol, a leading Canadian security firm whose services included the provision of uniformed security guards, mobile security patrols, polygraph testing, insurance and criminal investigations, and a broad range of specialized services, was faced with a number of challenges that threatened its future profitability. "Increasing competition, especially from large multinationals such as Pinkertons, is further reducing already low industry margins," Pat had said. He was also concerned about Metropol's reliance on the commodity-like security guard business for 90% of its revenue. "We have to find some way to meaningfully differentiate our services from those of our competitors," Pat observed. "That is essential if we are to achieve the kind of growth we desire."

COMPANY BACKGROUND

Metropol was founded in Winnipeg, in 1952 by George Whitbread, a former RCMP officer. He perceived the need and profit potential in providing security services to the

Written by Stephen S. Tax under the supervision of Professor Walter S. Good as a basis for classroom discussion rather than to illustrate either effective or ineffective handling of an administrative situation. Copyright by Case Development Program, Faculty of Management, University of Manitoba.

business sector, particularly at large industrial sites such as hydro installations and mines in northwestern Ontario. At the time, most businesses' security needs were not being met.

By 1970, the company had grown to such an extent that Mr. Whitbread could not run and control the operation on his own, so he hired a couple of assistants. That turned out to be a big mistake, as the assistants proved to be relatively ineffective.

By 1975, Mr. Whitbread had become so frustrated trying to manage the business on his own that he hired former Manitoba Premier Duff Roblin to act as a consultant to the firm. Mr. Roblin ended up purchasing the firm.

Pat Haney joined the firm in 1976. He was hired to run the Winnipeg operation, which at the time was 80% of the firm's business. It was also expected that Pat would develop an overall marketing program for the company. "My experience was in the computer field," declared Pat. "When I first heard about Metropol Security I thought it was a stocks and bonds company."

In the late 1970s and early 1980s, Metropol expanded into Saskatchewan and Alberta and was aggressively seeking acquisitions. Finally, in 1984, it merged with Base-Fort Security, the leading security firm in Alberta and a major competitor in British Columbia and a number of other areas in Canada. Pat believed this move offered economies of scale, as well as other benefits, and was an important step toward making Metropol a national company.

Sales topped $30 million in 1985, making Metropol the third-largest security company in Canada. Offices were maintained in British Columbia, Alberta, Saskatchewan, Manitoba, Quebec, the Northwest Territories, and Newfoundland, with 70% of the business coming from western Canada.

THE SECURITY INDUSTRY

Security products and services were purchased by individuals and businesses as a means of reducing the risk of loss or damage to their assets. The amount of security purchased depended on individual risk preferences, their perception of the degree of risk involved, and the value of the assets to be protected. Security, therefore, was very much an intangible product subject to individual evaluation.

The industry offered such services as unarmed uniformed security guards, mobile patrols, investigations, and consulting and education, as well as "hardware" products such as alarms, fences, locks, safes, and electronic surveillance devices (ESDs) and monitoring equipment. Most companies purchased a package combining various services and hardware systems. "It would not make much sense to have 50 television monitors and only one person watching them," Pat pointed out, "nor would it be wise to have 50 security guards roaming around a building which had no locks on the doors."

There were a number of factors that contributed to the competitive nature of the security industry. All a firm needed to enter the business was to open an office. Startup costs were minimal, and no accreditation was required by the company or its employees. Clients considered the cost of switching from one firm to another quite low, so their business often went to the lowest-cost provider. Most customers really did not understand the difference in services provided by the various competitors in the security business, which made differentiation very difficult. Pat found, in studying the financial statements of the large multinational security firms, that most security companies earned pretax profit margins of about 4% on gross sales.

The 1985 security guard and private investigation markets in Canada were worth about $400 million retail. ESDs and other types of "hardware" added close to another $400 million to this figure at retail prices.

Growth was expected to continue in the security field for a variety of reasons, including a general increase in the level of risk around the world, the rising cost of insurance, economic growth, technological innovation that created new security problems, and the increasing sophistication of security system purchasers. The ESD and security guard segments were expected to outpace basic hardware sales growth (Exhibit 1).

On the negative side was the industry's poor reputation for the quality and reliability of its services. This perception threatened to limit growth and provide an opportunity for new competitors to enter the market.

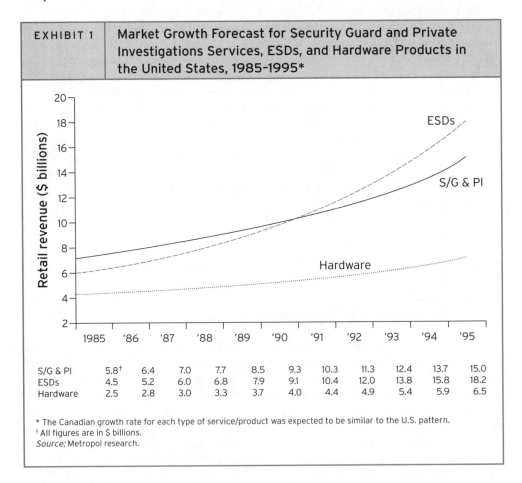

EXHIBIT 1	Market Growth Forecast for Security Guard and Private Investigations Services, ESDs, and Hardware Products in the United States, 1985-1995*

	1985	'86	'87	'88	'89	'90	'91	'92	'93	'94	'95
S/G & PI	5.8†	6.4	7.0	7.7	8.5	9.3	10.3	11.3	12.4	13.7	15.0
ESDs	4.5	5.2	6.0	6.8	7.9	9.1	10.4	12.0	13.8	15.8	18.2
Hardware	2.5	2.8	3.0	3.3	3.7	4.0	4.4	4.9	5.4	5.9	6.5

* The Canadian growth rate for each type of service/product was expected to be similar to the U.S. pattern.
† All figures are in $ billions.
Source: Metropol research.

COMPETITION

Metropol's competition came in both a direct and an indirect form from a variety of competitors. "We compete with other firms who primarily offer security guard services as well as a number of companies that provide substitute products and services," observed Pat.

There were literally hundreds of security guard businesses in Canada ranging in size from one or two ex-policemen operating out of a basement to large multinational firms such as Pinkertons, Burns, and Wackenhut. Metropol was the third-largest firm in the country with a 7% market share (Exhibit 2). It was the leading firm in western Canada with a 25% share of that market.

EXHIBIT 2	Major Security Guard Companies Operating in Canada (ranked by market share)		

Company Name	Canadian Revenue ($ millions)	Employees	Market Share (%)
1. Pinkertons	50	4600	12.5
2. Burns	30	4500	7.5
3. Metropol Base-Fort	30	2000	7.0
4. Wackenhut	12	2000	3.0
5. Canadian Protection	12	1700	3.0
6. Barnes	12	1500	3.0
7. Phillips	10	1200	2.5
Canada	400	40 000*	100%

*In-house guards could raise this figure by as much as 100%. However, a better estimate would be 50–60%, as in-house accounts use more full-time staff. This means that there are more than 60 000 people working as guards or private investigators at any time. Further, with turnover at close to 100% annually, there are over 100 000 people working in this field over the course of a year.

Source: Metropol Research.

Hardware products served as the foundation of a good security system. Although items such as fencing, lighting, alarms, safes, and locks were to some extent complementary to the security guard business, they also competed with it—firms could substitute some portion of either their security guard or hardware expenditures for the other.

Insurance had been long a favourite substitute for security and other loss-prevention services. Business spent more on insurance than all forms of security products combined. However, falling interest rates, a series of major disasters around the world, and a trend to more generous damage awards by the courts were making insurance a more expensive alternative. Faced with higher premiums, lower limits, and higher deductibles, businesses were likely to consider spending more on loss-prevention products and services.

The various levels of government also provided some basic protection services to companies (fire, police, etc.). However, their services were geared more to personal than business protection. These government services tend to set the base level of risk in a community. Tight civic budgets were not permitting these services to keep pace with the growth in crime and the increase in value of corporate assets. This provided the private security business with an opportunity to fill the void.

Businesses were spending almost as much for ESDs and related services as for security guard services. There were a number of different ESD products ranging from small electronic gadgets to the very popular central station monitoring systems. ESDs were the fastest-growing segment of the security industry. The principal attribute of these products was that they provided accurate and reliable information to whoever was responsible for responding to a problem situation. Thus, to a large extent, these products were really productivity tools that enhanced the performance of security guards, the fire department, and/or the police force. They did tend to reduce the amount of security guard service needed. Some security-conscious firms with large-scale security needs hired their own internal (in-house) specialists. In most cases they would also hire guards from companies such as Metropol to do the actual patrolling.

The primary basis of competition in the security business was price. However, this was as much the fault of small, poorly managed firms and large multinationals trying to "buy market share" as it was a fundamental characteristic of the industry. "I've seen companies bid under cost," observed Pat, "and they did not necessarily know they were doing it. It is a very unprofessional business in that sense. If you offer superior service and give a customer what he wants, in most cases you don't have to offer the lowest price. Just recently the Air Canada Data Centre job went to the highest bidder. Lowering your price is very easy, but not the way to succeed in this business." However, because price was a key factor in getting jobs, cost control became crucial if profits were to be made. Pretax margins of 4 to 8% quickly disappeared if unanticipated costs occurred.

MARKET SEGMENTS

The market for security products and services could be segmented in a variety of ways such as by type of service, type of business, geographic location, sensitivity to security needs, government versus private companies, and occasional versus continuous needs. Metropol segmented its customers and the rest of the market using a combination of the above bases as outlined below and in Exhibit 3.

- *Large security-conscious organizations (private and public).* The common feature among these companies was that they had the potential for heavy losses if security was breached. They typically had high-value assets, such as computers or other high-tech equipment, or valuable proprietary information as in the case of research and development firms. These buyers were usually quite knowledgeable about security and rated quality over price. This group included firms in both local urban and remote, rural locations.

- *Organizations for whom security was a low priority.* This group was dominated by local companies, commercial property management companies, and branches of firms that were headquartered elsewhere. They were less knowledgeable about security and tended to have limited security programs. They were price-sensitive and principally utilized low-cost security guards.

- *Government organizations.* Government organizations (non-hospital) typically awarded contracts on the basis of a tendered price for a predetermined period of time, usually one to two years. The price for these contracts was commonly in the vicinity of the minimum wage plus 5%.

- *Occasional services.* These included anything from sporting or entertainment events to social or emergency services. Contracts were seasonal, as with a CFL or NHL sports team, or one-time affairs. Wages paid to the security personnel were usually quite low, but profit margins to the firm were above average.

BUYER BEHAVIOUR

The buyer of security services was commonly in a stronger position. This resulted from a multitude of firms offering what buyers perceived to be largely undifferentiated products and services and sellers trying to "win" business by providing the lowest price. Further, the cost of switching suppliers was low because of the customer's perceived similarity of their services. It was also quite simple for firms to bring the security function in-house if they believed they could achieve substantial cost savings or other improvements in their

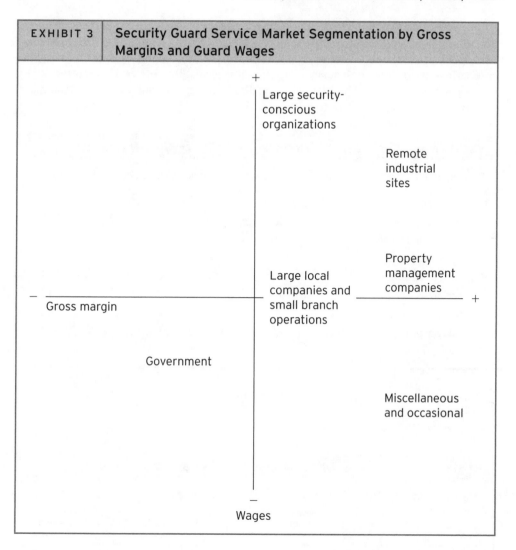

| EXHIBIT 3 | **Security Guard Service Market Segmentation by Gross Margins and Guard Wages** |

security programs. In addition, some buyers tended to give security considerations a low priority in their budgeting.

Firms purchasing security products and services had three levels of decisions to make: (1) a general policy on the role and risk-cost framework that security would play in their firm, (2) a decision regarding the types of products and services to be purchased, and (3) the selection of suppliers.

Each decision level involved new groups or individuals within the organization. Policy decisions were generally made at the senior executive level, whereas the product/service and supplier decisions tended to be made at the local level.

Most purchases were straight tender purchases based on a sealed bidding process. Firms with which security was a low priority and most government agencies tended to choose the lowest bidder. Companies that took a greater interest in the quality of their security program considered attributes other than price when deciding upon their security supplier.

As part of a study on the security industry, Metropol surveyed buyers' ratings of the importance of several selection criteria in choosing a security firm. It also had buyers rate Metropol's performance on those criteria. Among the most significant decision-making criteria identified were consistency and reliability, availability of service representatives, and price. Metropol scored highest on the quality of its representatives and the customers' view of the firm's reputation (Exhibits 4 and 5).

EXHIBIT 4	Customer Decision-Making Criteria—Survey Results*

How important are the following attributes to you when making a decision on security services?

	Not Important 1	2	3	4	Very Important 5	Average Score
Consistency and reliability	–	–	–	3	14	4.8
Quality of service representatives	–	–	–	5	12	4.7
Price competitiveness	–	–	3	8	6	4.2
Company reputation	1	1	–	7	8	4.2
Emergency services	–	2	4	7	4	3.8
Full range of products and services	–	4	2	6	5	3.7
Consulting services	–	6	6	3	2	3.1
National coverage	4	4	6	2	–	2.4

*The survey was a convenience sample of Metropol customers.

Source: Metropol Research.

EXHIBIT 5	Customer Decision-Making Criteria—Survey Results*

How would you rate Metropol Security on the following attributes?

	Poor 1	Fair 2	Set 3	Good 4	Excellent 5	Average Score
Consistency and reliability	1	1	5	7	3	3.6
Quality of service reps	–	2	–	11	4	4.0
Price competitiveness	–	1	4	10	2	3.8
Company reputation	–	–	2	10	5	4.2
Emergency services	1	1	6	7	3	3.6
Full range of products and services	1	2	7	6	1	3.2
Consulting services	–	4	5	5	2	2.9
National coverage	1	–	7	3	–	3.1

*The survey was a convenience sample of Metropol customers.

Source: Metropol Research.

METROPOL

Metropol organized its operations on a regional (provincial) basis. The Manitoba head-quarters developed a centralized policy and operating guidelines procedure that was instituted in all offices. While sales representatives dealt with the day to day needs of customers, top management was involved in making sales presentations to large accounts.

Services

Despite Metropol's variety of services, supplying unarmed, uniformed security guards accounted for most of its revenue. Its sales revenue breakdown by service type was:

Security guards	90%
Mobile security checks	8%
Other (investigation, polygraph testing, retail services, consulting, and education)	2%
Total	100%

Providing security guard services involved more than just sending guards to industrial or office sites. Metropol had to train, pay, uniform, and insure the guards. It also had to supervise and dispatch its people, as well as provide reports to its clients.

"We have attempted to provide greater value to our customers than our competitors have," stated Pat. "For example, we have a 24-hour dispatch service, while all the other firms use an answering service. There is a $100 000 [annual] difference in cost, but we can respond much faster to any situation. Some customers will say they just consider price in their purchase decision but end up liking and buying the extra service."

Metropol also gave its guards special training on the procedures to follow in the case of such emergencies as bomb threats, hostage takings, and fire evacuations. Again, this was an attempt to differentiate its services from those of other security guard companies.

The mobile security business was contracted out to local firms. This market was not considered to be a growth area, and Metropol did not invest a great deal of resources in it.

Investigative and polygraph services were contracted out to a couple of ex-RCMP officers. Metropol had maintained these investigators on its staff at one time, but found that demand for these services was not great enough to justify having the high-salaried people as full-time employees.

Education programs were another means Metropol used to create added value and increase switching costs for its customers. Pat explained, "We give seminars on such topics as 'The Protection of Proprietary Information' for our clients and even invite some companies we don't currently serve. We want our clients to realize that if they switch security firms they will be losing something of value."

Metropol did not sell hardware products such as fences, alarms, and locks. However, it could arrange the purchase of such equipment for its clients. It was presently considering working in conjunction with a systems engineer so that the company would be able to provide a total security package to its customers.

Costs

Metropol divided its costs into two groups: direct and administrative. A "typical" job had the following cost characteristics:

Direct costs	83-86%
Selling and administrative costs	8-9%
Pretax profit margin	4-7%

Given these figures, cost control was a key success factor for Metropol and the security industry in general. Metropol's margins were, in fact, higher than the industry average of approximately 4%. "We use a job costing process," volunteered Pat. "Every pay period [two weeks] we look at what we made on each job. We consider and analyze every expense item very closely to see if there was any deviation from what was budgeted."

Direct costs included wages, uniforms, bonding, transportation, and supervision. Metropol did a good job of keeping its costs as low or lower than its competitors despite offering a higher level of service. Some of this was a result of economies of scale in purchasing such items as uniforms and was achieved because of its comparatively large size. The company also did a superior job in collecting its outstanding receivables within a two-week period.

Pricing

Prices were determined by identifying the direct costs associated with a job, allowing for a contribution to selling and administrative overhead, and providing for a profit margin. Consideration was also given to any particular reason there may be for pricing a bid either particularly high or low. "We once bid at very close to our direct cost for a job in a town where we had no competition in order to discourage other firms from entering that market," noted Pat. He also suggested that it was important to anticipate competitors' likely pricing strategy when bidding on a job as well as recognizing that some projects had greater potential for cost overruns.

Promotion

Metropol individually identified the companies in each of its trading areas that were potential clients, and concentrated its promotional efforts on that group. In Manitoba this "club" numbered about 500 firms.

Once these firms were identified, strategies were developed either to sell to those potential accounts that presently had no security service or to become the logical alternative for those businesses who were using competitive services. "We want to put pressure on these incumbent firms to perform," explained Pat.

Metropol used, among other things, its educational seminars to stress to its clients that it offered superior services. At times firms using competing security companies were invited as a means of encouraging them to switch to Metropol.

Employees

Metropol employed approximately 2000 people, 1900 of whom were security guards and 100 who were selling, administrative, or management personnel.

Security guards came principally from three backgrounds: (1) young people (18–25) who could not find other work, (2) older people (50–65) looking for a second career, or (3) ex-military or police personnel who liked the quasi-military nature of the job.

Annual employee turnover in the security guard industry was very high, estimated to be in the vicinity of 100%. Metropol's turnover rate was in the same range. Reasons for the high level included a combination of low wages, generally boring work, and a lack of motivation or support from senior management.

"We have some employees who have been with the company for 15 years," Pat pointed out. "However, the wages we pay are based on our billing rate, which often only allows for minimum wages to be paid to employees." Intense competition and clients who wanted to pay a bare minimum for security guard services forced companies to pay their guards the legal minimum wage. This caused high turnover rates, which, evidently, did not bother some clients. Other customers, concerned with employee turnover, specified a higher minimum wage rate that the security company had to pay its guards. Pat liked this attitude because it allowed him to pay his people a higher wage and still be competitive.

Metropol's supervisors and customer service representatives (salespeople) did a good job servicing their accounts and handling any crises that arose. They helped maintain Metropol's reputation as a competent and reliable security company despite the generally poor reputation of the industry.

THE FUTURE

Pat turned his attention to the future. He believed that the way business was conducted in the security guard industry would not significantly change in the near future. He did expect the business to become somewhat more professional with guards being trained in formal, standardized programs. The pressure on profit margins was expected to continue and perhaps even intensify as the larger, multinational firms fought for market share and smaller independents struggled for survival. Pat was thinking about how he could use Metropol's present position and reputation in the security guard sector to expand into more profitable segments of the industry or improve the company's general standing within the guard sector. Some of the opportunities he was considering were:

- Geographic expansion
- A focused strategy
- Expanding the range of security products and services offered by the company
- Diversification into other service areas outside the security field
- Serving the consumer home security market

Geographic Expansion

"To be a national company in Canada you need a presence in southern Ontario," observed Pat. Even though many companies' security needs were handled at the local level, there was considerable potential for a national accounts program. To be involved in providing a national service, a company had to be active in the Toronto area, where most national companies' security decisions were made. In addition, the Ontario market offered substantial local business. Pat explained, "We handle Northern Telecom's [now Nortel's] security guard needs throughout western Canada, but not in Ontario. Northern Telecom has three times the business volume there as it does in all of the western provinces combined."

There were three ways Metropol could enter the Ontario market: (1) by purchasing a local security firm, (2) through merging with another company, or (3) by bidding on contracts in Ontario and opening up an office once a contract was obtained.

Pat believed that the "merger method" was the most appealing, since it offered the potential for increased profits with virtually no additional cash investment. He had discussed the possibility with two firms that had head offices in Ontario and were also minor competitors in the Winnipeg, Edmonton, Calgary, and Vancouver markets. The western offices of the merged firm could be closed down and the business operated under the Metropol name. "The gross margin on their western contracts would go right to the bottom line," suggested Pat. "Because all the current Metropol offices could meet their administrative needs and absorb any incremental expenses."

A restricting factor in this strategy was Metropol's limited product/service line. To provide a complete security package for any company on a national basis, it was necessary to offer the hardware and ESD packages in addition to the security guards.

A Focused Strategy

This alternative was really a continuation of Metropol's current strategy. Following this approach, Metropol's principal objective would be to become the fastest-growing security guard firm in western Canada, with the highest profit margin and return on equity, the lowest employee turnover, and the most satisfied customers in the business of providing contract, unarmed security personnel. This strategy required an increased emphasis on developing a formal marketing program and increasing the value added to Metropol's security guard and support services. Tighter control of costs and employee motivation would be critical success factors, as would the need to carefully segment the market and identify the most profitable clients.

The strategy would be designed to match the distinct competencies and resources of Metropol with the needs of the marketplace. Pat believed that while the strategy "sounded good," it would be very difficult to implement. "Even if you offer the highest-quality service, you might not get the job," he observed. "Too many contracts, particularly those involving the government sector and Crown corporations, are based solely on price, and simply supplying a higher service level in the provision of security guards is not likely to change that."

Expansion of Security Products and Service

From the customer's point of view there was an advantage to having one firm coordinate and provide the complete security coverage required by the business; the security system was more effective and efficient. If the customer had to contract with different firms for guards, fences, locks, lights, alarms, and ESDs, there was likely to be a lot of overlap and, in some cases, gaps in the overall system. Also, it was likely to be more expensive. Pat considered an investment in the production of hardware equipment much too costly given his firm's limited resources, but he was investigating the possibility of arranging a deal with a large multinational distributor of security hardware and ESD products.

Pat explained, "We would like to have an exclusive relationship whereby they [large multinationals] would provide us, at wholesale, with all the hardware and ESD equipment we needed on a private label basis [Metropol brand] and they would train our people. We could offer them our monitoring services and access to new markets." Metropol would package the system, which would include hardware, software, and people in whatever mix its clients needed. The products would be sold to the client or leased on a five-year arrangement.

The expanded product line strategy would deliver significant benefits to Metropol. Hardware and ESD equipment offered better margins than security guard services and, in some cases, were subject to becoming obsolete. This provided opportunities to sell upgraded systems. For example, television monitoring devices had already gone through several generations of change despite their relatively recent entry into the security product mix. Service contracts to maintain the equipment would provide another source of additional revenue. Finally, the need of these systems for close monitoring and servicing increased the dependence of the customer on Metropol. This higher dependence meant that switching costs for the customer were much higher than with security guard services. This would be especially true if the equipment was leased for a five-year period.

Diversification into Other Service Areas

This alternative would capitalize on Metropol's skills in hiring people for contract-type jobs and administering a payroll. Its current product line would be expanded to include one or all of the following additional services that could be provided on a contractual basis: secretarial services, nursing care, janitorial services, or landscaping services. The commercial sector would continue to be its primary target market.

Several years ago Metropol got into the dry cleaning business with poor results. "Businesses like janitorial and landscaping services are beyond our particular expertise," revealed Pat. "However, we are looking at providing people and handling the payroll for temporary clerical or nursing services. In those cases, we would be taking our established skills to another market."

Pat cited Drake International's experience as evidence that the strategy could work. That company went from providing temporary help to the provision of security guards.

The Consumer Market

Another alternative for Metropol would be to expand into the consumer market for security products and services. The major products of interest to residential customers were locks, supplementary lighting, fences, mobile home checks, house sitting, and alarm systems. This segment was growing slower than the business sector, but still offered substantial opportunity.

Pat was currently exploring Metropol's opportunities as a franchiser of home alarm systems to the numerous small Canadian alarm system dealers. "We could become the Century 21 of the alarm business," Pat suggested.

The alarm business in Canada was made up of a large number of small independent dealers and a few large multinationals. The "small guys" would buy their alarms from wholesalers in small lots that precluded much discounting. They also had to contract out their alarm monitoring to their competition, the large multinationals, because they could not afford the central station monitoring equipment. In most cases advertising and financing of installations for customers was too expensive to be carried out on a significant basis.

Pat thought a Metropol alarm franchise offered a number of important strategic advantages to independent alarm dealers: (1) by arranging with a large alarm manufacturer to produce a private label Metropol brand alarm line, it could pass on volume discounts to its dealers; (2) franchisees would have the Metropol name behind them; (3) co-op advertising would provide greater exposure; (4) an arrangement for consumer financing could be established; and (5) Metropol would set up a central monitoring system.

Consideration was also being given to making locksmiths sub-dealers of Metropol alarm systems. "Normally a customer must call a locksmith and an alarm specialist to secure his home," suggested Pat. "It would be more effective, especially from a selling perspective, if the locksmith could do both."

CONCLUSION

Pat realized that the alternatives he was considering were not merely incremental changes in Metropol's strategy. In fact, each option represented a distinct direction for the firm's future development. "We have to define our business's mission more specifically," Pat thought to himself. "Then we can choose and implement the strategy that best suits that mission."

Scotian Pride

Julia Sagebien

In December 1989, Rick Fraser, a private consultant and former mussel grower, was preparing an analysis of the mussel industry for the Nova Scotia Aquaculture Association (NSAA). Local mussel growers were concerned because competition from Maine controlled the low end of the market and "Island Blue" mussels from Prince Edward Island had positioned themselves at the high end. Rick was searching for an industry-wide marketing strategy that could give the Nova Scotia mussel growers a profitable and defendable market position. The report was due in a month.

RICK'S EXPERIENCE IN THE AQUACULTURE INDUSTRY

Rick Fraser had been a "roughneck" welder on oil rigs in Calgary. In 1978, he was laid off after a serious work accident. The accident, the slowdown in the Calgary oil boom, and the impending end of workers' compensation benefits forced Rick to make some serious decisions about his livelihood and his future plans. In 1980, Rick decided to go to university. By 1986, he had successfully completed both a B.Sc. and an M.Sc. in

This case was written by Julia Sagebien of Dalhousie University, Halifax, Nova Scotia for the Acadia Institute of Case Studies as a basis for classroom discussion, and is not meant to illustrate either effective or ineffective management. The case is based on material gathered by Ian McLeod for his master's research project at Saint Mary's University, Halifax, Nova Scotia. © 1992 Acadia Institute of Case Studies, Acadia University. Reprinted with permission.

biology at Acadia University, in Wolfville, Nova Scotia. As part of his thesis requirements Rick had conducted field research on aquaculture for two summers. During this time, he became convinced of the viability of an aquaculture business. In 1985, he and a partner, who had some previous entrepreneurial experience, bought some mussels and equipment and started Long-Line Farms (LLF) on the eastern shore of Nova Scotia.

Long-Line Farms was a modest operation. The partners knew they would need an increased sales volume to survive in the long run. They believed that a steady supply of high-grade mussels was key to gaining market power. A way to increase profitability would be to have a processing plant to clean, grade, and bag mussels, since this would allow them to go to market directly, rather than having to sell to other plant owners who had processing capabilities.

Since the growing cycle of mussels required two years before the product could go to market, LLF also faced a possible cash crunch. Rick's experience confirmed the sentiment among growers that banks rarely lent to small aquaculture operations and did not consider either equipment in the water or product inventory to be collateral.

In 1987, the partners wrote a business plan and applied to the Atlantic Canada Opportunities Agency (ACOA), a regional economic development fund, for financial assistance. The partners' equity and the loans and financial assistance they received allowed them to go into large-volume production and marketing. LLF bought equipment (e.g., anchors and buoys) and set up a processing plant.

In 1988, LLF sold 150 000 pounds of mussels directly to supermarkets in Nova Scotia such as the Atlantic Superstore and IGA, local brokers such as Walker's Wharf and Fishermen's Market, and Montreal and Toronto brokers. The operation showed a modest profit and the partners made plans to increase production by 25 to 30% a year for the next two years.

In September 1989, Rick attended a meeting of the NSAA. He had been a founding member of the organization and had been active in developing "Scotian Pride," the label the association's members could use if they qualified for certification. Rick and several members of the association had been discussing for some time the need to develop a marketing plan for the Nova Scotia mussel industry. At the meeting, the NSAA agreed to retain Rick as a consultant. Rick was quite certain that he would continue working in the industry, and he knew that any new venture he might get involved in would benefit from this plan. Even though the NSAA could only offer him a minimal fee, he decided that it was timely to undertake an industry analysis. His final report was due at the association's next meeting, slated for late January 1990. In order to concentrate on this project, Rick decided to sell his share of Long-Line Farms to his previous partner.

THE MUSSEL INDUSTRY—RICK'S RESEARCH FINDINGS

Rick had obtained several books, research reports, and magazine articles on the mussel industry. Most of his sources came from the Department of Fisheries and Oceans (DFO) and the magazine *Canadian Aquaculture*. To supplement his secondary research, Rick conducted interviews with mussel growers, brokers, and retailers in Canada and the United States, and government officials from Nova Scotia and Prince Edward Island.

Rick now had to analyze his research and develop a mussel industry marketing strategy for the Nova Scotia Aquaculture Association. This task was somewhat complicated because the reports analyzed were published in different years and the data was not always consistent.

WORLDWIDE MUSSEL PRODUCTION METHODS

In the 1990s three types of mussels were marketed worldwide: (1) long-line cultured, (2) bottom-cultivated, and (3) wild. Since the strategy for marketing each type of mussel was different, Rick had to pay special attention to growing methods and their strategy implications.

The majority of farms in the Maritime provinces used the long-line suspension method of growing cultured mussels. This method involved suspending "seed"—small mussels from intertidal zones—in plastic socks three metres long. The socks were suspended on a line supported by buoys at the surface and attached to the bottom by weights. Before winter, sandbags were attached to the lines to submerge them below the ice line. Winter harvesting was difficult and costly.

Compared to other types, the long-line mussel was cleaner (no pearls or grit) and had a prettier shell and higher meat yield. Because the growing method was more labour-intensive, the cost of harvesting long-line mussels, and consequently the market price for them, was greater than that for the wild or bottom-cultivated variety (Exhibit 1). Rick had noticed that retailers usually made more margin on bottom-cultivated mussels than on long-line mussels, because they were able to raise the price of the former and still have them look like a bargain compared to the latter.

EXHIBIT 1	Prices per Pound, March 1990 ($CDN)			
	Wild	Cultivated	Cultured	Long-line
Wholesale	n/a	0.35	0.95	1.20
Retail	n/a	0.49	1.29	1.49
Source: A survey of Halifax wholesalers and retailers. Seasonal fluctuations were wide.				

In 1989, the DFO conducted research on growing methods which Rick considered promising for long-line growers. New methods could improve growing yields and increase the industry margin of long-line cultured mussels by about 30 to 40% at current wholesale prices.

Prince Edward Island growers and provincial government officials had spent a considerable amount of time and money positioning their "Island Blue" mussels as the industry standard for high-quality mussels. Many Canadian and some U.S. white-tablecloth restaurants had featured them in their menus by name. In 1989, comparable cultured mussels from Nova Scotia commanded a lower wholesale and retail price than Island Blues (Exhibit 1). This meant that Prince Edward Island growers could realize substantially higher margins than Nova Scotia growers for essentially the same product, and that Nova Scotia growers had to be very careful with costs.

The Prince Edward Island government had made it easier for growers to obtain mussel licences and had thus encouraged the growth of the industry. The NSAA members were not happy that the licensing procedure for growing sites was much more expedient in Prince Edward Island than in Nova Scotia, and that the Nova Scotia government had not been as supportive as the Prince Edward Island government in terms of marketing assistance.

Maine growers had traditionally harvested bottom-cultivated mussels. In the spring, the seed mussels were dragged up from intertidal beds, put in small boats and transferred to deeper water. Free from the overcrowding of the intertidal bed that would stunt their growth, the mussels were able to grow to market size. After approximately 18 months, they were harvested by dragging, and prepared for market.

Bottom-cultivated mussels dominate the U.S. market and a considerable portion of the Canadian market. Even though most Atlantic Canadian growers believed there was a shortage of growing areas for bottom-cultivated mussels, DFO research indicated that this was not true and that, in fact, bottom-cultivated mussels were a viable option for growers in the Atlantic Provinces.

Wild mussels were harvested from in-shore areas using bottom dredges. The dredge was pulled across the natural mussel beds by a Cape Island–style fishing boat. The mussels were then handpicked from the dredged material. Like bottom-cultivated mussels, wild mussels had a reduced meat yield and a higher content of sand and pearls than long-line cultured mussels. Quebec consumed a high proportion of wild mussels.

Once harvested, all mussel types had a shelf life of seven to fourteen days if properly stored. They had to be processed for market (cleaning, sorting, etc.) and handled carefully during transport. Mussel shipments usually constituted part of a mixed load of seafood products.

From his interviews with retailers, Rick discovered that even though its shell was cleaner and the meat yield higher, to the average consumer the long-line cultured mussel was difficult to distinguish from the wild mussel and the bottom-cultivated mussel, whether in or out of the shell. Wholesalers and retailers themselves sometimes had a hard time differentiating the products and were in some cases completely unaware of the availability of three different products. According to retailers, only sophisticated mussel consumers, many of Mediterranean origin and living in major American and Canadian cities, were able to differentiate among them.

MARKETS

The information Rick gathered generally segmented the mussel market: geographically (U.S. and Canadian cities, Europe); by product type (wild, long-line cultured, and bottom-cultivated); and by sector (institutional or food service/restaurants versus consumer/retail).

The volume consumed by the food service sector versus that consumed by the retail sector varied considerably by city. According to one of the studies that Rick had reviewed, markets with a large retail sector volume offered good opportunities to long-line mussel growers because the retail sector catered to sophisticated consumers who could distinguish among the different types of mussels.

Another study suggested that the growth in North American demand for mussels in the 1980s could, in part, be traced to the dietary preferences of "yuppies": mussels are high in protein, low in calories and cholesterol, and considered "chic." Even though these dietary trends were not expected to change radically, there was always the caveat that mussel consumption might be a fad. Mussel consumption was clustered around large North American cities (Exhibits 2 and 3). Growth was anticipated in the restaurant sector in these cities because mussels were trendy. And the high markup of this menu item, particularly if bottom-cultivated mussels were used, made it attractive to restaurant managers. The retail trade, mostly supermarkets, was expected to grow much more slowly.

EXHIBIT 2	Canadian Market, Selected Cities, 1987, Institutional and Retail Combined (percentage breakdown by city)			
City	Tonnage	Bottom-Cultivated	Long-Line Cultured	Other
Montreal	750	15%	35%	50%
Quebec City	200	n/a	n/a	n/a
Ottawa	120	50%	25%	25%
Toronto	710	75%	15%	10%
Vancouver	120	n/a	n/a	n/a
Total	1900			

Source: Market Analysis Group (1988), Department of Fisheries and Oceans.

EXHIBIT 3	U.S. Market, Selected Cities, 1987, Institutional and Retail Combined (percentage breakdown by city)			
City	Tonnage	Bottom-Cultivated	Long-Line Cultured	Other
New York	2600	88%	5%	7%
Los Angeles	350	95%	3%	2%
Chicago	350	n/a	n/a	n/a
Atlanta	140	n/a	n/a	n/a
Seattle	165	50%	50%	–
Total	3604			

Source: Market Analysis Group (1988), Department of Fisheries and Oceans.

Canadian Market

The Canadian market, by industry sector, consisted of approximately 70% in the food service industry (mainly restaurants) and 30% in the retail trade (supermarkets, etc.). The retail trade was directed mainly at Mediterranean populations residing in large cities. The type of mussel consumed varied from city to city (Exhibit 2). The percentage breakdown accounted for by the food service industry versus the percentage consumed by the retail sector also varied among cities. For example, Montreal had a 50% food service / 50% retail split, while Toronto had an 80% food service / 20% retail split.

Even though Quebec purchased some Prince Edward Island mussels, the "Buy Quebec" preferential purchase policies in the province limited the market potential. Other market segments Rick had considered were processed products and export markets to western U.S. and Canadian cities. Even though transportation costs limited the potential of these markets, Rick knew that Island Blues were being flown to Los Angeles. Government research indicated that Europe was a mature market with few prospects for export.

United States Market

In 1987, the United States food service sector accounted for 80% of mussel demand, while the retail sector accounted for 20%. This breakdown also varied from city to city, Los Angeles having the greatest variation from the national norm with a 50% food service / 50% retail split. The type of mussel consumed also varied from city to city (Exhibit 3).

CANADIAN SUPPLY

In 1987, Canada supplied only between 1 and 2% of the world's mussels. In 1987, 2885 tonnes of mussels (mostly long-line mussels) were produced in Canada. Exports represented 20% or 577 tonnes. In addition, 800 tonnes were imported from the United States. Almost all of the imported mussels were bottom-cultivated. Most of the Canadian supply of mussels came from Atlantic Canada. Canadian west coast production still faced large technical difficulties.

Rick had seen the mussel industry grow at a considerably fast rate for a small cottage industry in Atlantic Canada. However, Rick also knew that the U.S. and Canadian markets were large and that Atlantic Canadians were missing out on many opportunities for export. In this context, Atlantic Canadian mussel production had grown in a somewhat slow and erratic way. A biologist's report stated that the environmental conditions in the Atlantic provinces could sustain a long-line cultured mussel capacity of 50 000 tonnes a year. This capacity could double if bottom-cultivated methods were used.

Some reports indicated that the industry was poised for meteoric growth. In 1987, overall Canadian production was expected to grow at 75% a year, with some areas, like Prince Edward Island, growing at 112% a year. Since there were relatively few barriers to entry (particularly in Prince Edward Island), there was always a danger of oversupply of long-line cultured mussels relative to market demand. Greater export efforts to the United States would be required in this case.

In 1985, research conducted by government agencies revealed that the major perceptions of retailers and wholesalers in the United States and Canada regarding Canadian domestic suppliers were: (1) price was the most important purchase requirement, and long-line cultured products (most of which came from Atlantic Canada) were considered too expensive compared to U.S. imports, particularly since there was no perceived difference in quality, (2) there were unreliable transportation systems in the Canadian east coast, and (3) the consistency of quality and delivery had to be improved.

CHARACTERISTICS OF ATLANTIC CANADIAN MUSSEL GROWERS

In 1986, Atlantic Canada's mollusc (e.g., mussels, oysters, quahogs, clams, etc.) production was valued at $16 million (2% of the landed value of all fisheries). Of the dollar value of production, 20% was mussels, 20% oysters, 5% quahogs, and 50% clams.

While the Atlantic provinces mussel industry had focused on the production and marketing of high-quality products at a premium price (long-line cultured), it generally ignored the low-to-medium-quality market niches (bottom-cultivated). Ninety-five percent of the mussels landed were long-line cultured.

East coast distribution patterns in 1987 showed that 56% of Atlantic Canadian production was sold in the Atlantic region (some of this volume was, in turn, sold by local brokers to brokers in other cities), 27% was shipped to other parts of Canada, and 17% was exported to the United States.

Prince Edward Island and Nova Scotia were the major players in the Atlantic mussel industry. Newfoundland and New Brunswick played relatively minor roles. Newfoundland supplied local markets, while New Brunswick served both the local and the United States market.

Prince Edward Island Mussel Production

Prince Edward Island had been the most important mussel producer in Atlantic Canada. Landings in 1987 were 1700 tonnes. The total investment in the industry in 1987 was $6.7 million. Virtually all production was long-line cultured.

Three large growers processed 80% of the landings. In 1982, Prince Edward Island producers organized a cooperative to process and market their products and to provide an effective lobbying group. Their efforts were successful, and in 1985 they incorporated under the name Atlantic Mussel Growers Corporation (AMG). The corporation had centralized processing capabilities where individual growers could have their mussels tagged (to trace original source), stored in tanks for up to two weeks, graded, cleaned, polished, boxed, and labelled with the "Island Blue" brand name. The inventory and storage system helped to smooth out demand and supply. The individual grower retained ownership of the product until it was sold by the corporation, which then credited the grower for the mussels. Mussels were then trucked to Halifax to be flown out to U.S. and Canadian markets. The plant was supplied by 15 growers, who had to provide AMG with 95% of their harvest. According to AMG sources, in 1989 the plant handled about 1369 tonnes a year. AMG prided itself on being a reliable supplier of a superior-quality product.

The Prince Edward Island provincial government had been very supportive of aquaculture development activities. The "Island Blue" label was developed by the AMG with the cooperation of the Prince Edward Island Development Agency. Prince Edward Island growers and government agents had been active in developing value-added products such as mussels frozen in the shell and mussels in wine sauce which they perceived as a good outlet for undersized mussels.

Prince Edward Island directed its products to Quebec (50%), Ontario (15%), and the United States (18%). Mussels were flown to Vancouver and to some United States cities or trucked to closer markets.

Nova Scotia Mussel Production

Government reports indicated that, in 1988, Nova Scotia mussel growers produced about 634 tonnes. Ninety-nine percent of the production was long-line. The total investment in the industry was $3.2 million. Even though the reports indicated that about 70% of the mussels were consumed in the province, Rick knew that a portion of these mussels were sold by local brokers to brokers in other provinces. Therefore, he would have a difficult time deciphering the exact size and characteristics of the Nova Scotia market.

In 1987, there were 62 active licensed growers. In 1989, many smaller growers were exiting the industry or were only part-time growers. Compared to Prince Edward Island growers, Nova Scotia growers were less organized and less informed about alternative growing methods, major markets, and competition from other Atlantic Canadian and Maine growers. Growers still regarded each other with suspicion and were secretive about company information. Growers sold their mussels to wholesalers and directly to the restaurant industry.

The Nova Scotia Aquaculture Association served a group of about 200 growers, scientists, and industry suppliers. "Scotian Pride," the label that the association's members could use if they qualified for certification, was a seal of approval which guaranteed product quality through adherence to the strict standards and specifications developed by the association. Standardization, centralization of ordering, and strict inspection criteria and documentation were very positive aspects of the program. Unlike Prince Edward Island growers, Nova Scotia growers had no central association-sponsored processing plant. Product identification and labelling were carried out by the individual association members which met the standards. Nova Scotia growers were ahead of Prince Edward Island growers in setting industry standards.

Rick's research sources stated that Prince Edward Island growers were well on their way to realizing the benefits of aquaculture. In Nova Scotia, growers would have to overcome many obstacles. The interviews he had conducted reinforced this assessment of the market. The Nova Scotian market had to contend with the following problems:

1. For the most part, growers were reactionary rather than visionary. They were disorganized and did not have a sophisticated understanding of their markets, industry trends, scientific advances, or business strategies.
2. Federal and provincial government support was slow and erratic.
3. Financing was difficult to obtain.
4. Marketing channel members (brokers, wholesalers, and retailers) and consumers were uneducated about the superior quality of long-line mussels.

UNITED STATES SUPPLY

Bottom-cultivated mussels grown by Maine companies dominated the U.S. mussel market. Maine mussels also had a strong presence in the Canadian market. In 1987, United States growers produced 17 000 tonnes of mussels. Recent developments in the Maine industry concerned Rick. Bottom-cultivating had been the prevalent growing method in the industry, but some growers were experimenting with long-line technology in anticipation of a more educated and demanding consumer.

Most of the 20 U.S. producers were located on the east coast. Four major operations (three of them in Maine) dominated the industry: Great Eastern Mussels, Maine; Blue Gold Seafarms, Maine; Abandoned Farm Inc., Maine; Penn Cove Mussel Farm Inc., Washington State.

TOXICITY, QUALITY, AND HEALTH STANDARDS

In 1989, mussel farming was an industry plagued by inconsistent quality standards, seasonal supply, environmental hazards, and problems of mussel toxicity. Both the "wild" landed catches and the aquaculture harvested products were susceptible to the toxic effects of human sewage, farm fertilizer runoffs, and the excrement of the mussels themselves.

The efforts of most of the private growers and producers with whom Rick came in contact were directed toward preventing a repeat of the December 1987 crisis, when two deaths and 134 cases of illness were attributed to toxic molluscs from Prince Edward Island. On the U.S. east coast, the "Red Tide" (a marine condition which makes mussels toxic) had created havoc in the mollusc industry there. Even though water temperature and other environmental conditions made the Red Tide a threat to Prince Edward Island waters, but not to Nova Scotia waters, consumers assumed that all Atlantic products were at risk.

Some of the newspaper clippings Rick had collected chronicled the events. Mollusc sales fell by 100% nationwide and sales of other shellfish and fish also fell considerably. Prices deteriorated severely and it took considerable time and effort to return them to their pre–December 1987 level. A quick and effective public relations campaign by the federal government, Prince Edward Island growers, and their provincial government helped restore confidence in the minds of consumers. After that incident, the federal government dedicated $2 million for a promotional campaign using television and point-of-sale materials. Some experts believed that the publicity might actually have helped the industry in the long run by creating awareness of the product and showing that authorities were responsive to health problems.

Still, Rick and other growers felt anxious about the industry's susceptibility to bad publicity. For example, in April 1989, the Saint John, New Brunswick daily *Evening Times-Globe* printed a story with the headline "Mussels Kill Quebec Man." The man had in fact died from a heart attack and not from bad mussels. However, prices immediately dropped and quantity demand lowered.

Industry self-regulation and government authorities had made improvements in quality control. The federal government had revamped its Shellfish Monitoring Program. This included testing of water quality by Environment Canada, testing of the product by the Department of Fisheries and Oceans, and policing of growing areas by various agencies in order to prevent harvesting in closed areas. Rick's plan had to develop tactics to support these activities.

A STRATEGIC MARKETING PLAN FOR THE NOVA SCOTIA MUSSEL INDUSTRY

Rick had spent two months gathering and analyzing information. He knew that a strategic marketing plan for the industry would need to address several key issues:

- Should growers use a cultured or a cultivated method of production? Which markets were more attractive? Could Nova Scotia growers be the overall cost leaders (over Maine) or should they concentrate their efforts on differentiating their product (from Prince Edward Island's)?

- If Nova Scotia growers wanted to grow long-line mussels, could some of the lines be located in Prince Edward Island in order to command a higher price? Would they have to be marketed through Prince Edward Island's Atlantic Mussel Growers Association in order to be considered true "Blues"?

- Could they adopt the new reduced-cost growing methods being developed by government scientists for long-line mussels and offer a lower priced but high-margin substitute for P.E.I. "Island Blues"? Was this advantage sustainable? Would Prince Edward Island soon follow?

- If a few growers switched to bottom-cultivating, how would local growers react to a competitor with a price advantage? Could these growers be persuaded to direct their production solely to the export market? Could they compete effectively with Maine?

- How could they take advantage of the Nova Scotia Aquaculture Association? "Scotian Pride" might allow them to brand all their products. It could help educate consumers on the difference between Maine products and Nova Scotia products. The label could perhaps even serve as a basis for competition with Island Blues.

- Could Rick encourage industry members to cooperate further in processing, grading, and marketing all their products? Should the Nova Scotia Aquaculture Association buy some of the smaller mussel farms which might be going out of business?

- Should the Nova Scotia Aquaculture Association work with the Atlantic Mussel Growers Association in an effort to compete effectively against Maine growers? Would growers be willing to cooperate at all? Would they think strategically? Should they set up a region-wide mussel marketing board?

- Could specific cities or market sectors be targeted for intensive marketing?

- How could stronger government regulation be encouraged in order to protect the market from unsafe products and unscrupulous practices? Would one more poisoning incident ruin the whole industry?

- How would the North American Free Trade Agreement and the 1990 Atlantic fishing industry crisis affect the local growers?

Atlantic Waterfowl Celebration

Gordon L. Fullerton

INTRODUCTION

It was an unusually sunny day in Sackville, New Brunswick early in December 1994 when Carol Currie, the managing director, and Lew Clarke, recently elected chair of the board of directors of the Atlantic Waterfowl Celebration (AWC), met to discuss the future of the organization. They knew the AWC had not been as successful as they had hoped in 1994, but its head was still above water. Lew felt that the AWC had lost the momentum gathered from its early successes. He believed that there was a need to examine all aspects of the AWC. More importantly, he saw that it must be infused with a number of keen and eager volunteers. Carol Currie also recognized that there was a need to revitalize the organization but that they could not spend too much time on assessment and analysis. The organization had to examine its past and start planning for the 1995 Atlantic Waterfowl Celebration, which was only eight months away.

This case was written by Gordon L. Fullerton of Saint Mary's University, Halifax, Nova Scotia for the Acadia Institute of Case Studies as a basis for classroom discussion, and is not meant to illustrate either effective or ineffective management. © 1995 Acadia Institute of Case Studies, Acadia University. Reprinted with permission.

HISTORY

Sackville, with a population of just over 5000, was located in the extreme southeast corner of New Brunswick on the isthmus of Chignecto, the small neck of land joining New Brunswick and Nova Scotia. The most dominant feature of the local geography was the Tantramar Marsh. Large parts of the marsh were used for agricultural purposes, as the moist fertile soil created high hay yields. The remainder of the marsh was a rich natural habitat for a large assortment of wildlife, particularly birds and waterfowl.

The historic economic base of the town was manufacturing. Until the 1970s, upwards of 1000 people were employed in two foundries (Enamel & Heating Ltd. and Enterprise Foundry Ltd.), both of which produced stoves and other consumer durables. One firm perished in the turbulent 1980s and the other firm reduced its payroll to under 100 people, most of whom were part-time employees. Mount Allison University and Atlantic Wholesalers Ltd., a subsidiary of Loblaws, were the largest employers. Sackville was also home to the Atlantic Canada Branch Office of the Canadian Wildlife Service, a unit within the federal Department of the Environment.

With the collapse of the manufacturing sector in the town, many people concluded that Sackville was just one of a large number of communities in eastern North America forced to make a transition from a manufacturing-based economy to a service-based economy. The presence of the marsh and its habitat was viewed by some visionaries as the building blocks for an entry into what would become the ecotourism industry. In 1988 the town in partnership with Ducks Unlimited Canada, the Canadian Wildlife Service, Mount Allison University, and the New Brunswick government built the Sackville Waterfowl Park, a 22 hectare preserve of wetlands on the periphery of the centre of town (see Exhibit 1). The main feature of the park was a walkway through a flooded marsh where people had the opportunity to observe birds and ducks in a natural marsh habitat.

Shortly after the creation of the park, a citizens' group formed with the goal of creating an event that would bring people to Sackville for a celebration built around the waterfowl theme. The park was the natural centrepiece of the event. Thus, the Atlantic Waterfowl Celebration was hatched.

At the time there was one other community event in eastern North America with a waterfowl theme. The Easton Waterfowl Festival was held annually in November in Easton, Maryland. This event generally coincided with the annual waterfowl migration through the area. This event was primarily an art show and sale featuring paintings, carvings, and photographs of waterfowl and their habitat. The target audience was upper-middle-class art collectors and duck hunters. Every year several thousand visitors attended the Easton Waterfowl Festival from a market area that extended from southern Pennsylvania–New Jersey to Virginia. The Sackville group realized that their event would have to have broader appeal due to the much smaller market. Nevertheless, they viewed Easton as a model for their own celebration.

PURPOSE

The founders agreed that the AWC would have three equally important pillars: artistic and cultural aspects of waterfowl and the marshlands, outdoor activities relating to the waterfowl theme, and environmental education relating to waterfowl and marshlands. These pillars represented three distinct and disparate markets: artwork collectors, hunters, and environmentally-concerned citizens. The AWC's vision of itself was that of an umbrella

EXHIBIT 1	Map of Sackville, New Brunswick Showing the Sackville Waterfowl Park

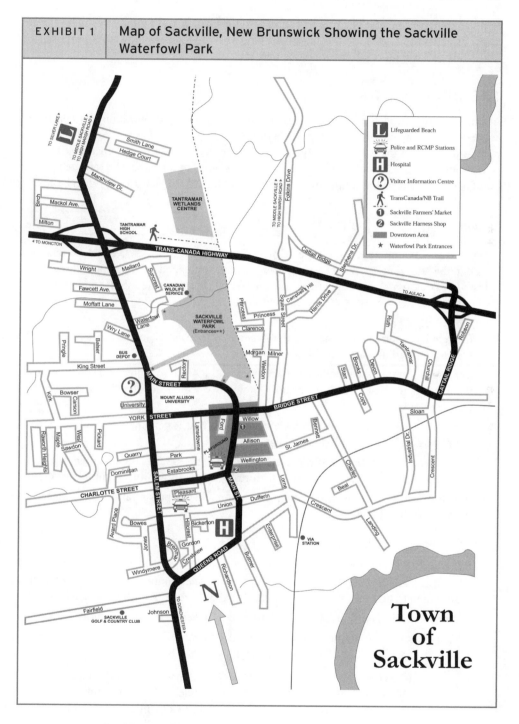

organization covering a series of events and activities which were interesting and relevant to the three markets. Despite the fact that there was wide agreement on its purpose, the AWC did not have a formal mission statement.

THE BEGINNINGS

Atlantic Waterfowl Celebration was incorporated as a nonprofit organization in 1989. It was not permitted to organize as a registered charity because significant aspects of its operations were in the tourism industry. Such organizations were not deemed to be "charitable" by the New Brunswick government. AWC was governed by a board of directors who reflected a number of interest groups in the community. Excerpts from the AWC bylaws are given in Exhibit 2.

EXHIBIT 2	Excerpts from the AWC Bylaws

Objectives: In conjunction with the "Objects" set forth for the AWC in its Letters of Patent, the "Atlantic Waterfowl Celebration" will be organized each year as a three day festival of outdoor recreation, arts, crafts and family fun dedicated to the appreciation of our natural heritage of wetlands and wildlife.

Our objectives are:

- to organize, promote and manage the Atlantic Waterfowl Celebration as an annual festival centred in Sackville, New Brunswick;

- to promote, through the themes and activities of the Atlantic Waterfowl Celebration, the kind of interest and pride in our community which encourages tourism and enhances business;

- to operate the Atlantic Waterfowl Celebration so that it generates enough revenue to become and remain self-supporting;

- to generate, whenever possible, enough revenue to provide financial support to our Sackville Waterfowl Park, and other features of our community's natural heritage;

- to support, in general, environmental education and the preservation and enhancement of wildlife habitat.

Article 1–Board of Directors

1.1   Board: The management and control of the business and affairs of the AWC shall be vested in a Board of Directors, consisting of such number of persons as shall from time to time be invited to join the Board of Directors, as herein provided.

1.2   Directors: The Board of Directors shall be composed of the following:

1.2.1   One representative (except as noted) delegated by each of the following organizations, invited to affiliate with AWC:

Town Council (2)	Canadian Wildlife Service
Chignecto Naturalist Club	Sackville Lions Club
Town Administration (2)	Ducks Unlimited Canada
Sackville Rod & Gun Club	Atlantic Wholesalers
SEDCO (Sackville Economic	Waterfowl Park Advisory
Development Commission) (2)	Committee

EXHIBIT 2	**Excerpts from the AWC Bylaws** (continued)

Sackville Rotary Club

Sackville Kinsmen Club

Mount Allison University

United Church Home for
Senior Citizens

Tantramar Tourist Association

1.2.2 Other individuals which the Board might choose to invite on the grounds of their participation in the work of the AWC.

Article 2—Officers and Committees

2.1 Officers and Executive Committee: The Board of Directors shall elect from among their number a Chairman, Vice-Chairman, Treasurer and Secretary to form along with the immediate Past Chairman, the core of an Executive Committee. These officers of the Board of Directors shall also be the officers of the Executive Committee.

2.5 Committees: The officers shall appoint such committees and coordinators as it deems appropriate to carry out the objectives of the AWC, and shall appoint chairpersons for each committee. In so far as possible, the Chair of each standing committee (identified below) will be a director on the Executive Committee.

2.5.1 Finance Committee: To control and supervise the finances of the AWC and its various committees, including the preparation of budgets, managing payments, income and investments, and presentation of annual statements to the board.

2.5.2 Fund-Raising Committee: To develop and recommend a fund-raising strategy from all appropriate sources, and to coordinate all matters concerning its implementation.

2.5.3 Marketing Committee: To develop and recommend the marketing and communication strategies for the AWC and to coordinate all matters concerning implementation.

2.5.4 Information and Sales Committee: To develop and recommend an overall strategy of selling tickets and souvenirs and distributing information, and to coordinate the volunteers, use of booths and all matters concerning the implementation of the strategy.

2.5.5 Facilities Committee: To make provision for and coordinate the use of all buildings, signs, parking, security, transportation, accommodations, and all other facilities required.

2.5.6 Events Committee: To develop and recommend an overall plan of events for the AWC, and to coordinate and oversee all scheduled events through those individuals responsible for each event.

2.5.7 Exhibitions Committee: To develop and recommend an overall plan of exhibitions, and to coordinate and oversee all such sanctioned exhibitions through those individuals and/or organizations responsible for each.

These committees shall have the power to act only as stated in these bylaws or as authorized by the Executive Committee or Board. All committees shall report to the Executive Committee or Board as requested by the Chairman of the Board and shall submit an annual report to the Annual General Meeting.

The first event was held in mid-August 1990. This time of year was chosen because it coincided with the annual migration of shore birds at nearby Dorchester Cape. It was felt that tours of this feeding area would be a main attraction of the AWC.

The volunteer board hired a full-time staff person to complete the legwork involved with setting up and running a community event of this magnitude. This person was responsible for the day-to-day running of the AWC and also spent considerable time coordinating the activities of the numerous volunteer and board committees. Exhibit 2 gives a description of the AWC committee structure.

FINANCING

In the year that led up to the first AWC, the board expended considerable effort on fundraising. A significant portion of the funding for the first AWC came from local, provincial, and federal governments; funding totalled approximately $45 000. Some of these grants were tied to specific purposes, usually in the form of wage subsidy grants such as Challenge or Employment and Immigration Section 25 grants.

Private donations and corporate sponsors contributed slightly under $43 000 in that first year. Revenues from AWC activities amounted to about $99 000, the largest part of which was earned from the sale of souvenirs and AWC memorabilia.

There were also significant startup costs involved with putting on the first AWC, including almost $61 000 spent on marketing and promotions. Despite this, the AWC managed to show a slight profit in its first year. It attracted slightly over 2000 visitors.

Over the next four years the AWC, like many other organizations in the public and non-profit sector, was forced to do more with less. Despite the increasingly constrained resources, the AWC was able to grow in size and stature. In 1992, the AWC received the Governor General's Award for Conservation from the Tourism and Industry Association of Canada. In 1994 it continued to be recognized by the New Brunswick Department of Economic Development and Tourism as one of the top 20 tourism-related events in New Brunswick.

The AWC was able to roughly break even in each of its first four years, although it continued to be heavily reliant on government funding. Lew had recently received the preliminary financial statements from the auditor which showed that the AWC lost just over $13 000 in 1994. Clearly, the AWC could not afford another year like 1994. Income statements and balance sheets from 1990 to 1994 can be found in Exhibit 3.

Lew and Carol recognized that the AWC was still quite reliant on government grants and support in 1994, even though government support had decreased over the years. They felt that their revenues from the public sector would continue to decline, so raising all other forms of revenue would have to be the priority.

EVENTS

The first AWC had a slate of events from each of the three pillars. Many of these events and activities would be held in subsequent years and would become flagship AWC events. The duck decoy auction was one of the most important events. It appealed to hunters, because many of the decoys at the auction were "working decoys" that could be used during the hunting season. This event also had considerable appeal to art collectors, because

EXHIBIT 3	Income Statements and Balance Sheets (1990-94)

Income Statements	1994 ($)	1993 ($)	1992 ($)	1991 ($)	1990 ($)
Revenues					
Grants: Province of New Brunswick					
• Government Grants Committee	2 990	3 395	8 075	9 205	9 305
• Regional Development Grant	1 041	6 000	9 035	12 700	6 000
• Dept. of Economic Dev. and Tourism	–	4 409	624	–	–
• Jet Stream	2 429	8 169	4 846	–	–
• Dept. of Labour	6 628	1 378	4 687	–	–
	13 088	23 351	27 267	21 905	15 305
Employment and Immigration:					
• Section 25 Operating	1 500	5 000	5 000	12 500	13 500
• Challenge Program	2 940	3 534	3 464	–	–
	4 440	8 534	8 464	12 500	13 500
Town of Sackville	18 000	18 000	18 000	30 140	10 000
ACOA	–	7 197	–	–	–
	35 528	57 082	53 731	64 545	38 805
Donations:					
• Foundations	–	–	5 000	5 000	–
• Corporate	6 000	17 400	11 000	6 219	9 907
• Private	5 650	3 800	3 877	5 370	23 690
• Event sponsors	7 350	1 000	1 250	6 100	9 100
	19 000	22 200	21 127	22 689	42 697
Revenues:					
• Admissions	6 581	11 199	7 641	10 102	12 258
• Souvenir sales	7 583	9 479	8 978	24 625	50 635
• Sale of prints and posters	561	1 685	5 029	802	15 929
• Sale of art	–	143	2 873	5 109	9 134
• Sale of castings	1 069	1 637	2 626	6 467	–
• Raffle tickets[1]	801	346	977	732	6 709
• Decoy and silent auctions	1 202	1 288	2 416	2 482	2 604
• Facilities rentals	1 817	2 838	2 474	2 815	1 560
• Other	–	–	914	18	411
	19 614	28 615	33 928	53 152	99 240
Total revenues	**74 142**	**107 897**	**108 786**	**140 386**	**180 742**

EXHIBIT 3	Income Statements and Balance Sheets (1990-94) (continued)				

Expenses

Events	10 135	10 092	10 877	21 161	13 159
Cost of sales	7 827	8 687	14 182	19 144	52 425
Marketing	8 770	32 072	27 811	44 976	61 647
Operating—office supplies, etc.[2]	15 605	11 870	11 397	–	–
Office wages	22 231	26 532	30 257	–	–
Grant-supported wages	16 504	14 465	5 887	–	–
Rent and utilities	3 411	4 004	5 051	–	–
Total (1990, 1991)	–	–	–	43 420	37 572
Inventory write-down	1 815	2 451	–	7 305	–
Audit and legal	1 100	611	601	2 118	3 041
Other[3, 4]	–	–	7 110	–	10 456
Total expenses	**87 398**	**110 784**	**113 173**	**138 124**	**178 300**
Excess (Shortfall)	**(13 256)**	**(2 887)**	**(4 387)**	**2 262**	**2 442**

Balance Sheets	**1994 ($)**	**1993 ($)**	**1992 ($)**	**1991 ($)**	**1990 ($)**
Assets					
Current assets:					
• Cash	10 429	6 387	2 094	3 560	15 212
• Accounts receivable	1 017	10 731	2 516	8 653	17 351
• Inventory	6 599	12 353	12 747	17 797	20 229
Total assets	**18 045**	**29 471**	**17 357**	**30 010**	**52 792**
Liabilities and Net Worth					
Current liabilities:					
• Town of Sackville	33 765	31 950	–	–	–
• Trade payables	106	91	–	–	–
• Total current (1990-1992)	–	–	17 040	25 306	50 350
Net worth	(15 826)	(2 570)	317	4 704	2 442
Total liabilities and net worth	**18 045**	**29 471**	**17 357**	**30 010**	**52 792**

1. 1990 amount includes revenue from sale of dance tickets.
2. In 1990 and 1991, operating expenses were not itemized by area.
3. AWC contribution to Waterfowl Park Security from a tied grant.
4. Opening "gala" for the first AWC.

the decoy was an art form that attracted collectors throughout Atlantic Canada. At the low end of the price scale, decoys sold for a few dollars while top-end decoys sold for as much as $1000. The AWC earned a 10% commission from decoy sales. Carol knew that the drawing power of this event was directly related to the quality of decoys available for auction. Carol expressed some concern that the event had decreased in stature due to a decline in decoy quality.

Another major "pillar" event was the waterfowl carving competition and exhibition, which attracted some of the major artists in Atlantic Canada. The competition provided the artists with the opportunity to test their carving skills against those of their peers. While most of the competitive works were not for sale, several exhibitors had other carvings for sale. The exhibition provided the artists with exposure to a group of collectors or potential collectors. In 1993, a taxidermy competition and exhibition were added, although the competition and exhibition were not as large as the carving exhibition and competition.

The competitions were held in the same venue as the AWC trade show. The trade show provided an opportunity for a number of businesses, nonprofit organizations, and government agencies to display and to sell products, and to communicate information. Typical exhibitors included: Ducks Unlimited, Environment Canada, competing and non-competing carvers, a carving equipment supplier, a canoe vendor, and a hunting supply dealer. In 1993 and 1994, approximately 30 exhibitors were present. Carol felt that exhibitors were satisfied in 1994 even though attendance was down.

Another important event was the art exhibition, sale, and silent auction. The exhibition permitted artists to display paintings, photographs, carvings, and other works that were available for sale. Once again, the AWC earned a commission on the sale of these items. Many artists donated works to be sold in a silent auction. The AWC received all of the proceeds from the sale of these donated items.

The Sackville Waterfowl Park was the site for a number of park tours that allowed visitors the opportunity to see and to learn about ducks and other birds inhabiting the park. The tours were led by a number of qualified guides, including experts from the Canadian Wildlife Service. The AWC also provided tours to a number of other sites, such as Dorchester Cape, to see the migrating shore birds, and Amherst Point (Nova Scotia), to see the bird sanctuary.

Over the next four years, the program of events was to be expanded but all new events were expected to fit with the basic theme of the AWC. The AWC hoped to add a new event, if it was possible to organize it and to fit it within at least one of the three pillars of the AWC. A few events, specifically the duck-calling competition and the retriever demonstration, have gathered a large following among people with an interest in duck hunting. Even though several events have been added, Currie and Clarke both considered the duck decoy auction, the carving and taxidermy competitions/exhibitions, the trade show, the tours, and the duck-calling competition to be the flagship events of the celebration, as they usually attracted large and enthusiastic crowds.

The AWC was fortunate, because there were a large number of venues available in Sackville. A significant amount of space was rented from Mount Allison University, but other indoor and outdoor sites were used in the community. Exhibit 4 provides a detailed program of events and venues from the 1994 AWC.

EXHIBIT 4	Program of Events from 1994 Atlantic Waterfowl Celebration

Friday, August 12

7:30-9:30 am	Walking Tour–SWP
8:00 am-8:00 pm	Wetlands Display–CWS
9:00 am	Primitive Village–LAN
9:00 am-9:00 pm	AWC Art Exhibition and Sale–TWE
9:30-11:30 am	Beausejour Salt Marsh Tour–THK
10:00 am-5:00 pm	Sackville in Print–LIB
10:00 am-5:00 pm	Omens Art Gallery Exhibition–OWE
10:00 am-8:00 pm	Rug Hooking Demo and Display–35
10:00 am-9:00 pm	Fog Forest Gallery–ANG
10:00 am-9:00 pm	Sackville Art Association Exhibit–BRI
12:00 pm-5:00 pm	Summer Show–Struts Gallery–STR
12:00 pm-9:00 pm	Downtown Party–PDP
12:00 pm	Trick Skipping–PDP
12:00 pm	Face Painting–PDP
1:00-2:30 pm	Natural Film Festival–VOG
1:00-9:00 pm	AWC Photography Competition–LIB
2:00-9:00 pm	Children's Art Competition–ATH
2:00 pm	Carving Competition Judging–ATH
2:00 pm	Taxidermy Competition Judging–ATH
2:00-4:00 pm	Nature Walk Ages 3 to 5–SWA
2:00-9:00 pm	Silent Auction–ATH
2:00-9:00 pm	Fundy Eco-Fair–ATH
3:00-5:00 pm	Waterfowl Tea–ARM$
3:30-5:30 pm	Fundy Shorebird Tour–THK

Saturday, August 13

7:00-10:00 am	Lion's Club Breakfast–LIO
7:30-9:30 am	Amherst Point Bird Sanct. Tour–THK
7:30 am-7:00 pm	Primitive Village–LAN
7:30 am-12:00 pm	Archery Competition–LAN
8:00 am-8:00 pm	Wetlands Display–CWS
9:00 am-12:00 pm	Register for Volksport Tours–TOU$
9:00 am-9:00 pm	AWC Art Exhibition and Sale–TWE
9:00 am-9:00 pm	AWC Photography Competition–LIB
9:00 am-8:00 pm	Silent Auction–ATH
9:00 am-8:00 pm	Children's Art Display–ATH
9:00 am-8:00 pm	Fundy Eco-Fair–ATH
9:00 am-8:00 pm	Carving Exhibitions–ATH
9:00 am-8:00 pm	Taxidermy Exhibitions–ATH
9:00 am-5:00 pm	Summer Show–Struts Gallery–STR
10:00 am-12:00 pm	Nature Walk Ages 6 to 12–SWA
10:00 am-3:00 pm	Canoe Lessons–SIL$
10:00 am-12:00 pm	Kite Flying Workshop–FOR$
10:00 am-8:00 pm	Rug Hooking Demo and Display–35
10:00 am-5:00 pm	Fog Forest Gallery–ANG
10:00 am-5:00 pm	Craft Demonstration and Sale–CRA
10:00 am-9:00 pm	Sackville Art Association Exhibit–BRI
10:00 am-8:00 pm	Quilt Fair–UNI
11:00 am-2:00 pm	Retriever Demonstrations–LOU
12:00 pm	Kite Flying–FOR

EXHIBIT 4	Program of Events from 1994 Atlantic Waterfowl Celebration (continued)

Friday, August 12

7:00-9:00 pm	Atl. Reg. Duck Calling Champ.–BRU
8:00 pm	Gates Motel–Live Bait Theatre–WIN$
9:00 pm-1:00 am	Dance–Blue Suede–CUR$
9:30 pm	Fireworks–RUG

Saturday, August 13

12:30-3:30 pm	Clay Bird Shoot–LAN
1:00-5:00 pm	Omens Art Gallery Exhibition–OWE
1:00-2:30 pm	Natural Film Festival–VOG
1:00-4:00 pm	Decoy Auction View–ARM
1:30-3:30 pm	Carver's Forum–MCH
1:30-3:30 pm	Acadian History Tour–THK$
	Sackville in Print–LIB
2:00-4:00 pm	Decoy Auction–ARM
4:00-5:30 pm	Black Powder Shoot–LAN
4:00-7:00 pm	Fundy Shorebird Tour–THK$
4:30-6:30 pm	Surf and Turf Bar-B-Q–BAN$

Sunday, August 14

7:30-9:30 am	Walking Tour–SWP
10:00 am	Golf Tournament–GOL$
10:00-11:00 am	Magic Show–ATH
10:00 am-4:00 pm	Wetlands Display–CWS
10:00 am-5:00 pm	Sackville Art Association Exhibit–BRI
10:00 am-5:00 pm	AWC Photography Competition–LIB
10:00 am-5:00 pm	AWC Art Exhibition and Sale–TWE
10:00 am-5:00 pm	Craft Demonstration and Sale–CRA
11:00 am-5:00 pm	Children's Art Competition–ATH
11:00 am-5:00 pm	Carving Exhibitions–ATH
11:00 am-5:00 pm	Taxidermy Exhibitions–ATH

Locations

Code	Location
ANG	St. Paul's Anglican Church
ARM	Sackville Armoury
ATH	Athletic Centre–Mount Allison
BAN	Sackville Band Stand
BRI	25 Bridge Street
BRU	Brunton Auditorium–Mount Allison
CRA	Crabtree Alcove–Mount Allison
CUR	Sackville Curling Club
CWS	Canadian Wildlife Service
DRD	Dorchester Recreation Department
FIR	Sackville Fire Hall

| EXHIBIT 4 | Program of Events from 1994 Atlantic Waterfowl Celebration (continued) |

Sunday, August 14

	Locations
11:00 am–5:00 pm Fundy Eco-Fair–ATH	FOR Fort Beausejour
11:00 am–5:00 pm Silent Auction–ATH	GOL Sackville Country Club
11:00 am–1:00 pm Retriever Demonstrations–LOU	HOS Sackville Memorial Hospital Atrium
12:00–4:00 pm Mount Allison Alumni Picnic–SWA	LAN Landing Road
1:00–2:30 pm Children's Nature Walk–SWA	LIB Sackville Public Library
1:00 pm Dorchester Marsh Walk–PDP	LIO Lions Club
1:00–5:00 pm Omens Art Gallery Exhibition–OWE	LOU Lounsbury's Parking Lot
1:00–2:00 pm Moncton Police Repelling Team–FIR	MCH McConnell Hall–Mount Allison
1:00–5:00 pm Rug Hooking Demo and Display–35	OWE Omens Art Gallery–Mount Allison
1:30–3:30 pm Acadian History Tour–THK$	PDP Pizza Delight Parking Lot
2:00–3:00 pm Kinsman Duck Race and Bar-B-Q–FIR$	RUG Rugby Field–Mount Allison
2:00–3:15 pm Percussion Ensemble–VOG$	SIL Silver Lake, Sackville
2:00–4:00 pm Sackville in Print–LIB	STR Struts Gallery
3:00 pm Stunt Kite Flying Exhibition–SAL	SWA Swan Pond–Mount Allison
5:30–7:30 pm Fundy Shorebird Tour–THK$	SWP Sackville Waterfowl Park
	THK Town Hall Kiosk
	TOU Sackville Tourist Bureau
	TWE Tweedie Hall–Mount Allison
	UNI Sackville United Church
	VOG Vogue Cinema
	LIB Windsor Theatre–Mount Allison
	35 35 Bridge Street
	$ Ticket price not included in AWC pass

Source: Company files.

CUSTOMER ANALYSIS

In 1993, groups of marketing students at Mount Allison University conducted projects on the AWC as part of the requirements in a marketing research course. The AWC already had a good knowledge of the geographic market area, because visitors were asked to complete a ticket stub providing their name, address, and phone number when they purchased event tickets or passes. Exhibit 5 presents a geographic profile of AWC visitors from 1993. The 1993 profile was thought to be similar to the visitor profile from previous years.

A sample was randomly selected from the pool of ticket stubs available from the 1992 AWC. Selected visitors were contacted and asked to complete a lengthy questionnaire by mail. This market research provided a more detailed demographic and attitudinal profile of AWC visitors. Lew Clarke noted, "This work was useful because it enabled us to find out who our customers were so that we could better develop events that would be interesting to them." Carol Currie commented, "The AWC marketing committee had used this information in the hope that advertising and communications could be used to reach more people similar to the current visitors." Some of the major findings of these student projects are given in Exhibit 6.

EXHIBIT 5	Geographic Profile of AWC Visitors, 1993 (includes event tickets, day passes, 3-day passes)
Sackville and Immediate Area	53%
Southeastern New Brunswick	15%
Northern Nova Scotia	11%
Other New Brunswick	8%
PEI and rest of Nova Scotia	6%
Other Canada	4%
United States	3%
Other international	1%
Source: Company files.	

EXHIBIT 6	Major Findings of Student Projects (1992 visitors)		
Family Life Cycle		**Average Household Income**	
Young single or couple	15%	Under $25 000	10%
Full nest I or II	31%	$25 001 to $40 000	19%
Empty nest I	37%	$40 001 to $60 000	36%
Empty nest II or single elderly	17%	$60 001 to $80 000	20%
		Over $80 000	15%
Occupation		**Sex of Respondent**	
Blue collar	20%	Male	54%
White collar / clerical	18%	Female	46%
Professional / managerial	48%		
Retired	13%		
Unemployed	1%		

EXHIBIT 6	Major Findings of Student Projects (1992 visitors) (continued)

Attend any AWC prior to 1992:

No	53%
Yes (Both 1990 & 1991)	25%
Yes (1991)	18%
Yes (1990)	4%

Respondent perception of the AWC. Respondents were asked to state how well the following image described the AWC by using the following scale:

Perfectly	1	2	3	4	5	6	7	Not at all

Image	Mean
Tourist-oriented	2.6
Hunting-oriented	3.7
Adult-oriented	2.3
Relaxing	2.1
Entertaining	2.3
Child-oriented	3.4
Interesting	3.9
Fun	3.1
Lacking content	5.5
Original	2.2
Environmentally friendly	2.0
Action-packed	4.2
Boring	6.2
Family-oriented	2.1
Educational	1.8

For all questions ($n = 163$); overall response rate = 70%.

Source: Company files.

CAROL'S ARRIVAL IN 1993

Carol was hired as managing director in late June 1993, when the previous managing director resigned in order to move to another community. "I arrived in the office and I was expected to manage this celebration that was taking place in six weeks, but I first had to find out what it was all about," said Carol, talking about her first few weeks on the job.

Even though Carol was new to the job of managing director, the 1993 AWC was arguably the most successful AWC to date. Lew felt that the 1993 AWC was successful because of the high level of activity existing in the town during the three days of the celebration. "Clearly," said Lew, "our high spending on promotion did its job, but in the end we lost money."

The communications goal in 1993 was to generate awareness and interest throughout the entire Maritime provinces, not just southeastern New Brunswick and northern Nova Scotia. Lew admitted that a few board members felt that the 1993 communications campaign had gone overboard in its efforts.

MARKETING AND COMMUNICATIONS

Since its inception, the AWC had always taken marketing seriously. In the early years, the AWC retained a close association with a local advertising agency. An agency was commissioned to design a poster for the 1991 celebration which won an international advertising award for community events.

The poster was an important part of the communications program. For each of the first four years of the AWC, a poster was designed around a strong visual image that related to the celebration or one of its pillars. "The AWC poster is a marketing tool but it is also a work that is important in its own right because of the strong visual imagery contained in the poster," said Carol Currie. Every year, several hundred posters were distributed to retail stores, motels, bed-and-breakfasts, and tourist information centres in New Brunswick. Posters were also sold as souvenirs. It was also recognized that posters from previous years continued to provide benefit to the AWC.

Lew Clarke summed up the view of the executive as follows: "I am sure that I could walk into a 'bed and breakfast' somewhere around St. Andrew's and see our 1991 poster displayed in the lobby. Now mind you, the date and year would be wrong, but some tourist from Connecticut walks into this B&B today and instantly they are aware of the AWC and they have a pretty strong sense of what we're all about from this poster. Our hope is that they will become interested enough to seek more information from tourist information centres."

The AWC printed a brochure which was primarily distributed through provincial and community tourist information centres. Every year approximately 10 000 brochures were required. Lew acknowledged that the brochure was an important tool in reaching tourists, who seek information about things to do in New Brunswick when they enter the province. In 1993, another Sackville advertising agency did substantial redesign work on the brochure. Printing and redesign work cost $12 000 in 1993, although several thousand brochures were still available for use in 1994. By the end of 1994, the AWC had run out of brochures and a reprint was necessary in 1995.

The AWC also made sure that the event was listed and identified in the section outlining festivals and events in the large New Brunswick tourist information guide.

Throughout its history, the AWC has used radio as a communication medium. In the early years, the radio buy was concentrated on stations in Moncton, New Brunswick and Amherst, Nova Scotia. The Moncton stations had good reach throughout southern New Brunswick, while the Amherst station reached the local market, including Sackville. Radio can be an expensive medium, but most stations offer a one-for-one (one free advertisement for every purchased advertisement) and supplement the bought time with public service announcements. In 1993, the marketing committee recommended a strategy of expanded radio coverage. As a result, AWC bought time on stations in Halifax (C-100, CJCH), Truro (CKTO), Antigonish (CJFX), and Amherst (CKDH) in Nova Scotia, and Moncton (CKCW, CFQM), Saint John (C-98), and Fredericton (CIHI) in New Brunswick. The AWC also purchased some airtime on CHMA, the campus radio station at Mount Allison

University. Carol Currie stated, "This radio buy was part of our strategy to widen the appeal of the celebration. How can we expect people in Halifax, Truro, or Saint John to make the decision to drive to Sackville for the day or weekend if we haven't made them aware of the Atlantic Waterfowl Celebration?"

The AWC benefited from a New Brunswick Department of Tourism subsidy program that paid for 50% of the buy in out-of-province media. It did not provide any subsidy for printing or creative development. The AWC successfully applied for this program in 1993 but did not qualify in 1994 because the budget had been allocated by the time AWC applied to the program, even though they had met the formal application deadline. Carol has found out that the 1995 application had been approved.

The AWC also made extensive use of signage on the highway near the Sackville exits and in the town during the weeks leading up to the event.

PLANNING FOR THE 1994 CELEBRATION

Everyone involved with the AWC felt that it would be difficult to top the success of the 1993 AWC. Funding became a top priority. Lew Clarke had the following comments about the 1994 fundraising plan: "Everyone felt that we had to reduce our reliance on government money. The reality is that government funding is risky because it can disappear at any time. We had to reduce our reliance on government funding by developing a stronger corporate business and personal sponsorship program." The AWC had always sought money from the business sector in two ways: large regional businesses were approached as corporate sponsors while smaller local businesses were identified as possible event sponsors. In 1993, corporate sponsors included Irving Oil, Atlantic Wholesalers, and Pizza Delight, while the event sponsors included a local grocery store and an auto dealership.

In addition to its problems on the revenue side, the AWC also found itself in the middle of a debt crunch. At the end of 1993, the AWC had an accumulated debt to the town of about $31 000. This debt existed because the AWC managing director was formally on the payroll of the town of Sackville. The town paid the employee and the AWC reimbursed the town. This practice stemmed from the early days of the AWC when it operated out of an office in the back of the town hall. In early January 1994, the executive committee met with the Sackville mayor and the town comptroller in order to work out a debt repayment plan. It was agreed that the AWC would repay $9000 in each of the next three years and the remainder in the fourth year. There would be no interest charges during this time; however, the town would no longer act as paymaster for AWC employees. The AWC executive were somewhat relieved that the town did not ask for immediate payment in full. They took this generosity as evidence that there was still considerable support for the event among local politicians. As of December 1994, all the current portion of the debt to the town of Sackville was outstanding.

The need for positive cash flow led to the development of a very ambitious corporate sponsorship program. "We all thought we could raise $30 000 from the corporate sector and $10 000 in individual event sponsorships," stated Carol. Carol, the former chairperson of the board and the chair of the marketing committee, had a number of meetings with Atlantic Canadian businesses in the early months of 1994. "We were quite disappointed with the results of our work but we learned that we had to start earlier in the year and be much more aggressive in our dealings with corporations," said Lew, when discussing the 1994 efforts. The AWC was able to raise only $6000 in the form of corporate sponsorships in 1994, much less than it had raised the year before. The results of the event sponsorship campaign were better, even though they fell quite short of their objectives. In 1994, the AWC raised $7350 from individual event sponsorships.

Also in 1994, the AWC undertook a more aggressive direct mail campaign. It had a list of previous donors and a list of previous visitors to the celebration. Carol commented, "Raising money from personal donations has always been difficult because we couldn't provide a tax receipt. We have gone to the same well too many times, we have to broaden the donation base. Previous visitors to the celebration were a natural target because they had at least some interest in the AWC and our purpose." The personal donations program was moderately successful in 1994, raising $5650.

By early 1994, the AWC's committee structure had disintegrated. Few, if any, committees met on a regular basis. Carol found that she was spending more of her time organizing AWC events rather than on coordinating the activities of the volunteer committees. Carol took her direction from a small five-person active executive committee that was extremely dedicated to the organization. The full board of directors retained the format outlined in the bylaws and it met the required three times per year, but the full board generated few new ideas. The board seemed content to let the executive run the show and the executive committee was content to run the AWC without much input from a broader group.

Just prior to the 1994 celebration, two of the five members of the executive committee announced they would be leaving Sackville to take jobs in other communities. Lew Clarke commented, "We originally thought we were looking to fill two key executive positions, but the more we thought about our situation, we realized we had some serious troubles with our whole structure." He went on to say, "The formula outlined in the bylaws was great as a means of representing important groups in the community, but it was lousy for getting things done." There was still a strong core of volunteers to complete specific tasks. Lew noted, "The AWC wasn't really short of volunteers during the celebration or in the weeks leading up to it, but Carol was doing most of the work and the executive seemed to be putting in a lot of time."

The marketing program for the 1994 AWC was less elaborate than the 1993 campaign. The biggest change was that the AWC produced a poster that was less elaborate than those produced in previous years. Design and print work for a four-colour-separation poster could cost over $3000. Carol said that the low-budget poster was purely a promotional device rather than a creative work that would last for years. Lew pointed out that there was an expectation both in and outside the community that a collectible poster was an important part of the AWC's marketing program. "When we produced a piece of junk," said Lew, "it sent a signal to the community that all was not well in our little organization." The AWC did manage to scrape together a few dollars for a radio campaign on local stations CKDH (Amherst) and CKCW/CFQM (Moncton) during the days leading up to the celebration.

One other change made in 1994 was the pricing. In previous years, visitors could buy three-day passes, one-day passes, or individual event tickets. The price of a three-day pass was raised to $25 from $14 and the price of a one-day pass to $10 from $7. Individual-event tickets were eliminated. Carol said that the goal was to significantly raise AWC's revenues from event attendance, but they fell far short of that goal. Some members of the executive committee felt that the AWC was a premium-quality event and that a premium-quality price was required. Lew noted that the price increase decision was made by the executive committee without much consultation from the full board. "Perhaps," said Lew, "this is the best example illustrating how out of touch we had become."

THE 1994 CELEBRATION

The 1994 celebration was successful on some fronts and a disappointment on others. Carol was enthusiastic about the number of new exhibitors and competitors entering the carving and taxidermy competitions. She was also excited about the number of new vendors who rented booths in the Fundy Eco-Fair (the new name given to the trade show). "We felt that the word trade show had a meaning which was not what we wanted. We were more interested in creating a type of market where vendors producing or selling artwork and outdoor-type products could reach our visitors," Carol said, commenting on this event.

Perhaps the greatest disappointment and the most embarrassing shortcoming of the 1994 AWC was the cancellation of the duck-calling competition at the very last minute. "We had tickets sold and an audience in the hall, but only two competitors," said Currie. We gave a very interesting impromptu duck-calling demonstration but it was clearly not the event that we or the audience expected." Lew and Carol agreed that the competition fell apart because of conflict among the volunteers charged with organizing the event.

Attendance and revenues were down from 1993. Carol and Lew were not sure how much of this decline could be attributed to the lower profile resulting from less advertising, how much was a result of a negative reaction to the price increases, and how much of it could be attributed to other factors, including the weather and competing events in the region. The 1994 AWC was held on the same weekend in August as the Acadian Homecoming, held in many francophone communities in southeastern New Brunswick. "Originally, we thought this one-time event would bring a large pool of visitors to the region from Quebec, elsewhere in Canada, and the southern U.S., and that we would receive some spillover," said Carol Currie. "As it turned out, many people in the area attended events held in conjunction with the Acadian Celebration and chose to not attend the AWC this year," continued Carol. Lew was worried that the AWC no longer had the support or interest of the community.

THE CALL

As they were discussing the immediate and long-term future of the organization, Carol took a call from a local town councillor. The councillor reported that the town finance committee had completed its preliminary budgeting exercise for 1995 and it would reduce its grant to the AWC in 1995 by about $8000 and that none of this would be disbursed until the AWC had paid the current $9000 portion of the debt owed to the town.

Carol and Lew agreed that this new information made a major impact on both the reorganization and the development of a marketing plan in 1995.

Dillon Controls, Ltd.

James E. Nelson and
Mark S. Johnson

"The choices themselves seem simple enough," thought Jac Dillon, "either we enter the U.S. market in Pennsylvania and New York, we forget about the U.S. for the time being, or we do some more marketing research." Dillon was president of Dillon Controls, Ltd., located in Brantford, Ontario. The company was formed in 1980 and, after a slow start, had grown steadily to its present size of 25 employees and annual revenues of about $1.6 million. About 2% of these revenues came from sales to U.S. accounts.

THE AQUAWATCH SYSTEM

Dillon Controls' product line centred about its AquaWatch System, a design of computer hardware and software for the monitoring and control of pressurized water flows. Most often these water flows consisted of either potable water or sewage effluent as these liquids were stored, moved, or treated by municipal water departments.

The System employed an AquaWatch microcomputer installed at individual pumping stations where liquids are stored and moved. Often, stations were located many kilometres

This case was written by Professor James E. Nelson and Doctoral Student Mark S. Johnson, University of Colorado. It is intended for use as a basis for class discussion rather than to illustrate either effective or ineffective administrative decision making. Some data are disguised. © 1990 by the Business Research Division, College of Business and Administration and the Graduate School of Business Administration, University of Colorado, Boulder, Colorado, 80309-0419. Reprinted with permission.

apart, linking geographically dispersed water users (households, businesses, etc.) to water and sewer systems. The microcomputer performed a number of important functions. It governed the starts, stops, and alarms of up to four pumps, monitored levels and available capacities of storage reservoirs, checked pump capacities and power consumptions, and recorded pump flows. It could even measure amounts of rainfall entering reservoirs and adjust pump operations or activate an alarm as needed. Each microcomputer could also be easily connected to a main computer to allow remote control of pumping stations and produce a variety of charts and graphs useful in evaluating pump performance and scheduling needed maintenance.

The AquaWatch System provided a monitoring function that human operators could not match in terms of sophistication, immediacy, and cost. It permitted each individual substation to control its own pumping operations; collect, analyze, and store data; forecast trends; transmit data and alarms to a central computer; and receive remote commands. Alarms could also be transmitted directly to a pocket-sized receiver carried by one or more operators on call. A supervisor could continually monitor pumping operations in a large system entirely via a computer terminal at a central location and send commands to individual pumps, thereby saving costly service calls and time. The System also reduced the possibility of overflows that could produce disastrous flooding of nearby communities or contamination of potable water.

Dillon Controls personnel would work with water and sewage engineers to design and install the desired AquaWatch System. Personnel would also train engineers and operators to work with the System and would be available 24 hours a day for consultation. If needed, a company engineer could be physically present to assist engineers and operators whenever major problems arose. Dillon Controls also offered its clients the option of purchasing a complete service contract whereby company personnel would provide periodic testing and maintenance of installed systems. The contract called for clients to pay Dillon for all direct costs of the service plus 15% for overhead.

An AquaWatch System could be configured a number of ways. In its most basic form, the System would be little more than a small "black box" that monitored two or three lift station activities and, when necessary, transmitted an alarm to one or more remote receivers. An intermediate System would monitor additional activities, send data to a central computer via telephone lines, and receive remote commands. An advanced System would provide the same monitoring capabilities but add forecasting features, maintenance management, auxiliary power backup, and data transmission and reception via radio. Prices to customers for the three configurations in early 1991 were about $1500, $2800, and $4800.

AQUAWATCH CUSTOMERS

AquaWatch customers could be divided into two groups—governmental units and industrial companies. The typical application in the first group was a sewage treatment plant having some four to 12 pumping stations, each station containing one or more pumps. Pumps would operate intermittently and—unless an AquaWatch or similar system were in place—be monitored by one or more operators who would visit each station once or perhaps twice each day for about a half-hour. Operators would take reservoir measurements, record running times of pumps, and sometimes perform limited maintenance and repairs. The sewage plant and stations typically were located in flat or rolling terrain, where gravity could not be used in lieu of pumping. If any monitoring equipment were present at all, it typically would consist of a crude, on-site alarm that would activate whenever fluid levels rose or fell beyond a preset level. Sometimes the alarm would activate a telephone dialling function that alerted an operator some distance from the station.

Numerous industrial companies also stored, moved, and processed large quantities of water or sewage. These applications usually differed little from those in governmental plants except for their smaller size. On the other hand, there were a considerably larger number of industrial companies having pumping stations and so, Dillon thought, the two markets offered about identical market potentials.

The two markets desired essentially the same products, although industrial applications often used smaller, simpler equipment. Both markets wanted their monitoring equipment to be accurate and reliable, the two dominant concerns. Equipment should also be easy to use, economical to operate, and require little regular service or maintenance. Purchase price often was not a major consideration—as long as the price was in some appropriate range, customers seemed more interested in actual product performance than in initial outlays.

Dillon thought that worldwide demand for these types of systems would continue to be strong for at least the next ten years. While some demand represented construction of new pumping stations, many applications were replacements of crude monitoring and alarm systems at existing sites. These existing systems depended greatly on regular visits by operators, visits that often continued even after new equipment was installed. Most such trips were probably not necessary. However, many managers found it difficult to dismiss or reassign monitoring personnel who were no longer needed; many were also quite cautious and conservative, desiring some human monitoring of the new equipment "just in case." Once replacements of existing systems were complete, market growth would be limited to new construction and, of course, replacements with more sophisticated systems.

Most customers (as well as non-customers) considered the AquaWatch System one of the best on the market. Those knowledgeable in the industry felt that competing products seldom matched AquaWatch's reliability and accuracy. Experts also believed that many competing products lacked the sophistication and flexibility present in AquaWatch's design. Beyond these product features, customers also appreciated Dillon Controls' knowledge about water and sanitation engineering. Competing firms often lacked this expertise, offering their products somewhat as a sideline and considering the market too small for an intensive marketing effort.

The market was clearly not too small for Dillon Controls. While Jac Dillon had no hard data on market potential for the United States, he thought that annual demand there could be as much as $30 million. In Canada, the total market was at least $4 million. Perhaps about 40% of market demand came from new construction while the rest represented replacements of existing systems. Industry sales in the latter category could be increased by more aggressive marketing efforts on the part of competitors in the industry.

DILLON CONTROLS' STRATEGY

Dillon Controls currently marketed its AquaWatch System primarily to sewage treatment plants in Canada as opposed to industrial companies. Approximately 70% of its revenues came from Ontario and Quebec. The company's strategy could be described as providing technologically superior equipment to monitor pumping operations at these plants. The strategy stressed frequent contacts with customers and potential customers to design, supply, and service AquaWatch Systems. The strategy also stressed superior knowledge of water and sanitation engineering along with up-to-date electronics and computer technology. The result was a line of highly specialized sensors, computers, and methods for process controls in water treatment plants.

This was the essence of Dillon Controls' strategy, having a special competence that no firm in the market could easily match. The company also prided itself on being a young, creative company, without an entrenched bureaucracy. Company employees generally worked with enthusiasm and dedication; they talked with each other, regularly, openly, and with a great deal of give and take. Most importantly, customers—as well as technology—seemed to drive all areas in the company.

Dillon Controls' strategy in Canada seemed to be fairly well decided. That is, Dillon thought that a continuation of present strategies and tactics should continue to produce good results. However, an aspect that would likely change would be to locate a branch office having both sales and distribution functions somewhere out west, most likely in Vancouver. The plan was to have such an office in operation within the next few years. Having a branch office in Vancouver would greatly simplify sales and service in the western provinces, not to mention increase company sales.

Beyond establishing the branch office, Dillon was considering a major strategic decision to enter the U.S. market. The North American Free Trade Agreement, which came into effect in 1989, was prompting many Canadian companies to look southward. Among other things, the agreement eliminated all tariffs on computer products (such as the AquaWatch System) traded between Canada and the United States. In addition, Dillon's two recent visits to the United States had led him to conclude that the market represented potential far beyond that of Canada and that the United States seemed perfect for expansion. Industry experts in the United States agreed with Dillon that the AquaWatch System outperformed anything used in the U.S. market. Experts thought that many water and sewage engineers would welcome Dillon Controls' products and knowledge. Moreover, Dillon thought that U.S. transportation systems and payment arrangements would present few problems.

Entry would most likely be in the form of a sales and service office located in Philadelphia. The Pennsylvania and New York State markets seemed representative of the United States and appeared to offer a good test of the AquaWatch System. While the two states represented only 12% of the U.S. population, they accounted for almost 16% of U.S. manufacturing activity. The office would require an investment of some $200 000 for inventory and other balance sheet items. Annual fixed costs would total upwards of $250 000 for salaries and other operating expenses—Dillon thought that the office would employ only a general manager, technician, and secretary for at least the first year or two. Each AquaWatch System sold in the United States would be priced to provide a contribution of about 30%. Dillon wanted a 35% annual return on any Dillon Controls' investment, to begin no later than the second year. At issue was whether Dillon could realistically expect to achieve this goal in the United States.

MARKETING RESEARCH

To estimate the viability of a U.S. sales office, Dillon had commissioned the Browning Group in Philadelphia to conduct some limited marketing research with selected personnel in the water and sewage industries in the city and surrounding areas. The research had two purposes: to obtain a sense of market needs and market reactions to Dillon Controls' products and to calculate a rough estimate of market potential in Pennsylvania and New York. Results were intended to help Dillon interpret his earlier conversations with industry experts and perhaps allow a decision on market entry.

The research design itself employed two phases of data collection. The first consisted of five one-hour interviews with water and sewage engineers employed by local city and municipal governments. For each interview, an experienced Browning Group interviewer scheduled an appointment with the engineer and then visited his office, armed with a set of questions and a tape recorder. Questions included:

1. What procedures do you use to monitor your pumping stations?
2. Is your current monitoring system effective? Costly?
3. What are the costs of a monitoring malfunction?
4. What features would you like to see in a monitoring system?
5. Who decides on the selection of a monitoring system?
6. What is your reaction to the AquaWatch System?

Interviewers were careful to listen closely to the engineers' responses and to probe for additional detail and clarification.

Tapes of the personal interviews were transcribed and then analyzed by the project manager at Browning. The report noted that these results were interesting in that they described typical industry practices and viewpoints. A partial summary from the report appears below:

> The picture that emerges is one of fairly sophisticated personnel making decisions about monitoring equipment that is relatively simple in design. Still, some engineers would appear distrustful of this equipment because they persist in sending operators to pumping stations on a daily basis. The distrust may be justified because potential costs of a malfunction were identified as expensive repairs and cleanups, fines of $10 000 per day of violation, lawsuits, harassment by the Health Department, and public embarrassment. The five engineers identified themselves as key individuals in the decision to purchase new equipment. Without exception, they considered AquaWatch features innovative, highly desirable, and worth the price.

The summary noted also that the primary use of the interview results was to construct a questionnaire that could be administered over the telephone.

The questionnaire was used in the second phase of data collection, as part of a telephone survey of 65 utility managers, water and sewage engineers, and pumping station operators in Philadelphia and surrounding areas. All respondents were employed by governmental units. Each interview took about ten minutes to complete, covering topics identified in questions 1, 2, and 4 above. The Browning Group's research report stated that most interviews found respondents to be quite cooperative, although 15 people refused to participate at all.

The telephone interviews had produced results that could be considered more representative of the market because of the larger sample size. The report had organized these results about the topics of monitoring procedures, system effectiveness and costs, and features desired in a monitoring system:

All monitoring systems under the responsibility of the 50 respondents were considered to require manual checking. The frequency of operator visits to pumping stations ranged from monthly to twice daily, depending on flow rates, pumping station history, proximity of nearby communities, monitoring equipment in operation, and other factors. Even the most sophisticated automatic systems were checked because respondents "just don't trust the machine." Each operator was responsible for an average of 15 stations.

Despite the perceived need for double-checking, all respondents considered their current monitoring system to be quite effective. Not one reported a serious pumping malfunction in the past three years that had escaped detection. However, this reliability came at considerable cost—the annual wages and other expenses associated with each monitoring operator averaged about $50 000.

Respondents were about evenly divided between those wishing a simple alarm system and those desiring a sophisticated, versatile microprocessor. Managers and engineers in the former category often said that the only feature they really needed was an emergency signal such as a siren, horn, or light. Sometimes they would add a telephone dialer that would be automatically activated at the same time as the signal. Most agreed that a price of around $2000 would be reasonable for such a system. The latter category of individuals contained engineers desiring many of the AquaWatch System's features, once they knew such equipment was available. A price of $5000 per system seemed acceptable. Some of these respondents were quite knowledgeable about computers and computer programming while others were not. Only four respondents voiced any strong concerns about the cost to purchase and install more sophisticated monitoring equipment. Everyone demanded that the equipment be reliable and accurate.

Dillon found the report quite helpful. Much of the information, of course, simply confirmed his own view of the U.S. market. However, it was good to have this knowledge from an independent, objective organization. In addition, to learn that the market consisted of two, apparently equally sized segments of simple and sophisticated applications was quite worthwhile. In particular, knowledge of system prices considered acceptable by each segment would make the entry decision easier. Meeting these prices would not be a major problem.

A most important section of the report contained an estimate of market potential for Pennsylvania and New York. The estimate was based on an analysis of discharge permits on file in governmental offices in the two states. These permits were required before any city, municipality, water or sewage district, or industrial company could release sewage or other contaminated water to another system or to a lake or river. Each permit showed the number of pumping stations in operation. Based on a 10% sample of permits, the report had estimated that governmental units in Pennsylvania and New York contained approximately 3000 and 5000 pumping stations for waste water, respectively. Industrial companies in the two states were estimated to add some 3000 and 9000 more pumping stations, respectively. The total number of pumping stations in the two states—20 000—seemed to be growing at about 2% per year.

Finally, a brief section of the report dealt with the study's limitations. Dillon agreed that the sample was quite small, that it contained no utility managers or engineers from New York, and that it probably concentrated too heavily on individuals in larger urban areas. In addition, the research told him nothing about competitors and their marketing strategies and tactics. Nor did he learn anything about any state regulations for monitoring equipment, if indeed any existed. However, these shortcomings came as no surprise, representing a consequence of the research design proposed to Dillon by the Browning Group some six weeks ago, before the study began.

THE DECISION

Dillon's decision seemed a difficult one. The most risky option was to enter the U.S. market as soon as possible. There was no question about the vast market potential of the U.S. However, the company's opportunity for a greatly increased bottom line had to be balanced against the threat of new competitors who were, for the most part, larger and more sophisticated than Dillon Controls. In fact, a friend had jokingly remarked that "a Canadian firm selling microprocessor controls in the U.S. would be like trying to sell Canadian semiconductors to the Japanese."

The most conservative option was to stay in Canada. Of course, Dillon Controls would continue to respond to the odd inquiry from the United States and would continue to fill orders that the company accepted from U.S. customers. However, it would not seek this sort of business in an aggressive fashion. Nor would it seek representation in the United States through an agent or distributor. The latter option put Dillon Controls out of the picture as far as controlling sales claims, prices, product installation, service, and other important aspects of customer relations was concerned.

In between the two extremes was the option of conducting some additional marketing research. Discussion with the Browning Group had identified the objectives of this research as to rectify limitations of the first study as well as to provide more accurate estimates of market potential. (The estimates of the numbers of pumping stations in Pennsylvania and New York were accurate to around plus or minus 20%.) This research was estimated to cost $40 000 and take another three months to complete.

Marketing In-Focus, Inc.

H. F. (Herb) MacKenzie

In the fall term of 2002, Donna Mason was considering what she would like to do after completing her undergraduate business degree. She was in the last academic year of study at an eastern Canadian business school. She was at one time considering going into the family furniture business with her two older brothers, but the closer she came to graduation, the less attractive this option seemed. She had applied to several consumer goods companies for a marketing position, and she was confident that at least one would result in a job opportunity. However, Donna's first choice was to open her own small consulting firm, Marketing In-Focus, Inc.

Donna first started to think seriously about consulting after talking to one of her marketing professors. He told her that there was a dramatic increase in demand for marketing consulting in recent years. Donna decided to do some investigating on her own, and she found an article in *Consultation* titled "The Management Consulting Profession: An Empirical Description" by Terry L. Maris. The article stated that a higher percentage of consultants serviced the manufacturing sector than any other sector.

As she continued her search, Donna found that there was little published information that would help her decide where opportunities might exist, although she found a lot of information in trade magazines related to consulting. Specifically, Donna wanted to know who in companies made the decision to hire a consultant, what types of consulting were most commonly needed, what criteria were used to decide which consulting firms were selected, and most importantly, whether companies preferred to use large consulting firms or if they would consider using small independent consulting firms such as the one she wished to start. Donna decided to conduct her own marketing research.

MARKETING RESEARCH STUDY AND RESULTS

Donna decided that she would focus specifically on manufacturing firms with 20 or more employees, located in principal cities within a two-hour drive from where she hoped to operate her business. Following a search of *Scott's Directories* for that region, she was able to identify 681 firms. She randomly chose 100 of these firms for her research sample. Donna divided the sample into four equal groups, and convinced three of her friends to each conduct 25 telephone surveys for her. She did the first 25 surveys herself to ensure that there were no problems with the questionnaire. Among the 100 companies chosen for the study, 7 had gone out of business or had disconnected telephones and could not be located by company name, 6 were abandoned by interviewers after a minimum of three callbacks, and 5 refused to cooperate.

Among the 82 firms that cooperated, only 30 used management consultants (36.6%). The average number of employees among these firms was 274; those firms that did not use consultants averaged only 67 employees. There was one firm included in the sample that employed 2300 people, and another that employed 1100 people. All other respondent firms had less than 1000 employees. If the two largest firms were dropped from the sample, the average number of employees of companies that employed management consultants was 173.

Exhibit 1 provides the questions Donna asked in her survey, along with a summary of respondent answers.

EXHIBIT 1	Survey Questionnaire and Summary Results

Question 1

Has your firm used the services of an external consultant or consulting firm within the past three years?

Yes	30	(Go to Question 2)
No	52	(Go to Question 8)

Question 2

Who in your firm decides which external consultant or consulting firm is to be hired?

Title	Responses	Percent
President/CEO	17	(30.4)
Vice-President	8	(14.3)
COO/General Manager	12	(21.4)
Director	3	(5.4)
Controller	3	(5.4)
Manager	11	(19.6)
Owner	2	(3.6)

EXHIBIT 1	Survey Questionnaire and Summary Results (continued)

Question 3

For what reasons has your firm hired an external consultant or consulting firm within the past three years?

Purpose for Hiring	Responses	Percent
Human resources	16	(33.3)
Operations issues	11	(22.9)
Computers	5	(10.4)
Technical issues	4	(8.3)
General management	4	(8.3)
Strategic planning	4	(8.3)
Marketing / sales management	2	(4.2)
Reorganization	2	(4.2)

	Not Very Important				Very Important
When your firm chooses an external consultant or consulting firm, how important is their experience in your choice?	1	2	3	4	5
When your firm chooses an external consultant or consulting firm, how important is their past performance in your choice?	1	2	3	4	5
When your firm chooses an external consultant or consulting firm, how important is the reputation of the individual who will be managing the project in your choice?	1	2	3	4	5
When your firm chooses an external consultant or consulting firm, how important is the reputation of the firm in your choice?	1	2	3	4	5
When your firm chooses an external consultant or consulting firm, how important is it that the individual be recommended to you in your choice?	1	2	3	4	5
When your firm chooses an external consultant or consulting firm, how important is it that the firm be recommended to you in your choice?	1	2	3	4	5
When your firm chooses an external consultant or consulting firm, how important is price or fees in your choice?	1	2	3	4	5
When your firm chooses an external consultant or consulting firm, how important is the size of the firm in your choice?	1	2	3	4	5

EXHIBIT 1	Survey Questionnaire and Summary Results (continued)

Criteria	Mean Response
Experience	4.57[a]
Past performance	4.40
Reputation of individual	4.40[b]
Reputation of firm	4.00[b]
Individual recommended	3.57
Firm recommended	3.50
Prices/fees	3.47[b]
Size of firm	2.00

a. Significantly different from the next-highest mean, $p < .10$.
b. Significantly different from the next-highest mean, $p < .05$.

Question 5

Are there any other criteria that your firm uses when choosing an external consultant or consulting firm? If *yes*, what are they?

Criterion	Responses
Personality fit	4
Appropriate expertise	3
Fit with organization culture	2
Availability / flexibility of hours	1
Presentation	1
Diagnostic ability	1
Government subsidization	1

Question 6

Consider the last external consultant or consulting firm your company hired. Did your company choose a small, independent consultant or one of the large management consulting firms such as Ernst & Young or PricewaterhouseCoopers? *Also:* If your company considered a second alternative, how would you describe that second alternative?

	Only Alternative	Second Alternative
Small, independent firm	9	7
Larger management consulting firm	6	8

EXHIBIT 1	**Survey Questionnaire and Summary Results** (continued)

Question 7

Consider the last external consultant or consulting firm your company hired. What criteria did you use to evaluate their performance?

Criterion	Responses
Accepted by client people	8
Experience with consultant	5
Practical recommendations	4
Results on time	4
Maintained good relationship	4
Met objectives	3
Ability of client to carry on	2
Flexible schedule of consultant	2
Ethics of consultant	1
Involvement of consultant	1
Organized approach to project	1
Walked client through process	1
Cost control	1

Question 8

Can you tell me why your firm has not used an external consultant or consulting firm within the past three years?

Reasons	Responses	Percent
We had no requirement	17	(37.0)
We have in-house expertise	9	(19.6)
Head office decision	9	(19.6)
We are too small	8	(17.4)
They are too expensive	3	(6.5)

Eyckline Farms

Jane Funk and Thomas Funk

Wilhelm Van Eyck turned his pickup into the lane of Eyckline Farms and stopped at the mailbox. Pulling out the day's mail, he found the usual collection of advertisements, magazines, and personal letters. He noted that his wife would be pleased to get her latest *Good Housekeeping* and that he had received a letter from cousin Charlie in British Columbia. Wilhelm and Charlie had corresponded regularly since their immigration to Canada 30 years ago. They had gone through public school together and then worked on a local farm while taking evening courses at a Dutch agricultural college. When they left the Netherlands and came to Canada, Charlie settled in British Columbia and Wilhelm came to Ontario. Wilhelm and Charlie spent most of their yearly visits in heated debates about the relative importance of various inputs in their broiler operations, and Wilhelm had little patience with Charlie's belief that he would increase his profits once he found the "magic feed" formula. Wilhelm always answered that no grower would ever have consistently outstanding crops: "too many variables, Charlie. Better trust your own judgment, not some magic formula. You need healthy chicks and proper management as well as good feed." Charlie never listened, of course. That's what made their yearly visits so interesting.

This case was prepared by Jane Funk and Thomas Funk of the Ontario Agricultural College at the University of Guelph, Guelph, Ontario, Canada. It is intended as a basis for classroom discussion and is not designed to present either correct or incorrect handling of administrative problems. © 1998 by Thomas Funk. Reprinted with permission.

Wilhelm had done well for himself and was quite pleased with his operation which included capacity to produce 100 000 broilers a year, a 300-sow farrow to finish operation, and 809 hectares of crops. Wilhelm was also pleased because his two sons, Harold and Martin, were actively involved in the operation. Although Wilhelm made most of the key management decisions on the farm and was mainly responsible for the broiler operation, Harold had primary responsibility for the swine operation and Martin looked after the crops and the maintenance of all equipment. Harold's wife, Marcia, was very skilled in computers, so she looked after keeping records, ordering supplies and paying bills. Harold and Marcia lived just a half-mile from the main operation of Eyckline Farms while Martin, who was not married, lived at home. Harold graduated from the Ontario Agricultural College at the University of Guelph four years ago with a degree in Animal Science. Although Martin had no formal education past high school, he had taken a number of equipment maintenance courses at a local community college and was considering applying for the Diploma in Agriculture program at the University of Guelph.

Eyckline Farms also employed Adrian Vandenburg as a full-time employee who helped in all the operations, but spent most of his time with the broilers. This gave Wilhelm enough time to look after general farm management issues. Prior to joining Eyckline Farms, Adrian had a small broiler operation of his own so he was very knowledgeable in this field of agriculture. Wilhelm liked Adrian and often sought his opinion on decisions relating to the broiler operation. While Wilhelm felt diversifying into crops and hogs was a good business decision and spread his risk, he was always partial to the broiler operation, perhaps because it was how he got started.

As Wilhelm climbed back into his pickup, he tossed the mail on the seat beside him and continued down the lane. No doubt about it, he had come a long way in the thirty years since he and Charlie stepped off the boat. He surveyed the orderly spread of Eyckline Farms and admired the new siding on the house and the new broiler barn built this year. "Yessir, if you make a dollar you sometimes do well to put it back into the business," he said to himself. He appreciated the advice the building representative had given him on ventilation for the new facility. Of course, it seemed a bit extravagant given Wilhelm's budget, but once he adapted it to his own operation, it worked out fine. He appreciated good advice. Brushing a speck of dust off the steering wheel of his new pickup, Wilhelm gathered the mail and went into the house where Polly Van Eyck was preparing lunch.

"Here's your *Good Housekeeping*, Polly," Wilhelm said, "and I got a letter from Charlie, too."

"Anything from my sister?" asked Polly.

"No, just advertisements. These guys never give up. Wait, here's one from Master Feed. I wonder what they want. I just saw Jim yesterday and he didn't seem to have anything to say—seemed in a hurry, as usual."

Master Feed was Van Eyck's current feed supplier for his broiler operation. He had been with Master Feed for two years despite two price increases. The last price increase had annoyed him somewhat since it seemed designed to cover an increase in extra salesman services which Van Eyck did not use. However, he had stayed with Master Feed because results were reasonably good. He had to admit that the last crop had not been up to par, but he decided he would wait until he got the next results before considering a switch. All the same, he thought, as he looked at the letter, it would have been appreciated if Jim Sellars, the Master Feed salesman, had stopped by to check up on his last results. "I guess he's too busy carting the neighbour's birds to the vet," Wilhelm thought to himself. Since

Jim knew Wilhelm preferred to take his own birds to the vet, he rarely stopped by except to take an order.

Although Eyckline Farms purchased broiler feed from Master Feed, they purchased hog supplement from Smith Feeds. Chuck Hustead, the Smith Feed rep, and Harold had become very close friends at university so Harold was anxious to do business with Chuck. In addition, Smith Feed had an excellent reputation in the swine industry for products that would deliver high performance under superior management conditions.

Wilhelm gave no more thought to the letter from Master Feed until later that afternoon when he, Harold, Martin, and Marcia met in the farm office for their weekly management meeting. Marcia had just finished summarizing the results from the last broiler crop which she presented to the others. Much to Wilhelm's disappointment, feed conversion had slipped again for the third crop in a row. The decline was not great, but there appeared to be a consistent trend. Harold suggested that they might do better with something less expensive. Then Wilhelm remembered the letter. Opening it, he discovered a form letter explaining Master Feed's new policy which required their contract growers to assign proceeds from the processing plant to the feed supplier who then deducted the cost of feed and chicks before sending the balance to the grower. Wilhelm had never contracted with Master Feed though he bought both feed and chicks from the company. He preferred to choose his own processor, and it annoyed him that he should have received a form letter meant only for contract producers. He put down the letter and glanced again at the performance results. It was irritating that Jim Sellars had not taken the time to make sure his non-contract customers did not receive the letter. "Too busy giving out expensive advice about medication and high brooder temperatures," muttered Van Eyck. Even more alarming was the policy itself which seemed almost an insult and further evidence to Wilhelm that the producer who contracted with an integrated firm lost much of their independence. "I don't want anybody telling me what to pay for feed or chicks or when to ship my crop," Wilhelm said to the others.

During the meeting, Marcia also mentioned her growing frustration with billing problems from several suppliers, especially Master Feed. Marcia prided herself on always getting cheques prepared and in the mail in enough time to earn early payment discounts. The fact that occasionally these were not properly handled was becoming annoying. "It makes me wonder how good their products are when companies are sloppy in how they handle administrative matters like accounting," she noted. "In addition, it causes me a lot of unnecessary work. I have enough to do without having to check every statement that comes in. In an operation like ours we get over 30 every month."

The next morning Van Eyck was on his way to the barn when his neighbour Fritz Lonsdorf stopped by. Lonsdorf was one of the larger broiler producers in the area and Wilhelm enjoyed comparing notes with him. They chatted for awhile about the weather, then Wilhelm mentioned the new Master Feed policy and their carelessness in sending him the form letter. They had discussed the price increase earlier and Wilhelm's disappointing crop.

Fritz suggested trying Domar, the brand he had been using for a number of years. "My cockerels weighed over 2.1 kilograms at 38 days on the last crop," exclaimed Fritz.

"I remember you telling me," said Wilhelm, lighting his pipe. He also remembered checking with the processor and finding that Fritz's cockerels had actually been killed at 42 days and averaged 2.07 kilograms. "Nice fellow, Fritz, but you have to take what he says with a grain of salt," Wilhelm told Harold at the time. "Dad," Harold laughed, "you say that about everybody. Fritz does brag a little, but you and I both know 2.07 kilograms is a darned sight higher than our last average, even with our more expensive feed."

He and Fritz continued chatting about John Stern's new farrowing house and the best cure for "bent beak syndrome." Fritz mentioned a new remedy which he had seen advertised in *Canada Poultryman*. Wilhelm remained skeptical: "I wouldn't take a chance Fritz. I'd get my birds to the vet as fast as I could if I were you. Maybe take them to the university. See what they think of your idea before you try it." Fritz said he would consider it and the two of them made further plans to visit the London Poultry Show later in the month. "Always look forward to seeing the new displays and talking with the other producers," Wilhelm said as Fritz left.

That evening Wilhelm spread the reports Marcia had prepared on the kitchen table and noticed again the poor results of the last crop. Not drastic, he thought, but he would hate to see it continue, especially given the higher price he paid for Master Feed. Fritz's results kept running through his mind. He thought Master Feed was much the same as other quality feeds but the latest price increase and the poor results made him wonder. He considered the other major variables in his operation to see if they could be responsible for the disappointing performance. His buildings and equipment were the latest design and he handled the management himself with Adrian doing most of the work. In the past, Adrian had been a little careless—failing to clean the waterer or some other little thing, but lately he was really shaping up. The chicks, also purchased since he started his operation from a Master Feed affiliate, were top-quality. Wilhelm personally rushed them to the university or the lab at the slightest sign of disease. Lately, Jim Sellars seemed anxious to do this for his customers, but Wilhelm preferred to be right there to give the vet the benefit of his own ideas. He found the vet's advice sound, though he never followed it without first airing his own idea. "Nobody knows my operation as well as I do," he remarked to the vet.

Chicks, management, and equipment were all checked out. That left feed. With the latest price increase, the slightest rise in feed conversion could cause a significant decrease in return per bird. "Beyond a certain price, quality isn't that different," Wilhelm often told cousin Charlie. He looked at the entries in the record book which detailed his feed purchasing history from the beginning of his operation:

Feed Company	Purchase History
Starlight Feeds	Five years until the company was purchased by Supersweet
Supersweet Feeds	Three years
Chance Feeds	Two years until the company was purchased by P & H
P & H Feeds	One year
Full-O-Pep Feeds	Three years until the company was purchased by Master Feed
Master Feed	Current supplier

Wilhelm remembered how he had been quite happy with Starlight Feeds and stayed with them even after they were purchased by Supersweet. Soon Supersweet discontinued the Starlight brand and tried to switch customers to their Supersweet brand by offering an initial price reduction. Wilhelm had used Supersweet for three years even as the planned price increases were implemented because he was reluctant to switch. Finally, he could not agree that there was a quality difference worth the $8–$10 a ton (1 ton = 0.91 tonne) premium which Supersweet was charging. When the Chance Feeds salesman came around and offered $10 a ton less, Wilhelm gave their feed a try and found it was every bit as good as the higher-priced Supersweet product. Not only was it less expensive the feed conversion was equally good.

Wilhelm stayed with Chance Feeds for two years, even after they were purchased by P & H Feeds. Once again the price started to go up about $2–$3 per crop. "Seems to be the story of my operation," Wilhelm muttered to himself. P & H was now at the same price level as Full-O-Pep, and Wilhelm had heard about Full-O-Pep results from other growers so he decided to give it a try. The results were good and Wilhelm stayed with them even after their operation was purchased by Master Feed. Soon Master Feed phased out the Full-O-Pep line, replacing it with their own brand. Since Master Feed was competitively priced, Van Eyck made the change and had been satisfied. Then Master Feed began to raise their price. After two price increases they were one of the most expensive brands in the industry, priced in the range of Supersweet. Neither price increase had been announced and Wilhelm had noticed it only after the feed bills arrived. Though not immediately alarmed, Wilhelm had become uneasy when his latest crop results were less than spectacular. "And here I am," Wilhelm said. "Every time one of those big fellows takes over, price goes up and service goes down."

Wilhelm felt he was pretty realistic about his feed expectations, unlike cousin Charlie. He also appreciated that Jim Sellars didn't pressure him to sign a contract but wished he would stop by every now and then for a chat just to see how things were going. Wilhelm enjoyed chatting with salesmen about market changes, growers' results, and disease problems, but he became annoyed when they brought out their "outstanding grower results." He also disliked paying (through price increases) for services which he did not use. It seemed that Jim Sellars was too busy running around the country taking birds to the vet and dispensing "free" advice on feeder space, temperature, and ventilation, all areas where Wilhelm relied on his own experience. When he wanted advice, he'd ask for it, thank you, and he'd ask somebody who knew what they were talking about.

Wilhelm put down the performance report and wandered into the living room. Polly was at a church meeting and Martin was at a ball game, so he picked up the day's mail, turned on the radio, and sat down. Glancing through *Canada Poultryman*, he noticed the ads for Chance Feeds and Ralston Purina. Both featured a testimonial by an "outstanding poultry producer," neither of whom was known to Wilhelm. "Sure they get great results," Wilhelm thought. "They probably have two million dollars' worth of equipment!" An ad for new feeding equipment caught his eye and he made a note to ask Harold, Martin, and Adrian what they knew about it. Continuing on he saw the medication mentioned by Fritz and made another note to ask the vet about it next time he was at the clinic. Then he heard a car drive in the lane and, looking out, saw Dave Crawford, the salesman for Domar in Elmira, walking toward the house. Crawford was a pleasant fellow, not much older than Martin. He had been with Domar for about a year and had been trying to get Wilhelm to consider their broiler feeds. It would be pleasant to pass some time with Crawford.

"Hello, Dave. Good to see you. Come on in and have a coffee."

"Thanks, Wilhelm. I was in the neighbourhood and thought I'd stop by to give you this article on a new feeding system. I saw it in *Ontario Farmer* and thought you would enjoy reading it."

"That's real thoughtful of you, Dave. I was considering a new system," Wilhelm answered, thinking how Jim Sellars had never even bothered to stop by to see the new broiler barn, let alone bring a bit of unsolicited information.

"My pleasure, Wilhelm. I figured you'd be alone tonight with the women off at the church meeting and Martin at the ball game. Of course, I also wanted to see that new broiler barn. It's the talk of the neighbourhood."

They chatted for awhile about local events, latest marketing board activities, and Fritz Lonsdorf's problem with bent beak syndrome. Then Dave said, "Wilhelm, the mill is taking a group of growers to the London Poultry Show and I thought you might be able to join us."

Wilhelm thanked him but explained that he and Fritz had already planned to go. Dave then casually remarked, "I hear Master Feed upped their prices again."

Wilhelm acknowledged that this was so. "Well," Dave went on, "They've got a good feed there, no doubt about it. Are you still pleased with the results?"

Wilhelm hesitated, then admitted his last crop was a little disappointing.

"I can understand your feelings, Wilhelm. I really believe Domar can give you equal or better results. You know our quality and feed conversion ratios are competitive and our price is a good $5 a ton lower. Someone who is as experienced as you are knows we have to offer a quality product to stay in business. Why not let us feed the next crop and see how our feed performs in your barn?

"Dave, I'm just not ready to make a change yet, but I sure will give your offer some thought," Wilhelm answered. "Adrian is encouraging me to try Smith Feeds because of his past experience with their brand and the fact that Harold likes it for the hog operation. I'll let you know in a week or so."

"Sure, Wilhelm. I understand. I appreciate your considering us. I remember that Adrian used Smith Feed when he had his own operation. I thought he was disappointed with their performance."

"Is there anything I can do to help you better understand the value of our Domar product?" asked Dave. "I would be pleased to bring our company nutritionist out in a couple of days to discuss your situation in more detail and provide a professional opinion."

"Thanks, Dave," Wilhelm said, " but I don't think that will be necessary right now. I have a pretty good feel for my own operation."

"Fine, Wilhelm, talk to you later," Crawford said as he rose to go. "Better get on, the women will be home soon."

The next day Wilhelm took a load of birds to the vet. He drove past the P & H dealer but didn't stop, remembering that their prices were at least as high as Master Feed. Besides, not one of their salesmen had stopped by since he had switched several years earlier. While at the vet, Wilhelm mentioned his dissatisfaction with Master Feed and asked the vet's opinion about Domar. The vet agreed that above a certain price range quality was quite comparable and results would probably be much the same using either feed.

Driving home, Wilhelm passed Chuck Hustead, the sales rep for Smith Feeds. Hustead pulled over and asked if Wilhelm had a few minutes to spare. Wilhelm glanced at the birds in the back, but said he could give Hustead a few minutes. Hustead climbed into the truck, dropping his portfolio in the process and scattering papers. Wilhelm sighed and glanced at his watch and the chicks sitting in the sun in the back, while Hustead tried to rearrange the papers.

"I was just by your place, Wilhelm. That's some broiler barn you have there. I was a little surprised at the ventilation, though."

Wilhelm filled his pipe and looked at Hustead pointedly. "Is that right, Chuck? Well, I did what I thought best."

"Sure, Wilhelm, but I thought those reports I showed you gave some pretty good suggestions," Hustead said.

"They were a little too experimental for me, Chuck. Now what can I do for you?"

"Well, I thought I would stop by and explain our new program. You know we're quality- and price-competitive, especially after that latest Master Feed price increase. And Harold is very pleased with the performance of our hog feed. Did Marcia show you how the average number of pigs per litter has increased since you started using our new sow ration?"

Wilhelm's pipe went out and the chicks seemed to be getting more restless. Chuck didn't seem to notice as he continued. "Look at these broiler reports! I'll bet you've never seen better results than these."

"My results aren't so bad, Chuck. Besides, I told you before, I don't hold with these consistently outstanding results. You know as well as I do that excellent crops are as much the result of chance and good management as they are of feed."

"Well, have it your own way Wilhelm, but these figures don't lie."

Wilhelm looked at him silently. "Besides we'll deliver whenever you want and take your birds to the vet so you don't have to waste your time running around," Hustead continued.

Wilhelm's pipe went out again. "Speaking of birds, Chuck, you may have noticed mine are getting nervous, so I'd best be getting on."

"Oh—sure, sure! I'll leave these results with you. Once you look them over I'm sure you'll be impressed. By the way, have you considered doing business with Fairview Hatcheries? They have good-quality chicks. Hardly ever get sick. Probably save you in the long run. Not nearly as nervous as yours."

"See you later, Chuck," said Wilhelm closing the door and driving away.

"I'll be hearing from you soon," shouted Hustead. Wilhelm drove on.

Smith Feeds had a good reputation, especially in swine, and they were price- and quality-competitive, but Wilhelm was annoyed at Hustead's continual harping on "excellent grower results." It was the same every call. Besides, "the ventilation is fine in my new chicken house and it's my business which hatchery I choose!" At least Jim Sellars never pushed him to try a new hatchery! Wilhelm knew that Harold was very happy with the performance of Smith Feeds in the hog operation. Harold often urged Wilhelm to at least give them a try in the broiler operation. So far Wilhelm prevailed with the argument that Smith Feeds does not have a comparable reputation among broiler producers. Not having seen any performance results, Harold could not argue otherwise.

When he arrived home, Wilhelm put the chicks in the chicken house and went into the kitchen, dropping Hustead's reports on the table. Polly came over with the dishes and, glancing at the reports, said, "Do you need these, Wilhelm?"

"What? Oh, those. No, Polly, throw them away," Wilhelm said as he opened the evening paper.

In the days that followed, Wilhelm continued thinking about his feed situation but made no move to change suppliers, as he still had a couple of bins of Master Feed product on hand. He knew he would have to decide soon. Crawford stopped by several times and so did Hustead. Jim Sellars came by once, but Wilhelm was out. He left a message to have Wilhelm call if he had any problems. Wilhelm knew there were other feed suppliers in the immediate area and he was not opposed to travelling a few miles further, though he thought local feed was probably fresher. Their prices were all pretty competitive with Smith and Domar and the quality was similar, at least in his view. There were also several large companies with prices similar to those of Master Feed and P & H, but he suspected the price difference went into their flashy advertising and not the quality of their feed. "Maybe it isn't worth it to change," he thought. Just then Jim Sellars passed him on the road and waved. Wilhelm thought he might be coming for a chat, but Jim drove on. Wilhelm turned in to Eyckline Farms. He had made his decision and would place the call after dinner.

"Greener Pastures": The Launch of StaGreen™ by HydroCan

Anne T. Hale

Stone Age Marketing Consultants was founded five years ago by Cari Clarkstone, Karen Jonestone, and Robert Sommerstone. Their target clients were small, startup firms as well as medium-sized firms looking to expand operations. Their newest client, HydroCan, had a meeting scheduled for the following afternoon and the three founders were discussing the results of their market analysis. HydroCan was a startup company that was obtaining patents in both the United States and Canada for a new type of lawn-care product. Since the company was made up of four agricultural engineers and a financial accountant, they were in need of marketing advice concerning their new product, StaGreen™. This product, when applied to most types of grass, enabled the root system to retain water longer, thus reducing the need for both extra watering and frequent fertilizing. They were anxious to take this product to market; however, they desperately needed answers to several questions, including which segment to target, how to position their new product, and what type of launch strategy they should use. They approached Stone Age Marketing Consultants approximately four weeks ago with their needs. The marketing consultants had analyzed the markets, costs, prices, and communications options. Their last task was to formulate a comprehensive strategy for the launch of StaGreen.

Prepared by Anne T. Hale, Visiting Assistant Professor of Marketing, Faculty of Business, University of Victoria, Victoria, British Columbia, as a basis for class discussion. © 1996 by Anne T. Hale. Reprinted with permission.

INITIAL MEETING WITH HYDROCAN

During the initial meeting between HydroCan and Stone Age, the engineers outlined the product and its potential benefits. The product was very similar in appearance to most brands of common lawn fertilizer. In fact, StaGreen was classified as a chemical fertilizer, but with one very important difference. Its primary benefit was its effect on the root system of most of the common types of grasses used for lawns. The small pellets attached to roots and attracted and retained moisture. Extensive laboratory testing demonstrated that StaGreen reduced the need for manual watering on most types of grass by up to 40%. Obviously such a product would have high demand. The first question that HydroCan needed addressed was what market to target initially with this product. Gary Gillis, CEO of HydroCan, wanted to target the consumer lawn and garden market as their initial target segment. Carla Humphreys, on the other hand, was more inclined to target the commercial lawn and garden market. Since these two markets required very different launch strategies, selecting the appropriate segment was the primary concern. And, due to the fact that both Mr. Gillis and Ms. Humphreys were extremely biased toward their position, the consultants knew that they would have to present strong reasons to support their recommendation. To make this task manageable, they divided the research and analysis along the following lines: Cari Clarkstone was to investigate the viability of a consumer launch, Karen Jonestone was to investigate the viability of a commercial launch, and Robert Sommerstone was to obtain all necessary financial information.

THE CONSUMER MARKET

In 1995, Canadians spent nearly $2.3 billion, at the retail level, on gardening. This figure includes $945 million for grass (both sod and seed), trees, and plants, $620 million on lawn maintenance (fertilizers accounting for 52% of the total), and $815 million on hand tools, pots, window boxes, books, magazines, landscaping services, etc. In other words, gardening is big business in Canada. Lawn care is, however, a highly seasonal business, with 70% of sales occurring in the second and third fiscal quarters (i.e., April to September).

According to Cari Clarkstone's research, if HydroCan was to target this segment, they would be competing primarily with fertilizers. The consumer fertilizer market is extremely competitive, with the top two firms, Scotts Co. and Ortho Chemicals, controlling approximately 50% of the total consumer market. Both firms are headquartered in the United States (with divisional offices in Canada), and both have extensive international operations. The market share leader is Scotts Co., with their two powerful brands, Turf Builder and Miracle-Gro (acquired in May of 1995 from the privately held Stern's Group). Turf Builder is a slow-release fertilizer that reduces the number of applications required for a healthy lawn. This slow-release technology is relatively new—having been available to the consumer market for less than two years. Slow-release simply means that the fertilizing chemicals are released gradually over a number of months. Thus one application of slow-release fertilizer could last for a maximum of two years (although most manufacturers recommend applications every year).

Turf Builder is priced slightly lower than most Miracle-Gro products, which are advertised as maximum-growth products, and not specifically (i.e., exclusively) aimed at lawn care. Ortho's products are priced competitively with Turf Builder—their added value comes

EXHIBIT 1	Competitor Prices for the Consumer Market	
	Size(s)	Retail Prices(s)
Scotts Turf Builder	10 kg	$24.50
Scotts Turf Builder	25 kg	$59.99
Scotts Turf Builder	5 kg	$ 14.75
Miracle-Gro–plant/crystals	200 g	$ 8.50
Miracle-Gro–lawn/garden	2.5 kg	$ 12.95
Miracle-Gro–liquid	1 L	$ 7.99
Ortho (with pesticide)	10 kg	$23.99
Ortho (with pesticide)	30 kg	$68.79

from the inclusion of pesticides within the fertilizer that prevents most common lawn infestations. See Exhibit 1 for pricing information on the major branded fertilizer products.

Market research has shown that four out of ten consumers in this market have no concrete brand preferences. They rely heavily on in-store advertisements and sales staff for information and recommendations. Many consumers cannot recall a brand name or a manufacturer of fertilizer. The product with the highest brand-name awareness is Miracle-Gro; however, most associate this brand name with their plant foods rather than their lawn fertilizers. Because of consumer behaviour and attitude toward this product category, most manufacturers relied on a strong push strategy.

Most lawn care products are sold by three distinct types of retailers: discount stores, such as Canadian Tire, Wal-Mart, and Sears; specialty stores, including nurseries; and home improvement stores. The discount stores, who buy direct from manufacturers, place strict requirements on their orders and expect price concessions and special support. Marketing expenses for both Scott and Ortho went up by approximately 10% between 1994 and 1995, with the bulk of the increase devoted to promotions to discount retailers. This indicates the relative importance of this channel—it is estimated that 60% of all consumer fertilizer sales are made in discount stores, compared to approximately 30% of sales being made in specialty stores and 10% of sales being made in home improvement stores. Discount stores have, in fact, been spending millions in renovations in order to accommodate larger lawn and garden areas within their stores. The same is true with home improvement stores, such as Home Depot, which has 21 locations in Canada.[1]

Specialty stores, the vast majority of which are nurseries, tend to be independently owned and thus much more numerous. While the 9 top discount chains across Canada control over 89% of all sales from discount stores, the top 50 specialty garden stores account for less than 28% of all sales from this store type. The most recent research indicates that there are over 1000 specialty garden stores in Canada. Most of these stores purchase from large horticulture wholesalers, and receive little, if any promotional assistance from the major manufacturers. Home improvement stores are growing in numbers, and tend to be large, powerful chains, such as Home Depot. While these stores do not represent a large portion of current sales, they are expected to grow in importance. Like discount stores, home improvement stores buy direct from the manufacturers and require price concessions and promotional support.

The large manufacturers of fertilizer products generally spend approximately 20% of sales on marketing activities. The bulk of this money goes toward the sales force, and selling in general, and trade promotions. Due to the three different channels in which their product is sold, most fertilizer manufacturers recognize the importance of a strong sales force. In terms of trade promotions, they provide in-store literature, displays, and sales training—especially to the large discount stores and the home improvement stores. Less important is advertising. Miracle-Gro is the most heavily advertised brand on the market, and they generally spend 4% of sales on advertising (which probably accounts for the high brand-name awareness). Scotts advertises Turf Builder, but only during the early spring when demand for lawn fertilizers is at its peak. Most companies run their advertisements for their existing brands and any new brands they may be launching during the spring and early summer months. Thus, advertising expenditures are generally at their highest in March, April, May, and June, and zero at all other times. Only Miracle-Gro is advertised year-round, with different messages at different times of the year. For example, Miracle-Gro advertises its benefits for house plants during the winter months, and its benefits for fruits, vegetables, and flowers during the spring and summer months.

THE COMMERCIAL MARKET

The commercial market consists primarily of Canada's 1800 golf courses, but also includes commercial properties such as office complexes and apartment buildings. The most lucrative market, however, are golf courses. Currently under fire for being a major source of groundwater pollution, due to the high and frequent levels of fertilizers used to keep courses green, most owners are actively looking for ways to cut both water and fertilizer usage. Course owners spend, on average, $300 000 to maintain their golf course during the year, of which 42% represents water usage costs and 24% represents fertilizer purchases. For extremely large, complex courses, this figure can run as high as $800 000, and for smaller inner-city public courses, as low as $104 000. Tests have indicated that StaGreen will reduce water usage by half and fertilizer usage by a third. This is the primary reason why Ms. Humphreys was so adamant that the company select the commercial market as their primary target.

The game of golf has been enjoying a renewed popularity after a drastic decrease in participation during the 1980s. The growing number of public courses with reasonable fees, the continued aging of the Canadian population, and the development of better equipment have all contributed to this growth in popularity. It is estimated that the number of golf courses will increase by 22% to 2200 within five years. Most golf courses are independently owned and operated. Only 4% of all courses are owned by a company that owns more than one course. Courses are dispersed throughout Canada, but British Columbia, and Vancouver in particular, boast the highest number of courses.

Currently, golf courses purchase maintenance supplies from wholesalers who specialize in products uniquely designed for the type of grasses used. Manufacturers of these fertilizers tend to be small firms, or divisions of the larger chemical companies. The market share leader in golf course fertilizers is Sierra Horticultural Products, a subsidiary of Scotts Co. Scotts purchased Sierra in 1993, and it represents only about 2.2% of Scotts' total sales. Their biggest competitor in Canada is Nu-Gro Corporation, an Ontario-based horticultural products company founded in 1992. Unlike the firms competing in the consumer lawn maintenance market, these firms spend only about 9% of sales on marketing activities. These firms engage in little advertising, preferring to spend their marketing funds on sales calls to golf courses. They provide free samples of their products to non-users and try to build solid, long-lasting relationships with course owners. They know that it takes a tremendous selling effort to get a golf course owner to switch brands. If satisfied with their current brand, many course owners are unwilling to risk switching to a new product that may not perform as well. Since the condition of the course is the most important attribute in a consumer's selection of a course to play, course owners tend to be highly brand-loyal.

Course owners, however, have two overriding concerns. The first concerns the growing public debate on the groundwater pollution caused by golf courses. Heavy use of fertilizers and constant manual watering results in a chemical buildup in nearby reservoirs. In fact, according to the U.S. Environmental Protection Agency, golf courses are the major source of groundwater pollution in the United States. More and more negative publicity, in the form of newspaper and magazine articles, has resulted in golf course developers being denied permits to construct new courses. Thus, addressing the issue of groundwater pollution is a major concern with course owners.

Their second problem is that of shrinking profits. While golf is growing in popularity, and more courses are being built to accommodate demand, the actual number of golfers that can be accommodated on any one course cannot be expanded. With some courses engaging in green-fees price wars, profit margins for many of the public courses have become strained. Thus, while loyalty may play a role in fertilizer purchases, these difficult problems will also influence purchase behaviour.

Estimated to be about one-eighth the size of the golf course market is the balance of the commercial lawn care market, consisting of apartment and office complexes. Their needs are much less complex than those of golf courses, resulting in purchasing behaviour that mirrors that of the consumer market. Little concrete information is available concerning the number of office complex and apartment buildings, although estimates have put the total figure around 2900, of which 16.5% represent multiple holdings by one corporation. These commercial real estate property firms spend a disproportionate amount on lawn maintenance—they account for nearly 26% of the total dollars spent in this sector of the commercial maintenance market. This sector of the commercial market tends to purchase in bulk through wholesalers—generally the same wholesalers who service the specialty stores in the consumer market.

HYDROCAN

HydroCan was incorporated nearly one year ago. They have leased their production facilities, and have purchased and/or leased all of the equipment and machinery necessary for use in the production of StaGreen. Their production facility has the capacity to produce 180 000 kilograms of StaGreen per month. The owners of HydroCan have suggested a quality/value-added pricing strategy. They believe that they have a superior product that will save the end user both time and money, due to the reduced need for fertilizer products and reduced need for manual watering. The founders of HydroCan outlined their ideas for the launch year marketing strategy for both the consumer and the commercial lawn-care markets.

If HydroCan elects to target the consumer market, they will package StaGreen in a 10 kilogram bag, which market research indicates was the most popular size with consumers.

They will set their price to trade (i.e., wholesalers and retailers) at $22.50, with their variable costs representing 52% of sales. On average the large discount stores and home improvement stores take a 25% markup on lawn maintenance products. The smaller specialty stores take a larger markup of 35%. Wholesalers (if used) take a 15% markup. Fixed production costs include $700 000 in annual rental (for the site and the equipment), general and administrative expenses of $80 200, research and development expenses of $20 650, and miscellaneous expenses of $12 350. Distribution costs (including freight, warehousing, and storage) represented a significant yearly expense due to the seasonal nature of demand. Production of StaGreen would be continuous year-round; however, sales would be highly concentrated in the months of April through September. This means that the company would have relatively high distribution costs, estimated to be $426 000 per year. Not yet included in any of their financial statements are the salaries for the four founding partners of HydroCan. They would like to earn $50 000 per year (each), but are willing to forgo their salary in the launch year.

Their marketing budget has been set at $555 000, and HydroCan has suggested this amount be allocated to the various tasks, as shown in Exhibit 2. Seasonal discounts are price discounts offered to retailers and wholesalers as an incentive to purchase well in advance of the peak selling season. HydroCan plans to offer these discounts, estimated to be 20% off the trade price for each bag purchased, to wholesalers and retailers in the months of November and December as a method to reduce warehouse and storage costs. The displays will cost approximately $250 each (which includes promotional materials, such as brochures), and will be furnished to discount stores, home improvement stores, and as many nurseries as possible. The sweepstakes is used to increase awareness and interest in StaGreen. Consumers will have the chance to win several valuable prizes including a year of free lawn maintenance, lawn and garden equipment and supplies, and other related prizes.

EXHIBIT 2	Allocation of Marketing Budget for Consumer Market Launch
Marketing Task	**Total Expenditure (estimates)**
Seasonal discounts	$225 000
In-store displays	$ 92 000
Magazine advertising	$104 000
Newspaper advertising	$ 84 000
Sweepstakes	$ 50 000

In terms of the sales force, HydroCan has planned on hiring 20 sales reps at an average cost of $25 000 per rep (salary and commission). The sales reps will be responsible for selling the product to the various channels as well as offering sales training seminars.

If HydroCan elects to target the commercial market, then the size of the product will be increased to a 50 kilogram bag, which they will sell to wholesalers or end users at a price of $150. Because they would be charging a slightly higher price under this option, variable costs as a percentage of sales drop to 40%, resulting in a relatively high contribution margin of 60% of sales. Wholesalers, who generally sell directly to the commercial users, take a 15% markup. Fixed expenses will remain nearly the same as for the consumer market option, with the exception of marketing and distribution costs. None of the promotional activities, such as displays, seasonal discounts, sweepstakes, or advertising will be used in the commercial market. Instead, the size of the sales force will be increased to 30 to handle the lengthy sales calls necessary to golf courses. In addition, $100 000 has been set aside for free samples to be distributed to potential customers by the sales force. Finally, distribution costs decrease if the commercial market is chosen because demand tends to be slightly less seasonal. Thus costs for freight, warehousing and storage decrease to $225 000 under this option.

THE DECISION

The three founding partners of Stone Age Marketing Consultants were in the conference room discussing the results of their research and analysis. As Karen Jonestone pointed out, "A strong case can be made for both target markets! Each has its own advantages and limitations." Rob Sommerstone countered with the fact that HydroCan was a startup business. "Their financial resources are extremely limited right now. They cannot increase their production capacity for at least two years, and if they hope to acquire expansion capital to increase their total capacity, they need to show a profit as early as possible." Cari Clarkstone was considering a more creative solution—targeting selected parts of either or both the consumer and commercial markets. Before the group could begin to assess the viability of HydroCan and its product, StaGreen, they had to decide on which market to target and how to position StaGreen in that market, and then they had to develop a viable marketing strategy for the launch year. The final pressure for the group was the fact that HydroCan needed to launch in February—just prior to the peak selling season; thus, the consultants knew there was no time to acquire additional market research. The decision had to be based on the information at hand.

Notes

1.   *Maclean's*, April 22, 1996, pp. 62–63.

NCA Microelectronics

Alan McLean

It had not been a great year for NCA Microelectronics in 1990. Some good products had been developed, but financial success still seemed as far off as ever. Losses had forced severe staff cutbacks. The management group met in a planning session, in 1991, knowing that they had only one more chance to get it right. Harvey Nickerson looked at his partner Lewis Cobb and said, "If we don't avoid the problems we had with the R1000 and R2000, then the Chameleon project will '10' NCA Microelectronics. We'll lose the company and Saint John will have one less high-tech startup."

"Relax," said Lewis. "We know more about technology marketing since 1990, and anyway, we don't have a federal lab to complicate the development."

THE COMPANY

NCA Microelectronics was formed in 1987 by Harvey Nickerson and Lewis Cobb, two young electrical engineering graduates of the University of New Brunswick. Each had become disenchanted with the idea of being a "salaryman" in a large organization and felt excited by the challenge of creating a successful electronics design company in their home province of New Brunswick.

This case was prepared by Professor Alan McLean of the University of New Brunswick for the Acadia Institute of Case Studies as a basis for classroom discussion, and is not meant to illustrate either effective or ineffective management. © 1992 Acadia Institute of Case Studies, Acadia University. Reprinted with permission.

The first step in raising investment capital to augment their own resources was the preparation of a business plan. As a guide, they used the handbook *Making Technology Happen* by the well-known technological entrepreneur Denny Doyle. Denny, among other achievements, founded the Control Data Corporation operation in Canada. Eventually their plan and their personal enthusiasm attracted the interest of Bill Stanley of Cable Management, a company which controlled a group of companies involved in the cable TV industry. Stanley saw some potential synergy between his companies and a young high-tech microelectronics company. In January 1987, after an exchange of shares for equity, NCA Microelectronics was incorporated and set up operations in Saint John to provide high-tech electronic engineering services to the rest of the world. There were few, if any, other electronics design companies in New Brunswick.

The company's mission statement was "to generate customer satisfaction and corporate profitability through the design and manufacture of quality electronic products."

Initially, the company's only expertise was that of Harvey and Lewis and they chased energetically after any work which was within their technical competence. This strategy was reasonably successful, and by 1989, NCA had a staff of 15 and an annual revenue well in excess of $1 000 000.

HARVEY NICKERSON AND LEWIS COBB

Both Harvey and Lewis were native New Brunswickers, and like most Atlantic Canadians had a strong attachment to their home province. After graduating with his master's degree in electrical engineering in 1982, Harvey worked as a research engineer at newly formed CADMI Microelectronics Inc., a technology development facility on the campus of the University of New Brunswick (UNB). Subsequently, he took a position as a design engineer with Process Technologies Limited in Oromocto, New Brunswick. Concern with the uncertain future of this company contributed to his desire to establish his own enterprise.

Lewis, who graduated with his master's in electrical engineering in the fall of 1983, worked for a year with MacDonald, Detweiler and Associates in Richmond, British Columbia, on satellite image processing. He returned to New Brunswick, also to work with CADMI, and renewed his acquaintance with Harvey. They shared their desires to own and operate a business, and decided to branch out together.

PRODUCTS AND SERVICES OF NCA

Initially, the work that Harvey and Lewis brought in was varied. It included consulting, contract research, conceptual design, and equipment development and modifications. Clients came from the private sector and government, including the military. Most projects involved some aspect of control systems. Gradually the company began to carve out a niche in the design and development of microprocessor-based monitoring and control systems. NCA was able to secure several contracts from Saint John Shipbuilding, a company engaged in the construction of a series of ultramodern frigates for the Canadian Armed Forces. This work led NCA straight into the issue of quality assurance. The very demanding military standards forced them to examine existing quality control systems very critically and the company was obliged to become qualified to the Z2993 standard of the Canadian Standards Association. This attention to quality, originally driven by the military contracts, helped the company build an excellent reputation with private-sector customers.

A typical project for NCA was the Chat-R-Box developed under subcontract for Edmonton Transit. This product was originally designed to replace the endless-loop taped messages used in the transit industry to announce stops and other relevant information. Chat-R-Box could store up to four minutes of digitized as opposed to synthesized speech, accessible as a number of small phrases or as continuous audio text. Chat-R-Box could be used for anything from talking signs and traffic signals to talking garbage cans.

The company had electronics manufacturing facilities suitable for custom construction or for small runs of product. Other manufacturing requirements, such as equipment housing fabrication, could be contracted out.

THE R1000 STORY

In the spring of 1988, NCA won a $10 000 contract from the Department of Communications (DOC) to replicate a prototype of the Interact system. DOC was mandated to monitor and prevent illegal use of the airwaves. Continuous, routine monitoring of radio traffic, especially short-range traffic in remote locations, was expensive and impractical. The Interact system, then used in prototype form by DOC, had been designed by a DOC engineer, Mike LeBlanc, also a UNB graduate, to help with this problem. The unit could be transported to location and could be interrogated remotely using ordinary telephone lines. DOC was interested in having a second copy of their prototype made and was also prepared to transfer the technology to any company who was interested in and capable of marketing it commercially.

This seemed a perfect opportunity to Harvey and Lewis and they entered enthusiastically into discussions with DOC personnel, principally Marty MacLellan and Mike LeBlanc of the Moncton Office of DOC. The DOC technology transfer expert from Ottawa was brought in and, according to Marty, "the project seemed doable." Negotiations, which were never actually completed, began on the terms of the technology licensing agreement. The Interact system, although effective, was IBM PC–based and bulky. The NCA team saw two tasks before them: further development of the technology to make the system more acceptable to the marketplace and development of a marketing strategy.

A $100 000 contribution was made to the technology transfer process from the National Research Council, under the Industrial Research Assistance Program (IRAP), and NCA budgeted a further $100 000 from their own resources. Additional staff were hired and the technology development team began work, in April 1989, on miniaturizing the system and making it more robust. The process was planned to take 12 months. It was decided that the final product would be named the R1000.

Harvey and Lewis, realizing that their marketing expertise fell well short of their technical expertise, enlisted the help of a marketing expert from Fundy Cable, a company controlled by Cable Management, to help them assess the market prospects for the product.

The Interact system had been the subject of a paper presented by DOC personnel at an international communications conference in Europe and the technology had attracted a lot of interest. Also, the Ottawa office of DOC was actively involved in the provision of technical assistance to developing countries that wished to improve their ability to regulate and control their airwaves. The Interact/R1000 technology was demonstrated at a tradeshow to participants in a training program and was received enthusiastically. Influenced by the DOC's enthusiasm, the marketing expert from Fundy Cable became excited by the prospects not only for North American sales but also for overseas sales.

A marketing strategy was developed which involved the appointment of Canadian and U.S. distributors. A demonstration unit was shipped to a distributor in the Far East and was exhibited at a trade fair in Singapore.

A key to the overseas sales was the purchase by DOC of a unit for their own use. This would then become a reference point for potential overseas customers. Unfortunately, as the technical modifications developed, a difference developed between NCA and DOC over what features the final version of the R1000 should have. The NCA project team felt that the features desired by the DOC could not be achieved within the development budget and would make the final product unnecessarily expensive. This would detract from the marketability of the product. According to Harvey, "they wanted a Cadillac but would only pay for a Ford." Eventually, a compromise was reached and NCA agreed to develop an R900 version which could be upgraded at a later date to the "Cadillac"—that is, the fun-feature R1000. The main marketing effort would be directed to promoting the R900 with its lower cost.

The main competition for the R900 seemed to come from the German company Rohde and Schwartz, whose product sold for about $1 000 000, well over ten times the projected cost of the R900. This product had many more features than the R900, although it could not be operated remotely.

The marketing prospects still looked good for the R900, not only to NCA but also to a second marketing consultant hired to evaluate the situation. Quotes were requested by the governments of India and Uganda and visits to the plant were made by prospective buyers.

Unfortunately, by the spring of 1990, the DOC began to feel the brunt of budgetary restraint and informed NCA that they would no longer be in a position to purchase any R900s. It also emerged that the regional office of DOC, with whom NCA had been dealing, was the only one interested in the R900. Other regions appeared to have different ideas as to how to tackle the problem of remotely controlled radio spectrum monitoring. "It seemed that the NIH ('not invented here') syndrome was working to the detriment of NCA," claimed Harvey.

Realizing immediately that sales to foreign governments would be seriously jeopardized if the Canadian government did not purchase the R900 or the R1000, Harvey and Lewis reviewed their options. They could either drop the project completely, develop other markets for the R900, or try to find other applications for the core technology. Because they had faith in the technology, they decided to pursue the second and third options.

In their efforts to develop other markets for the R900, NCA contacted several agencies and government departments. "We realized that, while DOC and similar government departments overseas are interested in regulating the use of airwaves, law enforcement agencies may be interested in what is being said on the air," said Harvey. "We approached the RCMP and the Drug Enforcement Agency (DEA) in the U.S., thinking that our equipment could be used to gain information on drug smuggling. Each organization seemed interested and we eventually loaned a unit to the RCMP for a counter-smuggling operation in Newfoundland. Although the use of our equipment led to arrests, or so we understand, it unfortunately did not lead to a sale. Our experience with the DEA was also frustrating. The key to a successful sale of sophisticated technology depends very much on personal contact. We would laboriously build a relationship with someone and then they would 'disappear.' The employer would even refuse to acknowledge that our former contact had ever existed. I suppose this is the nature of law enforcement agencies, particularly those engaged in the war against drugs; however, they are extremely hard for a small company to do business with. Perhaps they were concerned about our security," said Harvey ruefully.

With respect to finding another application for the unique aspects of the R900, Harvey and Lewis agreed that the most important feature to pursue was the ability to use ordinary telephone lines to carry out interrogations of remote facilities.

The transmission towers used in the broadcasting industry are usually situated on hill-tops, often in remote locations. Since the facilities are automatic, maintenance by direct inspection is inconvenient and expensive. The NCA staff concluded that this would be a natural opportunity to apply their expertise in remote monitoring. The potential market was studied by examining competitors' products and by talking to equipment suppliers and distributors. There seemed to be an opportunity, and a development plan was struck for a new product. Since about 50% of the R900/1000 technology was transferable, it was decided to call the new product the R2000. Work began on the development of the R2000 before the R900 project was finally terminated.

By September 1990, the R2000 was ready The system was user-friendly, modular and therefore expanded easily, and programmable by the user, meaning it could be customized for a wide variety of situations. A marketing manager had been hired and the marketing campaign, which had been carried out in parallel with the technology development, seemed successful. There had been good response from trade shows and from customers who had agreed to test preliminary versions ("beta" products). The team had also created a telephone demonstration. A potential customer could phone, using a 1-800 number and a simulated transmission tower, and experiment with the interrogation features of the R2000. This was extremely popular and the phone hardly stopped ringing. About 12 units were sold, at about $10 000 per unit.

Unfortunately, sales stopped abruptly. Radio stations, hit by a sudden drop in advertising revenues brought about by the recession, drastically cut back on their capital spending.

Although there was still a certain amount of business from the defence industry, the NCA had tied its future to the success of the R2000. The negative cash flow brought about by the nonperformance of the R900, and now the collapse of the market for the R2000, was unsupportable. By November 1990, the company had no alternative but to reduce the staff to three: Harvey, Lewis, and Mark Sanford, a production engineer who had been one of the first employees. The drastic decline in staff meant that the company could no longer provide technical support to the R2000, and the product had to be taken off the market.

THE CHAMELEON PROJECT

Because of their association with Fundy Cable, Lewis and Harvey had already considered developing products for the cable TV industry. The cable TV industry was, however, not technology-conscious but very cost-conscious, and did not seem a fruitful market for high-technology products. The new reality, brought about by the collapse in demand for the "R" series of products, forced a second look at the situation and a niche seemed to emerge.

The theft of pay-TV signals was a growing problem for cable television companies, especially in the United States. In some regions, the theft rate was estimated to be as high as 50%. The theft was accomplished by bypassing or otherwise defeating the signal scrambler supplied by the cable TV company. The construction and sale of bootleg signal descramblers was a thriving cottage industry.

Sophisticated scramblers were available at a cost of about $150 per subscriber; how-ever, small-to-medium-sized cable companies with a large investment in older, more easily defeated scramblers could not afford this investment. NCA reckoned that the solution to the problem these companies faced was their new product, the Chameleon. This was a cir-cuit board that would fit existing scramblers and would sell for under $50. A feature of the board was a special chip that contained about 100 scrambling algorithms and that used a random number generator. The great advantage was that the scrambling algorithm could be changed by a signal from the "head end," that is, from equipment operated by the cable company itself.

General Instruments made, by far, most of the commonly used older-style scramblers, and the Chameleon was designed to fit easily into this equipment. Millions of these units were in service in North America and would not be completely replaced until 1997. Even then, the equipment would be in use in South America for many more years, further extending the market window.

NCA expected to sell about 160 000 units in the first year of full production; 35 000 of them would be sold in the Maritime provinces. At an estimated wholesale price of $50, the first year's gross revenue would be $8 million. Future revenues would depend on the degree of difficulty of penetrating the various sub-segments of the market, but the poten-tial existed for sales of as many as 500 000 units per year for the following four years.

THE PLANNING SESSION

"You're right, Lewis," said Harvey. "The situation is simpler and we have learned a lot, but selling to the cable TV industry is different again. These guys are not from an R&D cul-ture. Everything depends on proof-of-payback and improved service is not something they stay up late worrying about."

"OK, OK, but we can show them proof-of-payback! That's not the problem! The prob-lem is how do we sell them a $50 item? We are used to thinking in terms of marketing rel-atively small numbers of highly specialized products. The Chameleon is virtually a consumer item with large volumes and low markups."

"And speaking of low markups," interrupted Mark Sanford, "how will we handle the manufacture of this little goody? We will have to decide whether to set up our own line or contract out the manufacture once the design is frozen. If we make it ourselves, we can control the quality better, but we will get stuck with setup and inventory costs. If we con-tract it out, it will be easier on our capital, but we will have to take a smaller markup."

By this time, Harvey was staring out the window over the empty parking lot. "We must figure out the best way of marketing the little suckers. If we've learned anything, we've learned how difficult it is to market technically complex systems. The professional mar-keters don't understand the technology and we don't know enough about the science of marketing. The cable companies are interested, at least according to their reaction at the trade shows, but who will make the decision or push our product for us? We have to work through distributors. We can't market directly. I was talking to the head of Fundy Cable's repair section about it. She reckons that most small cable TV companies in the U.S. con-tract out their repair and installation work. She reckons we should market to the repair companies through their distributors. They are the ones with the know-how, not the cable companies themselves."

"Well, Louise knows how many beans make five all right, but it's the cable companies' money we are trying to protect," Lewis pointed out. "Surely they have the motivation to tell the repairers to install Chameleon? Another problem we have to face is whether we should be betting the company on one product again."

"Wait a minute!" cried Harvey, turning back from the window. "It's not our only product. We still have Chat-R-Box and how about the work we are doing for Thomas Equipment? If we can get the bugs out of the onboard computer we are developing for their skid loader, things could work out well."

Lewis grudgingly agreed, "But, there is a danger in developing a product line for only one client. We are too small to play hardball with them."

"We won't be small for long," grinned Harvey. "However, we have a number of issues to straighten out before we get rich. We need to develop a marketing game plan for the Chameleon and, as Mark pointed out, we need to decide whether to make or buy. I guess we should really look at other work we want to go after. It's not smart to bet the company, but there are only the three of us and we don't have the money to invest in all the opportunities. I would dearly love to be able to get back to the R2000 game though …"

"Yes," sighed Lewis. "It was great technology—pity nobody wanted to buy it."

PharmHealth Inc.

Carmel Augustyn,
Katy Kuzminski,
and Thomas Funk

Dr. Janet Ripley, director of marketing for PharmHealth, gazed out her 11th-floor office window at the snow-capped mountains in the distance. She thought of the ski season that was about to begin at Lake Louise and wished she was skiing on the hills instead of sitting in her Calgary office worrying about the dismal sales projections for 1995. Her major concern was PharmHealth's best-selling large-animal product, Wheez-Ease, a bovine injectable antibiotic that many in the company felt would face stiff generic competition within the next year. Several of Janet's colleagues at PharmHealth had been more than eager to share their particular strategies on how to deal with the expected generic threat to Wheez-Ease. Janet had three main options to choose from, but as yet she had not decided which was best. Her president, Les Richards, would be calling within the hour and would be expecting her recommendation.

THE CANADIAN ANIMAL HEALTH MARKET

The Canadian livestock industry has been hard hit by the recent recession. This dreary trend is expected to continue far into 1995. During the last five years, rising input costs

This case was prepared by Carmel Augustyn, Katy Kuzminski, and Thomas Funk of the Ontario Agricultural College at the University of Guelph, Guelph, Ontario, Canada. It is intended as a basis for classroom discussion and is not designed to present either correct or incorrect handling of administrative problems. Some data in the case have been disguised to protect confidentiality. © 1996 by Thomas Funk. Reprinted with permission.

and stagnant prices have reduced margins further and made beef producers more skeptical of returns and profitability. Recently, there has been a vast exit of unprofitable livestock producers, leaving fewer, better managers with cost cutting plans in place. A reduction of costly routine medication programs has been a high priority.

The Canadian animal health industry comprises three major product categories: feed additives, pharmaceuticals and biologicals. Feed additives are medications mixed into the feed at a local mill and fed orally to animals on a low-dose daily basis. A prescription from a veterinarian is not required. For example, a pneumonia outbreak in a swine herd may be treated by feeding a low dose of penicillin mixed with soybean meal and added to the regular feed rations.

Pharmaceutical products are medicinal drugs, usually available through professionals such as veterinarians and dispensed on a "prescription only" basis. Pharmaceuticals classified under veterinarian use only can include many diverse products such as antibiotics, anti-inflammatory preparations, dietary products, hormone substitutes, and insecticides.

Biologicals are vaccines produced from live antigens to inoculate an animal against major viral and secondary bacterial diseases. The use of biologicals as a preventative measure is well established in the pet market with the use of vaccination programs against rabies for dogs and cats.

Competition in the animal health industry has become more aggressive in recent years. Companies are well prepared to roll back prices and offer deals to maintain unit sales and market shares. As a result of current pressures on the industry, and the acute need for reduced input costs on the farm, a ripe opportunity has been created for relatively low-cost generic animal health products to enter the marketplace.

Generic products are relatively new entrants in the animal health industry. Companies that make generic products copy the formulation of well-established brand products when patent protection expires. Generic companies have not had to incur the up-front costs involved in research and development. As a result, they have not experienced the substantial product development costs that begin in the laboratory and end with a satisfied customer in the marketplace. Many generic products command significant market share as they enter the market priced 20 to 30% below the average selling price of branded products.

ANIMAL HEALTH INDUSTRY SALES

The Canadian animal health market has been sluggish over the past few years. Average annual growth rates of this industry have been low, but steady at 4 to 6%. Unfortunately, expert projections for 1995 and 1996 are not much better. The pharmaceutical sector is expected to be the poorest-performing, with a growth rate of 4 to 5%. Growth rates of biologicals are projected at a strong 12 to 14% for 1995 (see Table 1).

Table 1	Canadian Sales of Animal Health Products		
	1993 ($000)	1994 ($000)	Growth Rate (%)
Pharmaceuticals	$123.3	$128.8	4.5%
Feed additives	$ 57.4	$ 60.7	5.7%
Biologicals	$ 30.0	$ 33.0	10.0%
Total	$210.7	$222.5	

The entire animal health industry is also feeling the pressure from free trade. Significantly lower-priced U.S. products are now crossing the border and competing with Canadian products in all segments of the market. Tough economic times have severely affected product loyalty with veterinarians and producers. Current users of animal health products appear to be more price-sensitive than a few years ago.

CANADIAN LIVESTOCK SECTOR

Industry livestock numbers are currently static or decreasing, depending on the species. Dairy cattle and swine numbers are decreasing at 5% and 2% per year respectively. The beef sector is experiencing a slight recovery as beef cattle numbers are expected to increase 3% in 1995 and 1% in both 1996 and 1997, due to the large number of feeder cattle being exported to the United States (see Table 2).

Table 2	Canadian Livestock Inventory, July 1994		
	Beef	Dairy	Swine
Newfoundland	661	4 825	15 625
Prince Edward Island	12 977	18 318	106 728
Nova Scotia	27 629	28 913	133 640
New Brunswick	22 627	23 330	76 093
Quebec	187 498	514 542	2 909 251
Ontario	389 659	442 996	2 924 936
Manitoba	411 131	56 106	1 287 196
Saskatchewan	898 339	45 324	808 968
Alberta	1 635 727	105 905	1 729 870
British Columbia	242 742	74 919	223 776
Total Canada	3 828 630	1 315 178	10 216 083

THE COMPANY

PharmHealth, established in 1955, originated as a leader in beef herd health. Since that time, it has grown to employ 90 staff and expanded its product line to include all farm and companion animal species. Despite industry-wide pressures, PharmHealth has been able to hold its own in sales and earnings over the last few years. With 29 companies competing in a small marketplace of $222.5 million, PharmHealth is fortunate to still rank in the top five with 1994 sales of $28.3 million. Tables 3 and 4 provide the firm's 1994 balance sheet and income statement.

Table 3	PharmHealth Balance Sheet, October 31, 1994		
Assets		**Liabilities**	
Current assets:		**Current liabilities:**	
Cash	$ 1 134 200	Short-term debt	$ 2 370 000
Accounts receivable	$ 2 031 080	Accounts payable	$ 1 317 680
Inventory	$ 2 370 800	Taxes payable	$ 900 000
Work-in-process	$ 1 290 400	**Long-term debt:**	
Fixed assets:		Mortgages payable	$ 2 687 410
Plant and equipment	$ 10 752 700	Other	$ 1 790 590
Goodwill	$ 1 567 300	**Shareholder equity:**	
Less: Acc. dep.	$ 3 690 000	Common stock	$ 2 960 000
		Retained earnings	$ 3 430 800
Total assets	**$15 456 480**	**Total liabilities**	**$15 456 480**

Table 4	PharmHealth Income Statement, October 31, 1994		
Total revenue			$28 285 000
Cost of goods sold			$ 11 166 917
Gross profit			$ 17 118 083
Operating expenses			
Research and development		$ 1 599 011	
Selling		$ 7 212 221	
Administration		$1 847 844	$ 10 660 076
Gross operating income			$ 6 458 007
Depreciation			$ 1 643 988
Net operating income			$ 4 814 019
Other expenses			
Mortgage interest		$ 537 360	
Debenture interest		$ 300 000	$ 837 360
Net income before taxes			$ 3 976 659
Income taxes (50%)			$ 1 988 330
Net income			$ 1 988 329

In the last five years, feed additives and biologicals have been added to complement PharmHealth's solid pharmaceutical line. Feed additives have been the most profitable products sold by PharmHealth, with an average gross profit margin of 76%, followed closely by companion animal products with a 65% margin (see Table 5).

Unfortunately, producers are now using less feed additives on a routine basis as a means of cutting their input costs. As a consequence, sales of PharmHealth's feed additives have been steadily declining (see Table 6).

Table 5	1994 Sales by Product Group		
Product	Sales	Gross Profit ($)	Gross Profit (%)
Feed additives	$ 10 465 450	$ 7 953 742	76%
Pharmaceuticals:			
Large animal	$ 12 728 250	$ 6 109 560	48%
Small animal	$ 4 242750	$ 2 757 788	65%
Biologicals	$ 848 550	$ 296 993	35%
Total	$28 285 000	$17 118 083	60%

Table 6	Product Group as a Percentage of Sales	
Product	1989 % of Sales	1994 % of Sales
Feed additives	42%	37%
Pharmaceuticals:		
Large animal	49%	45%
Small animal	9%	15%
Biologicals	0%	3%

Sales and Marketing

PharmHealth recently has been experiencing a frustrating plateau in sales and has not achieved its projected sales goals for the last two quarters. The company has an image with its customer base as a conservative, premium-priced organization that rests on its research laurels. PharmHealth is not known for its flexible pricing or lucrative discounting policies.

PharmHealth does very little media advertising with only quarterly corporate ads placed in the *Canadian Veterinarian Journal*. Most market communication focuses on the "science" of the products, rather than the features and benefits to different customer segments. This marketing approach has resulted from the fact that the majority of PharmHealth's senior managers have received their formal training in veterinary medicine, with limited expertise in business and/or marketing. It is, however, for this very reason, that the company has a solid reputation for research and very effective products.

PharmHealth has a strong commitment to personal/value-added selling, with one of the largest salaried sales forces in the industry. PharmHealth has 22 sales representatives in contrast to their next closest competitor who has a sales staff of 14. Most companies in the industry put their promotional efforts into advertising and direct mail campaigns, while PharmHealth still prefers to sell face-to-face with their many different customer groups. PharmHealth's sales staff are the best equipped in the industry, as they are provided with laptop computers, the most advanced territory management software, and cellular phones.

The majority of animal health companies in Canada use specialized, commissioned sales representatives who focus on clients of a specific type. For example, a sales representative may only see veterinarians who specialize in dairy herd health management.

PharmHealth tends to follow a geographic protocol in their sales approach. Sales territories for PharmHealth reps include vets, industry specialists, producers, feed mills, and distributors. Currently, sales reps feel overburdened with territory management and unclear of their selling objectives and priorities (see Table 7).

Typical sales activities for PharmHealth sales representatives include calls on small- and large-animal veterinarians to promote the top pharmaceutical products. Representatives also visit the feed mills in their territory to discuss the volume and movement of their feed additive products with mill managers. Depending on the season, reps also call on their larger beef, dairy, and swine producers to emphasize the benefits of PharmHealth products and address any concerns. At the end of each week, sales reps are required to take half a day for administration and fill out sales call activity and gross profit reports for their territories.

Table 7	Sales Force		
Province	Sales Reps	Customer Base	$ Sales
British Columbia	1	A,D,F	$ 2 048 000
	1	B,E	$ 652 000
Alberta	4	A,D,E,F	$ 6 689 000
Saskatchewan	1	C,D,E,F	$ 4 103 000
Manitoba	1	C,C,E,F	$ 2 804 000
Ontario	5	C,D,E,F	$ 3 066 000
	1	B	$ 1 834 000
Quebec	4	A,D,E,F	$ 2 536 000
	1	B	$ 764 000
Maritimes	3	C,D,E,F	$ 3 789 000
Total	22		$28 285 000

A = Large-animal vets
B = Small-animal vets
C = Large- and small-animal vets
D = Feed mills and feed sales reps
E = Vet product distribution centres
F = Large producers

Product Line

PharmHealth has over 100 products. The extent of this product line is not typical of other animal health companies. A large portion of the products are old or rapidly aging, and targeted toward therapeutic markets in beef, swine, and dairy. A large portion of the products have marginal sales and contribute very little to the overall profit of PharmHealth. The top 15 products represent nearly 80% of the firm's total sales (see Table 8). The company also has a very limited range of products to adequately meet small-animal and equine health needs.

Table 8	Top Fifteen Products in 1994	
Category	**Product**	**Factory Sales**
Large animal	Wheez-Ease	$ 2 290 216
	Topazone	$ 1 970 380
	Udder Gel	$ 1 659 040
	Parabanum	$ 1 360 790
	Epilog	$ 1 030 980
	Synavet	$ 978 630
	Pig-Kem	$ 728 249
Small animal	M.P.G.	$ 1 147 390
	Vita-Tablets	$ 967 414
	Faxix	$ 505 264
	Pred-D	$ 486 506
	Sibrin	$ 416 157
Feed additives	Ampromed	$ 3 756 842
	Sur-Gro	$ 2 920 170
	Premiere	$ 2 187 439
Total		**$22 405 467**

Wheez-Ease

PharmHealth's biggest-selling large-animal product is Wheez-Ease, a bovine injectable antibiotic used to treat respiratory disease (bacterial pneumonia) in cattle. This product has been on the Canadian marketplace for 14 years. Bovine respiratory disease is the leading cause of death among immune-suppressed calves and a financial menace to producers. Typically, producers are forced to treat calves when they are most vulnerable, between 150 and 200 kilograms in size. On average, it is estimated that 40 to 50% of Canadian beef cattle are affected by the disease. During an especially wet season, the pneumonia incidence rate can reach as high as 80% in some herds.

Wheez-Ease competes at the premium end of the antibiotic market for beef cattle in Canada. This indicates that the product is recognized for its overall effectiveness when compared to lower-priced antibiotics such as penicillin. Producers fighting a disease outbreak are more than willing to pay for a premium antibiotic, as cattle often become resistant to penicillin products used in high doses. In Canada, the bovine premium injectable antibiotic market was estimated to be slightly less than $10 million in 1994, with very little growth expected in the future. Presently, there are four dominant players in the market (see Table 9).

Wheez-Ease is a broad-spectrum antibiotic prescribed by veterinarians in a moderate treatment dose of 1 milligram per 10 kilograms live weight, once a day for three days. Wheez-Ease's main competitor is Tetrabovine, a one-shot antibiotic with a required dosage of 5 milligrams per 10 kilograms live weight. Veterinarians find Tetrabovine very convenient, but not always as effective. Speering manufactures Bovocillin, widely considered the

Table 9	Bovine Injectable Antibiotic Market	
Company	Product	Market Share
Koopers	Tetrabovine	26%
PharmHealth	Wheez-Ease	32%
Speering	Bovocillin	20%
Techford	Oxysteer	22%

cheapest antibiotic available, but it requires a large dose, which is difficult for producers to administer safely. Oxysteer has experienced moderate sales success in the last few years, although the long withdrawal period is a significant disadvantage (see Table 10).

Wheez-Ease is very beneficial to the producer, as the product has a "zero-hour" withdrawal period. Typically, a producer must not send an animal to slaughter until a certain amount of time has elapsed since the last medication, for example, 72 hours. However, with Wheez-Ease, cattle can go directly to slaughter. This can significantly reduce feed costs and labour time for the producer, which gives Wheez-Ease a distinct advantage The fact that the product does not carry any meat residue at all could be a very important feature in the future because of rising food safety concerns. To date, this food safety advantage has not been fully explored by management.

Table 10	Key Product Features of Main Competitors			
Features	Wheez-Ease (PharmHealth)	Tetrabovine (Koopers)	Bovocillin (Speering)	Oxysteer (Techford)
Withdrawal	None	10 days	10 days	22 days
Injection	Intra-muscular	Intra-muscular	Intra-muscular	Intra-muscular
Dosage	1 mg/10 kg, 1 × 3 days	5 mg/10 kg., for 1 day	4 mg/10 kg, 1 × 4 days	1 mg/10 kg, 1 × 3 days
Expense	Most expensive	Moderate	Least expensive	Moderate
Packaging	6 g vial; 2 g vial	6 g vial	10 g vial; 6 g vial	4 g vial; 2 g vial
Advantages	Broad spectrum, no residue	Single injection	Inexpensive	Very effective
Drawbacks	Bacterial resistance	Narrow spectrum	Large-volume injection	Long withdrawal
Time on market	14 years	6 years	20 years	12 years

1 g = 1000 mg

The product is available in a two-gram and a six-gram vial package size, which retails for $22.15 and $64.20 respectively. Of the total Wheez-Ease sales in 1994, 60% was derived from the sale of the six-gram size.[1] Although veterinarians feel that Wheez-Ease is an effective product, some think it is overpriced for the average-to-smaller producer.

Biological Products

With the advent of better-skilled producers striving for minimal disease herds, the new biological (vaccine) market is becoming very popular in the 1990s. PharmHealth is at the forefront of developing a new vaccine for respiratory disease in cattle, which will meet the needs of producers more interested in prevention than treatment. The new vaccine is expected to be approved and registered by Agriculture Canada for distribution in late 1997. There are plans for the biological line to eventually include vaccines for swine, canine, and feline health needs.

Using new bioengineering techniques, it is possible to produce a new vaccine in two years. The cost of this process is approximately $650 000. It takes another 12–18 months for Agriculture Canada to test and approve the product.

Veterinary Product Distribution

PharmHealth's veterinary product distribution practices follow the industry norm. Seven regional buying groups across Canada purchase products directly from manufacturers. The buying groups then sell to veterinarians who, in turn, distribute to producers. A common practice is for veterinarians to purchase a membership in the closest distribution centre, share in buying group discounts, and capitalize on volume order prices. Such a cooperative system gives an advantage to all veterinary clinics, as they are not forced to stock large quantities of required products at their own expense. However, this approach creates a semi-controlled pricing structure for animal health companies, as it is difficult to give special deals and rebates to targeted areas and clinics. There are also strict regulations governing the advertising and promotion of veterinary products; for example, tactics such as "buy one and get the second one free" is strictly prohibited.

Buying groups operate on a 12% margin, while veterinarians normally receive a 20% margin on prescription products such as Wheez-Ease.

PHARMHEALTH'S DILEMMA

Marketing decisions in the animal health industry are affected by many factors such as livestock prices, consumer trends, and the overall agricultural economy. Aggressive competition from numerous companies is also an imposing factor. All these elements, and others, were currently pressuring PharmHealth into making some critical decisions for the near future. Compounding the complexity of the situation was the fact that the senior managers of the company suggested vastly different solutions to the stagnant sales performance and impending generic invasion (Exhibits 1 to 3).

After contemplating all the facts before her, Janet knew that something had to be done before it was too late. PharmHealth was currently operating in an unusually difficult environment. In the past, the company had made short-term decisions with relative ease. Today, however, not even her own colleagues were able to provide a unified direction. Janet was deep in thought when the ringing of the phone snapped her back to reality and she suddenly realized an hour had passed.

EXHIBIT 1	Inter-Office Memo

PharmHealth
Calgary, Alberta

TO: Dr. Janet Ripley, Director of Marketing
FROM: Hugh Whitehall, Director of Operations
DATE: November 14, 1994
SUBJECT: Under-Utilized Manufacturing Capacity

As you are aware, our manufacturing plant, which has a capacity of making 500 lots of Wheeze-Ease annually, is currently operating at only 60% of its capacity. I believe this underutilization presents PharmHealth with a great opportunity to decrease our production costs and increase our sales volume by manufacturing our own unlabelled form of Wheez-Ease. I have a tentative commitment from another animal health company to buy up to 150 lots of unlabelled Wheez-Ease at $5.75 per gram during 1995.

My colleagues and I are convinced that the likely introduction of a generic form of Wheez-Ease by a competitor in the near future will result in the loss of market share and units sold. Using our manufacturing capacity as I've suggested will ensure that we increase our throughput and alleviate the need to reduce production staff. This strategy will also allow us to bring in additional revenue from manufacturing, while placing no additional burden on our sales force.

Attached are current production costs for Wheez-Ease. For many valid reasons, I'm sure you'll agree this manufacturing opportunity deserves your utmost consideration.

Hugh

Wheez-Ease Production Costs at Current Volumes

	Quantity	Unit Cost	Total Cost
Direct Costs			
Raw materials:			
Tetracline	630	$ 2.35	$1 480.50
Methylparaben	280	$ 1.97	$ 551.60
Propylparaben	110	$ 1.30	$ 143.00
Total	**1 020**		**$ 2 175.10**
Packaging materials:			
Bags	1 020	$ 0.14	$ 142.80
Back labels	1 020	$ 0.05	$ 51.00
Shippers	50	$ 1.00	$ 50.00
Total			**$ 243.80**
Labour (hours):			
Manufacturing	8	$ 35.00	$ 280.00
Quality control	3	$ 44.00	$ 132.00
Packaging	5	$ 30.00	$ 150.00
Total			**$ 562.00**
Total direct costs			**$2 980.90**

EXHIBIT 1	Inter-Office Memo (continued)

Indirect Costs

Depreciation	$ 30 000.00
Administration	$100 500.00
Quality control	$ 81 000.00
Engineering	$ 61 800.00
Total indirect costs	$273 300.00
Indirect costs per lot	$ 911.00
Direct and indirect costs per lot	$ 3 891.90
Cost per gram	$ 3.89

Unit = 1 gram vial
Lot size = 1000 units
Yield−98%

EXHIBIT 2	Inter-Office Memo

PharmHealth
Calgary, Alberta

TO: Dr. Janet Ripley, Director of Marketing
FROM: Penny Gosling, Corporate Business Development
DATE: November 14, 1994
SUBJECT: Sell Generic Form of Wheez-Ease

Intensifying threats from generic competitors should be encouraging us to consider the manufacture of our own generic bovine injectable antibiotic.

As you are well aware, the 15-year patent on Wheez-Ease expires in 1995. Rumblings in the industry suggest that Global Pharmaceuticals will produce a generic Wheez-Ease and aggressively market it within the next 12 months. Since we will be competing with generics anyway, I see no reason why PharmHealth should not introduce our own generic form of Wheez-Ease. This strategy will make better use of our currently underutilized manufacturing plant, and will increase our sales volume (which as you know has been slightly under budget for six months now). Generics are typically priced 20–30% below branded products. The lower contribution of the generic will be more than offset by the increase in sales volume.

I have been in contact with a firm that is interested in distributing our product for a 12% commission. The company has eight sales reps who currently sell various animal health products throughout the country. I believe they could do an excellent job for us. Or better yet, we could use our own sales force for distribution, and cut down on the additional costs that would be required with third-party distribution. I strongly believe we could do this without jeopardizing our relationship with current customers or sales staff.

After extensive research for this proposal, I have taken the liberty of providing a three-year sales forecast for selling our own generic bovine antibiotic. As I'm sure you will see, the future could look very rosy.

I would be interested in hearing your thoughts.

Penny

EXHIBIT 2	Inter-Office Memo (continued)

Four-Year Sales Projection, Generic Wheez-Ease

Year	Two-Gram	Six-Gram	Total Grams
1995	33 070	17 850	173 240
1996	40 530	23 210	220 320
1997	42 050	26 880	245 300

EXHIBIT 3	Inter-Office Memo

PharmHealth
Calgary, Alberta

TO: Dr. Janet Ripley, Director of Marketing
FROM: Joey Turkstra, National Sales Manager
DATE: November 14, 1994
SUBJECT: Our Sales Slump Is Short-Term

I am concerned that senior management is about to make a strategic decision that will be detrimental to our long-term viability and sales force motivation and effectiveness. I do not believe that production of our own generic Wheez-Ease product or private labelling for a competitor are desirable actions to pursue at this time.

I am convinced that the poor sales performance we are currently experiencing is due to the agricultural recession and the limited resources we have allocated to our sales and marketing efforts. Pursuing other drastic actions at this premature stage is completely unnecessary and, in time, may prove to be very harmful to our sales figures. The only approach we need to take at this time is to implement an innovative sales plan that provides better selling tools and financial incentives for our sales staff.

PharmHealth should begin an aggressive promotional program that demonstrates the unique features and benefits of Wheez-Ease. If we do encounter any future competition from generics, now is the time to heavily promote the "value-added" concept of a branded product. This campaign should include a focus on customer needs and meet those requirements with better service and flexibility in our pricing policies.

I have outlined a promotional budget that includes marketing and selling activities that are essential to not only maintaining, but increasing, our Wheez-Ease sales figures. My proposal includes increasing our marketing expenditures as a percentage of sales from 2.5% to 15% for Wheez-Ease. I am confident that this strategy will give us the revenue we require, at a minimal outlay of resources.

Joey

EXHIBIT 3	Inter-Office Memo (continued)

Increased Marketing and Sales Costs

Marketing Cost

Catalogue/trade publications	$ 30 000
Journal advertising	$ 25 000
Direct mail	$ 5 000
Displays	$ 18 000
Detail materials	$ 8 000
Special promotions (discounts)	$ 50 000
Symposiums/speakers	$ 20 000
Conferences	$ 20 000
Translation costs	$ 4 000
Total marketing costs	$ 180 000

Sales Activity

Samples	$ 40 000
Trade shows	$ 14 000
Incentive bonus	$ 45 000
Sales training	$ 75 000
Clinic seminars	$ 15 000
Total sales costs	$ 189 000
Total increased marketing and sales Costs	**$369 000**

Notes

1. This results in a weighted average retail price of $10.85 per gram.

Zeneca Group PLC

Ralph Sykes, Thomas Funk,
and Steve Hawkins

In March 1999, Steve Hawkins had been assigned the task of recommending whether Reglone, the brand name used in Canada, Europe, Australia, and over 75 other countries, should become a global brand and replace Diquat, the brand name used in the United States. Diquat was one of his company's most profitable chemical products. Steve was North American product manager for Diquat/Reglone and he reported to Fred Johnson, North American business manager for Zeneca Group's non-selective herbicides. Fred also had asked Steve to recommend a brand migration strategy to prepare for the possibility that the brand name would be changed. In May 1999, after two months of data gathering, Steve was ready to develop recommendations.

INDUSTRY AND CORPORATE BACKGROUND

Zeneca Group PLC was a multinational life sciences company with its headquarters in the United Kingdom. The corporation had four principal lines of business. Zeneca Pharmaceuticals researched and developed ethical medicines for serious health conditions. Salick Health Care, Inc. provided cancer and kidney failure diagnostic and treatment services through seven comprehensive treatment centres in California, Florida, Kansas, and New York. Zeneca Agrochemicals marketed crop protection products designed to improve crop yields and food quality. And Zeneca Specialties supplied a broad range of products for customer industries including health care, agrochemical, paint, leather, and imaging applications.[1]

The principal products of Zeneca Agrochemicals were herbicides, insecticides, and fungicides. Herbicides replaced or reduced mechanical weeding and were either selective or non-selective. Selective herbicides destroyed certain weed types without significantly affecting the host crop, but non-selective herbicides affected all vegetation. Insecticides controlled insect pests that damaged crops and caused food quality problems. Fungicides prevented plant diseases that reduced crop yields and quality.

The agricultural chemical industry was relatively concentrated. Ten large, integrated life sciences or chemical companies based in Western Europe or North America accounted for 75% of worldwide sales of agrochemicals. Competition within the industry was based on innovation, product differentiation, geographical coverage, and customer service. In all major markets, agrochemical products were subjected to comprehensive registration and re-registration procedures that mitigated the effects of patent expiry on a product's market position and price.[2]

THE GLOBAL BRANDING CHALLENGE

Zeneca Agrochemicals marketed an important crop desiccant around the world. This product was a non-selective herbicide that was sprayed on potatoes, sunflowers, and canola just prior to harvesting. The herbicide dried up foliage on the plants, simplifying the harvesting process and reducing drying costs. The main ingredient in Zeneca's crop desiccant was a chemical called "diquat." Zeneca's diquat desiccant "killed" foliage within one week of contact, and only affected the plant parts it contacted. This feature meant that the product could be used on seed and food crops. A consistent formulation of the diquat desiccant has been sold in all markets served by Zeneca.

Zeneca's crop desiccant was sold under the brand name "Reglone" in Canada, Europe, Australia, and over 75 other countries (excluding the United States). The product has been sold under the brand name "Diquat" in the United States for over 30 years. Reglone/Diquat accounted for US$245 million of Zeneca's US$9 billion global sales, but was very important because it had generated a gross margin significantly above most Zeneca products.

At the beginning of 1999, Zeneca had reorganized its marketing group and appointed global brand managers. The newly appointed global brand managers were charged with implementing global branding whenever a global brand was advantageous. In February 1999, executives at Zeneca's headquarters started investigating where global brand names should be adopted in its various business divisions. Zeneca's marketing executives realized that, in the right circumstances, global branding would generate marketing efficiencies.

The Reglone global brand manager had requested Fred Johnson, the North American business manager for non-selective herbicides, to appoint a strong manager to investigate and recommend whether the Diquat brand should be converted to Reglone. In addition, in order to be ready with an action plan in the event of a decision to make the change, the manager was to recommend a strategy for migration of the Diquat brand to Reglone.

SHAPING THE TASK

When Steve Hawkins met with Fred Johnson to discuss his global branding and contingent brand migration strategy assignment, Fred explained the importance of Diquat to Zeneca. Within the United States the target market of the Diquat branded product was consistent with Zeneca's global targets: 94% to potato crops and 6% to canola, sunflower, and other crops. Diquat annual sales were approximately US$25 million, with only 1.5% of sales revenues spent on product promotion.

Fred Johnson stated that the desiccant had to deliver on seven key U.S. marketing objectives (Exhibit 1) independently of how the product was branded in the United States. One marketing objective was to communicate a formulation change to be implemented January 1, 2000. The chemical content of the product would remain the same, but the appearance of the product when in its container would change from dark, opaque, and viscous to dark red/brown and translucent. The reformulation was necessary because the product had settled out of its spray solution on a few occasions when used in areas with poor water quality. The reformulation did not change Zeneca's product costs.

Fred Johnson also told Steve that a new market entrant was expected in the United States in 2000. A competitor would introduce Rely, a non-selective herbicide that would desiccate non-seed potato vines. Its main ingredient was glufosinate, a systemic chemical that permeated the vine and killed the entire plant in about three weeks. Rely was projected to enter the U.S. market at a cost per acre (1 acre = .4 hectare) of about 15% less than Diquat and would add a new competitive force that could shift some power to customers. Rely's entry meant that the Diquat/Reglone migration had to be undertaken in an increasingly competitive market.

Fred Johnson concluded the meeting with Steve Hawkins by explaining that Steve's recommendations on whether Diquat should become Reglone, and his recommendations on a brand migration strategy, had important corporate implications. Throughout Zeneca worldwide there was resistance to the changing of domestic brand names, and Steve's recommendation on whether Diquat should become Reglone would influence similar decisions for other products. In addition, if the brand migration strategy were successful, it would provide a template for other brand migrations in Zeneca. Getting the right answers on Diquat clearly would generate internal resource leverage for the North American business unit within Zeneca. Steve felt the considerable weight of his new responsibility.

INFORMATION GATHERING, RESEARCH, AND ANALYSIS

Hawkins had begun his research by reviewing marketing textbooks, journals, periodicals, and newspapers, and conducting an extensive Internet search. Steve discovered that decisions on global branding were multifaceted and complex. He also identified a relationship between a decision on global branding in the Diquat/Reglone circumstances and the concept of brand equity. Steve summarized his findings on global brand decision-making (Exhibit 2) and his findings on calculating brand equity (Exhibit 3). Steve also summarized selected financial data that would be needed to calculate brand equity for Diquat in the United States and for Reglone in all countries excluding the United States (Exhibit 4). Finally, Steve found a chart summarizing the sources of brand equity in a marketing textbook (Exhibit 5).

Steve's research determined that brand migration had not received a lot of attention in the available literature. However, the literature on corporate name changes, product line extension, family branding, product introduction, and product rejuvenation struck Steve as analogous to brand migration. Steve summarized the best examples in the hope that they would be helpful (Exhibit 6).

Next, Steve reviewed the customer segmentation work done by Zeneca on its Diquat customers. Individual psychographic profiles of more than 50% of Zeneca's potato-growing customers had been prepared. This data classified the customer base into three segments (Exhibit 7). Interestingly, each segment contained approximately one-third of Zeneca's U.S. customer base. Segmentation allowed Zeneca to identify the marketing mix most appropriate for each segment, to customize its marketing message by segments, to analyze trends within and between segments, and to evaluate the return on investment by segment.

Zeneca had commissioned a study using customer focus groups to determine whether it was worthwhile to build a segment-specific marketing mix. The study confirmed Zeneca's hypothesis that its three segments would be receptive to segment-specific advertisements and promotional materials. Zeneca deliberately arranged for some of the focus groups to involve Idaho potato farmers because these farmers generally used sulfuric acid as a desiccant. A consequence was that Diquat had only a 10% market share in Idaho versus an average of over 60% for potato acreage throughout the rest of the United States. The study revealed that all three segments in Idaho preferred acid and would be unlikely to consider Diquat.

Steve reviewed the results of a brand share and pricing survey Zeneca had completed in the fall of 1997. This survey identified market shares in North America. It revealed that both Diquat (in the United States) and Reglone (in Canada) enjoyed a high level of unaided brand-awareness in their respective North American markets (Exhibit 8). The survey also revealed that both brands had significant market shares in their respective markets (Exhibit 9).

The 1997 brand share and pricing survey also provided the data needed to determine whether Diquat (in the United States) and Reglone (in Canada) were priced optimally. The data showed that lowering the price of Diquat would increase the total acres treated. This increase in volume would come from farmers not currently using a chemical desiccant, but it would not be sufficient to increase total revenue. From this finding, Steve Hawkins concluded that the demand for Diquat was relatively price-inelastic and that in 1997 Diquat was priced optimally.

Steve next turned his attention to the 1999 results of a Diquat brand-value survey commissioned by Zeneca. This survey identified why customers valued Diquat and how Diquat users might react to the entry of a generic competitor called "Alpha." The survey revealed many reasons why producers liked Diquat (Exhibit 10), a number of reasons why producers disliked Diquat (Exhibit 11), and a number of reasons producers offered for choosing the product (Exhibit 12). The survey also indicated farmers' propensity to use Diquat and competitive products at varying price levels (Exhibit 13).

Finally, Steve gathered some information related to the implementation of a U.S. brand name change, should Zeneca decide to go that route. Both Diquat and Reglone had been protected by trademarks and name registration in the United States many years ago. Nevertheless, federal and state regulatory approvals would be required for a product name change. For planning purposes Steve decided to assume that regulatory approvals would be obtained quickly, although he knew that there was a risk of late approvals. Steve estimated that regulatory approval would cost approximately $40 000 in one-time legal fees, not including Zeneca staff time.

The customer segmentation work, focus groups, brand share and pricing survey, and brand-value survey were all routine marketing projects undertaken by Zeneca independently of the global branding challenge.

Steve estimated that unbudgeted one-time costs for logo redesign, printing templates, training materials, and a variety of other costs related to a product name change (not including marketing staff time) would total approximately $60 000. Steve also calculated that the annual product promotion budget for the United States would shrink from $375 000 to $250 000 as a result of packaging and promotion economies of scale and media overlap benefits with Canada if the decision were made to use the Reglone name.

ALTERNATIVES, EVALUATION AND RECOMMENDATIONS

Steve Hawkins leaned back in his office chair and stared at the pile of information and surveys he had gathered, and at the various working papers in which he had analyzed all the available data. He recalled Fred Johnson's admonition that the product had to deliver on seven key marketing objectives independently of whether the product's name was Diquat or Reglone in the United States. Steve also recalled the profitability of the product, and the importance of his recommendations to the leverage of the North American business unit within Zeneca worldwide. Was changing the name of Diquat in the U.S. market to Reglone the right thing to do? Of course there were benefits, but what about the risks?

As Steve thought about the challenge and the importance of the project, he was both apprehensive and excited. Time had become a big factor because the year 2000 budgeting process would begin soon and Fred Johnson needed a basis for financial planning.

For the global branding question Steve decided that he would calculate appropriate brand-equity values and relate the theoretical arguments for and against global branding to the Diquat/Reglone situation. On the possible brand migration strategies, Steve decided that three approaches were worthy of exploration:

1. An abrupt and complete name change from Diquat to Reglone on January 1, 2000 (a "stop and go" strategy)

2. Communicating to the market throughout 2000 that a name change was coming and changing the name on January 1, 2001 (a "slow and easy" strategy)

3. Incorporating the ingredient name (diquat) into the Reglone brand name and introducing the "co-brand" on January 1, 2000 (a "tank mixing" strategy)

To find a successful brand migration strategy, Steve decided that he would evaluate these and possibly other strategies against the product marketing objectives. Steve turned on his computer and started to think about what he would say in his report.

EXHIBIT 1	Diquat/Reglone U.S. Marketing Objectives

1. Maintain product positioning as a consistent, convenient, fast-acting desiccant, allowing producers to schedule harvest and produce a quality crop.

2. Continue to target the existing market niche, particularly potato producers in the potato-growing regions of Maine, the Red River Valley, and the Pacific Northwest.

3. Continue Zeneca's psychographic market segmentation strategy.

4. Maintain existing 60% market share.

5. Maintain or enhance brand equity.[3]

6. Communicate a formulation change to be implemented in the year 2000.

7. Stay within the product's $375 000 promotional spending budget for the year 2000.

EXHIBIT 2	Global Branding: Why or Why Not?

The worldwide trend to reduce trade barriers and open markets has encouraged globalization by many suppliers of goods and services. Companies that decide to expand beyond domestic markets for the first time must decide whether to take domestic brands abroad or develop country-specific brands. Companies with global operations resulting from past acquisitions or growth also face difficult decisions on whether to continue country-specific brands or convert them to global brands.

The culture of some companies is highly centralized and, as Kapferer[4] suggests, decision-makers in these companies have a "singularity of thought" when it comes to branding. They simply disregard all arguments concerning local brands. At the other extreme, highly decentralized subsidiaries blindly guard local brands that have stood the test of time domestically. Most globally operating organizations exist somewhere between Kapferer's extremes, and make decisions on global branding after studying the advantages and disadvantages.

Two trends are often cited as the motivation for global branding: (1) television, affluence, and travel are causing tastes and styles throughout the world to become more homogeneous and (2) there is a growing desire around the world for the best-quality products and services.[5] At the same time, variations in competitive contexts from country to country, a tendency in some countries to buy "homegrown," and the fact that specific names and symbols have a damaging meaning (or are preempted) in certain countries, all discourage global branding.

In his book *Managing Brand Equity*,[6] Aaker identified five advantages for global branding:

- Image of strength and staying power
- Economies of scale in packaging and promotion
- Benefits from media overlap
- Brand-awareness facilitated when customers travel
- A desirable home country association

EXHIBIT 2	Global Branding: Why or Why Not? (continued)

To any list of global branding advantages, Keller[7] would add:

- Brand image consistency
- The ability to replicate domestic marketing successes quickly and efficiently

It is also important to note that the potential to enhance brand equity[8] may be another significant advantage of global branding. Generally speaking, global branding will be attractive when the brand equity inherent in a global brand exceeds the sum of the values of brand equity inherent in the related but separate national brands.

In his book *Strategic Brand Management*, Keller identified the disadvantages or constraints of global branding as differences in:

- Legal environments
- Marketing institutions
- Competitive environments
- Consumer needs, wants, and usage patterns
- Consumer response to marketing mix elements
- Administrative procedures

Aaker would supplement these disadvantages, arguing that:

- Names and symbols that will work everywhere are not optimally effective.
- Global branding can preempt local marketing ideas that may be more effective than big-budget, centralized efforts.

Notwithstanding the constraints on global branding, many companies feel compelled to develop global brands in order to grow revenues and benefit from economies of scale in packaging and promotion. The startling global successes of Coca-Cola, MacDonald's, Sony, Volkswagen, and many others act as a catalyst to encourage the international growth of countless other brands.

EXHIBIT 3	Calculating Brand Equity

Aaker has defined brand equity as a "set of brand assets and liabilities linked to a brand, its name and symbol, that add to or subtract from the value provided by a product or service to a firm and/or to that firm's customers." [9] Keller documents at least seven other definitions for brand equity and acknowledges that from the mid-1980s until the mid-1990s there was a good deal of confusion, and even frustration, with the term. Today, most marketing observers would probably accept Keller's notion that brand equity represents the "added value" endowed to a product as a result of past investments in marketing for the brand.[10]

In the Millennium Edition of Kotler's benchmark text, the author observes that a high value for brand equity provides a company with competitive advantages,

EXHIBIT 3	Calculating Brand Equity (continued)

including: (1) reduced marketing costs, because of consumer brand-awareness and loyalty, (2) more trade leverage in bargaining with distributors and retailers, because customers expect them to carry the brand, (3) the ability to charge higher prices, because the brand has higher perceived quality, (4) some defence against price competition, and (5) a greater ability to launch extensions, because the brand carries high credibility.[11] However, the value of brand equity is easier to conceptualize than it is to quantify and record.

Conventional accounting practices allow the identifiable costs of *acquired* brands to be recorded on company balance sheets, but not the value or costs of "*homegrown*" brands (except in the United Kingdom). For this reason, values for brand equity are generally only used by marketing professionals to measure their own brand stewardship over time, or by corporate managers to evaluate the brand stewardship of their marketing departments. This means that brand-equity calculation methods need to generate a consistent estimate of the going-concern, current-use, economic value of a brand.[12] As a result, professional brand valuators generally ignore breakup values, third-party values, and the value of future options.

The extensive literature on brand equity identifies at least eight different approaches to brand-equity valuation. An early notion was to assign values to brands on the basis of *consumer-related factors* such as recognition, awareness, and esteem.[13] But these factors are difficult to measure, and there is no known method to weight and combine them in order to arrive at a reliable valuation.

Two other valuation approaches are *historical cost* and *replacement cost*. One major problem with historical cost is that the relevant costs are hard to identify. Do you include all costs since the birth of the brand? What do you do if some of the costs were ineffective? How do you account for historic inflation? Another problem is that the historical cost of brand development ignores such qualitative factors as the degree of creativity in marketing initiatives, management expertise, and the organization's culture. Furthermore, calculating a replacement cost is equally problematic, because it is never clear what the replacement for a particular product might be, nor what costs would be relevant.

A fourth approach sometimes suggested is to value brand equity on a *market value* basis. Brand valuators do not favour this approach for several reasons:

1. Brands are almost never developed with the intention of selling them.
2. Each brand is unique.
3. There is no market for brands where values are regularly established by "arm's length" trades.
4. When brands are sold, the prices generally represent the value to a particular buyer for a particular purpose (not the going-concern, current-use, economic value of the brand).

Another approach involves calculating the *price premium* of a branded product over a similar non-branded product and multiplying the price premium by the volume of sales of the branded product. This method of valuing brand equity is problematic,

EXHIBIT 3	Calculating Brand Equity (continued)

because it is often difficult to find a comparable non-branded product and not all brands pursue price premium strategies. Furthermore, it is unclear over what time period the sales volume should be calculated.

The sixth approach often discussed in relevant literature is the *royalty payments* method. Here the royalty that a brand owner would receive from licensing the brand to an independent third party is multiplied by an earnings multiple or used in a discounted cash flow calculation. The problems with this approach are that market royalty rates are available for very few brands, and it is usually impossible to separate out the portion of a royalty related to use of a brand from the portion of a royalty related to other rights granted by the license.

Sometimes brand valuators will attempt a *discounted cash flow* approach to valuing brand equity based on the theory that the value of any asset is equal to its expected stream of incremental cash flows in future periods discounted at an appropriate rate.[14] Discounted cash flow valuations are so sensitive to the discount rate selected and the reliability of projected cash flows that the method is far better suited to valuing financial instruments than product brands.

The brand-equity valuation method that is most popular among professional brand valuators is the *earnings multiplier* approach. This method involves multiplying expected brand earnings by an appropriate multiplier. Although fairly popular, this method is not problem-free. In the first place, projecting expected earnings is a complex task and always subjective. Second, choosing an appropriate multiplier is also subjective and usually requires the application of considerable judgement.

The choice of an appropriate multiplier is often tied to a measure of brand strength. A consulting company that uses this approach for calculating brand equity is Brand Metrics Inc. (BMI). BMI rates brands on several key factors to determine brand-strength scores. The scores are then used to determine an appropriate multiplier using an S-shaped curve developed by the company. The following six factors are used by BMI to measure brand strength:

- *Market leadership.* Degree to which the brand is a share leader in the market
- *Sales growth.* Degree to which sales are growing
- *Sales stability.* Degree to which sales are stable from year to year
- *Internationality.* Degree to which the brand is well known throughout the world among target customers
- *Protection.* Degree to which the product and/or brand is protected by patent or trademark
- *Marketing support.* Degree to which the manufacturer provides effective marketing support for the brand.

The relationship between brand strength and the earnings multiple developed by BMI is shown below.

EXHIBIT 3	Calculating Brand Equity (continued)

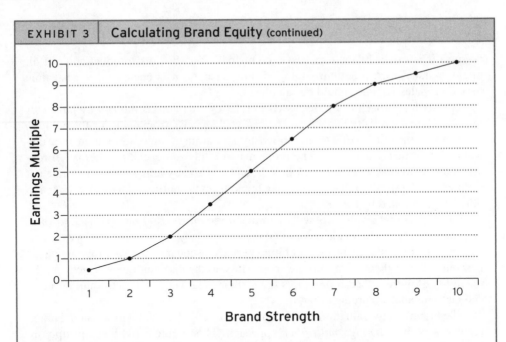

Brand Strength

Zeneca engaged the services of BMI to determine a multiplier for Diquat and Reglone. The following table shows the brand-strength ratings for Diquat and Reglone developed by BMI in 1999.

Factor	Weight	Diquat	Reglone
Market leadership	0.3	9.0	7.0
Sales growth	0.1	3.0	4.0
Sales stability	0.1	8.0	8.0
Internationality	0.1	0.0	8.0
Protection	0.2	6.0	6.0
Marketing support	0.2	3.0	3.0
Weighted brand strength	1.0	5.6	5.9

Using their S-shaped curve (shown above), BMI converted the weighted brand-strength ratings to estimated earnings multiples of 5.9 for Diquat and 6.4 for Reglone.

After determining a multiple, BMI uses the following procedure to calculate brand equity:

1. Determine the branded product's expected sales and earnings.

2. Estimate the amount of capital that will be employed to produce the branded product's expected sales.

3. Calculate the expected product's earnings-not-related-to-the-brand by taking 5% of the capital that will be employed to produce the branded product's sales. (There is a presumption here that a generic product should earn a 5% profit on the capital employed.)

EXHIBIT 3	Calculating Brand Equity (continued)

4. Determine the expected earnings attributable to the brand by subtracting the expected product's earnings-not-related-to-the-brand (step 3) from the branded product's expected earnings (step 1).

5. Determine the expected brand net income by subtracting income taxes that would be payable at the maximum corporate rate from the expected earnings attributable to the brand (step 4).

6. Calculate brand equity by multiplying the expected brand net income (step 5) by the earnings multiplier identified by the BMI S-curve using the brand-strength factor determined in the brand audit.

At best, brand-equity values (even using BMI's earnings multiplier) are very rough estimates of value. The difficulty separating out brand earnings and the uncertainty and subjectivity inherent in projecting sales, earnings, and capital to be employed are the reasons generally accepted accounting principles preclude the recording of brand-equity values in balance sheets. Nevertheless, many marketing managers favour the regular calculation of brand-equity values in order to demonstrate their brand stewardship. It has also been argued that regularly valuing brand equity usefully shifts a company's focus from short-term profit to investing wisely for the long term.[15]

The support among marketing managers for regularly measuring brand equity is by no means unanimous. A cross-America study of consumer goods and industrial/business-to-business companies in 1994 found that only 43% of these companies were measuring brand equity.[16] Interestingly, among those that did measure brand equity, only 55% felt their valuation method was satisfactory. The researchers found that companies tended to monitor brand equity using such qualitative factors as customer satisfaction and customer loyalty.

EXHIBIT 4	Selected Financial Data

	Diquat in the U.S. (US$)	Reglone in All Other Countries (US$)
Projected sales	$25 000 000	$245 000 000
Projected earnings	$ 5 000 000	$ 30 000 000
Capital employed to generate projected sales	$40 000 000	$270 000 000
Applicable income tax rates	37%	40%
BMI earning multipliers	5.9	6.4

Notes:
1. The sales, earnings, capital employed, and income tax data are estimates based on the figures, ratios, and explanations published in the 1998 Zeneca Group PLC annual report.
2. The BMI earnings multipliers are those determined by the 1999 BMI audit.

EXHIBIT 5 | **Sources of Brand Equity**

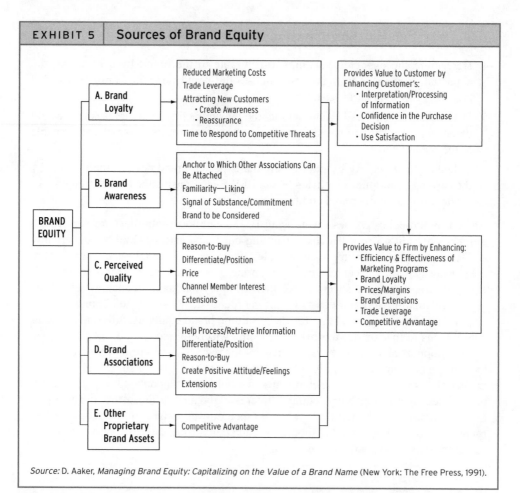

Source: D. Aaker, *Managing Brand Equity: Capitalizing on the Value of a Brand Name* (New York: The Free Press, 1991).

EXHIBIT 6 | **Some Historical Brand Change Examples**

When Coca-Cola's marketing department became defensive about Pepsi's taste comparisons, the company abruptly introduced a new product taste under the Coke brand. The consumer backlash to the sudden product change was so extreme that it forced Coca-Cola to reintroduce their original taste under the label "Coke Classic."[17]

In 1985, Black & Decker purchased the small appliance business of General Electric (GE) and abruptly changed the GE name to the Black & Decker brand name. By all indications, the Black & Decker small appliance business went on with great success and did not suffer from the lost equity of the GE brand. However, this brand-name change was accompanied by a multimillion-dollar promotional strategy.[18]

During the 1980s, the Nissan Corporation had established itself as a competitor in the North American automotive industry under the Datsun brand name. Over a four-year period the Datsun brand was changed to Nissan by a gradual acclimation process.

EXHIBIT 6	**Some Historical Brand Change Examples** (continued)

Nissan's North American sales plummeted during this period, although it must be acknowledged that North American auto sales also slumped at about that time.[19]

Another gradual name change was the global change of ICI Paints to the "Dulux" brand name. The market was sensitized to the new brand over two years by getting the ICI sales group to "buy in" to the name change through training and other internal processes. The internal brand conversion was translated into a very positive external message delivered by committed sales staff. The global establishment of the Dulux brand was successful, although it was admittedly supported by a relatively large promotional budget.[20]

In between abrupt and gradual brand changes are strategies involving dual branding or co-branding. Euro Disney failed as a brand name because the French did not see the theme park as European, and Europeans considered the park French on the basis of its location. In effect, consumers perceived no equity in the Euro Disney brand, because the "Euro" component did not fit the target market. The park was subsequently rebranded as Disneyland Paris.[21]

When the Philips Company purchased Whirlpool, they decided to capitalize on Whirlpool's solid brand equity. Philips rebranded the product as Whirlpool by Philips. This co-branding approach was very successful during the brand migration process, and has been successfully continued since.[22]

EXHIBIT 7	**Customer Segment Profiles**

Segment 1: Pole Positioners

Like a particular group of racecar drivers, these farmers strive for the best starting position, because they want to optimize their chances of winning. Pole Positioners are open to new product innovation, carefully research alternative farming methods, and are extremely comfortable operating in a rapidly changing environment. Like pole positioners in the world of racing, these farmers seek out leading-edge technology, are very confident in their ability to make choices, and rely only minimally on input suppliers for advice. Much like the incomes of race circuit winners, the profits of Pole Positioners tend to be high and stable, and they are not generally sensitive to input prices.

Segment 2: Tail-Enders

In contrast, just like racecar drivers who frequently lag behind the majority in any car race, these farmers are not focused on winning and therefore have little interest in learning new farming practices. Tail-Enders tend to lag behind industry changes and are not proactively looking for new technology. These farmers are not confident in their ability to make choices and rely heavily on input suppliers' advice and support to decrease their "burden." Tail-Enders are not particularly loyal to brands or manufacturers and, much like the incomes of laggard racing teams, the revenues and incomes of this group of farmers tend to be low.

| EXHIBIT 7 | Customer Segment Profiles (continued) |

Segment 3: The Pack

Sandwiched between Pole Positioners and Tail-Enders in any auto race is the Pack. In farming, the Pack includes traditional, conservative, and very experienced farmers. This group generally has difficulty keeping up with changing practices and is likely to resist new technologies. However, the Pack is environmentally concerned and cares about its community. These farmers have long-term relationships with local dealers and value service. Before adopting new products, important prerequisites for the Pack are seeing Pole Positioner neighbours succeed with those products, and running small trials on their own farms.

| EXHIBIT 8 | Unaided Brand Awareness by Segment (% of growers) |

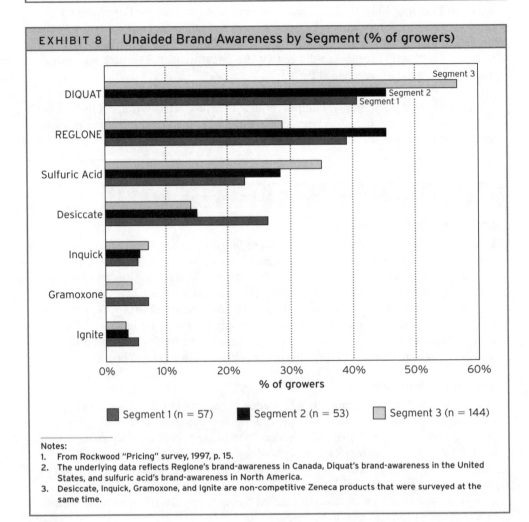

Notes:
1. From Rockwood "Pricing" survey, 1997, p. 15.
2. The underlying data reflects Reglone's brand-awareness in Canada, Diquat's brand-awareness in the United States, and sulfuric acid's brand-awareness in North America.
3. Desiccate, Inquick, Gramoxone, and Ignite are non-competitive Zeneca products that were surveyed at the same time.

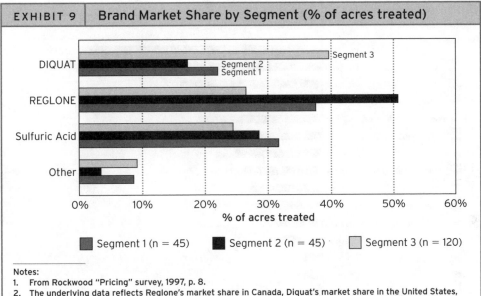

| EXHIBIT 9 | Brand Market Share by Segment (% of acres treated) |

Notes:
1. From Rockwood "Pricing" survey, 1997, p. 8.
2. The underlying data reflects Reglone's market share in Canada, Diquat's market share in the United States, and sulfuric acid's market share in North America.

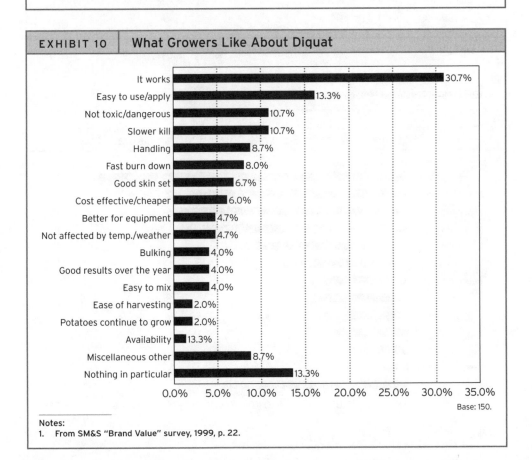

| EXHIBIT 10 | What Growers Like About Diquat |

Base: 150.

Notes:
1. From SM&S "Brand Value" survey, 1999, p. 22.

EXHIBIT 11	What Growers Dislike About Diquat

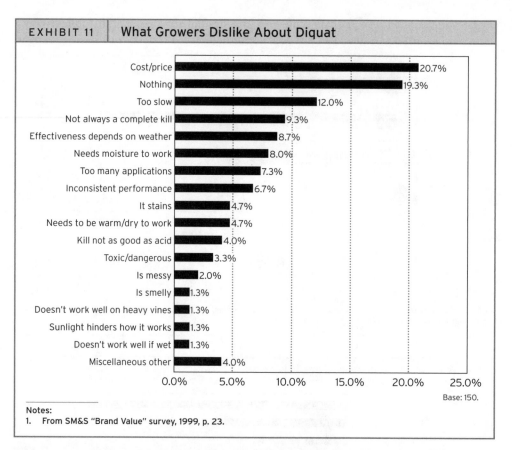

Cost/price — 20.7%
Nothing — 19.3%
Too slow — 12.0%
Not always a complete kill — 9.3%
Effectiveness depends on weather — 8.7%
Needs moisture to work — 8.0%
Too many applications — 7.3%
Inconsistent performance — 6.7%
It stains — 4.7%
Needs to be warm/dry to work — 4.7%
Kill not as good as acid — 4.0%
Toxic/dangerous — 3.3%
Is messy — 2.0%
Is smelly — 1.3%
Doesn't work well on heavy vines — 1.3%
Sunlight hinders how it works — 1.3%
Doesn't work well if wet — 1.3%
Miscellaneous other — 4.0%

Base: 150.

Notes:
1. From SM&S "Brand Value" survey, 1999, p. 23.

EXHIBIT 12	Primary Reason Growers Choose to Use Diquat

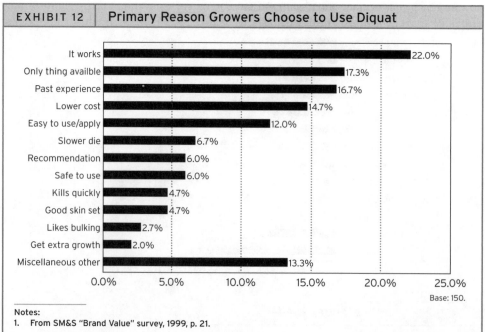

It works — 22.0%
Only thing availble — 17.3%
Past experience — 16.7%
Lower cost — 14.7%
Easy to use/apply — 12.0%
Slower die — 6.7%
Recommendation — 6.0%
Safe to use — 6.0%
Kills quickly — 4.7%
Good skin set — 4.7%
Likes bulking — 2.7%
Get extra growth — 2.0%
Miscellaneous other — 13.3%

Base: 150.

Notes:
1. From SM&S "Brand Value" survey, 1999, p. 21.

EXHIBIT 13	Share of Gross Treated Acres on which Indicated Desiccants Will Be Applied, Price of Alpha Changing

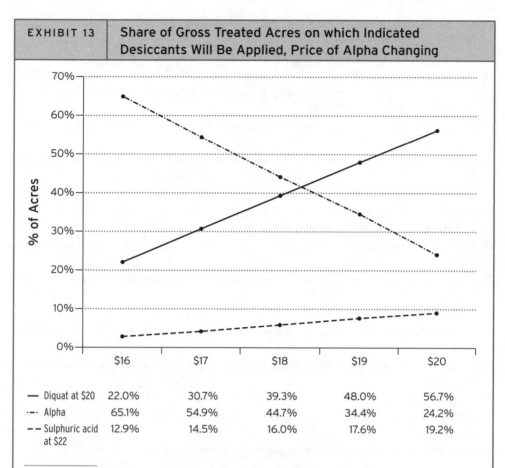

	$16	$17	$18	$19	$20
— Diquat at $20	22.0%	30.7%	39.3%	48.0%	56.7%
-·- Alpha	65.1%	54.9%	44.7%	34.4%	24.2%
-- Sulphuric acid at $22	12.9%	14.5%	16.0%	17.6%	19.2%

Notes:
1. The underlying data reflect the findings of Zeneca's 1999 SM&S "Brand Value" survey.
2. There is a core 22% of growers that are loyal to Diquat at its existing price positioning.
3. In the event Diquat was not available, loyal users would migrate to another chemical desiccant rather than to sulfuric acid.
4. Diquat brand loyalty declines (and thus brand equity declines) with even a $1 per acre price advantage for a generic competitor.
5. With greater pricing differences favouring the competitor, users of Diquat are quickly reduced to the loyal core. (Probably this threat is mitigated significantly by the fact that Alpha's pricing would be constrained by a relatively high unit cost of production.)
6. As a generic competitor's pricing advantage increases, most switching growers move to the generic and not to sulfuric acid.

Notes

1. Zeneca Group PLC, "Annual Report and Form 20-F," 1998, p. 2.
2. Zeneca Group PLC, "Annual Report and Form 20-F," 1998, p. 23.
3. For an understanding of brand equity, see Exhibit 3.
4. J. Kapferer, *Strategic Brand Management* (New York: The Free Press, 1992).
5. D. Aaker, *Managing Brand Equity: Capitalizing on the Value of a Brand* (New York: The Free Press, 1991).
6. D. Aaker, *Managing Brand Equity: Capitalizing on the Value of a Brand* (New York: The Free Press, 1991).

7. K. L. Keller, *Strategic Brand Management: Building, Measuring, and Managing Brand Equity* (Upper Saddle River, NJ: Prentice Hall, 1998).

8. For a discussion of brand equity, see Exhibit 3.

9. D. Aaker, *Managing Brand Equity: Capitalizing on the Value of a Brand* (New York: The Free Press, 1991).

10. K. L. Keller, *Strategic Brand Management: Building, Measuring, and Managing Brand Equity* (Upper Saddle River, NJ: Prentice Hall, 1998).

11. Philip Kotler, *Marketing Management: The Millennium Edition* (Upper Saddle River, NJ: Prentice Hall, 2000).

12. P. Barwise, C. Higson, A. Likierman, and P. Marsh, *Accounting for Brands* (London: London Business School and the Institute of Chartered Accountants in England and Wales, 1989).

13. L. de Chernatoney and M. McDonald, *Creating Powerful Brands* (Oxford: Butterworth-Heinemann, 1998).

14. P. Barwise, C. Higson, A. Likierman, and P. Marsh. *Accounting for Brands* (London: London Business School and the Institute of Chartered Accountants in England and Wales, 1989).

15. Paul Feldwick, "What Is Brand Equity Anyway, and How Do You Measure It?" *Journal of the Market Research Society*, April 1996.

16. S. Davis and D. Douglass, "Holistic Approach to Brand Equity Management," *Marketing News*, January 16, 1995.

17. T. Oliver, *The Real Coke, the Real Story* (Dallas, PA: Offset Paperback Manufacturers, 1986).

18. D. Aaker, *Managing Brand Equity: Capitalizing on the Value of a Brand Name* (New York: The Free Press, 1991).

19. D. Aaker, *Managing Brand Equity: Capitalizing on the Value of a Brand Name* (New York: The Free Press, 1991).

20. J. Kapferer, *Strategic Brand Management*, rev. ed. (Milford, CT: Kogan Page US, 1997).

21. J. Daniels and L. Radebaugh, *International Business: Environments and Operations*, 7th ed. (Addison-Wesley, 1995).

22. J. Kapferer, *Strategic Brand Management*, rev. ed. (Milford, CT: Kogan Page US, 1997).

Restored Vision Inc.

Brock Smith

INTRODUCTION

Restored Vision Inc. is a clinic for refractive eye surgery operated by a group of four doctors in Vancouver, British Columbia. We have been open for business since March 1995 but this type of surgery has been performed in Canada since 1990. It has only recently been given approval in the United States. The surgery uses a laser to reshape the cornea of the eye, restoring vision, and freeing people from the confines of their glasses or contact lenses. Between March 1995 and January 1996 we did approximately 250 laser procedures. Unfortunately, our monthly revenues have only just begun to match our expenses. We need some help developing a marketing plan to reach our goal of 60 treatments per month in our third year.

COMPANY HISTORY

In 1990, when excimer photorefractive keratectomy (PRK) laser eye surgery first became available in Canada, two of us initially became interested in the procedure.

Rather than jumping into the market with an unproven product, we waited until there was a sufficient track record to assess the different laser technologies and the risks to our patients. In 1994, after conducting an initial business analysis we invited two additional surgeons to join the group, and Restored Vision was formed. Our group share a common style of practice and are dedicated to quality patient care. Each of us runs our own private ophthalmology practice and works from half a day to two days a week in the clinic.

The first key decision we had to make was which of the various laser technologies to adopt. There are about 50 different makes of excimer laser machines. Visx is a brand adopted by many of the early entrants in North America. It uses a pulsing beam that shines down on the cornea and uncouples a layer of corneal tissue with each pulse. While this process is very precise and can produce good results in the low ranges of shortsightedness, it does not do farsightedness or astigmatism very well. It can also produce a side effect called "central islands" in which fluid builds up in the centre of the cornea, causing distorted vision.

We chose a new European technology that uses a scanning beam to uncouple corneal tissue. This process distributes the beam more smoothly and evenly across the surface of the cornea, cutting down the amount of haze on the cornea. It produces a better visual outcome and seems to eliminate the "central islands" problem. This machine is more expensive than those using the pulse technology but it handles farsightedness and astigmatism. It also has a better maintenance record.

The price of the excimer laser scanner was about $800 000. However, we took out a lease agreement in which we pay $1000 to the manufacturer for each operation. We have a nominal buyout option after 900 cases. We decided to lease our machine so we could change models when new technology became available. Some of our competitors will be hesitant to adopt new technology, as they will still be paying off their first machines and these will have little resale value.

We then turned our attention to finding rental space for our office. We chose a location on a major transit route in downtown Vancouver. We have about 149 square metres that is set up for consultation rooms, an examining room, a technical room, and a laser room. We have a nice reception area and a very friendly receptionist. One of the doctors had a flair for office decorating and we spent about $14 000 in furnishings and fixtures (see income statement, Exhibit 1).

It became apparent that none of the doctors had time to manage the business, so we hired an office manager and contracted a freelance marketing consultant. Neither of these people worked out, and our anticipated opening date was delayed by a month. We hired a new office manager and an advertising agency and finally opened our doors to the public in March 1995.

ISSUES

As with any new company, we experienced our fair share of problems. We got off to a bad start by having to delay our opening by a month. We have also found that patient consultations, which normally took 15 to 20 minutes in our regular practices, took up to an hour, due to the newness of the excimer laser treatment.

In the beginning we tried to make all important business decisions by consensus. This did not work very well. To streamline the decision-making process, a subcommittee of two officers was formed and tasks were allocated more efficiently. This has cut down on the amount of time we spend running the business but it still takes 5–8 hours a week for the officers.

Another problem we still face is our lack of sales experience. Although we have taken a sales training seminar with Dale Carnegie, we still feel somewhat uncomfortable with selling a medical service. Up until very recently it has been illegal for doctors to advertise in Canada. It is still considered "unprofessional" in some circles, so we must always be conscious of what the public and the College of Physicians and Surgeons might think. Consequently, we tend to undersell our services for fear of ethical and professional backlash.

Recently, we have faced additional issues. One such issue is budgeting, specifically for marketing. Initially, Restored Vision started off small, but due to high levels of spending by our competition, we have had to double our expenditures. In addition, with four doctors and one examining room, we are realizing that we need additional space or at least another set of examining equipment so patients do not have to wait very long for a consultation.

The business has also been stressful. Each of the doctors invested $50 000 dollars to start the business and operating expenses are divided between us. Our growing pains have been expensive; for example, we spent $5000 with our first marketing consultant and ended up with a logo we never used. We got off to a slow start and the bills have been piling up. Some of us are still putting $2000 more a month into the business than we are taking out. Some of the doctors are working harder than others to make the business a success and that has also created some tension in the group. We have tried to put some incentives in place to reward the people who put in more effort.

We did not get into the business to make a great profit. We wanted a way to be involved in this leading-edge technology and provide a quality service to our patients while maintaining our general practices. The government has no plans to fund this procedure and the universities do not have the budget. We saw an opportunity to provide a community resource where other physicians could service their patients and pay us a facility fee. Hence, our goal is to have as many people as possible involved with the centre, making it easier for us to make a profit without having to do all of the treatments and cover all the overhead ourselves. Our competitors have taken a different approach. They have full-time corrective laser surgery practices. Still, we would like to recover our investment soon.

CURRENT STRATEGY

Our mission is to provide quality facilities, technical procedures, and personal services for conducting PRK surgery. We service the general public of the Pacific Northwest and the community of ophthalmologists who would like to learn and apply these procedures to their own patients.

Our goals are to operate a profitable business and maintain a reputation of excellence. We want to be the excimer laser clinic of choice for British Columbia because of our reputation among clients for exceptional customer service and our reputation among health care professionals for excellence in treatment standards.

Our specific business objectives are:

1. Invoke the laser equipment buyout option by the end of year 3.
2. Hold shareholder loans to $50 000 with payback in year 3.
3. Average 60 treatments per month in year 3.

Restored Vision differentiates itself from the competition in primarily two ways: quality of service and superior technology. First, we are positioning ourselves as the clinic with the highest quality of service. We have four experienced ophthalmologists with university affiliation operating the business who have numerous years of individual practice. Where our competitors rely a great deal upon technical help and non-medical optometric personnel, we offer a high degree of doctor-patient interaction, greater security, and a higher quality of personalized care. Our state-of-the-art laser allows us to provide a broader range of treatments than our competitors and we achieve excellent visual outcomes.

PRODUCT STRATEGY

We offer a full-service package. This includes the pre-treatment consultation with the doctor, computerized eye measurement, the laser treatment itself, eyedrops, sunglasses, and 10 to 14 followup visits. Our service also includes re-treatments for the 2 to 4% of cases that require it to get the best result.

After the pre-treatment consultation, the procedure can be done in an hour. The patient comes in, we put anesthetic drops in the eye being treated, wait half an hour, do 10 to 15 minutes of preparation in the laser room, and then do the treatment. The treatment itself takes three minutes or less. The laser is programmed to eliminate the patient's refractive error. It removes a minute layer from the surface of the cornea less than the width of a human hair, until the correct shape for the cornea is obtained. We then put a protective contact lens on the eye, give the patient sunglasses to wear when outdoors, and instruct them how to apply the eyedrops they need to apply at home.

The patient comes back for a checkup the next day, and every two or three days for a week or two after that. After about five days we take out the protective contact lens. Sometimes the patient's vision is blurry for the first week. After about two weeks, the patient's vision should be very good. We give out our home phone numbers and patients can call us any time they think there is a problem. Our competitors do not provide this level of service.

Of the half-million eyes that have been treated worldwide, there have only been about ten serious problems where a corneal transplant has been needed. While this is significant to those few people, the percentage risk is low. Less than 1% of patients experience corneal hazing and end up having poorer vision with their glasses than they had before. Everyone experiences better vision without their glasses than they had before. We cannot guarantee 20/20 vision but worldwide success rates (at least 20/40 vision) have been in the 96% range. This means that most clients will be able to see, at least 20 feet away without their glasses, as well as perfectly sighted people can see 40 feet away.

PRICING STRATEGY

Price is an important consideration during the decision-making process; it is often the first question asked by prospective clients. As a "special" promotion during the first month we charged $1500 per eye. Then we went with $2400 per eye, which was $100 more than our competitors. We found that clients were coming to us for the advice then going to the competition to save the $100. So after a few months we dropped our price to $2200. We hoped this strategy would help increase volume and broaden word-of-mouth referrals. Clients seem to find it hard to evaluate our services and perceive little differentiation. We have a flexible pricing policy for family and friends of the doctors (typically $1650 per procedure). This discount comes out of the doctor's fee (usually $700) and not the contribution to the clinic ($500).

COMMUNICATION STRATEGY

A new advertising agency took over our account in May 1995. In June, and through the summer months, we focused on mass market print advertising (ad) running two campaigns: "Throwing Away Your Glasses" and "You Do Have a Choice." Both were awareness campaigns that promoted the immediate benefit of laser eye surgery. Summer ads made reference to the freedom of not having glasses while "in the water, on the courts, or cruising the beach." These campaigns were placed in all the municipalities making up the greater Vancouver region.

In August, and continuing through the fall, we ran a transit campaign called "20/20" which consisted of an overhead ad and three-fold brochures for takeaway. This was run on Vancouver's Skytrain system because of rider demographics: business commuters aged 25–55 with medium-to-high disposable incomes, and tourists, primarily from the United States.

At the same time, we selectively placed Restored Vision brochures into Fitness Centres. We also placed a print ad, "Eye Can See Clearly Now," in *Whistler* magazine, which targets ski enthusiasts, particularly those visiting from the U.S. We also targeted magazines which featured refractive laser eye surgery articles.

In the fall, we developed a more informational ad, "Goodbye Glasses," and a decision-evoking ad "To Be the Best." The placement schedule was designed so that awareness ads were followed three weeks later by informational ads and the decision evoking ads followed three weeks after that. We have tried to assess the effectiveness of these advertisements by tracking calls and treatments (see Exhibit 3).

PERFORMANCE

In 1995 we lost $116 238 (see Exhibits 1 and 2). However, our revenues only reflect ten months of operation, while the expenses reflect the full year. Our forecast for January 1996 suggests that we will almost break even (on a monthly basis) and we expect to show a modest profit in 1996.

OUR CUSTOMERS

Our target market includes those people currently using corrective vision devices such as glasses and contact lenses (about 30% of the population). Originally we thought we would attract the white-collar professional crowd that has more discretionary income. Most of our clients have been blue-collar workers with more modest incomes. About 53% of the people we have treated are male, 50% live in Vancouver, 45% live in the Vancouver region, and 5% are from out of town. About 75% of clients are aged 26–55. Some of the benefits they might seek are:

- Freedom from the hassle of glasses or contact lenses
- Greater ability to participate in, or enjoy, recreational sports

- A more natural appearance without glasses
- Engage in careers/activities where glasses are prohibited or inconvenient
- Improving night vision
- Avoiding the cost of maintenance of correctional devices
- Wanting to improve self-esteem and attractiveness

Refractive surgery is limited to those clients who:

- Are 18–70 years of age
- Have had stable vision for one year
- Have no complicating injuries/diseases
- Are not pregnant or nursing
- Are comfortable with the risks
- Have eyes in a correctable range of vision (90% of the population)
- Are prepared to pay the full cost of the elective surgery

Greater Vancouver Region (1.7 million people)	British Columbia (3.4 million people)		Pacific Northwest
Extremely active	Populations with Incomes Above $25 000 (in thousands)		Up until very recently (1996) the refractive laser eye surgery procedure had not been approved in the United States. Consequently American ophthalmologists have not had the same level of experience with the procedure as Canadians. With a 30% exchange rate working in our favour, we expect many Americans to elect doing this surgery in Canada.
Recreation-oriented			
Health- and fitness-conscious	Age	Male	Female	
Relaxed, carefree attitudes	25-34	274	128	
Not very conservative	35-44	444	195	
	45-54	366	151	
	55-64	205	66	

OUR ENVIRONMENT

There are three other groups in direct competition with us. One such group, the Downtown Laser Centre, is located quite near us and is run by two ophthalmologists who have also retained their own ophthalmology practices. The Laser Centre has been in business for the last four years and has generated up to 40% of their business from the United States. They have performed about 500 procedures to date and charge $2400 per eye. We estimate their gross revenues per year at over $300 000. One source of their referrals is an optometry clinic in Delta, B.C., 20 minutes from Vancouver. They have used testimonials in local newspapers to their advantage and have a professional-looking information package to distribute. Their laser equipment allows them to treat common refractive problems (myopia and astigmatism), but not other problems that are less common.

A third doctor recently separated from the Downtown Laser Centre and set up shop two blocks from us. This ophthalmologist is focusing his marketing in Asia. We do not know how well he has been doing.

A third clinic, the Vancouver Eye Surgery Centre, is located 30 minutes south of Vancouver. It is operated by an ophthalmologist considered a pioneer of this procedure. This doctor and his associates have been in business for four years and practise refractive surgery on a full-time basis. The Vancouver Eye Surgery Centre has been using television, radio, and print advertising to actively market their services in British Columbia and the United States. They have also been running a 30-minute infomercial but we do not know the reach or frequency. This group conducts seminars throughout British Columbia and have an information package that includes a video. This group did about 2000 procedures this year (at $2275) and have done more than 5000 to date. Their laser technology allows them to treat myopia, astigmatism, and low degrees of hyperopia.

In addition to these clinics, there are competitors in Kelowna (643 kilometres northeast of Vancouver) and Victoria (48 kilometres west of Vancouver, on Vancouver Island). We expect two more clinics to open in the Vancouver area in the next year or two. We also expect a bit of a shakeout in the industry with some clinics being taken over by large multinational health organizations.

Finally, industry observers are predicting continued acceptance, growth, and prominence of laser refractive surgery in the coming years. The safety, predictability, and superior visual correction that the technology offers will be the keys to long-term success. We expect a steady growth of refractive laser surgery in the 10–15%-per-year range. Some industry forecasters predict a day when glasses will no longer be worn. Advances in excimer laser technology are also expected. As the industry matures, we expect a proliferation of vendors, new product features, and lower costs to clinics such as ours.

POLITICAL CLIMATE

Our company is concerned with two major stakeholders in the macro environment: the B.C. College of Physicians and Surgeons, and the general public. The College of Physicians and Surgeons self-governs the practice of medicine in British Columbia and acts as a consumer watchdog to ensure the quality of medical care in the province. Until very recently, doctors have been forbidden to advertise their services. Although the College has relaxed this rule, there is still a sentiment among our colleagues, and the general public, that it is not appropriate to aggressively promote elective surgery. Our facility is approved by the College of Physicians and Surgeons.

CONCLUSIONS

We have probably made a few mistakes along the way but we are learning more every day about running a small business. Before we get too far into January we need to reflect on our experiences in 1995 and come up with a marketing plan for the new year. If you were running this business, what would you do?

Appendix A

Frequently Asked Questions

1. How long does it take?

   Laser eye surgery itself takes only a few minutes. The entire procedure including pre-operative preparation and a post-surgery eye examination, takes about an hour.

2. Do I have to go to the hospital?

   No. The surgery is performed in our clinic.

3. Will I be awake during the surgery?

   Yes. The laser procedure takes only a few minutes and clients are awake throughout. If desired, the doctor will administer a mild sedative prior to surgery.

4. Will it hurt?

   No. The treatment is virtually painless. The discomfort patients feel after treatment is minimal and pain-relieving medication is rarely needed.

5. How long does it take to recover?

   Most patients notice better vision right away, with further improvement over the next few weeks. Normal activities can usually be resumed within a few days of the treatment.

6. Can I drive home after the surgery?

   We suggest that you do not drive yourself after the treatment, particularly if you have had any sedation.

7. When can I go back to work?

   Provided you do not work in an excessively dirty or smoky environment and do not have to engage in extreme physical activity, you may return to work immediately after treatment.

8. What happens after the surgery?

   After the surgery, your doctor will monitor your progress through regular eye examinations. These checkups will occur at approximately one day, three to five days, two weeks, one month, three months, six months, and one year. In most cases, these appointments can be booked through your regular eye care provider.

9. Are both eyes done at the same time?

   In most cases, each eye is done separately with an interval of several weeks between procedures. It may be possible to shorten this interval and, in exceptional cases (e.g., when a patient has come from afar) both eyes may be done at the same time.

10. Will I still have to wear glasses or contacts after surgery?

    Even though everyone sees better after treatment, some patients may have to continue wearing glasses or contact lenses for specific activities, usually on a part-time basis.

Appendix B

What Our Customers Say About Us

"In the beginning I did perceive it to be a risky thing, but I wanted it badly enough that I was willing to look into it. I went to a couple of clinics and the information that I got led me to believe that it wasn't really a risky thing, but you're always kind of apprehensive about someone operating on your eyes because you only have one set of eyes. I heard about Restored Vision over the radio so I made an appointment and went down there and from day one they were very professional. They explained the procedure to me step by step. They made me feel confident that this operation would be a benefit to me."

—Andy Peters

"I'm 58 years old. I've had 20/500 vision for most of my life and I've just been sick and tired of glasses and contacts. For about five years I considered radial keratectomy but I just didn't feel it was an exact enough science to do it. But then I read about laser surgery and I attended two seminars on it. I still can hardly believe that I walked into his office that morning and spent 20 minutes getting my eyes numbed and 20 more minutes in the laser room getting prepped and having a two-and-a-half-minute laser treatment. Then I got up from the chair, went into the examination room and immediately read 20/30 on the eye chart. It was unbelievable!"

—Carol Smith

"I don't know too many people who like wearing glasses and having to rely on contacts (which I never really liked) and since I play a lot of sports it's something that I'm very happy now that I did."

—Andy Peters

I have recommended it to many, many people. I took brochures with me to Hawaii when I went. I took them down to California when I went to my painting seminar. I carry them in my purse!"

—Carol Smith

I would recommend the Restored Vision Clinic to all my friends because they were excellent. They were very helpful and friendly. They explained everything and answered all my questions. Very helpful."

—Koren Jordan

"You almost start taking it for granted now that you don't have contacts or glasses. It's kind of strange actually. But you know, I'd definitely recommend it."

—Andy Peters

Appendix C

Glossary of Terms

Astigmatism Astigmatism is when both distant and near objects are blurry. This results when the eye is not spherical and symmetrical and light is focused on multiple points in front of, and behind, the retina.

Cornea The transparent, circular part of the front of the eyeball. The curvature of the cornea determines most of the eye's refractive (light-bending) power.

Hyperopia Hyperopia is farsightedness. As a result of insufficient curvature of the cornea or too short an eyeball, light entering the eye is focussed behind the retina. Distant objects can be seen clearly but near objects are blurry.

Ophthalmologist A medical doctor who specializes in the eye. To become an ophthalmologist one must first obtain a medical degree (an M.D. in North America) and then complete further specialty training.

Retina The light-sensitive nerve layer that converts light images into electrical signals for transmission to the brain. The retina is analogous to the film of a camera.

EXHIBIT 1	Restored Vision Inc. Income Statement[1]	
	Jan. 1–Dec. 31, 1995	Forecast Jan. 1996*
Revenue:**		
Revenue–principal doctors	$ 447 000.00	
Revenue–associate doctors	32 200.00	
Interest income	1 300.00	
Total revenue	$480 500.00	$88 000.00
Expenses:		
Laser rental	$ 250 000.00	$ 40 000.00
Office rent	40 000.00	3 330.00
Telephone	6 000.00	280.00
Other overhead	25 000.00	950.00
Medical/pharmacy	15 700.00	750.00
Fees–associates	11 805.00	2 800.00
Fees–principals***	79 800.00	25 200.00

EXHIBIT 1	Restored Vision Inc. Income Statement[1] (continued)	

	Jan. 1–Dec. 31, 1995	Forecast Jan. 1996*
Equipment lease	13 600.00	1 220.00
Insurance	1 233.00	70.00
Wages and benefits	600 000.00	5 750.00
Marketing/advertising	77 200.00	7 200.00
Travel	2 000.00	200.00
Legal/accounting	14 400.00	450.00
Total expenses	**$ 596 738.00**	**$88 200.00**
Net income before taxes	**($116 238.00)**	**($200.00)**

*   Based on 40 treatments per month.
**   Revenues reflect charges to clients for 250 treatments (10 months).
*** Fees ranged from $150 to $800 during startup.
1.   Numbers in this Exhibit have been disguised to protect confidentiality.

EXHIBIT 2	Restored Vision Inc. Balance Sheet, as at Dec. 31, 1995[1]	

Assets		Liabilities and Equity	
Current assets:		**Current liabilities:**	
Cash	113 692.78	Accounts payable	110 520.00
Accounts receivable	64 851.21	WCB payable	136.80
Prepaid expenses	4 608.97		
Total current assets	183 152.96	Total current liabilities	110 656.80
Fixed assets:		Loans from principals	220 000.00
Furniture and fixture	14 403.31		
Equipment	5 652.31	Share capital	65.59
Leasehold improvement	4 044.31	Retained earnings	(6 089.97)
Computer equipment	1 141.53	Current earnings	(116 238.00)
Total fixed assets	25 241.46		
Total assets	**$208 394.42**	**Total liabilities and equity**	**$208 394.42**

1.   Numbers in this Exhibit have been disguised to protect their confidentiality.

EXHIBIT 3	Restored Vision Inc. Advertising Effectiveness, June–Dec. 1995

	% of Total Calls	% of Total Budget	% of Total Consults	Treatments
Print:				
Daily print media	20.0%	24.0%	18.0%	
Urban print media	15.0%	18.0%	11.5%	
Community media	18.0%	12.0%	20.0%	
Specialized	12.0%	17.0%	11.0%	
Radio	15.0%	14.0%	23.0%	
Skytrain	8.0%	12.0%	6.0%	
Phone book	5.0%	–	4.5%	
Word of mouth	7.0%	–	4.0%	
Other	0.0%	3.0%	2.0%	
Total	**100.0%**	**100.0%**	**100.0%**	
Marketing-generated totals	946.0	$62 500.00	224.0	130.0
Privately solicited totals			113.0	120.0

Notes:
Treatments can exceed consults, since two eyes are usually treated with one client. Numbers in this Exhibit have been disguised to protect confidentiality.

Zeneca Ag Products

Thomas Funk and Colin Steen

"We may be behind some other companies in biotechnology, but our new precision agriculture technology should be a huge help to us in selling our more traditional products. In addition, it should be a profitable product in itself." So thought Colin Steen, Manager of Pulse and Oilseed Products for Zeneca Ag Products (Zeneca), as he began thinking about his upcoming presentation to management on the introduction of some exciting new precision agriculture technology Zeneca had developed for disease detection in Saskatchewan lentils (peas).

Agriculture in Western Canada and the world had undergone a significant shift over the past five years. The crop protection industry, which once relied on traditional chemistry as a source of sales and profits, now used biotechnology to develop crops that contained traits never before seen. A good example of this was herbicide tolerance as exemplified by Monsanto's Roundup Ready technology. Using genetic engineering, Monsanto was able to develop new crop varieties that were resistant to Roundup, their popular non-selective herbicide. After planting these varieties, farmers could spray a field with Roundup and kill all vegetation except the crop they wanted to produce. This industry shift occurred very quickly, and left Zeneca trying to catch up to other companies leading the biotechnology movement. Though Zeneca was investing significant research dollars in biotechnology, the company was at least five years behind the industry in this area. Colin was sure that the new precision agriculture approaches would help Zeneca maintain the perception of technological leadership until other new high-tech products were developed.

ZENECA AG PRODUCTS

Zeneca, created from a demerger of ICI, the large British chemical manufacturer, was a leading global supplier of crop protection products. The company's products included herbicides, insecticides, and fungicides for a broad range of crops. In Canada, Zeneca was a major supplier of crop protection products.

Zeneca had substantial strength in fungicides, chemical products designed to control disease problems in plants. Zeneca brands in this category included Bravo, Quadris, Amistar, Heritage, and Abound. According to market research, Zeneca was the world leader in fungicide sales in 1999 with products registered for use in over 43 crops in 46 countries. Key crops requiring fungicides were potatoes, rice, and turf in the United States and canola and lentils in Canada. The fungicide portfolio was among the fastest-growing line of products manufactured by Zeneca, and sustaining this growth was very important to the future of the company.

PRECISION AGRICULTURE TECHNOLOGY

Zeneca Ag Products had invested significant resources in developing a broad range of precision agriculture technologies over the last five years. To date, the most promising technology was photo imagery that allowed farmers to identify disease symptoms that may not be present to the naked eye. Using high-resolution images from orbiting satellites or fixed-wing aircraft, Zeneca could determine the presence of disease symptoms long before visible symptoms occurred. Based on the premise that unhealthy plants reflect a different band of colour than healthy plants, this technology had the potential to save farmers thousands of dollars in lost yields due to disease pressure. Zeneca also felt it could boost fungicide sales and be a profitable service they could provide customers.

Zeneca had some initial success with this technology in tomato and turf crops in the United States, identifying disease in advance of symptoms and preventing yield and profit reductions. By being able to identify diseased plants before visual symptoms occurred, farmers would be able to apply a fungicide to control the disease, and therefore avoid the economic losses associated with the disease. In addition, this breakthrough technology had the potential of giving Zeneca the perception of technological leadership, even in the absence of a line of biotech crops and products.

Zeneca expected that when the process was in operation, it could provide reports to a farmer within 24 hours of an initial request. The report generated for the farmer consisted of a series of field maps that outlined the relative health of crops. An example of a field map is shown in Exhibit 1. The map measures relative crop vigour. The lighter areas are healthy crop while the darker areas are unhealthy crops. Moving from NW to SE, the crop worsens and disease pressure increases.

Initial estimates placed the cost to Zeneca of providing a photo at approximately $2.50 per acre (1 acre = 0.4 hectare).

LENTIL PRODUCTION IN WESTERN CANADA

Lentil production in western Canada was very important to the success of Zeneca. Acreage in Saskatchewan had increased dramatically over the past five years, reaching 1.6 million acres in 2000. The lentil acreage was divided into three markets: large-seeded green, small-seeded green, and red lentil. The Crop Development Centre, based at the University of Saskatchewan, had been responsible for the influx of lentil varieties well suited to the Saskatchewan climate. Exhibit 2 illustrates the growth in lentil acres in Saskatchewan since 1978.

Lentil growers in Saskatchewan faced plant diseases that potentially could affect yield and quality. Depending on when the farmer detected the disease, the financial impact could vary from minimal to severe. The main diseases that affected lentil production were ascochyta and anthracnose.

EXHIBIT 1	Example of Field Map

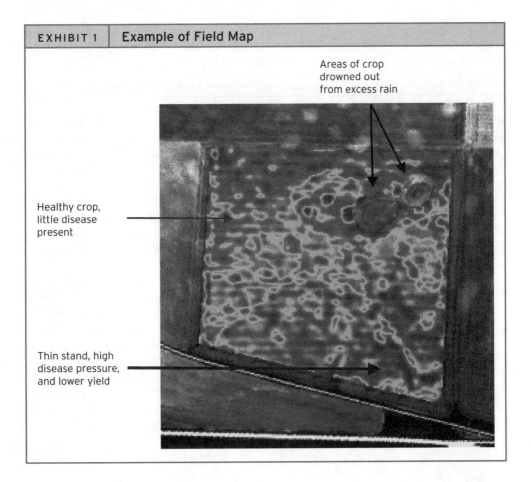

Areas of crop drowned out from excess rain

Healthy crop, little disease present

Thin stand, high disease pressure, and lower yield

EXHIBIT 2	Lentil Production in Saskatchewan, 1980-2000

Year	Acres (000s)*
1980	50 000
1982	100 000
1984	100 000
1986	100 000
1988	400 000
1990	300 000
1992	400 000
1994	700 000
1996	1 000 000
1998	1 300 000
2000	1 600 000

*   1 acre = 0.4 hectare.

Ascochyta (*Ascochyta lentis*) was a stubble- and seed-borne disease primarily affecting seed quality and, in severe cases, also affecting yield. Primarily spread by rainsplash throughout the growing season, ascochyta was prevalent in most areas of Saskatchewan. An application of Bravo at 0.8 litres/acre, which cost a farmer approximately $10.25/acre, stopped the spread of infectious spores in the crop by preventing new infection from forming. A second application of Bravo was sometimes necessary if weather conditions continued to be moist. The lesions that developed from ascochyta were cream-coloured with a tan margin and black spores in the centre. Under severe disease conditions, ascochyta blight seeds became partly or wholly brownish in colour, resulting in economic losses due to poor quality. The losses from poor-quality lentils due to ascochyta could range from 5 to 70% of the value of the crop. Ascochyta also could reduce the yield of lentils in cases of severe infection in a range of 10 to 50%.

Severe anthracnose (*Colletotrichum truncatum*) resulted in significant impacts on yield. Anthracnose lesions developed on the leaves and stem, causing plants to turn golden brown when they coalesced, resulting in plant death. Anthracnose was primarily stubble-borne, and spread from leaf to leaf via rainsplash throughout the growing season. Bravo was the only product registered for the prevention and control of this disease. An application of Bravo at 0.8 litres/acre prevented the formation of new lesions on what was already a healthy crop. A second application was sometimes necessary later in the growing season to protect new crop growth from lesion development. As anthracnose attacked the lower part of the stem, it was important to apply Bravo early in the growth stage, preferably just before flowering. Bravo served only as a protectant, and did not cure disease already present. This underscored the importance of early detection of lentil disease. Exhibit 3 shows the potential financial impact to farmers if they did not use a fungicide to prevent these diseases from spreading through the crop canopy.

EXHIBIT 3	Economic Returns per Acre* for Bravo Applications in Lentils		
		Disease Pressure	
Bravo Applications	High	Medium	Low
One application	$60 per acre	$50 per acre	$40 per acre
Two applications	$140 per acre	$100 per acre	$70 per acre

*1 acre = 0.4 hectare.

Source: University of Saskatchewan agronomic research.

Farmers were limited in the ways they could deal with disease problems in lentils. The most satisfactory method was to use Bravo. Zeneca estimated that 40% of lentil acres in 2000 were treated with this fungicide. Some farmers felt they could not justify the use of a fungicide based on likely economic returns. Other farmers felt that once they saw visible signs of disease it was too late for a fungicide to do any good.

Over the past several years, researchers at the University of Saskatchewan had developed several varieties that were resistant to lentil diseases. Although resistant to disease, most of these varieties had a 10 to 15% lower yield potential than non-resistant varieties.[1] This made them less attractive to farmers resulting in relatively low adoption. In 2000, disease-resistant varieties were seeded on approximately 20% of lentil acres in Saskatchewan.

In addition to Bravo, Zeneca also offered three other products for lentil production—Touchdown (glyphosate), Venture (grass herbicide) and Reglone (desiccant). This broad product line, and the visibility of Zeneca among growers, made lentils a very important crop to the success of Zeneca in Saskatchewan.

MARKETING THE IMAGERY TECHNOLOGY

Although Colin was excited about the new imagery technology, and the impact it could have on Bravo sales, he had little idea how farmers might react to the product. To gain additional insight he decided to retain the services of Agri Studies, a Calgary-based marketing research firm, to determine farmer reaction to the new technology. Appendix A contains a summary of the key results of this research.

Colin felt the research supported the introduction of the new technology. Even at the highest price level tested, the research showed a high proportion of farmers who said they would try the imagery. Colin knew, however, that to say they would try it in a research study, and to actually try it, were two different things. He also knew that trying the technology was only half the battle; the other half was making sure they were satisfied with the results and would use it again in subsequent years. To achieve a high level of trial and repeat buying required a solid marketing plan behind the product.

In developing the marketing plan, Colin first considered the target market. Obviously, the broad target was the 5000 lentil growers in Saskatchewan. Colin wondered whether there were smaller groups that would be better prospects for the new product.

The product itself was very simple—a colour satellite photo of a field with an accompanying legend indicating the degree of disease infestation. Colin felt he should stop short of including a recommendation for Bravo use, although he was not sure of this. He also wondered how he should position the new technology. Should it be positioned as a tool that would help farmers better manage fungicide use? Or a tool that could help farmers maximize returns per acre from lentils? Or was there some other positioning that should be used?

The price of the service was also something that was not determined. In the marketing research, three price levels were tested—$6 per acre, $8 per acre, and $10 per acre. Although the $6 per acre would undoubtedly promote faster adoption of the technology, higher prices would increase the contribution margin on the imagery product significantly.

Distribution was a real dilemma because there were different ways to approach this. The first was to distribute the images through the same dealers that sold Bravo. Under this plan, farmers would place orders for an image with a chemical dealer. The dealer would forward the request to Zeneca who would then arrange to have the photo taken and couriered or sent electronically to the dealer. The dealer would then deliver this to the farmer. Under this system the dealer would receive a margin on the sale. Colin was not sure what margin was appropriate but felt something in the range of 20% (the same margin they received on the sale of Bravo) was reasonable.

In Saskatchewan, there were approximately 100 dealers that sold fungicides for use on lentils. Of these dealers, 25 sold approximately 75% of the total fungicide used. Colin felt there might be some merit in restricting distribution to the top dealers.

A second distribution approach was for Zeneca to sell the product directly to farmers. Colin thought this could be done by sending farmers information on the imagery product and having farmers order by calling a 1-800 number or by visiting the Zeneca Web site. The photos would be delivered by courier, or electronically if the farmer had the appropriate computer technology to receive them in this manner.

The final area Colin needed to address was promotion. Here, of course, there were many options available, including the following main ones:

- *Farmer meetings where groups of 25 to 50 farmers could be assembled and introduced to the technology.* These meetings usually featured an information session followed by a meal. To do a session in the right way would cost approximately $20 per farmer.

- *Advertising in publications specifically oriented to lentil growers.* The most obvious choice here was the magazine *Lentils in Canada*, which was published quarterly. A full-page colour ad in this publication cost $6500.

- *Direct mail targeted at all lentil growers.* To produce and distribute a high-quality direct mail piece would cost about $20 per farmer.

- *Personal sales calls.* Since the time of the existing Zeneca rep was fully committed with current activities, any personal selling would have to be done through part-time reps hired specifically for this purpose. Colin felt that summer students might be a great choice. The total cost for a personal sales call was estimated to be $50.

A final area Colin wondered about was the possibility of bundling the imagery technology with sales of Bravo.[2] He was not sure if this was a good idea or how to put together such a program. One possibility was to offer a discount on Bravo purchases if a farmer had already purchased images.

Colin wondered what impact the imagery technology might have on Bravo sales. On the one hand, he felt it could boost Bravo sales because more farmers would be aware of disease problems and want to use Bravo to solve them. On the other hand, some farmers who in the past had sprayed Bravo to prevent disease, might now discover that they did not have a problem at all, or a problem only in certain parts of fields that might be dealt with using a spot treatment. Although spot-treating parts of a field that showed signs of disease seemed to make sense, it was not recommended by Zeneca. This was because once the spores associated with lentil disease got into a field they tended to move very fast and spot-treating may miss new infestations. Despite Zeneca's position on this, many farmers still followed the practice of spot-treating.

THE DECISION

As Colin pondered his decision, he was very aware of the fact that the imagery technology was new, and seemed to meet a real farmer need. He was almost sure it would have a positive impact on the brand image of Bravo, both in lentils and in other crops. The likely introduction of competitive products into the fungicide category in the next year or two made the establishment of a strong brand position all the more important.

Zeneca management felt the introduction of the imagery technology in lentils should cover additional overhead of $200 000 a year, which included a return on their investment in the technology as well as additional administrative costs of launching and providing the product. They would view the imagery product in a much more favourable light if it resulted in higher Bravo sales in lentils.

Appendix 1

Results of Marketing Research

In order to assess the potential of the new imagery technology, Zeneca carried out some marketing research in the summer of 1999 with a random sample of 100 Saskatchewan lentil producers. The sample was selected from a database maintained by Zeneca. Data were collected using personal interviews. Personal interviews were used because it was necessary to show farmers images of their own fields and explain the technology prior to asking questions. A brief summary of research findings follows.

After explaining the technology, each farmer was asked to indicate what he/she saw as the primary benefits of this approach. The following were the most frequently mentioned benefits:

- Save money on fungicides. Don't need to spray if the results show no disease is present.
- Facilitate spot treatment of a fungicide. Treat only areas of a field where there is evidence of disease.
- Monitor disease-susceptible varieties of lentils. Allows for better selection of disease-resistant varieties in future.

Respondents were also asked to indicate potential concerns with the technology. The following were the most frequently mentioned concerns:

- Accuracy of the imagery
- Possible misinterpretation of fertility problems for disease problems
- Amount of time it might take to get images
- Cost of the technology

Three price points were tested in the research—$6/acre, $8/acre, and $10/acre. One-third of the sample were asked their willingness to try the new technology at each of these prices. Results are shown below:

	$6	$8	$10
Definitely would try it	26%	14%	11%
Probably would try it	56%	36%	23%
May or may not try it	18%	44%	45%
Probably would not try it	0%	4%	11%
Definitely would not try it	0%	0%	0%

Regardless of the price, respondents who indicated they would try the technology indicated they would use it on 20% of their lentil acres in year 1, and if successful they would use it on 50% of their lentil acres in year 2 and on 100% of their lentil acres in year 3.

When asked how they currently used fungicides, the following were the responses:

- 20% said they used a disease-resistant variety so they didn't need to worry about spraying.
- 40% said they used a fungicide if disease was detected in a field after carefully examining the crop.
- 20% said they always used a fungicide as a preventive measure.
- 10% said they used a fungicide when weather conditions appeared to favour a disease problem.
- 10% said they would only use a fungicide if they saw a neighbour using one.

Lentil growers indicated varying degrees of disease problems in the past:

- 30% indicated they had past disease problems, but the associated economic losses have been small.
- 50% indicated they had past disease problems that resulted in significant economic losses.
- 20% indicated they had past disease problems that resulted in severe economic losses.

Notes

1. Many scientists believed that the "yield drag" associated with disease-resistant varieties would become smaller as additional plant breeding work was undertaken.
2. The contribution margin on Bravo was approximately 60%.

EJE Trans-Lite Inc.

H. F. (Herb) MacKenzie

In early 1994, Paul Edison, Marketing Director of EJE Trans-Lite Inc. (www.eje-translite.com), was trying to decide what to do concerning the price of the Digi-Lite, the company's principal product. Paul helped design the original Digi-Lite soon after he joined EJE in 1989. His technical background was in radio operations and electronic communications. He completed a course in this at Red River College in Winnipeg before spending eight years in the offshore oil industry immediately prior to joining EJE.

When the Digi-Lite was introduced in 1990, it was the world's smallest rescue light; it measured 4.2 x 5.0 centimetres and weighed only 33 grams (see Exhibit 1). It could be tied or sewn on any survival system (lifejacket, survival suit, or life raft) by means of a plastic tie, or specially designed patch. The light was visible for 1.2 nautical miles (about 2.2 kilometres), and the lithium battery, when activated, would last 12 hours, 50% longer than competitive products. The Digi-Lite was the only product that operated automatically when in contact with water, a great advantage in marine applications where the user could be unconscious or seriously injured.

Sales growth was rapid, and by 1993, it was sold through approximately 45 independent distributors in 40 countries. EJE had a sales agent in the United States who sold to the distributors there. Sixty percent of sales were to the United States, and 97% of sales were outside Canada. Two of the largest distributors that EJE had were Unitor and Jotron, both Scandinavian-based companies that sold a broad range of products to the marine industry. Unitor advertised daily delivery to 837 ports throughout the world, and it had offices and warehouses in many of these ports. Jotron sold mainly to independent distributors throughout the world, and it had EJE manufacture Digi-Lites for them with the Jotron brand name.

Besides distributors, EJE sold direct to cruise lines and manufacturers of water survival clothing. Both were considered original equipment manufacturers (OEM) accounts, and the volume justified lower pricing. In fact, price was the major decision criterion among OEM accounts, followed by availability of inventory. For distributors, the decision criteria varied depending on the size of the distributor. The larger distributors placed more emphasis on price, as they often sold to smaller distributors and sometimes to large user accounts. Smaller distributors generally sold in small quantities to final customers such as fishermen or recreational users, and price was less important, as the final customer was not so price-sensitive. Availability was often the most important purchase criterion, along with the convenience of being able to purchase many items from a single source of supply. In some instances, for example, EJE and Jotron sold to the same distributors. EJE had the price advantage when large orders were involved, but Jotron had the advantage when smaller quantities were involved as it could offer the convenience of a broad range of items that could be bought at one time.

Paul estimated that his 1993 North American market share was 35%, and his market share in the rest of the world was 46%. There were two main competitors, ACR Electronics in the United States and McMurdo in the United Kingdom. Both had larger units, required manual operation, and were slightly higher-priced. ACR Electronics sold about the same number of units as EJE in North America, but its total annual sales were at least ten times greater due to an expanded product line. It also sold strobe lights, buoy lights, search and rescue transponders, electronic positioning devices, and other electronic equipment.

The original unit, model A-12M was for marine applications. In 1993, Paul introduced model A-12A, a similar model for aviation applications, and had sold one trial order of 500 units. Government approval for general sale was expected at any time, and Paul expected to sell 6000 units in 1994. A final model was the A-12EWS, identical to model A-12M, but with a copper wire attached to it to ensure contact with the water in the event it was on an inflatable lifejacket and was too high from the water to be activated automatically. The Canadian Coast Guard purchased 3600 units in 1993, and were expected to buy another 4800 in 1994. Paul also expected to sell 7200 units of model A-12EWS to the U.K. in 1994. Paul estimated the world market would grow by 20.4% in 1994, but his own sales should increase by 23% because of expected increases in sales of models A-12A and A-12EWS.

EXHIBIT 1	EJE Sales and Profit Data, 1993				
Model	Units Sold	Cost	Selling Price	Contribution/Unit	Contribution/Total
A-12M	90 871	7.74	13.16	5.42	492 520.82
A-12A	500	7.74	13.16	5.42	2 710.00
A-12EWS	3600	8.94	15.20	6.26	22 536.00

All Digi-Lites, while designed by EJE, were assembled by another firm in St. John's, and sold to EJE in lots of 10 000 units. Exhibit 1 shows the sales and profit data for 1993.

In January 1994, Paul was contacted by one of his major distributors and informed that unless he dropped his price by 12½%, the distributor would have to buy elsewhere. Both competitors had dropped their prices, and although the distributor preferred to buy EJE Digi-Lites, the price differential was too great.

After a careful assessment, Paul determined that he stood to lose 27% of his 1994 projected sales; that is, he would only sell 85 274 units in total. He thought that he would maintain proposed sales of model A-12A as these would be domestic sales, and there was no competitive product. He also thought he would maintain proposed sales of model

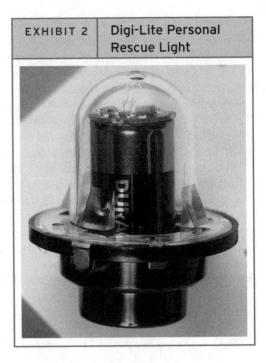

| EXHIBIT 2 | Digi-Lite Personal Rescue Light |

A-12EWS in Canada, but would probably lose the U.K. order. Model A-12M would account for the balance of lost sales.

Paul was trying to decide what to do. This was the first major pricing decision he had to make. He really didn't want to lower his price as he worked on a 70% markup over cost, and had used this markup for every product and every customer since the company started in business. EJE had just designed a unit with a slightly smaller, lighter lens that would be cheaper to produce, but, unfortunately, approval to design changes would take about a year, and production would delay introduction another six months.

Another alternative Paul had was to introduce units identical in size and appearance to the present units, only with flashing bulbs. These could be available in one month, would extend battery life to 40 hours, and would be the only flashing units on the market. It would cost about $15 000 for engineering and production setup; otherwise, the additional cost per unit would be $0.60 to EJE. If they were introduced in 1994, and Paul kept his full markup on all models, he expected that his sales would still be 22% below his 1994 projections. He also anticipated sales for model A-12A would change totally to flashing units due to the extended battery life; sales of model A-12EWS would remain totally with regular bulbs as many users were uncomfortable with flashing bulbs as they believed they might be less visible due to wave action that could hide them at times. For model A-12M, Paul thought that 30% of his sales would be for flashing units.

Atlas Chemical Company

Thomas Funk

Bob Aitken's mood matched the dreary November day as he guided his car along the Gardiner Expressway. The morning sportscaster droned on about the pathetic Maple Leafs. Undoubtedly, this would be another losing season. Why did he continue to cheer for them? Bob reached over and turned off the radio, putting his thoughts to the day that lay ahead. Today was it. If Atlas was going to launch its new line of micronutrient fertilizers on the Ontario and Quebec markets this spring, a decision would have to be made today. These decisions always made Aitken somewhat nervous. As manager of new product development he was responsible for initiating the launch of new, and presumably profitable products for the company. Initially he was very excited and enthusiastic about the micronutrient line, but lately he had become less sure. Was the product really profitable enough to go with? At what price level should they enter the market?

THE OPPORTUNITY

Atlas was a wholly owned subsidiary of its U.S. parent. Although the U.S. company had long been involved in agriculture through its complete line of dry and liquid fertilizers,

This case was prepared by Thomas Funk of the Ontario Agricultural College at the University of Guelph. It is intended as a basis for classroom discussion and is not designed to illustrate either effective or ineffective handling of administrative problems. © 2000 by Thomas Funk. Reprinted with permission.

the Canadian company had not yet entered this sector. Micronutrients would be the first agricultural product sold by Atlas in Canada, and could pave the way for other products in future.

Fertilizers are commonly used by farmers to provide essential plant nutrients to promote growth and higher yields. The most common major nutrients are nitrogen, phosphorous, and potash (N-P-K). Virtually all fertilizers contain one or more of these ingredients in significant volume. Micronutrients include magnesium, manganese, zinc, iron, copper, molybdenum, boron, calcium, and sulfur. Micronutrients are not used as often, or in the same volume, as nitrogen, phosphorous, and potash.

Atlas was proposing to enter the micronutrient market with three products imported from the U.S. company: Supergrow-M (Magnesium), Supergrow-Z (Zinc), and Supergrow-I (Iron). Although farmers could use up to twelve different micronutrients, the Atlas line presently consisted of only three. The three Atlas products were in liquid form and designed for foliar application at that point in a plant's growth when lack of these nutrients could limit the full development of grain or fruit. In addition to the micronutrients, each Atlas product also contained small amounts of nitrogen. This was included to give the crop an added boost at a critical stage in its development, and to promote a rich, green colour. It was felt that the added greenness would be an indication to farmers that the product was really working. With the added nitrogen, however, it became important that the product be applied in precisely the right manner to avoid burning the crop. When using the foliar method of application, conventional soil tests for micronutrient deficiencies were of limited value in gauging the extent to which micronutrients were needed. Visual signs, such as colour changes in leaves, were considered the best indicators of certain deficiencies, although these were far from being accurate.

Aitken felt the micronutrient market was questionable. Considerable debate had arisen recently as to the value of micronutrient fertilizer applications. While there was some industry evidence that the use of micronutrients could increase yields, most farmers had a very low awareness level of micronutrient deficiencies and products. What information was available to farmers from provincial departments of agriculture and Agriculture Canada did not support the use of micronutrients (see Exhibit 1). As well, the University of Guelph, which farmers looked to for technical information, was not promoting or recommending the use of micronutrients. Two major soil-testing labs in Eastern Canada had recently added both soil and tissue micronutrient testing to their line of services. These tests were relatively expensive and not widely used by farmers at this time.

On the other hand, some of the more progressive farmers were anxious to use micronutrients and considered the University of Guelph to be too conservative in its approach. They noted that many universities and farm publications in the United States were recommending the use of micronutrients.

Bob commissioned some marketing research among farmers and fertilizer dealers to provide additional information. Some key findings of this research included:

- Farmers and fertilizer dealers had a number of positive and negative attitudes concerning micronutrients. On the positive side, the most common attitude was that a lack of micronutrients could be a limiting factor which, when corrected, could dramatically increase yield potential.

- On the negative side, the most common attitudes were that micronutrients are not as important as other management practices; it is very difficult to know when real deficiencies exist; some fertilizer companies are pushing micronutrients without adequate

EXHIBIT 1	No Substitutes for Rotation*

Recently there has been a lot of interest in Ontario in micronutrients. There are numerous plots out this year with different formulations and mixes and ways of application on a variety of different crops. I am sure there will be a lot of discussion this winter about the subject.

Some things are becoming evident about micronutrients; at least I think they are. The first is that you cannot expect dramatic yield increases with individual micronutrients on small areas.

Secondly, none of the micronutrient sales staff have been able to explain the problem of over-applying micronutrients. They suggest if you put on too much potash you may tie up magnesium. If you put on too much phosphorus, you may need to put on more zinc and manganese. I believe, with our variable soils, in some fields you can put on too much zinc and manganese.

Finally, these micronutrients seem to be most attractive to growers with poor crop rotations. Some of your neighbours have gone to poor crop rotations and their yields have dropped. (You know: they are the ones that think Pioneer corn followed by Dekalb corn is crop rotation.) Now they are searching for something to pull their yield back to former highs. Micronutrients appear to them to be an answer.

What puzzles me is why some of you are willing to spend large sums of money on products you are not sure will work: shotgun micronutrients. We both know what the problem is. You have to get more crops into the rotation, especially perennial forages. I suppose the bottom line is when you hear your neighbour talking about all the micronutrients he is using. That's just a polite way for him to tell you he has a terrible crop rotation.

---

*   Article written by a soils and crops specialist with the Ontario Ministry of Agriculture, Food and Rural Affairs which appeared in *Cash Crop Farming*, a publication widely read by Ontario farmers.

research data; foliar application of micronutrients may cause some burning of plants in hot weather and does not result in lasting benefits. Foliar application was not widely used by farmers in Ontario and Quebec.

- Ten percent of all farmers in Ontario and Quebec had used micronutrients at one time or another during the past five years.

- The total long-run market potential for magnesium, zinc, and iron in Ontario and Quebec was conservatively estimated to be 7.5 million litres. (Market potential in this case was defined as the total litres of product that could be sold if every deficient acre of every crop were treated with the recommended application rate.)

- The potential for magnesium sales was much larger than that for zinc or iron.

- It was estimated that only 10% of the long-run market potential for magnesium and zinc had been developed at the present time, and that 50% of the long-run market potential for both these products would be reached within a five-year period.

- On average, farmers required a 5:1 benefit-to-cost ratio in deciding whether to use new chemical and fertilizer products.

All micronutrients in Ontario and Quebec were sold to farmers through local retail fertilizer dealers. Many of these dealers were directly controlled by large chain organizations such as Terra, Cargill, and the Co-op, while others were independently owned and operated. There were approximately 300 retail outlets serving farmers in Ontario and Quebec. At least 200 of these were branch operations of major chains. Micronutrient sales were a relatively small but growing part of overall dealer sales. There was considerable variation among retail outlets, even within the same chain, in their interest in and knowledge of micronutrients. Decisions to add new products by large chain organizations were made at both the head office and the branch level. The major factors considered when assessing a new product included margins, performance, testing, information, and technical backup.

COMPETITION

Aitken managed to gain considerable intelligence about current competition. There were two companies selling micronutrients in Ontario and Quebec: Stoller Chemical Company with about 60% of the market, and Frit Industries with the remaining 40%.

Bob knew that Stoller, one of the leading suppliers of micronutrients in the United States, had developed a very good reputation in Canada. It distributed a full line of dry and liquid micronutrients for all crop segments in eastern Canada. It was widely recognized for selling quality products using well-conceived marketing plans.

Stoller sold two types of products: ingredients and packaged micronutrients. The ingredients were sold to fertilizer dealers for mixing with bulk fertilizers. Fertilizer dealers would add micronutrients to their fertilizer products (N-P-K blends) on the basis of their own recommendations or at the request of customers. Customer requests were usually based on soil tests that would indicate a need for a certain level of one or more micronutrients. Micronutrients supplied in this manner would almost always be applied to the soil in the spring and, therefore, be available to the plant throughout the growing season.

The packaged products sold by Stoller were not intended to be mixed with other fertilizer ingredients. Instead, they were designed for separate soil or foliar application during the growing season. Most Stoller products in this category were designed for foliar application (directly on the leaves of the plant). All products in this category were attractively and conveniently packaged to meet the needs of specific growers. (As an example, Stoller sold Apple-Grow, a premix of the common micronutrients often needed for apple production. The micronutrients in this product included magnesium, zinc, manganese, copper, boron, and sulfur.)

All Stoller products were well supported with technical backup, product literature, sales people, and effective advertising. Its packaged products sold in the vicinity of $9 per litre.[1] Canadian prices were substantially above current U.S. prices for the same products. Stoller was headquartered in Indiana and sold its products in Canada through a major agricultural chemical distributor. The distributor, in turn, sold to local fertilizer dealers who then sold to farmers. The distributor operated on a 10% margin.

Frit industries also distributed a full line of micronutrients, but its product line was limited to ingredients sold to fertilizer dealers for mixing with bulk fertilizers. Consequently, Frit had a very low profile with farmers. Its products were sold on the basis of price, with little or no technical backup or marketing support. When expressed in comparable terms with Stoller and Atlas, Frit products would sell for $6 per litre and were used almost entirely on field crops such as corn and wheat.

Of the two major companies selling micronutrients in Canada, Stoller clearly had the products most similar to Atlas products, and therefore was considered by Bob to be the main competitor.

LAUNCH STRATEGY

Bob's tentative plan was to enter the market in the six crop segments that Atlas felt had the greatest short-run potential for the company's line of micronutrients. These were apples, tomatoes, potatoes, soybeans, tobacco, and vegetables. The segments were selected on the basis of potential volume, anticipated willingness of farmers to try new products, and concentration of production in small areas to facilitate initial distribution. According to the market research conducted by Atlas, the total long-run market potential in the above segments was 1 413 000 litres of magnesium and 162 000 litres of zinc. The potential for iron in all segments was too small to be of any consequence. The details of market potential in the six crop segments are shown in Exhibit 2.

EXHIBIT 2	Long-Run Market Potential for Micronutrients by Segment	
Specialty Crop Segment	Supergrow-M (litres)	Supergrow-Z (litres)
Apples	378 000	1 500
Potatoes	186 000	6 000
Tomatoes	36 000	3 000
Soybeans	399 000	150 000
Tobacco	408 000	0
Vegetables	6 000	1 500
Total	1 413 000	162 000

Aitken was aware that the ability to penetrate these markets would depend to some extent on price. A recent Atlas study on the economics of micronutrients for various crops revealed a considerable difference in the marginal value of the product among the six target crops. The details of the study results are shown in Exhibit 3 for magnesium and Exhibit 4 for zinc. Opinions concerning the ability of Atlas to penetrate these markets over the next five years were varied. Bob believed Atlas would have no difficulty gaining 10% market share for the six target crops in the first year if the products were priced in line with Stoller. He hoped that within five years Atlas would be able to capture 50% of the target market. This would depend, to some extent, on the pricing strategy Atlas used. Bob was considering three possible price levels for the micronutrients: $6, $9, and $12 per litre.

Bob felt that Atlas had three distribution options available: follow Stoller and sell through a chemical distributor, sell direct to fertilizer dealers in key market areas, or sell direct to farmers. Of the three, Bob favoured the second alternative. He estimated that 50 key dealers would provide good coverage in the six crop areas selected as initial targets.

Bob estimated various costs associated with entering the market. He knew dealers would require a 20% margin. On top of this he would need to put up $80 000 a year for a sales representative's salary and expenses to handle the product line, another $50 000 a

EXHIBIT 3	Economics of Using Magnesium			
Crops	Recommended Application Rates (litres/acre*)	Gross Revenue per Acre Without Micronutrients	Gross Revenue per Acre with Micronutrients	Other Benefits to Farmer
Apples	7.0	$4791	$5257	Improved appearance
Potatoes	3.0	1029	1192	Improved appearance
Tomatoes	2.5	1707	1835	Improved colour
Soybeans	2.0	361	430	Improved uniformity
Tobacco	4.0	2047	2402	Improved quality
Vegetables	2.0	1468	1593	Improved quality

* 1 acre = 0.4 hectare.

EXHIBIT 4	Economics of Using Zinc			
Crops	Recommended Application Rates (litres/acre*)	Gross Revenue per Acre Without Micronutrients	Gross Revenue per Acre with Micronutrients	Other Benefits to Farmer
Apples	1.0	$4791	$4824	Improved appearance
Potatoes	0.75	1029	1066	Improved appearance
Tomatoes	0.6	1707	1737	Improved colour
Soybeans	0.5	361	376	Improved uniformity
Tobacco	1.0	2047	2069	Improved quality
Vegetables	0.5	1 468	1501	Improved quality

* 1 acre = 0.4 hectare.

year on advertising and promotion, and $50 000 a year on product testing. To date, he had invested $40 000 in market research for the product line. In addition, Atlas would have to refit part of a Canadian manufacturing facility into a product formulation and packaging plant. Atlas would purchase the chemicals in bulk from its U.S. parent and then mix and package them into retail lots. This would cost approximately $300 000 and could be depreciated for taxation purposes at 10% per year.

Atlas's product costs were $1.90 a litre for Supergrow-M and $2 a litre for Supergrow-Z. These costs included raw materials, transportation, and the direct costs of mixing and packaging. Aitken knew that Atlas expected new products to break even within three years of launch. He also knew that Atlas was interested in agriculture as an area for future investment and needed a line of products to break into this market.

Notes

1. A product such as Apple-Grow actually sold for more that $9 a litre, because it contained several other micronutrients. The Stoller prices referred to in the case are comparable in value terms to Atlas products.

Canadian Novelty Printing

Joseph J. Schiele

Andy Cook, newly appointed president and CEO of Canadian Novelty Printing's Canadian Operations, located in Brampton, Ontario, faced the following problem. Company profits and the number of active distributors that remain with the company had been steadily declining during the last few years. After reviewing the situation, Andy wondered what action he should take next.

INDUSTRY OVERVIEW

The World Federation of Direct Selling Associates estimated that 1998 Canadian retail sales by direct selling sources amounted to $1.6 billion. The percentage of sales of major product groups was as follows: home and family care products (cleaning, cookware, and cutlery, etc.), 11%; personal care products (cosmetics, jewellery, and skin care, etc.), 30%; services and miscellaneous, 14%; wellness products (weight loss, vitamins, and nutritional supplements, etc.), 36%; and leisure items (books, toys, and games, etc.), 9%. Canadian retail sales by direct selling sources were expected to experience an average annual growth rate of 10 to 15% over the next five years.

Prepared by Joseph J. Schiele, Faculty of Business Administration, University of Ottawa. Support for the development of this case was provided by the Direct Selling Education Foundation of Canada. © 1999 by the Direct Selling Education Foundation of Canada. Reprinted with permission.

The location of these sales that were sold by an estimated 1.3 million distributors reported as a percentage of sales dollars was as follows: in the home, 75%; in the workplace, 10%; over the phone (in a followup to a face-to-face solicitation), 11%; and at temporary locations (fairs, exhibitions, shopping malls, etc.), 4%.

The sales strategies used to generate sales varied considerably. The methods used to generate sales, as a percentage of sales dollars, was as follows: individual one-to-one selling, 65%; party-plan or group selling, 29%; and customers placing an order directly to the firm (following a face-to-face solicitation), 6%.

CANADIAN NOVELTY PRINTING: GENERAL COMPANY BACKGROUND

In 1946, with a $1000 investment, Canadian Novelty Printing (CNP) was started by Rick Baily, a young Canadian entrepreneur. Mr. Baily was intrigued by the idea of manufacturing and selling personalized business cards and stationery to the expanding market for these products in Canada.

CNP was a subsidiary of a publicly traded company incorporated under the laws of the Province of Ontario, Canada. The registered office of CNP was located in Brampton, Ontario.

CANADIAN OPERATIONS

During 1999, CNP had an established Canadian network of 156 000 active distributors who marketed and sold the company's products to individuals and small businesses across Canada from 44 distribution centres.

PRODUCTS AND NEW PRODUCT DEVELOPMENT

Products

Historically, CNP was known for a product line that focused primarily on quality personalized business cards and stationery. However, over the past few years, CNP had expanded its product line to include such items as office furniture, office supplies, personalized apparel, unique value-priced gift items, books, and motivational artwork. CNP selected products that were competitively priced for the quality that they offered.

New Product Development

Over the years new products had been added to enrich CNP's product line. These items were added on the basis of management's belief that customers wanted a wider range of products to chose from. New product ideas were derived from a number of sources including existing distributors, customers, management, and various other CNP personnel.

Purchase volumes were based on estimated demand for products according to seasonal market consumption patterns. For instance, business cards and stationery sold more rapidly during the first few months of the year, whereas novelty gift items and personalized apparel sold more rapidly during the busy Christmas season.

COMPANY STRUCTURE

General Workforce

CNP employed approximately 100 people in a variety of general functions, including administration, marketing, information systems, and operations. There were no collective bargaining agreements in effect. The company enjoyed excellent ongoing relations with employees. Employees received competitive benefit and compensation packages.

Senior Management

CNP was managed by Andy Cook, President and CEO; Paul Haesler, Senior Vice-President and Chief Financial Officer; Chris Lauterbach, Senior Vice-President, Operations; Mary Steeds, Senior Vice-President, Marketing and Sales; and Christine Martini, Senior Vice-President, Merchandising. CNP senior management had spent most of their careers working in a direct marketing environment. They had come to believe from both their formal education and many years of practical work experience that the success of any direct marketing company was the result of an effective marketing plan. In order to be successful, CNP senior management believed that they needed to continually recruit and retain distributors that were highly motivated toward improving upon their customer base.

Distribution Centre Managers and Staff

Each of CNP's 44 distribution centres employed a manager, an assistant manager, and various general support staff. The people employed within these centres usually had distribution backgrounds. They had acquired their expertise from years of managing the flow of product from suppliers to distributors. Their jobs typically involved stock-keeping and order-filling. The people employed within each distribution centre had little or no marketing experience and could be seen as an operationally focused workforce.

Sales

The company's products were sold and distributed through a marketing system consisting of approximately 156 000 active distributors. Distributors were independent contractors who purchased products directly from the company for their own use and for resale to other consumers. Sales revenues were generated from four distinct segments:

- *Self buyer–family buyer.* The self buyer–family buyer segment represented approximately 30% of sales revenues. These distributors were people who shared CNP product catalogues with friends and family members. They used their status as distributors to either take advantage of the discounts offered on purchases for themselves or they passed these discounts along to their friends and family members. The average annual dollar amount spent by each self buyer–family buyer distributor was $135 per year.

- *Direct seller representative.* The direct seller representative segment represented approximately 40% of sales revenues. These distributors were people who saw themselves as independent business owners who actively distributed CNP product catalogues and recruited customers in order to make more sales and earn larger commission incomes for themselves. The average annual dollar spent by each direct seller representative distributor was $1900 per year.

- *Non-catalogue retail.* The non-catalogue retail segment represented approximately 19% of sales revenues. These were both distributors and non-distributors who purchased heavily discounted items that were advertised through flyers and various mailings and sold through the 44 retail distribution centres.

- *Fundraising.* The fundraising segment represented approximately 11% of sales revenues. These distributors were people who used the products sold by CNP to support fundraising activities. These items included personalized apparel, pins and key chains, and other similar items such as personalized coffee mugs or cups. The average annual dollar spent by each fundraising distributor was $2000 per year.

Marketing

CNP employed a system that enabled distributors to become involved on a part- or full-time basis. CNP concentrated its efforts on encouraging individuals to develop their own business, at their own pace, without the costly expense inherent to franchise operations or other startup enterprises. CNP gave individuals the opportunity to go into business without significant risk, yet offered them significant upside potential, albeit wholly dependent upon their own efforts.

The company's ability to increase sales was significantly dependent on its ability to attract, motivate, and retain distributors, and its ability to offer products and services that were well suited to the needs of their customers. Management attempted to do this through a catalogue marketing program which it believed was superior to programs offered by other network marketing companies. Typically, CNP product catalogues were mailed to distributors who circulated them to small businesses, friends, family members, and the like, in order to generate sales. Distributors could advertise through classified ads, hold home parties where information on the company and its products could be disseminated, go door to door, or use phone solicitation.

Customers would place their orders through distributors who would then contact a distribution centre where orders could be filled, picked up, and delivered to customers. Money for each order was collected directly from each customer by the respective distributor. This system allowed an individual distributor to leverage his or her time, talent, and energy to earn commissions from sales to all of the people that were introduced to company product lines. These methods had proven to be a simple and effective distribution model for CNP.

The marketing program offered by CNP provided financial incentives for distributors to earn income on the basis of the retail markup on product sales. Distributors purchased product from the company and resold the product at retail prices to consumers. The difference between the price paid by the distributor and the retail price was a distributor's profit or compensation. As a distributor sold more product the discounts offered would increase accordingly. These discounts ranged from 10% for cumulative sales under $250 to 50% for cumulative sales above $15 000. Three years ago, in an attempt to motivate sales, changes were made to the discount structure for distributors. Level 1 discounts were reduced from 20 to 10% and top-level discounts were raised to as high as 50%. (Exhibit 1 provides a comparison of the current and previous discount structures that corresponded to respective sales levels.)

EXHIBIT 1	Revised Distributor Discount Structure		
Discount Level	Sales Volume	Previous Discount	Current Discount
1	$0-$249	20%	10%
2	$250-$499	20%	20%
3	$500-$999	30%	30%
4	$1000-$2999	35%	35%
5	$3000-$7499	40%	40%
6	$7500-$14 999	40%	45%
7	Over $15 000	45%	50%

COMPETITION

Overview

CNP competed with many companies marketing products similar to those that it marketed and sold. It also competed directly with other marketing companies for the recruitment of distributors.

Not all competitors sold all the types of products marketed by CNP. Some competitors had more focused lines—others more varied lines. For example, some competitors were known for and were identified by the personalized stationery that they sold, while others were known for and identified by a wide array of product lines.

Another source of competition in the sale and distribution of CNP products was direct retail establishments, such as large retailers, independents, and non-category stores.

There were also many other companies with which CNP competed for distributors. (Exhibit 2 provides an outline of direct marketing companies that CNP competed with for product sales and distributors, including details on product lines offered, discounts offered, distributor support, and new distributor promotional programs.)

Future Outlook

The company believed that its success to date was due to its reputation for quality products and services offered; its in-stock, first-time delivery of items; its familiar, quality product lines, such as personalized business cards and stationery; and its appeal to distributors as a business opportunity for those interested in establishing their own direct sales business.

The company's primary objective for the future was to increase sales and profitability by capitalizing on its operating strengths in order to become a leading distributor of consumer products in each of its markets. The company intended to do this by introducing new products, attracting new distributors, and increasing company awareness and loyalty. (Exhibit 3 provides sales and earning projections for the next three years.)

Current Situation

Sales Trends

Over the last three years, the financial performance of the company had shown a steady decline despite attempts to enrich catalogue offerings and adjust discount structures for distributor segments. (Exhibit 4 provides financial results for the past four years.)

Declining Distributor Base

During the last three years the total number of CNP distributors had declined from 180 000 to 156 000 distributors. (Exhibit 4 provides distributor levels for the past four years.)

Stock-Outs and Other Inventory Problems

Over the last four years the number of stock-keeping units for CNP products had increased from 3700 to over 7900 units. Management believed that this increase might have contributed to stock-outs and the problems associated with managing the larger inventory levels needed to meet customer demand. During the last two years, distribution centres had been unable to provide in-stock, first-time delivery for 75% of orders.

EXHIBIT 2	CNP's Competitors			
Company	Product Line	Discount Structure	Distributor Support	New Distributor Promotional Programs
CNP	Personalized business cards and stationery, office furniture and supplies, apparel, unique value-priced gift items, books, and motivational artwork	10-50% on cumulative annual sales volumes	Support was offered through a 1-800 telephone line, regular non-catalogue flyers, and newsletters.	There was an additional 10% discount offered to new distributors, as well as free information packages and starter coupons for various products.
Company A	Over 5000 brand-name products from over 300 various companies, plus thousands of private-label products	30% on products, plus 3-25% on certain sale items, and commissions from a distributor's down-line sales network	Support was offered through product guarantees, written business plans, brochures, and interviews with successful distributors.	There were no special programs. New distributors had to purchase a sales starter kit for approximately $200.

EXHIBIT 2	CNP's Competitors (continued)

Company	Product Line	Discount Structure	Distributor Support	New Distributor Promotional Programs
Company B	Wide range of cosmetic products, including makeup and perfumes, as well as fashion items, jewellery, vitamins, toys, games, compact disks, and videos	10–50%, on the basis of current order volumes, plus special discounts on special items	Support was offered through district managers, a contact person who assisted distributors with questions and training, meetings, conferences, and various brochures.	Occasionally, the $20 signup fee for new representatives was waived or discounted.
Company C	Various office products, including novelty gift items, supplies, and stationery	30% on current orders	Support was offered through written material, regular sales training from supervisors, and an extensive distributor support network.	There were no special programs. New representatives had to purchase a sales starter kit for approximately $45.
Company D	Plastic household products and toys	25–35% on current orders	Support was offered through regular sales and information meetings, and phone consultation with other distributors.	Many programs existed, including product incentives, and new distributor parties. New distributors had to purchase a sales starter kit for approximately $125.
Company E	Office business cards and stationery	50% on current orders	Support was offered through extensive sales and product-related training sessions.	There were no special programs.
Company F	Household consumable food items, laundry and cleaning products, and personal health products	28–48% on current orders	Support was offered through local meetings, conferences, and conventions. An area supervisor was also available for consultation.	There were no special programs. New distributors had to purchase a sales starter kit for approximately $99.

| EXHIBIT 3 | Three-Year Sales Forecast ($C, 000 000) | | | |

	Current Year	1st Year Ended	2nd Year Ended	3rd Year Ended
Sales	$63.0	$69.3	$79.7	$91.7
Earnings before tax	(6.7)	(1.0)	5.1	9.8

Assumptions:
1st Year Ended: Sales grow by 10%; margin at 49%; expenses reduced by $3.4 million.
2nd Year Ended: Sales grow by 15%; margin at 50%; expenses grow by 2%.
3rd Year Ended: Sales grow by 15%; margin at 51%; expenses grow by 3%.

| EXHIBIT 4 | Comparative Results Prior Four Years Ended ($C, 000 000) | | | |

	4th Year Ended	3rd Year Ended	2nd Year Ended	Current Year Ended
Sales	$69.2	$72.3	$70.6	$63.0
Cost of goods sold	31.1	35.1	36.1	32.8
Gross margin	38.1	37.2	34.5	30.2
Operating expenses	34.1	35.6	41.1	36.9
Earnings before taxes	4.0	1.6	(6.6)	(6.7)
Number of distributors	172 000	180 000	176 000	156 000

MANDATE FOR TURNAROUND

Due to the losses experienced during the last few years, CNP's parent company decided to change CNP's status as an operating subsidiary to a discontinued operation. Unless Andy could find a way to turn the company around, CNP's parent company would be forced to either sell or close CNP permanently.

OTHER PROBLEMS ENCOUNTERED

Management believed that there were other factors that might have contributed to the decline in sales and distributor levels over the past few years. These factors included a mail strike two years ago that prevented the timely delivery of CNP product catalogues and advertisements, and a rise in inflation that caused significant price increases.

DECISION

Having reviewed the key information that he felt relevant, Andy wondered what action he should take next.

Parker Instruments Ltd.

Philip Rosson

Parker Instruments Ltd. (PI) is a British firm that operates as a manufacturer and an importer/distributor. Its field is electronic instruments, and the imported products account for about 75% of sales. One of the companies Parker Instruments represents in the United Kingdom is Electro Industries (EI), a Canadian precision instrument firm. PI and EI have been working together for about ten years. The relationship between the two companies was good for a number of years. Then things started to go wrong, and this was accentuated by an accident a year ago that robbed EI of its top two executives. George Parker feels strong ties to EI but is increasingly worried by the Canadian company's seeming indifference to its international operations in general and to the relationship with PI in particular.

George Parker locked the door of his car and walked across the parking lot toward the station entrance. Although it was a sunny spring morning and the daffodils and tulips provided welcome colour after the greyness of winter, Parker hardly noticed. Within a few minutes, the train from London would be arriving with Bruce MacDonald, the export sales manager for Electro Industries. Parker would be spending the day with MacDonald, and he wondered what the outcome of their discussions would be.

This case was prepared by Philip Rosson, Professor of Marketing, Dalhousie University, Halifax, Nova Scotia, as a basis for class discussion. Reprinted with permission.

PARKER INSTRUMENTS LTD.

George Parker was managing director of Parker Instruments Ltd., part of a small, family-owned U.K. group of companies. The company gained its first sales agency in 1923 (from an American manufacturer), which made it one of the most well established international trading firms in electronic instruments. PI sales were the equivalent of about $1 million, with 75% coming from imported distributed items and 25% from sales of its own manu-factured items. The company had a total of 15 employees.

PI was the British distributor for 15 manufacturers located in the United States, Canada, Switzerland, and Japan. Like many firms, it found that the 80/20 rule held true: About 80% of its import sales of $750 000 were generated by 20% of the distributorships it held. With current sales of $165 000, the Electro Industries distributorship was an important one.

ELECTRO INDUSTRIES

Electro Industries was a younger and larger organization than its U.K. distributor. Located in southern Ontario, it was founded in the mid-1950s and had current sales of $4 million and a workforce of 90. EI had developed a strong reputation over the years for its high-pre-cision instrumentation and testing equipment, and this led to considerable market expan-sion. The company had moved in a number of new product directions. The original products were very precise devices for use in standards laboratories. From this base it had more recently established a presence in the oceanographic and electric power fields.

As a result of this expansion, 80% of its sales were now made outside Canada, split evenly between the United States and offshore markets. In the United States, the company had its own direct sales organization, whereas indirect methods were used elsewhere. In the "best" 15 offshore markets, EI had exclusive distributors; in 30 other markets, it relied on commission agents.

WORKING TOGETHER

EI and PI first made contact in New York City, and the two companies agreed to work together. George Parker was on a business trip in the United States when he received a cable from his brother saying that a representative of EI wanted to get in touch with him. Parker and his wife met the senior executive in their hotel room and, after initial introduc-tions, settled down to exchange information. At some point, Parker, who had had a hectic day, fell asleep. He awoke to find that PI was now more or less EI's U.K. distributor, his wife having kept the discussion rolling while he slept.

The two firms soon began to prosper together. The distributorship gave PI a product line to complement those it already carried. Furthermore, the EI instruments were regarded as the "Cadillacs" of the industry. This ensured entry to the customer's premises and an interest in the rest of the PI product line. As far as EI was concerned, it could hardly have chosen a more suitable partner: PI's staff was technically competent, facilities existed for product servicing, and customer contacts were good. Moreover, as time passed, George Parker's long experience and international connections proved invaluable to EI. He was often asked for an opinion prior to some new move by the Canadian producer. Parker pre-ferred to have a close working relationship with the firms he represented, so he was happy to provide advice. In this way, PI did an effective job of representing EI in the United Kingdom and helped with market expansion elsewhere.

As might be expected, the senior executives of the companies got along well together. The president and vice-president of marketing—EI's "international ambassadors"—and George Parker progressed from being business partners to becoming close personal friends. Then, after nine successful years, a tragedy occurred: the two EI executives were killed in an airplane crash on their way home from a sales trip.

The tragic accident created a management succession crisis within EI. During this period, international operations were left dangling while other priorities were attended to. Nobody was able to take charge of the exporting activities that had generated such good sales for the company. Although there was an export sales manager, Bruce MacDonald, he was a relative newcomer, having been in training at the time of the accident. He was also a middle-level executive, whereas his international predecessors were the company's most senior personnel.

From Parker's point of view, things were still not right a year later. The void in EI's international operations had not been properly filled. Bruce MacDonald had proved to be a competent manager, but he lacked support because a new vice-president of marketing had yet to be appointed. A new president headed the company, but he was the previous vice-president of engineering and preferred to deal with technical rather than business issues. So despite the fact that MacDonald had a lot of ideas about what should be done internationally (most of which were similar to George Parker's ideas), he lacked both the position and the support of a superior to bring about the necessary changes.

While the airplane accident precipitated the current problems in the two companies' relationship, Parker realized that things had been going sour for a couple of years. At the outset of the relationship, EI executives had welcomed the close association with PI. Over time, however, as the manufacturer grew in size and new personnel came along, it seemed to Parker that his input was increasingly resented. This was unfortunate, because Parker believed that EI could become a more sophisticated international competitor if it considered advice given by informed distributors. In the past, EI had been open to advice and had benefited considerably from it. Yet there were still areas where EI could effect improvements. For example, its product literature was poor-quality and was often inaccurate or outdated. Prices were also worrisome. EI seemed unable to hold its costs, and its competitors now offered better value-for-money alternatives. Other marketing practices needed attention also.

THE OCEANOGRAPHIC MARKET

One area where EI and PI were in disagreement was the move into the oceanographic field. George Parker was pleased to see EI moving into new fields, but wondered if EI truly appreciated how "new" the field was. In a way, he believed the company had been led by the technology into the new field rather than having considered the fit between its capabilities and success criteria for the new field. For example, the customer fit did not seem even close. The traditional buyers of EI products for use in standards laboratories were scientists, some of whom were employed by government, some by industry, and some by universities. By and large, they were academic types, used to getting their equipment when the budget permitted. As a result, selling was "gentlemanly," and followup visits were required to maintain contacts. Patience was often required, since purchasing cycles could be relatively long. Service needs were not extensive, for the instruments were used very carefully.

In contrast, the oceanographic products were used in the very demanding sea environment. Service needs were acute, due not just to the harsh operating environment but also to the cost associated with having inoperable equipment. For example, ocean research costs were already high but became even higher if faults in shipboard equipment prevented taking sea measurements. In such a situation, the customer demanded service today or tomorrow, wherever the faulty equipment was located. The oceanographic customer was also a difficult type—still technically trained but concerned about getting the job done as quickly as possible. Purchasing budgets were much less of a worry; if the equipment was good, reliable, and with proven backup, chances were it could be sold. But selling required more of a push than the laboratory equipment.

When EI entered the oceanographic field, a separate distributor was appointed in the United Kingdom. However, the arrangement did not work out. EI then asked George Parker to carry the line, and with great reluctance he agreed. The lack of enthusiasm was due to Parker's perception that his company was not capable of functioning well in this new arena. Because PI was ill equipped to service the oceanographic customer, it was thought that there could even be repercussions in its more traditional field. Parker was unwilling to risk the company's established reputation in this way. However, while he preferred not to represent EI in the oceanographic field, he worried about a "one market, one distributor" mentality at EI.

THE CURRENT VISIT

George Parker had strong personal sentiments for EI as a company. In his opinion, however, some concrete action was required if the business relationship was to survive, let alone prosper.

Parker recognized the good sales of EI products, but also took note of shrinking profit margins over the last few years due to the increased costs PI faced with the EI product line. Since EI was slow to respond to service and other problems, PI had been putting things right and absorbing the associated costs more and more frequently. However, these costs could not be absorbed forever. Parker had been willing to help tide EI over the last difficult year but expected a more positive response in the future.

George Parker hoped that Bruce MacDonald would bring good news from Canada. Ideally, he hoped to drop the oceanographic line and rebuild the "bridges" that used to exist between his firm and the manufacturer. A return to the close and helpful relationship that once existed would be welcomed. However, he wondered if EI's management wanted to operate in a more formal and distant "buy and sell" manner. If this were the case, George Parker would have to give more serious thought to the EI distributorship.

Murray Industrial Limited

H. F. (Herb) MacKenzie

Murray Industrial Limited (MIL) was advertised as Newfoundland's most complete industrial supplier, and sold to industrial accounts throughout Newfoundland and Labrador from three locations across the province. Products sold included hydraulic hose and fittings, bearings, conveyor products, hand and power tools, fasteners (nuts, bolts, etc.), chain, packing, and general mill supply items.

According to Dave Rowe, "Our success has been largely due to our customer service strategy. We aim to provide superior service with a well-trained, motivated staff and a broad inventory of quality products. We have an ongoing commitment to in-house training and product seminars, and we have a 24-hour emergency service for all of our accounts."

Prior to 1991, MIL was a sub-distributor for Snowden Rubber, a Gates Rubber distributor located in Dartmouth, Nova Scotia. In 1991, an opportunity arose to become a distributor for one of North America's largest and best-known manufacturers of hydraulic hose and fittings when its Newfoundland distributor, Newfoundland Armature Works, went bankrupt.

Industrial distributors that sold hydraulic hose and fittings usually bought the more popular sizes and types of hose in full reel lengths and then cut it to fit particular customer applications. Frequently, distributors would attach hydraulic fittings or other special attachments to the shorter hose lengths as required by customers. When distributors bought full-length reels of hose (that varied in length with the size of the hose) or full-box quantities of fittings (that also varied with the size and style of fitting), they paid a standard distributor price for their inventory. If they desired to buy a cut-to-length piece of hose or a small quantity of fittings for special applications that might arise infrequently, they paid a 10% surcharge on the distributor price. For shipments that were needed urgently, manufacturers would often guarantee shipment within 24 hours, but charged a $10 special order handling charge.

At the time negotiations between MIL and the manufacturer began, the manufacturer had a distribution centre in Dartmouth, Nova Scotia and prepaid shipments from there to distributors throughout Atlantic Canada. It offered a prompt payment discount of 2%-25th following, and co-op allowances to share promotion costs with distributors. Within a month (and before an agreement was signed), the Dartmouth warehouse was closed and the salesperson was let go. Shipments were still prepaid but came from Toronto, and the salesperson that serviced the Atlantic Provinces operated from Quebec. After about three months, the manufacturer's policy changed, and shipments became F.O.B. Toronto, and the prompt payment discount was eliminated.

MIL increased sales by establishing sub-distributors in remote regions, and hydraulic hose eventually accounted for about 8% of the company's total sales, and helped increase sales for complementary products. The largest customer MIL had was Royal Oak Mines, a gold mine located about 1½ hours from Port aux Basques, and accessible only by air or water. It accounted for 35% of MIL's hydraulic hose sales.

Within a year, MIL began to have problems getting inventory. Back order rates increased. The manufacturer closed its Toronto and Edmonton distribution centres in 1993, and decided to supply the Canadian market from the United States. The manufacturer sales force was reduced from six to two representatives in Canada. Distributors were reduced from 140 to 40 (MIL was the 22nd largest at the time). All co-op policies were eliminated, and the Canadian price sheets were removed so that Canadian distributors had to purchase from U.S. price sheets and add exchange, duty, brokerage, transportation, and whatever markup they needed.

"Our biggest problem," said Dave Rowe, "was that they didn't plan for the change to the distribution system. Service continued to worsen from Toronto as inventory that was sold from there was not replaced, and we were told we couldn't order from the U.S. until July 1, 1993 when it would be organized to serve us. We haven't seen a salesperson since early 1993, and any contact we have had with them since then has been initiated by us. Service started to affect our relationships with our customers. We eventually lost the Royal Oak Mines account, and they started buying Gates Rubber products. We were stuck with about $50 000 in inventory that we stocked specifically for them. When we approached the manufacturer, they refused to help us beyond their normal return goods policy. They were willing to take back up to 2% of our annual purchases as long as the material was still in new condition and was still a standard item listed in their catalogue. We had to pay return freight and a 15% restocking charge. It was also their policy not to accept return of any hose products after one year as hose quality deteriorated with time. While their pricing and inventory management practices were standard for the industry, we felt they had an obligation to help us as they were largely to blame for our lost customer."

What responsibility should the manufacturer have for the lost account (Royal Oak Mines)? What can Dave Rowe do? What must he consider before taking any action?

Hannas Seeds

Thomas Funk and
Patricia Hannas

Patricia Hannas and Warren Stowkoski were engaged in a heated debate concerning the future direction of distribution at Hannas Seeds. Patricia, daughter of the founder Nicholas Hannas, and current president of the company, was a strong supporter of further development of the company's dealer distribution, while Warren, sales manager, was more inclined to favour direct distribution. As they sat in the company's head office in Lacombe, Alberta, Patricia commented, "Warren, I appreciate that direct distribution has a place in our company, but I cannot see building our long-term plans around this method of distribution. It's just too limiting in scope and would require hiring more people and incurring more marketing costs. In addition, it would take years to reach the volume objectives we have for the company." In reply, Warren commented, "I appreciate your point of view, Patricia, but further development of our dealer system will require more people too. And, of course, it means we have to compensate our dealers for selling our product. This is a costly activity. And our dealers are always complaining about something. Just last week, a couple of dealers mentioned again that they were not adequately trained to provide technical advice to customers. And we are get-

This case was prepared by Thomas Funk of the University of Guelph and Patricia Hannas of Hannas Seeds. It is intended as a basis for classroom discussion and is not designed to illustrate either effective of ineffective handling of administrative problems. Some of the information in the case has been disguised to protect confidentiality. © 2001 by Thomas Funk. Reprinted with permission.

ting more and more complaints about not protecting dealer territories. It just isn't worth the hassle." And so the debate continued as Patricia and Warren argued the pros and cons of dealer versus direct distribution.

COMPANY BACKGROUND

In 1956, Nicholas Hannas purchased Lacombe Seeds, which was a retail store selling forage seed (alfalfas, clovers, and grasses) for use as hay or pasture to area farmers. Shortly after buying the company, Nicholas changed the name to Hannas Seeds and continued to operate in Lacombe. For the next 15 years, the company consisted of both a garden centre that supplied packaged seeds, bulbs, tools, and chemicals to local customers and a warehouse for forage seeds sold to central Alberta farmers. The marketing program during this period consisted in the distribution of forage seed price lists by mail or by customer pickup at the store. Advertisements were placed in the local newspaper during the busy spring season. Sales came from repeat customers, referrals, walk-in traffic, and telephone inquiries. Little or no effort was devoted to aggressively generating new business. The company did not own a delivery truck, so all sales were picked up by customers.

The 1970s were a time of significant growth for Hannas Seeds. Sale revenues and volumes increased substantially as a result of the well-established presence of Hannas Seeds in Lacombe, the continually expanding client base, and the absence of significant competition in the area. In 1973, a grain-cleaning and -processing facility was purchased in the Peace River region of northwestern Alberta and converted to a processing facility for creeping red fescue seed. Creeping red fescue was a primary component in packaged lawn grass mixtures sold for residential lawns, playgrounds, golf courses, and parks. The demand for creeping red fescue was substantial, so the purchase of this facility provided Hannas Seeds with the ability to produce and market a product that could be sold into world markets. During this period, there were only a handful of companies in the creeping red fescue market. Export sales were generated through the use of commodity brokers so there was no need to market one's own product. Brokers would approach a seller of creeping red fescue with a bid from a prospective buyer. If interested in selling one or more loads of seed, the seller would agree or counter the bid. Conversely, the seller may approach the broker first with an offer and the broker would then search for an interested buyer. The identities of both the buyer and seller remained undisclosed until a transaction was completed. As there were only a small number of fescue processors and exporters, demand tended to be greater than supply and the sellers could be assured that they would attain very attractive margins.

The successful entry of Hannas Seeds into the export market was accompanied by similar rapid growth in the domestic market. In the early 1980s, the company began developing a dealer network to complement retail sales. Despite this growth, marketing and sales efforts remained more or less the same as in earlier years with the exception of targeting golf courses, oil and construction companies, and parks and recreation departments, as well as the traditional farm customers. Occasionally an employee would be assigned the task of contacting potential customers by telephone, but this was never a sustained activity.

The retail side of the business continued to develop in the early 1980s although not at the same pace as in earlier years. Several new seed companies sprang up in Alberta, and large eastern Canadian seed companies also sought to establish a presence in the province. Many of these companies entered the lucrative fescue market attracted by the possibility of attaining very high margins. Consequently, it was not long before the fescue market became saturated and margins declined accordingly.

Even with the entrance of new competition, Hannas Seeds did not alter its low-key approach to marketing. More advertising vehicles were used, such as radio, local newspapers, and the Yellow Pages, but there was no formal marketing program, nor was anyone hired or assigned to concentrate on marketing. The company continued to rely on its springtime mailing campaign to generate direct sales, and there was a small dealer network. Hannas Seeds dealers generally sold forage seed as a sideline to their existing farm or business operations and tended to order seed as they received orders from customers. Only a few dealers inventoried Hannas Seed products and attempted to sell them aggressively.

In the early 1990s, it became apparent that more effort should be devoted to marketing. In 1990 a Customer Appreciation Day was created on which customers were offered discounts on their forage seed purchases. That same year the company purchased a custom-designed display booth for use at various farm, turf, seed industry, and horticultural trade shows. Most competing seed companies had been attending such shows for years and it was felt that Hannas Seeds should establish its own presence at these shows in order to reach more prospective customers. More efforts were made to visit existing dealers in person as well as approach potential dealers. This was, however, not formalized into a job function and therefore not done on a regular basis.

An individual with a strong sales background was hired in the mid-1990s to focus on sales and marketing. In the last half of the 1990s, the company still was achieving some success in recruiting new dealers, especially in the eastern part of the province. At the same time, the number of customers who purchased directly from Hannas Seeds was increasing, although not as rapidly as dealer sales. In 2000, direct sales declined for the first time in many years.

FORAGE SEED BUSINESS

Forage crops were mainly used by farmers to produce hay and pasture for feed to livestock. The most common forage crops were alfalfa, clover, bromegrass, fescue, ryegrass, and timothy. Most of these crops were perennials, which meant that, once seeded, they would grow year after year. Even though this was the case, farmers usually reseeded every three or four years because after this period of time the forage crops started to lose vigour and production declined. Although Patricia was not sure how many pounds of forage seed were sold in Alberta each year, her best guess was approximately 8 500 000 pounds (1 pound = 0.45 kilograms), and that this had remained relatively stable for many years. The industry was hoping that the Canadian Seed Trade Association would start to collect and publish this type of information.

Although some seed companies developed their own proprietary lines of forage seeds, most accessed products from either public or private seed breeding organizations. Public seed breeders included universities and government agencies. The University of Alberta, for example, had an active forage seed breeding program. When they developed a new forage variety, they provided information about this variety to a number of seed companies and solicited bids from these companies. The company with the winning bid was then allowed to grow and distribute the variety and paid the developing organization a royalty. In addition to public institutions, there were a number of private seed breeders who developed varieties and provided them to seed companies on a similar royalty basis.

Most seed companies did not own seed production facilities. Instead, they contracted with farmers (seed growers) to produce seed on their behalf. The seed companies supplied seed growers with a small amount of the seed they want produced and then the growers multiplied this seed for the seed company under a contract. After the seed had been multiplied, it was transported to the seed company for cleaning and packaging under the company's brand name. In cases where more than one company had access to the same variety, seed companies often "traded" with each other. For example, if Hannas Seed had an excess supply of Alsike clover, they might sell some of this to a competitor who was short this variety.

There were a number of seed companies in the Alberta forage market. The seven most active were:

- *Agricore*, formerly the Alberta Wheat Pool, distributed forage seeds in all regions of Alberta through their system of grain elevators and local farm supply outlets located in most communities in the province. Agricore was estimated to have a market share of approximately 10%.

- *Western Seeds* out of Manitoba operated in central and southern Alberta, mainly through a dealer organization. Western Seeds had one sales rep in Alberta who spent most of his time managing the existing dealer organization and obtaining new dealers. The company experienced some growth in recent years by increasing their number of dealers. Hannas Seeds recently lost some dealer accounts to Western Seeds. Western Seeds was thought to have a 15% share of the forage market in Alberta.

- *Peace Seeds* was located in the Peace River region of Alberta and had its head office in Grande Prairie. Although primarily an exporter of creeping red fescue, Peace Seeds had a small dealer organization in northwestern Alberta and northeastern British Columbia. They did not have sales reps on the road, relying instead on telephone contact with their dealers. Their current share was thought to be about 5%.

- *International Seeds* was a Saskatchewan seed company that had developed some business in eastern Alberta. They were a division of a very large European seed breeding organization. Recently they created a division called Performance Seeds to set up a dealer organization in Alberta. Their estimated share of the market was 10%, but many thought it was likely to grow in the future.

- *North American Seeds* was an eastern Canada–based business with a division in Alberta. The Alberta division had a number of dealers, but also four sales reps who did a lot of direct business with larger farmers. They were probably the largest forage seed company in the province with an estimated share of 20%.

- *Alberta Seed Company* out of Edmonton sold in central Alberta. They sold only through a dealer organization and had approximately 10% of the market.

- *Canada West Seed* was owned by Continental Grain of Manitoba. They sold through independent dealers and their comprehensive network of grain elevators in many Alberta communities. In addition, they had five sales reps selling a complete line of seeds directly to large farm accounts. They currently had a market share of about 15%.

CURRENT OPERATIONS

By the end of the 1990s, three distinct divisions made up the operations of Hannas Seeds: the garden centre, international forage seed sales, and domestic forage seed sales.

The garden centre provided a wide assortment of competitively priced gardening products and accessories to Lacombe and area gardeners. Products included vegetable and garden seed, lawn grass seed, bird feed, horticultural supplies, ornamental concrete products, bedding plants, and nursery stock in an 167 square metre retail store and a 93 square metre greenhouse situated in downtown Lacombe. The garden centre accounted for approximately 5% of total company sales in fiscal year 1999/2000.

The international forage seed division exported high quality creeping red fescue seed to the United States, Japan, and eastern and western Europe. This division accounted for approximately 65% of total sales in fiscal year 1999/2000.

The domestic forage seed operation provided a wide selection of competitively priced, high-yielding seeds to western Canadian farmers for use in the production of annual and perennial legumes and grasses. Although these products were sold throughout western Canada, the primary market was central Alberta. Domestic forage seed sales accounted for approximately 30% of total company sales in fiscal year 1999/2000. Exhibit 1 provides a list of all products sold by Hannas Seeds in the domestic market and their prices as of March 2000.[1] Patricia felt the real growth opportunities for Hannas Seeds were in this area of the business. Although the size of the forage seed market in Alberta was not growing, Patricia felt the company could increase its current 15% share of the market.

All the forage seed products sold by Hannas Seeds were non-proprietary varieties of annual and perennial legumes and grasses. These varieties were developed in public institutions such as agricultural universities and provincial and federal government research departments. Hannas Seeds acquired the rights to sell these products and contracted with Alberta seed growers to produce certain quantities of seeds which were cleaned and shipped to Hannas facilities for packaging and distribution.

Marketing and sales were under the direction of Warren Stowkoski. Warren had been with the company for six years but had extensive prior experience as a sales rep for BMW Canada. Although Warren's responsibilities were to manage both the company's direct and its dealer sales of domestic forage seeds, time pressure meant that he spent most of his time working in the direct sales area of the company. Warren also attended a number of trade shows in Western Canada and industry meetings in both Canada and the United States. Patricia managed the company's modest advertising program, which averaged 2% of sales and mainly consisted of local newspaper and Yellow Pages ads.

Exhibit 2 shows the operating statement for the domestic forage division for the fiscal year ending July 31, 2000.

Direct Distribution

Hannas Seeds had been involved in direct distribution of forage seeds in the Alberta market since its inception. At first, distribution was through the retail store in Lacombe. Local farmers visited the store to purchase forage seeds, usually prior to or during the spring, summer, or fall planting seasons. This was an excellent method of reaching local farmers, but as Hannas Seeds wanted to expand outside the local area, other activities became necessary. In the early 1980s, the company started to advertise in community newspapers in areas up to 200 kilometres from Lacombe. The ads included a 1-800 phone number that prospective customers could use to obtain more information and place orders. Hannas Seeds also obtained a number of farmer lists it used for direct mail.

In 1989, the company purchased a custom-designed display booth for use in various farm, turf, seed industry, and horticultural trade shows. Most competing seed companies had been attending such shows for years and it was felt that it was time for Hannas Seeds to establish its own presence at these shows and reach more prospective customers.

EXHIBIT 1	Hannas Seeds Retail Price List, March 1, 2000

Alfalfas	**$/lb***		**Wild Rye**	
Alfalfa, Common No. 1	1.70		Altai wild rye, Common No. 1	6.75
AC Blue J	2.75		Altai wild rye, Prairieland	7.75
Algonquin	1.95		Dahurian wild rye, Common No. 1	2.15
Beaver	1.95		Dahurian wild rye, James	2.25
Hannas High Tech Brand	2.25		Russian wild rye, Common No. 1	2.50
Proleaf	2.50		Russian wild rye, Swift	(ask)
Rambler	2.20			
Rangelander	2.20		**Wheatgrass**	
			Crested wheat, Common No. 1	2.25
Clovers			Crested wheat, Fairway	2.75
Alsike clover, Common No. 1	3.10		Crested wheat, Kirk	2.75
Red clover, Common No. 1	0.90		Intermediate wheat, Common No. 1	1.90
Red clover, double cut	1.95		Intermediate wheat, Chief	1.95
Sweet clover, Common No. 1	0.70		Northern wheat, Common No. 1	17.95
Sweet clover, Norgold	1.25		Pubescent wheat, Greenleaf	2.50
White clover, Common No. 1	2.50		Slender wheat, Common No. 1	2.10
			Slender wheat, Revenue	2.25
Special Legumes			Streambank wheat, Common No. 1	11.00
Birdsfoot Trefoil, Common No. 1	2.50		Streambank wheat, Sodar	11.50
Birdsfoot Trefoil, Leo	2.75		Tall wheatgrass	2.75
Cicer Milk Vetch, Common No. 1	2.40		Western wheat, Common No. 1	8.95
Cicer Milk Vetch, Oxley	2.45		Western wheat, Rosanna	9.95
Bromegrass			**Special Grasses**	
Meadow brome, Common No. 1	3.25		Canada bluegrass, Common No. 1	2.95
Meadow brome, Fleet	3.95		Creeping foxtail, Common No. 1	2.70
Smooth brome, Common No. 1	0.90		Kentucky bluegrass, Common No. 1	1.95
Smooth brome, Carlton	1.30		Meadow foxtail, Common No. 1	2.70
Smooth brome, Manchar	1.95		Orchardgrass, Common No. 1	1.20
			Orchardgrass, Potomac	1.35
Fescue			Reed canarygrass, Common No. 1	3.50
Creeping red fescue, Common No. 1	1.70		Reed canarygrass, Palaton	3.75
Creeping red fescue, Boreal	1.75		Reed canarygrass, Rival	3.80
Hard fescue, Common No. 1	1.95			
Sheeps fescue, Common No. 1	4.25		**Timothy**	
Tall fescue, Common No. 1	1.25		Timothy, Common No. 1	1.25
			Timothy, Basho	1.75
Ryegrass			Timothy, Carola	1.75
Annual ryegrass, Common No. 1	0.60		Timothy, Champ	1.75
Italian ryegrass, Common No. 1	1.10		Timothy, Climax	1.75
Perennial ryegrass, Common No. 1	1.25			
			Special Seed	
*1 pound = 0.45 kilogram.			Fall rye, Prima	0.22
			Field peas	0.19

PRICES SUBJECT TO CHANGE WITHOUT NOTICE
HANNAS SEEDS
5039–49 Street, Lacombe, Alberta T4L 1Y2

EXHIBIT 2	Domestic Forage Seed Division, Operating Statement, Period Ending July 31, 2000		
Gross sales			$2 462 000
Less: Discounts			$ 55 440
Net sales			$2 406 560
Less: Cost of goods			$ 1 625 000
Less: Delivery			$ 65 480
Gross margin			$ 716 080
Expenses			
Marketing manager		$ 75 000	
Office staff		$ 90 000	
Bad debts		$ 13 000	
Advertising and promotion		$ 52 000	
Direct marketing		$ 60 000	
Customer Appreciation Day		$ 15 000	
Travel		$ 30 000	
Division overhead		$200 000	
Total expenses			$ 535 000
Division profit			$ 181 080

In 1990, an annual Customer Appreciation Day was created on which customers and prospects on the mailing list were invited to Lacombe for a one-day event where they could purchase forage seeds at a 10% discount. The day, usually scheduled for mid-March, also featured live entertainment, product seminars, and a great meal. Attendance at this event grew every year, reaching a peak of 250 in 2000. Company records indicated that approximately 33% of direct sales were made on this day. The event took a lot of staff time to organize and cost Hannas approximately $15 000 in out-of-pocket costs.

All of these efforts allowed Hannas Seeds to develop a direct marketing list of approximately 6000 customers and prospects by the year 2000. This list was used extensively: in 2000 Hannas spent approximately $60 000 on direct marketing activities, mainly direct mail. The direct distribution activities were carried out by Warren with the assistance of three office people who were all capable of assisting forage seed customers in person or on the phone.[2] These women would pass a "difficult" customer on to Warren when that customer required more technical information, had a complaint, or specifically asked to talk to "a man." Hannas Seeds also had a production manager who was responsible for all shipping and receiving. The office staff was responsible for maintaining the customer and prospect database. Warren enjoyed this part of his job, especially the customer contact.

Once an order was obtained, Hannas Seeds shipped the product to the customer. Because of the small volume purchased by each customer, shipping costs were relatively high at $0.10 per pound. Hannas Seeds paid the full cost of distribution to all direct customers except those who purchased and took delivery at a Customer Appreciation Day.

Direct sales of forage seeds in 1999/2000 were approximately 840 000 pounds. This was down about 50 000 pounds from the previous year.

Dealer Distribution

In the early 1980s, Hannas Seeds began to dabble in dealer distribution as well as direct distribution. Patricia felt this was an important step for the company to achieve significant sales growth.

There were four types of dealers available for seed distribution in western Canada: independent farm supply dealers, branches of large distribution companies, co-ops, and farmer dealers. Farm supply dealers varied in the type of product lines they carried. Some dealers carried a very narrow line such as fertilizer, seed, or feed, whereas others carried a broad product line including most of the items a farmer would need to purchase for his farm. Seed-cleaning plants often carried branded forage seeds to supplement their main business of cleaning grain for local farmers. In addition to the agricultural dealers, there were a few highly specialized dealers serving the oilfield and land reclamation markets.

Independent dealers were locally owned businesses that normally had one or two retail outlets. Although the number of independent dealers had been declining in Alberta, it was estimated that there were approximately 100 businesses in this category.

A growing percentage of farm supplies were sold by branches of large distribution companies such as Agricore, Continental Grain, and United Farmers of Alberta. With the exception of United Farmers of Alberta, the other large distribution companies had their own lines of forage seeds, making it difficult, but not impossible, for a company like Hannas to establish distribution in this channel. Each of the three major distribution companies in Alberta had approximately 50 retail outlets serving the province. Most of their retail outlets carried a full line of farm supplies.

Co-ops were farmer-owned retail outlets that operated much like independent dealers. Most co-ops had one or two retail outlets serving local farmers. Patricia and Warren felt there were probably 50 co-ops in their market area.

In an attempt to develop new sources of income, some farmers would become dealers for seed companies. Although some farmer dealers were very active in attempting to develop business, most were fairly passive, waiting for customers to contact them.

All forage seed dealers performed similar activities. They ordered supplies of forage seeds based on their sales forecast. Once received, these supplies were put in a warehouse for storage until purchased. This usually was done in the winter months as dealers prepared for the busy spring selling season. To the extent possible, they trained their inside and outside salespeople on forage seeds so they were able to advise customers on which varieties to purchase. If seed companies supplied them with point-of-purchase material, this was normally displayed in the retail store. With the exception of specialized seed dealers, most retailers did not make a special effort to push forage seeds; they simply attempted to answer questions and took orders.

Patricia took major responsibility for recruiting new dealers for the company and then Warren worked with the dealers once they were established. To date, Patricia had set up 37 dealers that carried Hannas Seeds products. Exhibit 3 shows a listing of all Hannas dealers. Exhibit 4 shows the sales of these dealers over the past four years.

Contact with dealers was minimal and irregular. Warren made it a point to personally visit each dealer at least once a year, and supplemented this with phone calls, letters, faxes, and emails. Most competing companies had sales reps that would call on dealers on a much more frequent basis.

Hannas dealers were allowed the industry standard 15% margin on all seed products they sold. So, for example, if a dealer purchased 1000 pounds of Climax Timothy, which had a retail price of $1.75 per pound, they would be invoiced for $1487.50.[3] Hannas Seeds paid all freight on dealer sales except in cases where dealers would place an order for a couple of bags they needed in a hurry. This was usually shipped via courier and paid for by the dealer. If a dealer wanted to pick up an order from the Hannas warehouse, the invoice would deduct the cost of shipping. Because of larger volumes, shipping costs to dealers averaged only $0.02 per pound. All accounts were expected to be settled in 30 days. In the case of a few very large dealers, Hannas would rent a large truck trailer, load it with seed, and drop the truck off at their yard. At the end of the season, Hannas would pick up the truck trailer and invoice them for what was sold.

Other than margin, payment terms, and shipping, Hannas had not developed any dealer policies in areas such as sales incentives, training, exclusivity, or territory protection. Although Patricia was pleased with the growth of dealer sales over the last ten years, she was sure this aspect of the business could be improved by expanding the number of dealers and by getting existing dealers to increase sales.

Many of the current Hannas dealers had been recruited in the early 1990s when this was a priority task for Patricia. Lately, growth in dealer numbers had declined because Patricia was not able to devote as much time to this activity. In fact, recruiting dealers was a very time-consuming process. The first step was to identify prospects, and then it was necessary to contact these businesses and sell them on the benefits of carrying Hannas products. If a prospect did not carry forage seeds, it was much easier for Patricia to sell them on the idea of adding this product line than it was to sell a dealer currently carrying forage seeds on changing brands or adding a second brand. Patricia had no idea how many potential Alberta farm supply dealers currently did not carry any forage seed products, but estimated it might be 20%. The data in Exhibit 3 shows Patricia's estimate of the number of competing brands of forage seed carried by existing Hannas dealers.

In addition to recruiting new dealers, Patricia felt there was a lot of opportunity in working with existing dealers to help them increase sales of Hannas products. In reviewing sales by dealer (Exhibit 4) she noted that there was a lot of variability from dealer to dealer and, for any dealer, from year to year. Only a few dealers had shown a steady increase in sales over the past five years. She was not sure why this was the case, but speculated that it might be due to dealers starting to carry more than one line of forage seeds or dealer dissatisfaction or apathy. In an effort to understand the perspectives of dealers more fully, Patricia interviewed a number of dealers on a fairly wide range of topics. These interviews revealed a number of issues:

- Some dealers were unhappy with the fact that Hannas sold seed direct as well as through a dealer system. They felt that some customers would come to their dealership to obtain information on forage seeds and then go to the Hannas Customer Appreciation Day to purchase their needs at a 10% discount.

- Other dealers expressed some concern over the fact that Hannas had established two or more dealers in proximity to each other leading to some local competition for sales. In a few cases these dealers said there was occasional price cutting at the local level to secure sales.

EXHIBIT 3	Hannas Seeds Dealers

Name	Product Line	Ownership	Other Brands Carried	Years as a Dealer
Agri Farm Supplies	General farm supplies	Independent	0	5 to 9
Alberta Agro Services	Fertilizer dealer	Independent	2	Less than 5
Alberta Ranch & Farm	General farm supplies	Independent	2	Less than 5
Alberta Seed Cleaning	Seed-cleaning plant	Independent	2	10 or more
Aylmer UFA	Feed dealer	Branch	0	Less than 5
Bruce Seeds	Seed dealer	Independent	2	5 to 9
Cedarview Co-op	General farm supplies	Co-op	1	10 or more
Clarence Seed Cleaning	Seed-cleaning plant	Independent	1	10 or more
Dartmouth Supplies	General farm supplies	Independent	0	10 or more
Drumbo Co-op	General farm supplies	Co-op	1	Less than 5
Eccles Co-op	General farm supplies	Co-op	2	10 or more
Eyckville Fertilizer	Fertilizer dealer	Independent	0	10 or more
Fowler Farm & Ranch	General farm supplies	Independent	0	10 or more
Francesville Agri Supplies	General farm supplies	Independent	1	Less than 5
Grimsby UFA	General farm supplies	Branch	1	Less than 5
Harry Krabbe	Farmer	Independent	0	Less than 5
Harvard Fertilizer	Fertilizer dealer	Independent	1	10 or more
Hi Tech Agro	Fertilizer dealer	Independent	1	10 or more
John Krug	Farmer	Independent	0	5 to 9
Laroche County Supply	General farm supplies	Independent	1	5 to 9
Lawrence Seed Cleaning	Seed-cleaning plant	Independent	1	10 or more
Len's Feed Store	Feed dealer	Independent	0	10 or more
Lloyd's Seed Cleaning	Seed-cleaning plant	Independent	1	5 to 9
Muller Feed Mill	Feed dealer	Independent	0	10 or more
Parkview Fertilizer	Fertilizer dealer	Independent	0	5 to 9
Philip Reynolds	Farmer	Independent	0	5 to 9
Purvis Seeds	Seed dealer	Independent	1	Less than 5
Richardson Supplies	Oilfield supplies	Independent	0	5 to 9
Riverside Supplies	General farm supplies	Independent	1	5 to 9
Sagamore Livestock Supplies	Feed dealer	Independent	0	5 to 9
Smith Feeds	Feed dealer	Independent	0	5 to 9
Smithville Co-op	General farm supplies	Co-op	2	5 to 9
Sunshine Seeds	Seed dealer	Independent	2	5 to 9
Valley UFA	General farm supplies	Branch	2	Less than 5
Western Farm Supplies	General farm supplies	Co-op	1	Less than 5
Western Forest Supplies	Reclamation supplies	Independent	0	5 to 9
William Torsten	Farmer	Independent	0	5 to 9

EXHIBIT 4	Hannas Seeds Dealer Sales

Name	Pounds Sold 1996-1997	Pounds Sold 1997-1998	Pounds Sold 1998-1999	Pounds Sold 1999-2000	Total
Agri Farm Supplies	4 460	3 430	4 230	7 735	19 855
Alberta Agro Services	0	950	750	9 060	10 760
Alberta Ranch & Farm	0	0	265	0	265
Alberta Seed Cleaning	9 655	165	1 895	165	11 880
Aylmer UFA	0	0	280	1 795	2 075
Bruce Seeds	5 150	14 467	9 290	22 055	50 962
Cedarview Co-op	8 712	9 870	18 604	165	37 351
Clarence Seed Cleaning	1 495	16 150	19 625	10 965	48 235
Dartmouth Supplies	47 370	36 525	42 663	34 305	160 863
Drumbo Co-op	0	3 525	15 497	11 256	30 278
Eccles Co-op	31 969	33 985	45 192	23 050	134 196
Eyckville Fertilizer	8 430	11 905	13 710	1 660	35 705
Fowler Farm & Ranch	12 930	29 335	12 139	18 515	72 919
Francesville Agri Supplies	3 765	0	0	535	4 300
Grimsby UFA	0	200	1 924	2 635	4 759
Harry Krabbe	0	875	1 750	55	2 680
Harvard Fertilizer	15 684	11 265	13 657	1 485	42 091
Hi Tech Agro	8 870	0	11 350	14 640	34 860
John Krug	29 060	36 265	25 370	33 545	124 240
Laroche County Supply	975	2 900	2 860	2 575	9 310
Lawrence Seed Cleaning	18 787	17 295	13 615	1 000	50 697
Len's Feed Store	2 098	1 510	2 885	1 500	7 993
Lloyd's Seed Cleaning	705	2 360	4 960	4 870	12 895
Muller Feed Mill	0	100	50	0	150
Parkview Fertilizer	12 898	17 475	46 261	50 674	127 308
Philip Reynolds	3 190	2 275	6 517	14 085	26 067
Purvis Seeds	51 533	81 010	61 808	49 465	243 816
Richardson Supplies	13 701	22 335	7 455	47 515	91 006
Riverside Supplies	2 745	2 695	630	2 355	8 425
Sagamore Livestock Supplies	15 385	10 770	15 288	9 341	50 784
Smith Feeds	350	1 760	5 655	3 715	11 480
Smithville Co-op	4 165	0	100	0	4 265
Sunshine Seeds	2 550	10 135	25 691	14 978	53 354
Valley UFA	0	1 200	6 710	5 250	13 160
Western Farm Supplies	0	700	6 111	11 745	18 556
Western Forest Supplies	26 850	19 085	15 218	37 395	98 548
William Torsten	10 640	6 045	2 868	9 245	28 798
	354 122	**408 562**	**462 873**	**459 329**	

- There was fairly general concern over the fact that Hannas did not provide sales support for its dealers. Although Hannas did provide brochures listing its products and some technical information on each product, this was the only thing Hannas did.

- A number of dealers mentioned that the financial rewards for carrying Hannas products were not adequate.

- Some dealers mentioned that they could not afford the time and expense to aggressively sell forage seeds. This line represented such a small portion of their business that it was not worth it to devote much effort to selling it. If farmers asked for a forage seed, they would take the order and fill it, but that was the extent of their involvement.

- A few dealers expressed concern over occasional delays in receiving orders.

FUTURE DIRECTION

Patricia and Warren were at odds in terms of how to expand sales of forage seeds in the Alberta market. Warren was strongly in favour of gradually phasing out dealer sales and putting major effort into direct sales. He felt it would not be possible to get a consistently strong effort from dealers to provide the sales growth Hannas Seeds required to meet company objectives. In his mind, using the margin currently allowed dealers to fund other marketing efforts would have greater payoff. Some of the activities he had in mind included the use of company sales people to call on large accounts, greater use of advertising and direct mail, the possibility of having Customer Appreciation Days at other locations in Alberta, and the use of the Internet. He also noted that a substantial increase in direct sales would require hiring at least one more person in the office, since the three current employees were operating at maximum capacity at the present time.

Patricia, on the other hand, had serious concerns about direct distribution. She felt that some face-to-face contact with customers was required to sell forage seeds and that it would simply be too costly for Hannas to do this itself. Having dealers allowed for this face-to-face contact at a reasonable cost. She was, however, concerned about the ability of the company to attract good new dealers and motivate existing dealers to sell larger volumes of seed. She realized the company needed to review its distribution policies, particularly those policies related to compensating and motivating dealers. She also wondered whether it was possible to operate a system of direct distribution along with dealer sales.

Notes

1. The average retail price of a pound of forage seed was approximately $2. Direct costs of producing and processing the seed were about $1.25 per pound.

2. Each of the office staff was paid $30 000 in salary and benefits. Warren's salary and benefits totalled $75 000 in 2000.

3. The difference between the retail value of $1750 and the purchase price of $1487.50 is the margin the retailer earns.

Toronto Door & Trim

Donna Bernachi,
John Blackie, and
David S. Litvack

INTRODUCTION

Gerry, accompanied by his friend John, was waiting around inside his newly leased building in Markham, Ontario, surveying the layout (see Exhibit 1).

"What do you think? Isn't it great? I like it more than the old building in Scarborough where I was for two years. It has the same amount of warehouse space, but it is better laid out. I can now use a forklift instead of doing everything by hand. This really saves me time. At the front there is an office and a service counter where I can deal with the contractors, and there is a large empty area in front of the counter."

"Gerry, it looks bigger than the old place."

"That's right, it is larger than the one I had in Scarborough, and of course, more expensive. The rent here is an additional $1500 per month. I'm either going to have to sell more doors or else cut costs to be able to afford this place. I thought that if I used the whole building for warehousing then I could sell doors to more contractors. But the dividing walls in the front are well built and would be expensive and difficult to move.

EXHIBIT 1	Layout of New Building

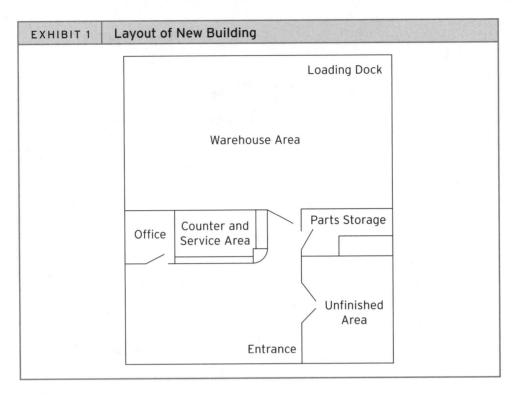

A contractor friend of mine estimated that the cost would be around $15 000 to remove the walls and renovate the area. What do you think, John?"

"Well, it looks like the front area was used as display space by the former tenant," John replied. "Maybe you can use the area to show contractors what products you offer. Or, instead, concentrate on selling your doors retail and bid on a few jobs from the larger contractors in Toronto."

Gerry responded, "The retail market has some interesting possibilities. A lot of people renovate their homes themselves, especially now during this recession. John, you've just finished your MBA—you could probably come up with some good ideas. What would you do with the extra space?"

TORONTO DOOR & TRIM

Toronto Door & Trim was started by Gerry Brown in January of 1992 as a wholesale business selling interior doors, wood trim, and casements to small contractors who build residential homes and small apartments. The product line offered consists of three categories:

1. Standard interior doors and accessories (door handles, hinges, and so on)

2. Specialty doors: French doors (solid wood and bevelled glass); closet doors (mirrored, sliding, and so on)

3. Wood mouldings and trim (required to finish the interior of residential and commercial buildings)

The doors are sold to small contractors in Toronto and surrounding areas. The new location is quite attractive, situated on the outskirts of the city across from a major nursery, which has a large clientele. It is easily reached by highway; a convenience for the customers since they can avoid travelling through the congested downtown traffic.

Gerry buys the doors and frames separately. He assembles the doors in the frames and sells them prehung to small contractors. This extra service saves the contractors installation time on the job site. He also offers measurement on site, delivery, and credit for the return of leftover products. According to Gerry, it is this high level of service that differentiates him from his competitors. This service and the quality products offered are what he feels have made him successful to date.

The current gross margin on products is 33%. Gary estimates products sold to large developers would yield gross margins of about 20% to 25%, and that retail gross margins would be 60% to 75%. (Exhibit 2 shows the income statement and the cost and selling prices of various doors.)

Although Toronto Door & Trim was opened during the recession period, Gerry's familiarity with the contractors in the area has contributed to the company's success to date. Before opening this business, he worked as a salesperson for a wholesaler of building products for ten years.

EXHIBIT 2	**Income Statement and Price List**			

Income Statement

	Standard	Specialty	Trim	Total
Sales Revenue	$850 000	$50 000	$300 000	$1 200 000
COGS	600 000	25 000	175 000	800 000
Gross margin	250 000	25 000	125 000	400 000
Other expenses				375 000
Net income				$ 25 000
Total assets	$400 000			
Total debt	$ 265 000			

Note: Other expenses includes the wage Gerry pays himself.

Price List

	Cost	Wholesale	Retail
Standard interior door	$ 60	$ 75	$ 80
Closet door (sliding mirror)	$ 70	$105	$ 125
French door (oak and bevelled glass)	$ 120	$225	$260
French door (oak and stained glass)	$230	–	$500

*   Available from supplier of bevelled glass doors. Retail price includes finishing door.

The staff consists of two employees who assemble the doors, and one commissioned salesperson who deals directly with the contractors. Most of the sales and marketing is done by Gerry himself. Should he decide to enter the retail market, an extra employee to serve at the counter would be necessary, and this would cost an additional $400 per week. He might also need to advertise to create some awareness.

CUSTOMERS

Most of the sales of Toronto Door & Trim are to the small contractors involved in building small apartments and residential developments. These contractors look for quality products at low prices and expect a high level of service from Gerry and his staff. However, price is the main determining factor when making a purchase.

Targeting the larger contractors, who build large apartment and row housing developments, is a feasible way for Gerry to increase sales. These customers have some similarities to his current market. However, low price becomes even more important with the larger contractors as does prompt delivery and the installation of precuts. These customers can be quite demanding at times, and they constantly seek ways to reduce costs.

The retail market consists of homeowners who are doing their own home renovations or are acting as their own contractor. Aside from quality products at a reasonable price, this group seeks service, advice, and a wide selection of products. Installation would be offered on an as-required basis.

COMPETITORS

Competition on the wholesale side of the business consists of both large warehouse-style stores and smaller specialty stores. Lumberyards such as Beaver Lumber are currently serving the retail market. They can sell doors at a competitive price because their volumes are high, but they do not offer a very wide selection of products. In the Scarborough and surrounding area there are about 15 companies other than Toronto Door & Trim that specialize in or offer doors as part of their product lines as industrial distributors to smaller contractors.

Entry barriers into this industry are minimal as a result of relatively low capital requirements to start operations, simple technology, and a relatively modest level of expertise and skills required.

INDUSTRY

Wholesale

This industry's activities have always closely followed cyclical trends in the level of new housing construction as well as interest in do-it-yourself and contracted renovation projects. Studies have shown that the small size and urban market dependency of most companies in this industry make it especially vulnerable to competitive market forces. The ability to give close personal attention to customers' needs, especially in urban centres, is important to a firm's success.

The recession, which started in 1991, brought an abrupt decline in the number of new housing starts. As fewer homes are built, fewer contractors need Gerry's products. However, at the same time, the potential for the retail market to remain unchanged during recessionary times exists as an interest in do-it-yourself or contracted renovations is sparked. Renovations can give your home a new look at a lower cost than buying a new home (see Exhibit 3).

Retail

The retail market is served in two ways: by large warehouse-type stores and high-end specialty stores. Nothing really exists to serve the segment between these two types of stores. The main renovation seasons are in the fall and the spring. The industry does experience price competition.

The aging population is expected to present large opportunities in all retail sectors. As children leave the home, homeowners find that they have more funds available for home renovations.

Another factor affecting this industry is the slow recovery from the current recession. Large numbers of job losses over the past few years have caused consumers to tighten their purse strings. Buyer confidence is slow to return and this is hampering the recovery.

QUESTION

John sat staring at the information he had gathered about Toronto Door & Trim, wishing he had paid more attention during his marketing courses. If you were John, what recommendations would you make to Gerry?

EXHIBIT 3	Renovations Help Take Up the Slack

New kitchens and bathrooms will make up a large put of building activity over the next year. Renovation spending is on the rise, several construction forecasters predicted recently, although the outlook for housing starts across the nation remains bleak.

Peter Anderson, principal of Toronto-based Anderson & Associates, called 1993 the "worst year in this [business] cycle in terms of housing starts." He said about 150 000 new homes will probably be built this year, followed by some recovery in 1994, with a high of 168 000 forecast. Renovations are expected to increase this year and next, but figures are deceiving, Anderson said. He explained that this is because so much renovation work forms part of the so-called underground economy—cash payments permit both homeowner and builder to avoid the goods and services tax.

Canada Mortgage & Housing Corp. said last week that it projects a 3.5% increase in renovation spending to $17.5 billion in 1994 from $16.8 billion this year.

But a recent study by the Canadian Home Builders Association said at least 45% of all building and renovation activity takes place in the underground economy and is not reported.

Current low interest rates are a major factor in the upswing expected in renovations, Anderson said. "People are refinancing their five-year mortgages, and with the

EXHIBIT 3	Renovations Help Take Up the Slack (continued)

rates [expected to be at] about 8% next spring instead of 12% in 1988, there's financing room for those thinking about redoing their kitchens or bedrooms," the real estate analyst told the recent CanaData construction forecasting conference.

Demographics may also work in favour of renovators. As people get older and their children grow up, they are more likely to make improvements to their homes. Anderson estimates about 60% of houses in Canada are more than 15 years old.

Gerry Proulx, CMHC's chief economist, agreed that as housing starts and sales of existing homes begin to increase next year, renovation activity should also rise. "Home sales tend to boost the renovation market because many improvement projects are done shortly before and immediately after a house is sold," he said. This represents at least a glimmer of hope for the construction industry, which has been devastated by the collapse of the real estate market in the late 1980s.

The Canadian Construction Association estimated that 120 000 workers have lost their jobs in the past five years. Anderson said homeowners will fuel the renovation market, not work on multiple units. He added that as more people switch to working at home, he sees a niche for home-office building or refurbishing.

David Ellis, vice-president of Royal LePage Appraisal & Consulting Services, said there may be some renovation work in commercial real estate as well. "You need to keep your tenants happy or they won't stay," he said. "This bodes well for the renovation and retrofit markets, but it will be offset by the fact that 50% of office space has been built in the last ten years."

Source: Financial Post, October 6, 1993, p. 14.

Union Station Clothing Store

Ian Spencer

In January 2001, four St. Francis Xavier University (StFX) students and one StFX staff member gathered in one of the Student Union offices on the 4th floor of the Bloomfield Centre to discuss how to increase sales of Union Station Clothing Store. The store was owned and operated by the Student Union, and its profits helped fund Student Union activities and events. All five participants felt greater sales and profits were possible. It soon became clear, however, that each had a different idea how that growth should be realized.

SUGGESTIONS FOR GROWTH

John Beaton, manager of the Bloomfield Centre, and the only non-student, favoured relocating Union Station from the 4th floor to the 2nd floor and, in turn, moving a dozen or so video games to the cafeteria on the same floor. John felt a higher-traffic location would be necessary to grow the business. John noted the proposed site would provide more space—about 51 square metres of sales area. He ended by mentioning the possibility of Union Station moving off-campus to a downtown location to really increase visibility and traffic.

This case was written by Ian Spencer, Professor of Marketing, St. Francis Xavier University, Antigonish, Nova Scotia. © Ian Spencer, 2001. The assistance of all participants in the meeting is gratefully acknowledged. Reprinted with permission.

The students also offered a number of opinions. Jocelyn Casford, Union Station Manager for 2000/01, felt the current location could handle more sales. It just needed more and better promotion. Jocelyn believed a lot of students didn't even know the store existed. Claire Barry, the Student Union vice-president for off-campus affairs and a former sales clerk at Union Station, thought the key to growth was to increase the variety of products bearing different StFX logos and embroideries. Leigh Anne Sturmy, the Student Union vice-president of finance, suggested simply moving to a larger office on the 4th floor. Leigh Anne felt more inventory and more display space would easily generate sales increases. Shane Dunn, Student Union vice-president for on-campus affairs, felt Union Station should develop a Web site—or perhaps a catalogue—and target StFX alumni, parents, and friends wherever they lived in the world. Shane observed, "If the market can't get to us, then we'll just have to go to the market."

UNION STATION OPERATIONS, MARKETING, MARKETS, AND RESULTS

Prior to the meeting, John Beaton had assembled the following background information on store operations, marketing, markets, and results.

Union Station Operations

Union Station opened in 1990. In the 1970s and 1980s, the 12' × 16' room was variously a Student Union office and a small meeting room. The store was open Monday to Friday from 10 am to 4 pm year-round, except for a four-week shutdown over Christmas. The store manager reported to the Student Union vice-president of finance, and part-time sales staff reported to the manager. Each year a new vice-president of finance and a new manager were appointed and a new staff were hired.

All available space was filled with wall and floor displays. The store also contained a small desk with a computer on it and a filing cabinet with a Visa and Interac machine on top. The telephone line into the store was dedicated to the Visa and Interac machine. Washrooms at the end of the 4th floor were used as change rooms.

The store paid no rent. The Bloomfield Centre was the Student Union Building, and any office space required on the 4th floor was provided as part of the arrangement with the university and the Bloomfield Board of Directors. If Union Station moved off the 4th floor, the capital cost of creating a new store would be borne by StFX and the Bloomfield Centre. However, some rent—possibly $5000 per year—would have to be charged. Operating expenses—primarily wages, but also including an honorarium for the manager and general operating expenses, such as the telephone line—averaged about $12 000 per year. Cost of goods sold averaged 75% of sales.

Union Station Marketing

Products sold included sweatshirts, t-shirts, golf shirts, fleece vests and jackets, rain gear, nylon jackets, jogging pants, hospital pants, key chains, mugs, hats, mittens, children's wear, and novelty items, such as towels, shot glasses, and plastic licence plate covers. The store had excellent supplier relations. Its main supplier was Russell Athletics. In 2000, Union Station promotional activities included:

- 8½" × 11" posters that hung in the Bloomfield Centre, the Oland Centre, and Nicholson Hall
- Sales booths at large alumni events, such as *Homecoming* and *Come Home 2000*
- 10% discount coupons in the Student Planners or Student Agenda Handbooks
- Semiannual sales (December and April) in the Bloomfield Centre MacKay Room

Retail prices at Union Station were below those of the competition. For example, a sweatshirt retailing for approximately $75 elsewhere would sell for approximately $55. The three largest competitors were the StFX Bookstore, located on the 1st floor of the Bloomfield Centre; the StFX Alumni Affairs Office, located across campus in Xavier Hall; and Jim's Shirt Locker, located on Main Street in the downtown business district of Antigonish, Nova Scotia. The Alumni Office targeted alumni exclusively and offered a limited selection of merchandise. Its main product was picture frames for grad photos and degrees.

Union Station Markets

The StFX student population was approximately 3600. Faculty and staff numbered approximately 600. There were 12 000 other Antigonish-area residents over 13 years of age. As well, about 28 000 StFX alumni were scattered throughout the world. In 1998, Statistics Canada reported the average independent clothing store in a mall in Canada achieved sales of about $3333 per square metre of sales area, and Canadians spent an average of about $900 on women's clothing and $600 on men's clothing.

Union Station Results

Until the fall of 2000 all store records were kept manually. At that time a computerized point of sale and inventory system was purchased and installed. Unfortunately, no historical records of sales by month, by market, or by product existed. Jocelyn Casford estimated sales to be about 75% to current StFX Students, 10% to StFX faculty, staff, and residents of the Antigonish area, and 15% to alumni and others who lived outside the area. About 90% of all sales were clothing, and about 25% of sales were made during special events such as the sales in the MacKay Room (15%) and booths set up at alumni events (10%). Union Station sales reached $100 000 for the fiscal year ending April 30, 2000.

With so many different opinions floating around the room, within 15 minutes of the start of the meeting everyone realized it would be a lively initial discussion indeed.

Amway Launches Quixtar.com

Joseph J. Schiele

On February 1, 1999, Jim Hunking, general manager of Amway's Canadian operations, located in London, Ontario, faced the following problem. Amway had just announced its commitment to launching a fully functioning e-commerce Web site, called Quixtar.com, on September 1, 1999. He realized that a number of challenges would have to be overcome and a great deal of planning and coordination would have to occur in order for this commitment to be met by the stated date. Jim wondered what action he should take next.

AMWAY CORPORATION

General Company Background

Amway Corporation was one of the world's largest direct selling companies with 1998 estimated retail sales of approximately US$6 billion. More than 2.5 million people in 45 countries had embraced the Amway business opportunity. Amway was founded in 1959 by two friends, Jay Van Adel and Rich DeVos, in the basements of their homes in Grand

Prepared by Joseph J. Schiele, Faculty of Business Administration, University of Ottawa. Support for the development of this case was provided by the Direct Selling Education Foundation of Canada. © 1999 by the Direct Selling Education Foundation of Canada. Reprinted with permission.

Rapids, Michigan. Amway's very first product was L.O.C.® (Liquid Organic Cleaner), an all-purpose cleaning solution containing biodegradable surfactants.

Ownership and Management

Amway Corporation was privately held by the DeVos and Van Andel families and was governed by the Amway Policy Board (which functioned as the corporation's board of directors), composed of both co-founders and eight second-generation members of the DeVos and Van Andel families. Amway management was led by chairman Steve Van Andel and president Dick DeVos, who shared management responsibility for the worldwide business and led a global management team of seasoned Amway executives. Amway's Canadian operation was managed by general manager Jim Hunking.

Jim Hunking, General Manager, Amway's Canadian Operations

Jim Hunking was employed as the general manager of Amway's Canadian operations. Jim had been with Amway for 21 years. Jim began his career with Amway as a financial accountant, then moved progressively through various positions including chief accountant and chief financial officer to his current position in 1995. In 1990 Jim also obtained his Certified Management Accounting designation from the Certified Management Accounting Association of Ontario.

As general manager of Amway's Canadian operations, Jim was ultimately responsible for the day-to-day operations for Amway in Canada including activities associated with distribution, marketing, finance, and customer service.

Company Vision, Mission, and Values

The founding families believed that it was vital for everyone at Amway to understand the philosophy upon which the business operated and the strategic direction by which it would move forward. This was outlined in the following vision, mission, and values statements.

Vision

To be the best business opportunity in the world.

Mission

Through the partnering of distributors, employees, and the founding families, and the support of quality products and services, Amway set out to offer all people the chance to achieve their goals through the Amway business opportunity.

Values

Amway identified the following six fundamental values, not to be compromised, as the essential and enduring standards by which it operated:

1. *Partnership.* Amway was built on the concept of partnership, beginning with the partnership between founders. The partnership that existed among the founding families, distributors, and employees was their most prized possession. They always tried to do what was in the best interests of their partners, in a manner that increased trust and confidence. Amway would reward all who contributed to its success.

2. *Integrity.* Integrity was essential to Amway's business success. It tried to do what was right, not just whatever "worked." Amway's success was measured not only in economic terms, but by the respect, trust, and credibility it earned.

3. *Personal worth.* Amway acknowledged the uniqueness present in each individual. Every person was worthy of respect, and deserved fair treatment and the opportunity to succeed to the fullest extent of his or her potential.

4. *Achievement.* Amway founders, distributors, and employees were builders and encouragers. They strove for excellence in all that they did. Their focus was on continued improvement, progress, and achievement of individual and group goals. They anticipated change, responded swiftly to it, took action to get the job done, and gained from their experiences. They encouraged creativity and innovation.

5. *Personal responsibility.* Each individual at Amway was responsible and accountable for achieving personal goals, as well as for giving 100% effort in helping to achieve corporate or team goals. By helping people help themselves, the company furthered the potential for individual and shared success. Amway also had a responsibility to be a good citizen within the communities where its people lived and worked.

6. *Free enterprise.* Amway was a proud advocate of freedom and free enterprise. Human economic advancement was clearly proven to be best achieved in a free market economy.

Taken as a whole, the above six points constituted the foundation upon which Amway felt it could achieve its vision of being the best business opportunity in the world.

Sister Companies

Amway Japan Limited was the exclusive distribution company for Amway Corporation in Japan. Amway Asia Pacific Limited was the exclusive distribution company for Amway Corporation in Australia, Brunei, New Zealand, Thailand, Taiwan, Malaysia, Macau, Hong Kong, and the People's Republic of China. Certain trusts, foundations, and other entities that were established by or for the benefit of the founders were the majority shareholders of each company. A minority of each company was publicly traded. Both companies were listed on the New York stock exchange: Amway Japan Limited as AJL and Amway Pacific Limited as AAP.

Facilities

Amway of Canada was based in London, Ontario. Manufacturing occurred at the Ada, Michigan world headquarters; Amway's Nutrilite facilities were in Lakeview and Buena Park, California; and there were facilities in South Korea and China. Amway's Artistry® cosmetics and skin care products were manufactured at the corporation's state-of-the-art manufacturing facility in Ada, Michigan for distribution on six continents.

Products were delivered to Amway distributors in the United States and Canada through ten Amway service centres. Amway had 46 affiliated operations worldwide, serving 80 countries and territories. Approximately 70% of Amway's business occurred outside North America. Amway and its affiliates employed more than 14 000 people worldwide.

Canadian Operations

Amway Corporation's Canadian operations were started as Amway's first foreign affiliate in October 1962, with a 56 square metre facility on Hyman Street in London, Ontario. In 1964, Amway moved to its present location on Exeter Road, into a 372 square metre facility that was ultimately expanded to 20 903.18 square metres. The Canadian headquarters, with approximately 300 employees, provided distribution of Amway's products and services to Amway's 76 000 Canadian distributors across the nation.

The number of new distributors joining the company in Canada had increased 9.5% annually over the previous five years. In addition, Amway of Canada's revenues—at estimated retail—for the fiscal year ended August 31, 1998 were approximately $203 million, up from $170 million the previous year. The average annual growth in Canada over the previous five years was 18%.

During 1998, Amway of Canada processed an average of 41 000 orders per month. The products were generally shipped out within 24 hours of ordering, to various locations across Canada.

Products and Services

Over time, Amway products and services had expanded to include more than 450 personal care, nutrition and wellness, home care, home tech, and commercial products, developed and manufactured by Amway, plus a variety of products and services carrying the Amway name. On the basis of 1998 sales, Amway was one of the world's largest manufacturers of branded vitamin and mineral supplements in tablet and capsule form.

Amway also offered goods and services from a variety of major companies, including the Amway Food Storage System created exclusively for Amway by Rubbermaid. Other products included thousands of brand-name items in Amway of Canada's *Personal Shoppers*® catalogue and other specialty catalogues, available in both English and French. These products included a wide range of food products, clothing, furniture, jewellery, appliances, televisions, and other home entertainment products, plus many other personal and commercial use items.

Amway of Canada Ltd. also marketed a variety of services, including AT&T Canada long-distance telephone service, Cantel cellular phone service, the Franklin Covey Day Planner System, and the Amway Auto Club, administered by the Dominion Automobile Association.

Sales and Marketing

As of 1998, a core force of more than 2.5 million distributors worldwide, including more than 76 000 Canadians, represented the primary distribution network for Amway products and services. These distributors were independent business owners, not Amway employees. They were sponsored and trained by active distributors, and they operated their businesses using the Amway Sales and Marketing Plan.

New distributors began by buying a Business Kit, valued at approximately C$204, which contained 13 of Amway's most popular products, as well as information on Amway products and programs. The kit was returnable if a distributor chose not to continue.

There were two ways in which an Amway distributor earned income. First, Amway distributors earned income from the markup on products and services they sold directly to consumers. Typically, this markup was 25 to 30% of the wholesale price, but distributors were entitled to determine independently the prices at which they sold products. In most cases, distributors sold to consumers in their homes; you could not buy Amway-branded products from store shelves.

The second method by which an Amway distributor could earn income was from bonuses earned from the down-line sales of distributors that they sponsored. A distributor would receive bonuses not only from his or her direct sales but also from the sales of those within their respective down-line sales organizations.

Although these distributors were independent entrepreneurs, distributors were not alone in building their business. New distributors were trained by a sponsor to ensure that they knew how to build their business. The Business Kit came with the Amway Sales and Marketing Plan that provided information on business principles. Ethical values were outlined in the Amway Code of Ethics, and rules of conduct were also provided to distributors before they were allowed to set out on their own.

Competition

Amway competed with many companies marketing similar products. Few competitors in the direct marketing industry marketed the number of products and services offered by Amway. Another source of competition in the sale and distribution of products was from direct retail establishments, such as large retailers, independents and non-category stores (e.g., drugstores).

Amway also competed directly with other network marketing companies in the recruitment of distributors. Some of the largest of these were Avon, Mary Kay Cosmetics, Tupperware, and NuSkin. The company competed for these distributors through its marketing program that included its commission or bonus structure, training and support services, and other benefits.

SITUATION

Changes in the Competitive Business Environment

As electronic commerce (e-commerce) emerged as a dominant way of conducting business, it became increasingly important for companies to utilize e-commerce as a way to maintain existing market share and to expand customer networks.

E-commerce was an electronic means of funds transfer from consumers to a variety of vendors that provided a vast array of goods and services via the Internet. In this new type of economic exchange, value changed hands without the involvement of physical currency, banknotes, cheques, or other type of physical medium. It was estimated that by the year 2003, worldwide sales via e-commerce would reach between $1.3 and $2.3 trillion.

E-commerce via the Internet provided a number of benefits to companies. These benefits included increased revenue streams, improved customer service, reduced internal costs, increased market share through access to new markets, improved order and inventory management, expedited cash flow, improved supply chain management, improved global partnerships, and the opportunity to take advantage of a wealth of information collected about customer spending patterns and preferences. These benefits, however, were also accompanied by a number of significant challenges.

Many direct selling companies had expanded their businesses and increased the level of service to their customers through the introduction of e-commerce company Web sites. These sites allowed individuals to gain more flexibility from the options they had for both ordering and receiving products. In addition, company sites allowed individuals to expand upon their direct marketing businesses, purchase products online, and gain wider access to a customer base that would not be available through traditional direct selling methods.

AMWAY LAUNCHES QUIXTAR.COM

The Announcement of Quixtar.com

On February 1, 1999, as a response to changes in the competitive business environment, Amway announced that it would launch a fully functioning e-commerce Web site, effective September 1, 1999, called Quixtar.com.

Quixtar.com would be a new Internet-based business featuring the unique convergence of e-commerce, member benefits, business ownership, and office services. Quixtar Incorporated would be based in Grand Rapids. The Canadian subsidiary, Quixtar Canada Corporation, would be based in London, Ontario.

Ownership and Management

Quixtar.com was owned by the families of Rich DeVos and Jay Van Andel, who also owned the Amway Corporation. Quixtar.com would be contracting many services from the Amway Corporation, including programming, warehousing, distribution, and product development. Quixtar.com's core management team would be assembled from numerous individuals who had led key functional areas for the Amway Corporation.

A Quixtar.com Business

Quixtar.com would allow entrepreneurs in the United States and Canada to start their own Internet-based business without the burden of having to invest in the necessary infrastructure or product lines generally required of startup Internet companies. These *Independent Business Owners* (IBOs) would direct their *Clients* to Quixtar to purchase a wide variety of products, earning income on the retail markup for those products. In addition, IBOs would recruit *Members* and other IBOs and earn bonuses based on the overall monthly sales volume of those individuals in their group.

Products, Services, and More

Quixtar.com would feature a wide variety of products and services similar to those already offered by Amway. A Quixtar Exclusives store would feature "My Home," "My Health," and "My Self" sections offering skin care and cosmetics, nutrition and wellness products, laundry care products, cookware products, and other high-quality product lines. In addition to these products, this section would feature personalized information providing solutions to everyday challenges plus a "Ditto Delivery" service that would offer shipments to customers automatically when they needed them.

A "Store for More" would feature hundreds of products from leading brand-name companies in many product categories. These categories would include apparel and athletic shoes for men and women, beauty care, over-the-counter medications, cameras, electronics, appliances, furniture, and many more. A "Hot Buys" section would contain many of these brand-name products offered at very special prices.

Finally, there would be dozens of links to partner stores, other e-commerce sites that would provide benefits to Quixtar.com Clients, Members, and IBOs. These were yet to be determined and would be announced just prior to Quixtar.com's launch on September 1, 1999. The categories these stores would fall into would include sporting goods, apparel, jewellery, collectable toys, gifts, designer eyewear, high-end luxury products, specialty foods, entertainment, flowers, art, gardening, music, tools, office supplies, computer hardware and software, and much more.

Independent Business Owners (IBOs), Members, and Clients

Quixtar.com would feature three basic levels of participation—IBOs, Members, and Clients. As of February 1, 1999, an overwhelming number of people across North America expressed an interest in joining Quixtar.com as either an IBO, a Member, or a Client.

Independent Business Owners (IBOs)

Quixtar.com IBOs would build businesses that allowed them to earn income on the basis of the business sales volume from their down-line networks. These networks would comprise other IBOs, Members, and Clients that a particular IBO would recruit. IBOs would also be able to take advantage of special business services, including a Virtual Office where they would be able to access detailed volume inquiries showing the invoices that made up the total sales of their down-line network. Some IBOs would, on the basis of individual sales volumes, qualify for access to Business Profile reports that would provide detailed and trending information about their businesses, such as product line movement and sponsoring activity. To become an IBO, a startup fee of $149 would be required. This fee would include $90 worth of products that could be selected by the new IBO.

Members

Quixtar Members would be preferred customers that were recruited by or were affiliated with IBOs, who obtained products at special discount prices and received special benefits through their association with Quixtar. Members would be able to earn Q-Credits for many

Quixtar.com purchases. Q-Credits would be earned in a number of ways and be redeemable for a number of items, including small appliances, gifts, and other household items. There would also be a special option allowing Members to convert Q-Credits into frequent flyer miles on an airline of their choice. To become a Member, a minimal startup fee of $30 would be required. In addition, a $15 annual fee would be required to maintain a Member's current status.

Clients

Clients would be individuals recruited by or affiliated with IBOs, who would be able to shop from a large selection of high-quality products and learn more about what they needed through expert advice on health, personal care, home maintenance, and more. There were to be no fees associated with becoming a Client. Clients needed only to be recruited by and be associated with an individual IBO.

Delivery to IBOs, Members, and Clients

Products purchased by IBOs, Members, and Clients would be shipped directly to an individual's home, and in most cases Members and Clients would know the particular IBOs who would be benefiting from each of their individual purchases.

DECISION

Amway had made a significant commitment to the public regarding Quixtar.com and the services that it would offer starting September 1, 1999. Nothing had been done to date to provide the infrastructure needed to support these commitments. Jim realized that a number of challenges would have to be overcome and a great deal of planning and coordination would have to occur in order for this commitment to be met. Jim wondered what action he should take next.

Wilderness Newfoundland Adventures

*Cori-Jane Radford and
H.F. (Herb) MacKenzie*

It was a beautiful January morning in St. John's, Newfoundland, and Stan Cook, Jr. was staring out of his office window, contemplating the 1999 promotional strategy for his family's ecotourism business, Wilderness Newfoundland Adventures (WNA). He was supposed to meet with his father on Friday to discuss it. It was already Tuesday, and time was short. Many advertising and promotional items should have been placed by now. Stan Cook, Sr. would be expecting a progress report. Stan, Jr. decided to review the 1998 promotional strategy to see which items should be continued, and which should be changed or dropped for 1999.

WNA'S PRODUCT

WNA offers single- and multi-day tours, including kayak day (approximately eight hours), half-day, and sunset trips. As well, they offer weekend tours, multi-day combination-activity tours, multi-day single-activity tours, and on-site and off-site equipment rentals. Tours include instruction and interpretation on sea kayaking, mountain biking, hiking, canoeing, orienteering, outdoor camping, and wilderness survival skills. WNA

---

offers a comprehensive program for beginner, intermediate, and expert paddlers, and adventurers of all ages.

WNA tours are all-inclusive. The adventurer is supplied with all food, camping equipment, sporting equipment, and safety gear. Participants only bring appropriate clothing and a backpack. WNA covers all sections of non-consumptive adventure tourism and caters to the traveller who is attracted to these activities. WNA also specializes in outdoor excursions that are modified for its clients.

WNA has been focusing recently on products that are thought to have national and international potential and are "market-ready." Sea kayaking is one of these products. According to the Canadian Recreation Canoe Association, sea kayaking is the fastest-growing paddling activity, with an annual growth rate of 20%. Many areas of Newfoundland are ideal for this activity. Newfoundland is an island with over 10 000 miles of fascinating coastline, dotted with caves, waterfalls, sea stacks, and arches. Icebergs are abundant from May through July, and thousands of humpback and minke whales visit from late June to mid-August.

WNA mainly uses two-person, ocean-going kayaks for all trips. These kayaks are very stable and seaworthy, and all use rudders to steer. The area that the Cooks picked to run their day trips, Cape Broyle, is beautiful and quite calm. Rarely has anyone ever fallen out of a kayak, although it has happened in knee-deep water when participants were pulling the kayak up on the beach. The guide-to-participant ratio is 1:6, one guide kayak (single-person kayak) to every three participant kayaks. WNA's guides are all trained in safety, rescue, and first aid techniques. Sea kayaking in these circumstances is not difficult; people of all ages and fitness levels can participate. In fact, WNA has taken an 84-year-old grandmother on one of the day trips.

HEADQUARTERS

After searching for three years, WNA decided to locate its operations in Cape Broyle, about 50 minutes south of St. John's on the province's Avalon Peninsula. The area has natural beauty (soaring cliffs, caves, waterfalls, varied topography), nature attractions (icebergs, bird sanctuaries, caribou herd), protection from the wind (7 kilometre fjord), an abundance of marine life (whales, seals, otters), proximity to a large urban population (St. John's), an historic property (85-year-old community general store), and cultural distinction (Irish Heart of Newfoundland). WNA believed this area to be a world-class area for sea kayaking, mountain biking, and hiking, and an ideal location for its site.

WNA has become the first adventure travel and ecotourism operator to utilize the opportunity that Newfoundland and Labrador offers with its unique culture and history. WNA has leased a heritage building for $150 per month in Cape Broyle. The building is suitable for barbecues and dinners for groups of up to 30 people. Together, the adventure tours and facilities highlight the cultural and historical identity most tourists and visitors welcome, and provide an unique and memorable experience.

SHORT SEASON

Newfoundland has a relatively short summer. Therefore, WNA has a short season to generate revenue. WNA presently has 12 two-person kayaks, but is considering purchasing 4 more for the 1999 season. Newfoundland's summer extends from late June until mid-September. Kayaking in May and early June is beautiful, but it can be cold and uncomfortable. Late September is a great time to paddle, but the tourist trade usually drops off. As well, once children are back in school, local people lose interest in summer activities. To counter this seasonal disinterest, WNA has contacted local high schools, and has encouraged them to take their students on kayaking field trips. Biology and physical education teachers were the targets of this promotion. Biology students were invited to take a close-up look at the marine life in Newfoundland's waters, and physical education students were invited to participate simply for exercise. This promotion was relatively successful; four of twelve schools participated in 1998. On average, schools have the potential to take at least two classes of students.

TRIP BREAKDOWN

WNA's day trips run from May until early October. People can book any day they wish, but a trip is cancelled if less than four people book in advance. An equal number of tourists and local adventurers participate in the shorter trips. During the peak whale and iceberg period, WNA runs a 5-day kayak trip; a 7-day kayak and mountain bike trip; a 14-day kayak, mountain bike, and canoe youth trip; and several "kayak weekends." In 1998, the numbers of participants for each of these types of trips were 12, 10, 12, and 16, respectively. Extended trips are made up entirely of tourists who come from all over the world, including Japan, Germany, the United Kingdom, the United States, and other parts of Canada. These trips often involve other areas of the province, such as Trinity Bay, Notre Dame Bay, and Terra Nova National Park. These trips begin when participants arrive at the St. John's airport, where they are met and then taken to the appropriate trailhead.

Tourists book reservations for these excursions months in advance, often by calling the WNA toll-free number. The provincial travel guide, WNA's Web page, the television program *The Great Outdoorsman*, and the Outdoor Adventure Trade Show seem to be the routes of discovery to WNA for international tourists. As well, wholesalers in both Ontario and the United States have expressed an interest in representing WNA to their markets. These wholesalers take WNA's price and mark it up 10–15% before advertising it to their customers. This requires limited marketing by WNA, and is a relatively stress-free option, although unpredictable. These wholesalers usually market trips to different locations each year.

WNA markets sea kayaking packages to both potential tourists and to visitors who come to the province. This forward strategy provided WNA with an early introduction in the industry, and allowed it to become the premier adventure travel and ecotourism company in the province.

COMPANY BACKGROUND

In 1970, Mr. Cook introduced commercial canoeing to Newfoundland. He provided all-inclusive canoeing trips that averaged five to ten days in length. These trips included instructions on canoeing operations, trout fishing, camping skills, and orientation with maps and compass instruction. The focus of the trips was placed on acquisition of life skills that are indigenous to outdoor experience. Cooperation, self-reliance, and appreciation of the great outdoors were main priorities with Mr. Cook. He guided and instructed both children and adults of all skill levels throughout the 1970s and early 1980s.

During the 1980s, Mr. Cook received numerous international inquiries about his abilities to coordinate and handle groups interested in canoeing and camping in Newfoundland. After joining the Marine Adventures Association of Newfoundland and Labrador in the late 1980s and becoming its secretary/treasurer, he noticed the interest that the province was generating for adventure travel. Mr. Cook believed that it was economically feasible to expand his current canoeing school, which was focused on the local provincial market, to encompass a larger, yet specific, international market interested in adventure travel and ecotourism. This would not only include the usual training in canoeing and portaging skills, but would also utilize the world-class sea kayaking and mountain biking opportunities that existed in the province and had not been properly marketed.

In 1995, Mr. Cook changed the company name from Stan Cook Enterprises to Wilderness Newfoundland Adventures, symbolizing the new focus on international business. The expanded product line was promoted to new target markets, and the business and Mr. Cook's reputation soon enhanced the Newfoundland and Labrador tourism industry.

Besides Mr. Cook, the company involved two other members of his family, and a number of seasonal workers. Stan Jr. was responsible for the daily operations of the business. He had an undergraduate business degree, and was available to manage the business during the earlier and later parts of the season when his father was still teaching physical education at one of the St. John's high schools. Much of the success of WNA can be attributed to its first marketing plan, developed and implemented by Stan Jr.

Mr. Cook's daughter, Cori-Jane Radford, started working with WNA in the spring of 1996, when she assumed responsibility for marketing. This allowed Stan Jr. to get more involved with daily operations, and to address issues that had previously been ignored. Many of the marketing ideas implemented during 1997 and 1998 were her creation. In September 1998, however, Cori-Jane decided to get her MBA, and her involvement with the business diminished.

During the summer of 1998, WNA employed five seasonal employees. There were three full-time guides and one part-time guide ($10/hour), and a junior guide ($7/hour). The full-time guides averaged 40 hours of work per week, the part-time guide averaged 15 hours of work per week, and the junior guide averaged 30 hours of work per week. All guides had specific outdoor qualifications before they were hired. Before being given responsibility to lead trips, all guides had a one-week training program, followed by a weekend expedition with Mr. Cook and Stan, Junior Guides were hired on the basis of their qualifications, personality, and knowledge of the history and culture of Newfoundland. See Exhibit 2 for a complete description of a guide's duties on a typical day trip and an overnight.

For 1999, WNA plans to increase the number of seasonal employees, and it will also attempt to increase the length of the season. This is an attempt to increase revenues and to market itself as a destination in the shoulder seasons as well. However, this strategy directly hinges on the ability of WNA to attract larger volumes of out-of-province travellers. WNA wishes to expand further into the international adventure market. To achieve this goal the company needs a larger workforce, and perhaps a full-time marketing and sales person.

This person would be expected to take the marketing responsibilities from Stan Jr. so that he can concentrate on other important matters. As well, this person would be responsible for generating individual sales, both locally and internationally. The 2-day sea kayak trip sells for $250, the 5-day trip is $625, the 7-day combo trip (sea kayak / mountain bike) is $875, and the 14-day youth combo is $980.

ADVENTURE TRAVEL AND ECOTOURISM IN NEWFOUNDLAND AND LABRADOR

The tourism industry in Newfoundland and Labrador has evolved to the point where traditional markets are being segmented into highly specific niche markets, such as soft and hard adventure, and ecotourism. However, in Newfoundland and Labrador, the ecotourism segment of the market is still in its developmental stages, with few quality operators. This category of tourism is particularly beneficial to the province, due to its careful use of the environment, and the tendency of nature-oriented travellers to spend more money during their vacations than recreational travellers.

Adventure travel is defined as a leisure activity that takes place in an unusual, exotic, remote, or wilderness destination, and is associated with high or low levels of activity by the participants. Adventure travellers expect to experience varying degrees of risk, excitement, or tranquillity, and to be personally tested or stretched in some way. Adventure travel is participatory, informative, interesting, unique, and in addition to excitement, it offers a wide range of challenges in an outdoor setting. A trip might be devoted to one activity or a combination of activities. The duration can be from several hours to several weeks.

Non-consumptive tourism uses the natural habitat without removing any of its resources (consumptive tourism removes resources, e.g., hunting or fishing). Non-consumptive adventure tourism can be subdivided into three areas: soft adventure, hard adventure, and ecotourism. WNA is most concerned with soft adventure and ecotourism but can offer participants hard adventure if they so desire. All three types of adventure tourism take place outdoors, involve travel to a particular natural attraction and some level of physical activity, and focus on activities that offer new or unusual experiences. Though these types of adventure tourism differ in degree of physical exertion, it is possible that all three can be combined into a single tour package.

Soft Adventure Travel

Soft adventure travel focuses on providing a unique outdoors experience or "adventure." However, it involves only a minor element of risk, little physical exertion, and no skill. It involves less physically demanding activities. All ages and fitness levels can participate.

Hard Adventure Travel

Hard adventure travel combines a unique experience in an outdoor setting with excitement and a degree of risk. It frequently demands physical exertion, a level of skill, and it often requires that the participant prepares or trains for the experience.

Ecotourism

Ecotourism is purposeful travel that creates an understanding of the region's culture and natural history, while safeguarding the integrity of the ecosystem and producing economic benefits that encourage conservation. An ecotour can be either soft adventure or hard adventure, but not both.

THE APPEAL OF ADVENTURE TRAVEL AND ECOTOURISM

Adventure travel and ecotourism form one of the world's fastest-growing tourism sectors. It holds appeal for travellers who are no longer happy with traditional vacations. Members of these groups look for the things that adventure travel and ecotourism offer: excitement, risk, unique experiences, education, and fun.

Analysts believe that the worldwide demand for adventure and ecotourism vacations will continue to grow well into the next century, with increasing demand each year. Currently, growth in this sector is leading the whole Canadian tourism industry, and it is actually outperforming the Canadian economy.

Newfoundland and Labrador are in a good position to profit from the increased demand for adventure travel and ecotourism. The province offers pristine environments, wildlife, unique flora and fauna, and exotic, challenging experiences. Almost every region of the province is trying to develop a variety of activities or products to draw visitors. However, the adventure travel and ecotourism business is highly seasonal with few operators open all year. Despite its potential, Newfoundland and Labrador attracts a small fraction of the North American market. Clearly, there are opportunities for growth in this business. This task is not easy because international competition has kept pace with the growth in demand. Today, consumers can chose from the wide variety of appealing activities and experiences available in many countries.

WNA believes its success in the international marketplace depends on both the quality of the experience it provides, and on how that experience is marketed and managed. The future success of Newfoundland and Labrador adventure travel and ecotourism will depend on how well operators are provided with tools to address challenges with informed, effective action.

TARGET MARKETS FOR ADVENTURE TOURISM

The target market includes travellers interested in visiting a specific place to engage in a new or unusual participative experience. This group of tourists has different product needs that change on a seasonal basis. Many market researchers believe the single most significant trend that will determine the nature of demand for the adventure product will be the ageing baby boomers. They are wealthier, not as interested in the hard "roughing-it adventure," have less time, and yet still seek new experiences.

Some interesting statistics about adventure travellers are:

- There are 30 to 40 million Americans that are potential candidates for an adventure trip of some kind.
- There are 787 000 potential adventure tourism clients in the United Kingdom. Thirty-five percent of British vacationers seek adventure and are looking for an active holiday where they can get in touch with their daring adventurous side.
- The outdoor sports segments, totalling 1.3 million people, represent potential for adventure travel.

These potential adventure travellers fit the following three main profiles.

Casual Adventure Travellers

These are the entry-level adventurers, experimenting with new and challenging outdoor activities. They take short trips (one or two days) to get a "taste of adventure." This market affords the greatest growth potential in the short term. Also, there is little difference between these travellers and the touring urban-based tourists. Therefore, the opportunity to attract city-touring visitors for short excursions is good, due to their closely related desires.

Committed Adventure Travellers

These travellers form the most affluent segment. They are fitness-conscious, in the middle- to upper-income brackets, 30 to 55 years old, well educated, and live in urban centres. They demand and are willing to pay for quality accommodations.

Expert Adventure Travellers

These are the adventurers who are on their way to mastering a sports-related skill or knowledge about a topic (e.g., wildlife), and for whom the motivation for a trip has shifted from general growth and exploration to the fine-tuning of a particular skill. This market tends to be younger, has less disposable income, and is more inclined than other groups to "rough it."

COMPETITION

It is important for WNA to understand and cultivate its target market and to know its competition. The main competition for WNA is not within the province. Since this province has very few quality operators, the real competition is coming from operators outside Newfoundland and Labrador who are offering similar travel experiences. Many of these operators are very good and have much to offer. Therefore, WNA is working hard to create better products. By monitoring its larger international competitors, WNA has been trying to improve its products, providing better value and, hopefully, attracting more customers.

The major competition for all adventure travel and ecotourism customers comes from outside Canada. Worldwide consumer demand for unique experiences and intriguing packages is fuelling international competition. However, current market opportunities support WNA's products. WNA remains highly competitive with its current pricing strategy, service quality, product uniqueness (i.e., sea kayaking with whales and icebergs), wilderness environmental appeal, and current currency exchange rates.

1998 PROMOTIONAL ACTIVITIES

Stan Jr. and Cori-Jane generated all of the ad concepts and material and decided the 1998 media plan (see Exhibit 1). Cori-Jane created the physical displays and then had films produced by the printer. This is quite inexpensive compared to hiring a marketing firm, although it is time-consuming. Stan, Jr. had limited involvement with the graphic design, but his involvement has been increasing due to Cori-Jane's decreasing involvement in the business.

EXHIBIT 1	WNA Media Budget, 1998			
Media	Date	Company	Form of Ad	Cost
TV	07/28/98	The Great Outdoorsman	Half-hour television show	$ 7 500.00
Radio	06/30/98	OZ-FM	60 × 30 sec. spots (2 weeks)	$ 1 750.00
	07/31/98	OZ-FM	60 × 30 sec. spots (2 weeks)	$ 1 750.00
	08/31/98	OZ-FM	60 × 30 sec. spots (2 weeks)	$ 1 750.00
Print	12/29/97	St. John's Visitor's Guide	¼-page ad–full colour	$ 575.00
	01/15/98	NewTel Communications	Yellow Pages–1/8-page ad– 1 colour	$ 1 200.00
	04/30/98	NFLD Sportsman	⅙-page ad–full colour	$ 400.00
	05/03/98	NFLD Sportsman	⅙-page ad–full colour	$ 400.00
	06/07/98	NFLD Sportsman	Full-page ad–full colour– accompanying story	$ 1 300.00
	12/29/97	Provincial Travel Guide	¼-page ad–full colour	$ 1 500.00
	04/30/98	St. John's Board of Trade	Front cover	$ 1 200.00
	03/31/98	Sterling Press Printers	Small brochure–full colour	$ 1 350.00
Sales promo	06/04/98	Gift certificates	25 half-day trips for 2	$ 2 500.00
Signage	05/02/98	Highway signage	Three 12' × 8'	$ 500.00
	04/26/98	WNA van signage	Full-colour, 4 sides	$ 500.00
Trade show	06/01/98	Kinetic Marketing	NFLD Sportsman Show, St. John's–Booth	$ 600.00
	02/14/98	National Event Management	Outdoor Adventure Show, Toronto–Booth	$ 2 000.00
				$26 775.00

Print Advertising

Newfoundland Sportsman

Newfoundland Sportsman magazine is a 70-page, full-colour, glossy magazine. This magazine prints 20 000 copies every two months. It has approximately 5000 subscribers and the other copies are distributed to retailers and news stands all across the province. This magazine is published in Newfoundland and marketed to adults interested in the outdoors. Most readers are between the ages of 18 and 55, and include both men and women in approximately equal numbers. Both consumptive and non-consumptive approaches are represented in this publication. In 1998, WNA placed three ads in this magazine. Two were 1/6-page ads, placed for recognition, and the third was a full-page, full-colour advertisement that appeared facing an article written by the magazine on sea kayaking, and, in particular, on WNA.

Newfoundland Travel Guide

The *Newfoundland Travel Guide* is a 200-page, colour brochure created by the provincial Department of Tourism. Interested potential tourists from all over the world contact the Department to request information. The *Guide* is then delivered free-of-charge to anyone expressing an interest in visiting the province. A new guide is published each year, listing accommodations, events, attractions, tours, and services.

All businesses relating to the tourist industry receive a free 100-word listing under their appropriate heading. As well, the Department provides pages in the publication for business that wish to purchase ad space. Rates for 1999 are double the 1998 rates.

Brochures

WNA has produced two brochures. A small brochure (see Exhibit 2 which displays the front and back of the brochure) was created to advertise WNA's sea kayaking cruises, although WNA was planning on changing its prices for 1999 to $100 per person for full-day cruises, and $65 per person for half-day and sunset trips. This was targeted at the local population and the tourists visiting the St. John's area. These brochures are placed throughout St. John's, in tourist chalets, hotels, motels, restaurants, and any stores that will accept them. These are two-sided, full-colour, high-quality brochures. They are printed on cardboard-type paper, cut to $3\frac{1}{3}" \times 8\frac{1}{2}"$.

WNA's larger brochures are mailed to people interested in extended trips. This brochure was created and printed in 1996. In order to keep the brochure up to date, there is a pocket inside the back cover that allows WNA to insert current prices and updated information. This brochure was expensive to produce, but most adventurers have been impressed by it.

Radio Advertising

OZ-FM (94.7) is a St. John's radio station that reaches approximately 182 000 people over 12 years of age each week. The target market for OZ FM is 18-to-49-year-old adults with active lifestyles, from all socioeconomic classes.

WNA ran three sets of 30-second ads throughout the summer. The duration of each set was two weeks. In conjunction with the advertisements, WNA arranged to have 6 pairs of free gift certificates given away on the radio during the Friday "morning drive" time slot. OZ-FM's morning drive is called the *Dawn Patrol*, and has three radio personalities. WNA invited all of them to participate on a free day trip. This proved to be a great idea, as, when they gave away the free passes, they were able to make first-hand and favourable comments about sea kayaking. In fact, they continued to promote WNA and sea kayaking with personal comments throughout all of the radio advertising campaigns.

Television Advertising

The Great Outdoorsman (TGO) is a half-hour Sunday night television program on the Life network (carried all over North America). The program host, John Summerfield, and his two-man crew travel all over the world seeking different types of adventure. John was

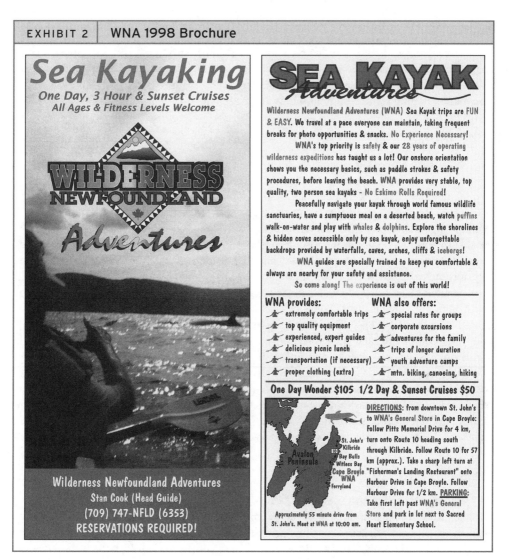

| EXHIBIT 2 | WNA 1998 Brochure |

Sea Kayaking
One Day, 3 Hour & Sunset Cruises
All Ages & Fitness Levels Welcome

WILDERNESS NEWFOUNDLAND *Adventures*

Wilderness Newfoundland Adventures
Stan Cook (Head Guide)
(709) 747-NFLD (6353)
RESERVATIONS REQUIRED!

SEA KAYAK *Adventures*

Wilderness Newfoundland Adventures (WNA) Sea Kayak trips are FUN & EASY. We travel at a pace everyone can maintain, taking frequent breaks for photo opportunities & snacks. No Experience Necessary!

WNA's top priority is safety & our 28 years of operating wilderness expeditions has taught us a lot! Our onshore orientation shows you the necessary basics, such as paddle strokes & safety procedures, before leaving the beach. WNA provides very stable, top quality, two person sea kayaks - No Eskimo Rolls Required!

Peacefully navigate your kayak through world famous wildlife sanctuaries, have a sumptuous meal on a deserted beach, watch puffins walk-on-water and play with whales & dolphins. Explore the shorelines & hidden coves accessible only by sea kayak, enjoy unforgettable backdrops provided by waterfalls, caves, arches, cliffs & icebergs!

WNA guides are specially trained to keep you comfortable & always are nearby for your safety and assistance.

So come along! The experience is out of this world!

WNA provides:
- extremely comfortable trips
- top quality equipment
- experienced, expert guides
- delicious picnic lunch
- transportation (if necessary)
- proper clothing (extra)

WNA also offers:
- special rates for groups
- corporate excursions
- adventures for the family
- trips of longer duration
- youth adventure camps
- mtn. biking, canoeing, hiking

One Day Wonder $105   1/2 Day & Sunset Cruises $50

Avalon Peninsula
St. John's
Kilbride
Bay Bulls
Witless Bay
Cape Broyle
WNA
Ferryland

Approximately 55 minute drive from St. John's. Meet at WNA at 10:00 am.

DIRECTIONS: from downtown St. John's to WNA's General Store in Cape Broyle: Follow Pitts Memorial Drive for 4 km, turn onto Route 10 heading south through Kilbride. Follow Route 10 for 57 km (approx.). Take a sharp left turn at "Fisherman's Landing Restaurant" onto Harbour Drive in Cape Broyle. Follow Harbour Drive for 1/2 km. **PARKING:** Take first left past WNA's General Store and park in lot next to Sacred Heart Elementary School.

interested in sea kayaking with whales and icebergs, and contacted Stan Jr. after meeting him at a trade show. In July 1997, TGO came to St. John's and filmed a show. The shooting went extremely well, and both John and WNA received considerable praise. John enjoyed Newfoundland so much that he decided to return to film another show with WNA (never before had he done two shows with the same company, with the same product). The Great Outdoorsman and his crew returned in July 1998 and filmed another show. This show aired in October 1998, and was scheduled for two repeats during 1999.

WNA has received many benefits and much recognition from these shows, although they were very expensive. WNA paid the air travel, accommodations, and meals of the TGO team for four days and three nights, a total of approximately $2500. As well, there was a $5000 fee payable to TGO to participate in its show.

Internet

WNA first created its Web site (www.wildnfld.ca) in the spring of 1997. It enlisted a small local Web design firm to assist in developing its online personality. The site gets updated about twice a year (before and after the regular season). WNA is currently investigating e-commerce, hoping to take both bookings and payments over the Web.

Signage

St. John's is the end of the line when driving east on the Trans-Canada Highway (TCH), as it is the most easterly city in North America. The TCH is the most used route into the city and many local businesses have signs along it, advertising to incoming motor tourists.

WNA decided to strategically place three signs. The first was placed along the TCH with all the other signs. The second was put on a highly used arterial within the city. The final sign was placed along the Southern Shore Highway. This highway follows the coast from St. John's, south past Cape Broyle, and then it loops back along St. Mary's Bay to the city, a route called the Irish Loop. The signs were designed by Stan Jr. and Cori-Jane, and were painted by an art student at Stan Sr.'s high school.

Additional signage was placed on a company van. WNA leased a forest-green Ford AeroStar in April 1998 ($500/month). This van is used for pickup and delivery of clients, shuttle of equipment, and transportation for the guides to and from the various sites. The van is only used for 16 weeks during the summer. It requires gas about twice a week, and costs $60 per fill-up. Cori-Jane thought that WNA should take advantage of the vehicle's visibility around St. John's and that it should be incorporated in the promotion strategy. She hired a local business that specializes in auto advertising to put WNA's logo and other information on all four sides of the vehicle. The final product was quite impressive, and a number of people commented that they had seen the "Green WNA Machine" around town.

Sales Promotions

In 1998, WNA gave away 25 pairs of "Half-Day Sea Kayak Adventures for Two" gift certificates to different individuals. Some people won them on the radio, while other tickets were given to local celebrities or other prominent people. WNA wanted to get people to try sea kayaking and thought this would be a good idea, although only 11 pairs were redeemed over the summer.

Trade Shows

The Newfoundland Sportsman Show, sponsored by *Newfoundland Sportsman* magazine, is the largest show of its type in the province. It is a consumer retail trade fair with its primary focus on the outdoor industry. Many types of land, air, and marine activities are represented, and it attracts 8000 to 14 000 interested consumers.

A new trade show, the Outdoor Adventure Sports Show (OASS), has been held in February in Toronto, Ontario for the past two years. At the OASS, attendees can try climbing the Pyramid wall, and can test-ride mountain bikes on a demo track, and canoeing or kayaking in an indoor pool. As well, outfitters from all over North America show what their province/company/activity has to offer the willing adventurer.

Attendance at the 1998 OASS included 23 320 people, with 62% either making an adventure purchase there or expressing an intention to make such a purchase as a result of the show. This attendance was 120% over the 1997 attendance, and it is expected to continue to grow for some time. WNA has participated both years. This show provides a venue for WNA to reach clients for their longer-duration adventures. These people will specifically come to Newfoundland for an excursion with WNA. Travelling, accommodation, and meal expenses amount to approximately $2000 for two people to attend OASS.

Other Methods

Excluding trade shows, the majority of WNA's personal selling has been informal. Mr. Cook and Stan, Jr. attend many local events, sporting rallies, and other activities that attract adventure-minded people. As well, WNA encourages its summer employees to promote sea kayaking on their own time by giving them a $10 bonus every customer they bring on a full-day kayak trip, and a $5 bonus for every customer they bring to half-day or sunset trips. This encourages the guides to get a group of friends together to go out kayaking. (At the beginning of the summer, each staff member also receives three free day passes for family and friends.)

In their first two years of operation, WNA had a difficult time attracting local customers. Due to unfamiliarity with sea kayaking, many people were very nervous. The only information people had accumulated previously was on the dangerous sport of river kayaking. River and sea kayaking are completely different sports, with very differently-shaped vessels and different objectives. Now that people have heard of sea kayaking, they are starting to differentiate WNA from other local outfitters by both reputation and value.

St. John's is becoming a popular tourist destination. An increasing number of businesses and associations are holding annual conferences in the oldest city in North America. Exhibit 3 presents a list of conferences planned in 1998 to come to St. John's in the summer of 1999.

Finally, WNA is considering the possibility of hiring a salesperson. So far, little thought has been given to what the sales person would do, how he or she would be compensated, and exactly what criteria would be important in hiring an appropriate person.

Public Relations

WNA has attempted to take advantage of the free publicity. Stan Jr. has invited several local reporters to participate on a free day trip in return for writing articles on WNA. So far, two reporters have participated, and both have written very positive articles on their experiences. The first appeared in *The Evening Telegram* (St. John's). It was a full-page article, accompanied by five full-colour photos. The second appeared in *Mount Pearl Pride*. Mount Pearl is a smaller city that borders St. John's. Again, it was a full-page article with full-colour photos. WNA received many phone calls following the printing of these articles.

CONCLUSION

Before making any decisions with respect to the 1999 promotional strategy, Stan Jr. decided to review the summary of responses to the customer satisfaction surveys collected

EXHIBIT 3	Upcoming Conventions and Events, St. John's, 1999	
Date	**Convention**	**Delegates**
May 10-13	Canadian Association of Principals	550
June 1-5	Co-operative Housing Federation of Canada	700
June 11-14	Canadian Council for the Advancement of Education	250
June 13-20	Canadian Corps of Commissioners AGM '99	400
June 17-20	Air Cadet League of Canada	150
June 23-27	CAMRT/CSDMU Joint Meeting	500
July 5-9	Canadian Orthopedic Association	700
July 11-16	Offshore Mechanics and Arctic Engineering	400
August 21-26	Canada Employment & Immigration Union	325
September 19-22	Risk & Insurance Management Society	500
September 27-30	Workers' Compensation Commission	100
October 1-3	International Association of Business Communicators	300

Source: Department of Economic Development and Tourism.

in 1998. Every person that participated on a day, half-day, or sunset trip between May 24 and September 6, 1998 filled one out. The summary of responses is provided in Exhibit 4.

Stan Jr. has a tremendous amount of planning to do and decisions to make over the next few days. How successful has the 1998 promotional campaign been? What items should be retained for 1999, and what items should be changed or deleted? How should WNA set its promotional budget? Stan Jr. knew his father would want answers to all of these questions at their Friday meeting.

EXHIBIT 4	WNA Customer Satisfaction Survey Results, Summer 1998						
Age	**Total**		**Sex**	**Total**		**Trip**	**Total**
10-19	48		Male	332		Full day	360
20-29	309		Female	388		Half day	180
30-39	239		**Total**	**720**		Sunset	180
40-49	76					**Total**	**720**
50-59	28						
60+	20						
Total	**720**						

EXHIBIT 4	WNA Customer Satisfaction Survey Results, Summer 1998 (continued)

How Did You Like Our Staff and Service?

Guides

Friendly	Ratings	Total	Knowledgeable	Ratings	Total
Dissatisfied	1	0	Dissatisfied	1	0
	2	0		2	0
	3	0		3	0
Satisfied	4	11	Satisfied	4	15
	5	33		5	28
	6	73		6	55
100% satisfied	7	603	100% satisfied	7	622
Total		**720**	Total		**720**

Physical Product

Food	Ratings	Total	Equipment	Ratings	Total
Dissatisfied	1	0	Dissatisfied	1	0
	2	0		2	0
	3	4		3	9
Satisfied	4	14	Satisfied	4	12
	5	32		5	33
	6	68		6	70
100% satisfied	7	602	100% satisfied	7	596
Total		**720**	Total		**720**

How Do You Feel?

Would You Return?	Ratings	No. of People	Recommend Us to Others?	Ratings	No. of People
No	1	0	No	1	0
	2	0		2	0
Maybe	3	38	Maybe	3	30
	4	66		4	69
Definitely	5	616	Definitely	5	621
Total		**720**	Total		**720**

EXHIBIT 4	WNA Customer Satisfaction Survey Results, Summer 1998 (continued)

Where Did You Hear About Us?	No. of People	What Influenced You to Try Sea Kayaking?	No. of People
Brochure (large)	10	Advertising:	148
Brochure (small)	99	Brochure	45
Gift certificate	11	Travel guide ad	8
Other	7	Sign on road	8
Phone book (Yellow Pages)	32	OZ FM ad	44
Radio	66	Television show	24
Referral (word of mouth)	175	Mount Pearl Pride	19
Repeat customer	53	Alpine Country Lodge recommendation	15
Television:		Always wanted to try sea kayaking	33
The Great Outdoorsman	19	Dept. of Tourism recommendation	13
Travel Agency	5	Familiarization tour	20
Web site	23	Family recommendation	26
Magazine:		For the adventure	15
Newfoundland Sportsman	35	Free invitation	10
Provincial Travel Guide	68	Friend of the Cooks	22
St. John's Visitor's Guide	12	Friend recommendation/ going with friends	112
Road sign:		Good reputation	44
Harbour arterial	31	Group from work going	55
Trans-Canada Highway	19	Guide recommendation	35
Southern Shore Highway	17	Hotel recommendation	22
Trade show:		New experience	10
Newfoundland Sportsman	33	OZ FM Dawn Patrol recommendation	55
Outdoor Adventure Show	5	Received gift certificate	16
Total	**720**	Repeat customer	53
		Wedding day activity	10
		Won on the radio	6
		Total	**720**

EXHIBIT 4	WNA Customer Satisfaction Survey Results, Summer 1998 (continued)

Overall Satisfaction with Your Excursion

Overall	Ratings	Total
Dissatisfied	1	0
	2	0
	3	0
Satisfied	4	8
	5	24
	6	96
100% satisfied	7	592
Total		**720**

Maritime Trading Company

Martha Lawrence
and Shelly McDougall

In February 1999, Kent Groves sat in a coffee shop thinking about his company's new site on the World Wide Web. As president of Maritime Trading Company (MTC), a small business he started in 1993, he still made most of the decisions.

Maritime Trading had had a Web site since 1995. Until recently, there had been no real strategy for the site. In 1995, some friends of Kent, who had developed skills in Web site development, had offered to create one for MTC for little cost. Kent's attitude toward this was "Let's throw it up and see what happens." From that time until the end of 1997, co-op students from a local university maintained it. The only purpose of the site was to be an online extension of the company's catalogue, giving people using the Internet access to the products.

In November 1998, Kent had the site redesigned to appear more professional and include complete, secure online ordering. He wanted to entice people to visit and order online. Kent wondered how to both draw traffic to the site and encourage customers to come back. His goal was to provide the most interactive and secure online shopping experience in Atlantic Canada.

This case was prepared by Martha Lawrence and Dr. Shelly McDougall of Acadia University as a basis for classroom discussion, and is not meant to illustrate either effective or ineffective management. © 2000 Acadia Institute of Case Studies, Acadia University. Reprinted with permission.

COMPANY BACKGROUND

Maritime Trading Company began as a mail order company specializing in foods and consumables unique to Nova Scotia. Its first catalogue was published in 1993 and products were only marketed in Canada at that time. Between 1993 and 1999, new products were added and subsequent versions of the catalogue were produced. Exhibit 1 provides a synopsis of the company's development.

MTC had been keeping track of its customers and sales in a database for several years. Although the company had customers from all walks of life, the typical customer had remained the same. Women in their late 30s to 50s, with considerable disposable income,

EXHIBIT 1	Synopsis of MTC's Development		
Year	**New products**	**Other developments**	**Sales**
1993	Gift boxes, jams, maple products, fruit syrups, fruitcake, handmade soap, herbal oils and vinegars, balsam Christmas wreaths	• First catalogue published	n/a
1994	Clothing, dried flowers, coffee, oatcakes, lobster pate	• Retail store opened in Halifax • Second catalogue produced	n/a
1995	More titles of east coast music	• More emphasis on Canadian east coast music • Vender kiosk opened on Halifax waterfront • East coast music catalogue produced • Expansion of retail store • Third catalogue produced • Started to explore the Internet	$350 000
1996	Toys, books, home decor items, King Cole tea, Ganong chocolates, live lobster	• Retail expansion continued • Fourth catalogue published • Hired co-op student to do new Web site design	$500 000
1997		• Full-page colour catalogue published • More advanced Web site; all products online • Expanded into wholesale	$700 000
1998	Jewellery, art, smoked salmon, maple syrup	• Sixth catalogue produced • Relationship with Icom Alliance begun • New Web site launched in December	$750 000

were the greatest consumers of the company's products. When it came to mail order sales, this typical customer was generally restricted from shopping in person by either geography or time constraints. Maritime Trading had never done very much prospecting for new business; 80% of its business had come from repeat customers over the last two years.

The company broke even in 1998. Kent felt this was appropriate, "It takes five years to build a critical mass in a direct-to-consumer venue." Maritime Trading had moved away from just marketing its products to the rest of Canada. Its new slogan, "Delivering Atlantic Canada to the World," clearly expressed its new scope.

COMPETITION

Maritime Trading Company was in the gift business, selling predominantly via mail order. The competition was almost any gift store and catalogue, anywhere. Three other organizations promoted regional Canadian products by mail order and the World Wide Web: Beautiful BC, Canadian Geographic, and Images of Canada. Kent considered these three organizations to be competition in only the loosest sense of the word.

Although several entrepreneurs had tried, no one had been successful in creating direct competition for MTC in the sale of Atlantic Canadian products. Kent believed these ventures did not have enough capital to be successful and did not anticipate any threats to his business in the near future.

DISTRIBUTION CHANNELS

Maritime Trading Company was a retailer and wholesale distributor for many small Maritime manufacturers and several medium-sized companies. It sold products from a retail location, a catalogue, and its Web site. Orders from the catalogue and Web site were received by mail, fax, or telephone. Products were also sold wholesale to other retail outlets.

Retail Outlet

The peak sales period for the retail store was August and September, the prime tourist season in Halifax. Approximately 75% of the store's sales came from visitors to the area.

The vice-president of retail marketing, Stephen Simpson, was responsible for the development of retail operations. Stephen, age 36, had joined Maritime Trading Company from a position as general manager in automobile sales. The level of opportunity for retail expansion was considered quite high and a major goal was to open a retail location in Boston within three years.

Kent preferred to spend his time with the mail order side of the company. Although he preferred to leave it up to Stephen, Kent realized retail was an integral part of mail order sales. Tourists coming into the store would be encouraged by the staff to register to receive a catalogue. The retail presence of MTC directly drove mail order sales.

Catalogue

In 1998, 20% of mail order sales came from the United States, while less than 3% came from the Atlantic Region of Canada. Seventy-seven percent of mail order sales were from customers across the rest of Canada.

November was the busiest month for the mail-order business. This was the result of past visitors and Atlantic Canadians buying holiday gifts. The catalogue had developed greatly over the past few years and was currently a full-format design (8.5" x 11") with 24 full-colour pages.

Wholesale

Kent was constantly searching for products to broaden the company's offering, especially for wholesale distribution, which made up approximately 15% of the company's sales. The challenge of this process was to find products that had sufficient margin for wholesaling to be worthwhile.

Wholesale customers included Alder's, a company that owned gift shops in several Maritime airports and Clearwater Fine Foods, a supplier of premium-quality shellfish and seafood. Kent saw the wholesale business as a definite growth area. However, the most popular high-margin products were fish products, which were sometimes in short supply. Kent was wary of sales growing to the point where he would be unable to meet the demand from his existing customers.

Web Site

Kent viewed electronic commerce (the sale of products and services online) as the future of MTC. With the new Web site in place, Kent was intent on increasing sales with the use of Internet technology. Kent did not see the site as a replacement for the current distribution channels, but as an extension of them. His focus was on an integrated marketing strategy, allowing the customer to order products via any desired channel. He was afraid that if MTC wasn't offering its products on the Web, some customers might be dissuaded from buying.

MARITIME TRADING COMPANY ON THE WORLD WIDE WEB

The Web site had evolved since 1995. Initially, it had been just an experiment. It was inexpensive and entertaining to see if a few people would fill out the online order form or print it and fax it in. It was completely insecure, with no protection for those who entered their credit card numbers online. Orders came occasionally but far from regularly.

At the time, the company did not have its own domain name; the URL was long and virtually impossible for a customer to remember. In 1995, the site was linked to the sites of a few of MTC's suppliers.

In 1996 and 1997, information management co-op students from a local university were hired to redesign and maintain the site. In 1996, Maritime Trading acquired the domain name *maritimetrading.com*. The site, shown in Exhibit 2, remained largely unchanged until December 1998.

By this time, Kent was no longer satisfied with the site. He felt it was too static; it did not make use of the interactive aspect of the Internet medium. He contracted Icom Alliance to redesign the site. Icom was a small, Halifax-based, information technology services company specializing in electronic commerce and Web-enabled business solutions. The new site is shown in Exhibit 3.

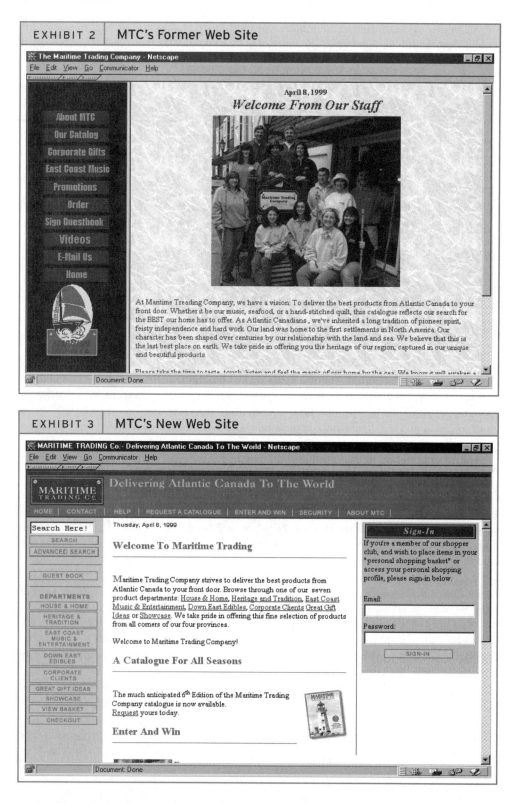

EXHIBIT 2 | MTC's Former Web Site

EXHIBIT 3 | MTC's New Web Site

Maritime Trading Company agreed to pay Icom Alliance $2500 for the initial design and a floating percentage of gross online sales (12.5%, on average). These payment terms were not typical but they involved a far lower up-front cost than the standard payment terms. Under standard terms, a site like the new Maritimetrading.com would have a startup cost of approximately $10 000 and monthly updating fees of $150. Kent thought that he was getting a better deal with Icom Alliance. Furthermore, he knew the Icom managers personally and felt comfortable doing business with them.

THE FUTURE OF MARITIMETRADING.COM

Kent felt he had some good ideas about what the new Web site could accomplish. He believed that his own three-step marketing strategy for the company—acquisition, retention, and extension—was applicable to the Web site as well. Acquisition meant getting customers to visit the site for the first time. Retention referred to keeping the customer coming back. The third step, extension, was motivating customers to buy across a broad range of product offerings on the site.

Kent viewed this three-step process as the building of relationships with customers. He felt that relationship-building was the only way to make the new site successful. His ultimate goal, of course, was to increase sales above and beyond what the catalogue brought in. In the meantime, Kent wanted to get customers comfortable with the Web as a shopping medium and provide a place where they could get useful and current information about MTC and its products. He was not exactly sure how he would know if the site was generating sales that would have come in from the catalogue anyway.

Site Promotion

In 1999, the URL was promoted on all business cards, letterhead, envelopes, and gift cards. It was also printed on all private labels, inserts, and hang-tags. The address was published on alternating pages of the general merchandise catalogue and in the music catalogue. Online promotion included links from suppliers, promotion by Icom Alliance, and targeted email. Kent's goal was to incur little or no additional promotional costs for the Web site.

In the past, Kent supported the idea of registering with search engines but felt quite differently about it by 1999. Although it was free to register with search engines, he wanted to avoid "getting lost in the sea" of search engine results. "What if in two years the whole search engine thing crashes? Then what are you left with?" Kent reasoned. He felt strongly that search engines were a thing of the past.

Kent also felt uneasy about using online promotion such as links from other sites and banner ads. He didn't want very many links or any ads on the MTC site, because he thought it would lead people away. He knew from searching the Internet himself that after going from link to link, it was difficult to remember what pages had been visited. Besides having links on the pages of a few suppliers and on Icom Alliance's site, there were not any other sites on the Web that included links to Maritimetrading.com.

For these reasons, Kent strongly felt traditional promotion was the way to go for the new site. He didn't want to pull customers to the site who had never heard of MTC. He wanted customers to see the URL on products and in the catalogues and then go to the site. This way, they would be familiar with MTC before they arrived.

Keeping people coming back was part of the retention step of the marketing strategy. Kent was still wondering how to retain customers effectively. In order to make a purchase or enter a contest on the Web site, the customer had to fill out an online registration form, which included his or her email address. This gave MTC a way to make contact at a later date and build a relationship.

The site also used "cookies"—pieces of information saved on the visitor's computer—that allowed the company to record how often a particular computer accessed the site and what kind of pages the visitor looked at while there.

Cookies and unsolicited email were a current issue of debate. The Canadian government was reviewing Bill C-54, "an act to support and promote electronic commerce by protecting personal information that is collected, used or disclosed, in certain circumstances…." This meant banning the use of information collected online for any purpose other than what the customer intended.

It was clear that any steps taken in the use of cookies and email would have to be careful. The permission of the customer was obviously important.

Goals

In January 1999, the new site had garnered 10 000 visits. Kent hoped to get 50 000 visits per month by the end of 1999. Sales on the old site had been roughly $500 per week. The new goal was to have weekly sales of $1000 to $2000 by the end of the year.

Kent didn't have figures on the length of the average visit but he knew that longer visits meant more interest and more time for a relationship to be built. Catalogue requests had been fairly good in the past, since they did not require a credit card number to be given online. However, Kent hoped for more activity with the new site.

Kent felt these goals were important as consumers became more comfortable with the idea of electronic commerce. He anticipated sales would become a significant measure of site effectiveness in the long term.

Gathering His Thoughts

As Kent sat in the coffee shop, he began to organize his thoughts about the Web site. Although his offline promotion of the site was quite extensive, he wondered if there was anything he could do to make it more effective on the shoestring budget he had for Web site promotion. The site had to be profitable in order to be worthwhile—it was already quite expensive and he needed cost-effective ideas. Kent was pretty sure offline promotion was the way to go, but he was a bit concerned after hearing that someone wanting to visit the site could not find it because they had not been exposed to the promotion of the URL.

Kent felt building a relationship online should be the main focus of the site. He was not sure how he could do this most effectively. The new site had cookies and the database of customers was growing. He really wanted to figure out how to build strong, lasting relationships with online customers. He knew he needed to give them something of value in order to keep them coming back.

Kent also realized that e-business could be more that just a Web site but he wasn't exactly sure what else he could do. The office used accounting software for invoices and inventory management, and much of the internal communication was done using email. Kent was puzzled as to how he could use e-business when dealing with suppliers, since only around 5% even had a fax machine, let alone Web-based ordering systems.

Kent was meeting with Icom Alliance next week. He had some thinking to do. He flagged down a waiter. "Can I get a refill on this coffee?"

The Holey War: Robin's Donuts Versus Tim Horton's

Ian Spencer

In July 2001, Wally Ballou, manager and part-owner of Robin's Donuts in Summerside, P.E.I., was wrestling with a tough problem: how to use media advertising, special promotions (incentives), public relations, and personal selling to increase Robin's sales and take market share away from Tim Horton's. As he pondered this challenge, Wally jotted down some relevant background information he planned to turn over to Tim Carroll, a retired marketing consultant and friend. Wally was enthused that Tim had agreed to help because he was just about out of ideas and needed a fresh approach. The following are Wally's jottings:

- Robin's opened in June 1999 and to date has gained only about 20% of the donut shop market in Summerside. The Tim Horton's franchise, which has operated for about ten years in Summerside, has the remaining 80%. Our shop is directly across the street from Tim Horton's on the way into town from the Trans-Canada Highway. My goal is to achieve a 30% market share, or about $500 000 in sales.

- Robin's Donuts has a small core of loyal customers. They like the coffee, the sweets, and the many deli items available at lunch. A few customers have patronized Robin's outlets in central or western Canada.

This case was written by Ian Spencer, Professor of Marketing, St. Francis Xavier University, Antigonish, Nova Scotia. © Ian Spencer, 2001. The assistance of all participants in the meeting is gratefully acknowledged. Reprinted with permission.

- Robin's sales are fairly consistent Monday to Friday, but fall off on the weekend. Sales are about 40% drive-thru, 40% eat-in, and 20% takeout.

- Most sales are to customers who live in or near Summerside. Other geographic market segments are people who live in western Prince Edward Island, but at least five kilometres away from Summerside, and visitors to Prince Edward Island.

- About 20 000 people live in, or within five kilometres of, Summerside.

- Last year a group of students at the University of Prince Edward Island conducted a survey for us. The survey revealed that almost everyone in the Summerside area had heard of Robin's and most had tried it. However, most also had returned to Tim Horton's. They had no real problems with Robin's. They just did not feel there was a good enough reason to switch.

- The thing is, we really are different than Tim Horton's. We have an extensive deli selection (salads, subs, and sandwiches) and several other items Tim Horton's does not carry (pizza pretzels, oatcakes, fruit sticks, and soon a line of deluxe pies).

- We have promoted Robin's quite aggressively:

  - Three commercials per week ($30 per spot) on Summerside radio station CJRW

  - A large sign in front of the building with messages changed each week or so

  - Discount coupons

  - Quarter-page ads ($200 per insertion) in the weekly newspaper, the *Journal Pioneer*

    As well, I have personally dropped off coffee and donuts to various businesses in town to let them try our products.

- I think there are several opportunities to grow:

  - Pulling in more business from the highway

  - Getting current customers to drop in more frequently

  - Getting people who eat lunch out to try Robin's

  - Getting regular Tim Horton's customers to spend at least some of their donut shop dollars at Robin's; that is, to switch shops

Royal Bank of Canada and Bank of Montreal: The Proposed Merger

Kerri-Lynn Parsons and
H.F. (Herb) MacKenzie

In November 1998, nearly 11 months after the best-kept secret in corporate Canada finally broke over the Canadian newswire, the members of the communications team for "Project Alpha" reflected on the day that shook the Canadian banking industry. Eight forty-five on the morning of January 23, 1998 had been the moment they'd worked day and night to prepare for during a whirlwind three-week period that saw the country's two largest banks—the Royal Bank of Canada (RBC) and the Bank of Montreal (BMO)—negotiate the biggest merger in Canadian history. The negotiations had been conducted very secretly, and the communications team, led by David Moorcroft, vice-president of public affairs and communications at RBC, and Joe Barbera, director of media and public relations at BMO, had been certain that the news of the blockbuster $40 billion merger plan between two of the country's fiercest competitors would stun everyone, including industry watchers, government officials, and the Canadian public.[1]

The crowded press conference provided an opportunity for the two CEOs, John Cleghorn of RBC and Matthew Barrett of BMO, to explain their decision to merge into the 22nd-largest bank in the world, with a market capitalization of $39 billion and $453 billion in assets[2] (see Exhibit 1):

This case was written by Kerri-Lynn Parsons under the direction of H. F. (Herb) MacKenzie, Memorial University of Newfoundland, Faculty of Business Administration, St. John's, NF A1B 3X5. It is intended as the basis for classroom discussion and does not illustrate either effective or ineffective business management. © 2000 by H. F. (Herb) MacKenzie. Reprinted with permission.

EXHIBIT 1	The Merged RBC-BMO Bank

Bank	Assets ($billions)	Revenue ($ billion)	Net Income ($ billion)	Employees	Branches	ABMs
BMO	208	7.2	1.3	34 286	1246	2035
RBC	245	9.3	1.7	50 719	1558	4248
RBC-BMO	453	16.5	3.0	85 005	2804	6283

Source: "Merger Mania: The RBC-BMO Deal," CBC.ca, The National Online <www.tv.cbc.ca/national/pgminfo/banks/mergerdeal2.html>, accessed November 8, 2002.

This merger will create a Canadian-based, internationally competitive bank with a strong North American platform which allows us to cost-effectively deliver quality products and services to Canadians and retain high-quality financial service jobs in Canada. Together, we will have the financial resources, technology, and skills to help Canada remain a global leader in financial services, just as other Canadian-based companies like Nortel, Alcan, and Bombardier are leaders in their respective fields.[3]

They also provided information about the merged bank's proposed structure. They would share leadership, each serving as co-chairperson of the new bank's board of directors. Cleghorn would also serve as chief executive officer and Barrett as head of the executive committee. The merger would result in RBC's shareholders receiving one share of the new bank for each RBC share they held, while BMO shareholders would get 0.97 of a share for each BMO share they held.[4]

The months following this merger announcement were eventful to say the least. Just four months later, in April 1998, the RBC-BMO proposed merger prompted a second merger announcement—this time between the Canadian Imperial Bank of Commerce (CIBC) and the Toronto-Dominion Bank (TD). If both mergers were successful, they would put approximately 75% of the assets, loans, and deposits of Canada's largest commercial banks in the hands of just two institutions.

The news of the mergers had not been well received by the Canadian public, whose long-standing abhorrence of their "big banks" escalated into a major public policy debate across the country. RBC and BMO attempted to respond to this growing sentiment by reassuring customers of the new bank's commitment through a communications campaign that addressed the concerns voiced by over 400 000 Canadians polled by the two banks during a seven-month period.[5] The banks began running a series of print ads in Canadian daily and community newspapers under the slogan "Two Banks. One Pledge," promising a reduction in service charges, improved customer service, and more branches. CIBC and TD had yet to launch any similar campaign.[6]

Canada's federal government, after monitoring public sentiment and reviewing competition implications for almost a year, was preparing to announce its decision on the proposed bank mergers—whether they would be allowed to proceed. RBC and BMO would certainly not be able to wait for the decision to continue planning for the merger. If the decision were favourable, they would have to have in place an appropriate long-term marketing and communications strategy to successfully launch the newly merged bank in both the domestic and the international market. Among the questions that they would need to answer before they could move further with implementation of the merger were:

How could the new bank position itself for international growth without alienating its equally important domestic customer base even further? With Canadians' already outspoken criticism of their big banks, how could the new bank convince Canadians that "even bigger" meant "even better"? How could the banks merge their unique marketing cultures and strong identities into one that would be meaningful to each bank's existing loyal customers, and to potential new customers in international markets. Should one of the existing brand names and identities be retained or should an entirely new one be developed? How should the new bank be positioned? Finally, how would this new positioning and identity be rolled out?

THE CANADIAN BANKING INDUSTRY

Evolution

The Canadian banking industry dates back to 1817 when the first bank emerged as a result of the efforts of nine Montreal merchants. The Montreal Bank, or so it was called at the time, eventually became known as the Bank of Montreal. The next 50 years saw a proliferation of Canadian banks as more than 30 were established. By 1998, Canada had more than 50 banks. They employed 221 400 people, managed $1.2 trillion in assets, and operated 8140 branches and 14 484 automated banking machines.[7] The banking industry in Canada was highly centralized relative to that of the United States and many other countries, dominated by a small number of banks cynically referred to as the "Big Six" by the Canadian public (see Exhibit 2).

In 1867, Confederation gave the federal government exclusive jurisdiction over money and banking in Canada. The Bank Act established the boundaries of bank power, and created order, safety, and some uniformity among banking activities. Significant revisions to the Act in 1992 resulted in a pivotal shift in the environment in which Canadian banks operated. These revisions dramatically increased domestic and international competition by permitting banks, trust and loan companies, and insurance companies to diversify into each other's markets. Coupled with rapid technological innovations, these changes also forced Canadian banks to reevaluate their strategic approaches. In particular, more aggressive marketing strategies were required by all banks in the industry in order to compete more effectively.

Stability

By 1998, Canada's banking system was one of the most stable in the world, and the banking industry was one of the most regulated industries in the country. The Office of the Superintendent of Financial Institutions (OSFI) carefully monitored banks' ongoing operations for financial soundness and compliance with the Bank Act. Banks were subject to securities and other financial-instrument regulation across the country and abroad. In addition, the banks were highly self-regulated through the Canadian Bankers Association (CBA), a professional industry association representing all chartered banks operating in Canada. The CBA had established joint standards of action, the Privacy Model Code (to protect the confidentiality of customers' personal information), and guidelines to combat financial crimes.[8]

EXHIBIT 2	Canadian Banking Industry Market Share Analysis				

| | | | Market Share | | |
Brand	1996 Rank	1997 Rank	1997	1996	Change in Share Points
Canada's "Big Six"					
Royal Bank of Canada	1	1	21.1%	22.5%	-1.4
Bank of Montreal	2	3	17.5%	16.5%	+1.0
CIBC	3	2	16.9%	17.7%	-0.8
Bank of Nova Scotia	3	4	16.9%	16.4%	+0.5
Toronto-Dominion Bank	5	5	13.5%	12.2%	+1.3
National Bank of Canada	6	6	5.3%	5.6%	-0.3
Other Domestic Banks					
Laurentian Bank of Canada	7	7	1.3%	1.5%	-0.2
Canadian Western Bank	8	8	0.2%	0.2%	0.0
Other domestic banks	9	9	0.1%	0.03%	+0.07
International Banks					
Foreign banks			7.2%	7.4%	-0.2

Source: "Report on Market Shares," *Marketing Magazine*, May 25, 1998.

Technology

In addition to its security, Canada's banking industry was at the forefront of technology. With over 14 000 automated banking machines across the country, only Japan had a greater per capita coverage than Canada. In addition, according to a 1997 Ernst & Young survey of 17 countries, Canada was the global leader in home banking, a trend that capitalized on the consumer demand for convenience by providing banking by telephone or by personal computer, 24 hours per day, 7 days per week. Some banks evolved the convenience concept even further by offering "virtual banks" which had no branches, and which operated entirely by electronic means.

Customers

Increased competition heightened Canadians' expectations for more information, choice, and convenience. Customers began to demand more innovative products, improved access to financial services, and lower fees and interest rates. By 1998, Canadians had developed a love-hate relationship with their banks. On the positive side, Canada's banks led all other industries in Canada in community support and charitable donations (more than $66 million in 1997), and employed approximately 1.6% of the total Canadian population.[9] In addition, due to their security, Canada's banks provided a safe haven for Canadians' life savings. Still, Canadians were increasingly distrustful and skeptical of the banks, mainly fuelled by media coverage linking exorbitant profits and multimillion-dollar executive salaries to excessively high service fees. This public frustration manifested itself in a trend that had become widely known as "bank-bashing," resulting in a climate of intensely cynical and negative media coverage surrounding banking issues.

In response to this growing negative sentiment among customers, in early 1998 the CBA unveiled a five-year, $20 million marketing initiative in an attempt to improve Canadians' perception of their banks. The president of the CBA stated, "It's no secret to anyone that our industry faces a communications challenge. Clearly we have work to do to improve our dialogue with Canadians."[10] The CBA campaign, called "Building a Better Understanding," involved a combination of advertising, pamphlets, conferences and seminars, and public relations initiatives, with the objective of increasing Canadians' understanding of the economy. The idea for the campaign came from a CBA study that found two-thirds of Canadians believed they would be better off if they knew more about the economy and how it affected them.[11] While the CBA reported a favourable consumer response, the campaign did not find favour among industry critics who saw the economics lessons simply as a way to justify the banks' exorbitant earnings. Carole Kerbel, an executive vice-president of Hill & Knowlton Canada Inc., a company specializing in corporate reputation management, stated, "I can't believe if people have a better understanding of the economy they will like banks better."[12] However, a representative working on the CBA's advertising effort stated more optimistically, "It's going to take a minimum of three years before we begin to see a change in attitude. The first thing we need to do is to get to the stage where the public is prepared to listen."[13]

In 1998, Canada's banking customers could be loosely categorized into four groups: retail, commercial and corporate, investment, and international. Retail banking involved accepting deposits, making loans, and providing services to private individuals. Commercial banking provided similar services to small- and medium-sized businesses, while corporate banking focused on larger corporations. Investment banking encompassed the selling of investment products and brokerage services. International banking involved retail, commercial and corporate lending in international markets, export financing, and treasury and investment services. From the international perspective, Canada's banks were attempting to become increasingly innovative at helping Canadian customers become more active in global markets, and at helping foreign clients become more active in Canada.

Millions of Canadian bank customers were also owners, holding shares in the country's chartered banks, either directly, or indirectly through RRSPs, pension plans, and mutual funds. In fact, it was estimated that, in 1998, one in every two working adults in Canada owned bank shares. More than $2.5 billion in common and preferred share dividends were distributed to Canadians in 1997, representing 34% of the banks' net after-tax income.[14]

Marketing

Bank advertising in Canada emerged in the early 1900s with "tombstone"-style ads that reported only bold facts and figures such as the names of directors, the extent of the banks' networks, and statements about assets and liabilities. In 1919, the Royal Bank of Canada established an advertising department to build goodwill and recognition.[15] By the 1920s, bank advertising, in general, attempted to become more closely related to the lives of average Canadians. The general public were becoming acquainted with banking services such as savings accounts, safety deposit boxes, and money orders. Despite its continued conservative nature, bank advertising was well established by 1930. A significant Bank Act revision in 1967 made it easier for banks to market a range of new consumer products such as Chargex, mutual funds, consumer loans, and electronic banking. This spurred a change in bank advertising as it became more product-oriented to support the increasing variety of banking products. For the first time, bank advertising on broadcast mediums began to emerge.

By the early 1990s, Canadian customers were generally ambivalent about their banks. This could be largely attributed to the historical lack of differentiation or brand development among the banks. The product-oriented advertising approach that continued from the late 1960s contributed to bank products being seen as commodities by customers. Additionally, with the historical concentration of power in the industry, Canada's domestic banks had not invested heavily in building their brand images. Consequently, research showed that, in general, customers did not see any major differences in the banks' abilities to service their needs. Overall, the traditional advertising efforts of Canada's banks were seen as boring and uninspiring. The Bank of Nova Scotia's vice-president of brand and marketing management explained:

> I think great brands is something you experience and we've not touched Canadians with having the feeling that the Scotiabank experience is different than the TD (Bank) experience or the Royal (Bank) experience.[16]

Fuelled by increasing competition in the Canadian marketplace, the late 1990s were beginning to see a turnaround in the banks' approach to advertising. More specifically, 1997 saw a tremendous growth in financial-sector image advertising.[17] This trend was expected to continue as the fight for market share became more aggressive.

Despite the traditional ambivalence of consumers with respect to advertising, there was still a strong indication of behavioural loyalty among Canadian banking customers. This may have been a reflection of Canadians' relatively strong level of conservatism and risk-aversiveness. It was thought that Canadians' apparent reluctance to change established banking arrangements could be attributed to inertia, rather than any emotional attachment to their banking institution. Some international banking competitors also reported that, despite Canadians' outspoken criticism of their banks, customers maintained a strong sense of loyalty to Canadian banks. An executive with Switzerland-based UBS stated:

> Loyalty is still amazingly high, even if you have a convincing value proposition. The Canadian market is really loyal to being Canadian. Even though UBS is a strong global brand, that isn't necessarily giving it a leg up in the Canadian market.[18]

However, while this seemed to be the case in 1998, it appeared that many international banks were willing to invest in changing consumer attitudes in order to compete effectively in the lucrative Canadian marketplace.

Competition

In 1998, because of regulatory and technological change, the level of competition in Canada's banking industry was becoming increasingly intense. Canada's Big Six competed intensely with each other, but also had a variety of other competitive influences to contend with. It was estimated that there were more than 2800 direct competitors in the financial services industry in Canada.[19] In his merger announcement speech, RBC's CEO gave an overview of the competitive situation for Canada's domestic banks, saying, "We compete with 50 foreign-owned banks, 50 trust companies, 2500 credit unions, 150 life insurance companies, 80 mutual fund companies, and major finance and leasing companies."[20] (See Exhibit 3 for an overview of the asset rankings of banks operating in the Canadian industry.)

CIBC and TD Bank

In April, following the RBC-BMO announcement, Canada's next two largest banks, Canadian Imperial Bank of Commerce (CIBC) and Toronto-Dominion Bank (TD), announced their intention to merge. If it went through, this merger would create a formidable domestic competitor for the newly merged RBC-BMO bank. A combined CIBC-TD bank would be the 10th-largest banking institution in North America in terms of market capitalization. It would have more than ten million customers in Canada and around the world, shareholder equity of more than $18 billion, and assets of $460 billion (see Exhibit 4). They also revealed that the new institution would be called "Canadian Imperial Bank of Commerce," as the name better represented a broadly Canadian financial institution.

EXHIBIT 3	Canadian Banking Industry Asset Ranking	
Brand	**Asset Ranking**	**Asset Size ($C billion)**
International		
Bank of Tokyo Mitsubishi	1	887.9
Deutsche Bank	2	781.1
Credit Agricole	3	654.2
Sumitomo Bank	4	631.0
Industrial & Commercial Bank of China	5	599.5
Dai-Ichi Kangyo	6	594.7
Fuji Bank	7	593.1
Sanwa Bank	8	585.8
Sakura Bank	9	579.5
HSBC Holdings	10	550.6
Domestic		
Royal Bank of Canada	50	231.5
CIBC	54	199.0
Bank of Montreal	65	169.8
Scotiabank	75	165.3
Toronto-Dominion Bank	86	130.3
National Bank of Canada	174	53.1

Source: The Banker Magazine, July 1997.

EXHIBIT 4	A Merged CIBC-TD Bank					
Bank	Assets ($ billions)	Revenue ($ billions)	Net Income ($ billions)	Employees	Branches	ABMs
CIBC	282	8.6	1.6	46 037	1374	3211
TD	177	5.6	1.0	28 582	913	2067
CIBC-TD	459	14.2	2.6	74 619	2287	5278

Source: : Toronto-Dominion Bank, "CIBC and TD Bank Announce Merger," press release, April 17, 1998, available <www.tdcanadatrust.com/tdbank/PressSearch/199804171.html>, accessed August 16, 1999.

Some industry watchers considered the CIBC and TD cultures more complementary than those of RBC and BMO. Both CIBC and TD had made attempts to become known as innovators in the banking industry. In announcing the merger, TD Bank's CEO stated:

> I believe that each of us has a winning strategy. … I was struck by the extraordinary fit offered by a merger with CIBC. Together, we will be the leader in high growth businesses, businesses of the next century. Strategically, we complement each other very well. In particular, we enhance each others' existing international businesses and the merger will allow us to leverage our growth to realize significant value for the customers, shareholders, and employees of both institutions.[21]

In reaction to the announcement, RBC and BMO issued the following statement on the proposed CIBC-TD merger:

> The proposed merger between CIBC and TD Bank, like our own merger, reflects how the rapidly changing global economy is affecting the provision of financial services everywhere, including Canada. These mergers will ensure that Canadians in every region of the country continue to have access to world-class products and competitive prices from home-grown institutions. They will ensure that Canadian businesses of all sizes continue to have a strong Canadian financial partner at home and abroad. And they will ensure that Canadians continue to reap the economic benefits that come from having globally competitive financial institutions headquartered in Canada.[22]

About a year before the proposed merger was announced, CIBC had started to position itself on its Canadian roots in an attempt to set itself apart from the seemingly faceless bank image of its competitors. In February 1997, CIBC launched a new image-based advertising campaign with the tagline "Seeing Beyond." It included TV and print elements that focused on stories about CIBC's Canadian heritage. For example, a tale of the bank's status as the government's official bank during the Klondike gold rush of the 1890s was clearly an appeal to Canadians' sense of pride. The bank also began to reemphasize its full name, "Canadian Imperial Bank of Commerce," versus the acronym, CIBC, widely used since 1987.[23]

By late 1998, CIBC announced that it had restructured to become a "customer-centric" organization, focused on different customer segments instead of different product lines.[24] In addition, it launched a new advertising campaign in an attempt to capitalize on research that revealed a positive consumer attitude toward electronic banking. The campaign's slogan was "Just Because You Can."[25]

Bank of Nova Scotia

In 1998, the Bank of Nova Scotia (BNS, also referred to as "Scotiabank") was one of the smaller of the Big Six. It had 1200 branches and $132.9 billion in total assets. Following the RBC-BMO proposed merger announcement, the BNS CEO became one of its most outspoken critics. The subsequent announcement in April of a proposed CIBC-TD merger meant that BNS would be among the two major Canadian banks not proposing a merger. Ranked fourth among the Big Six in terms of market share in 1997, BNS' position in the Canadian marketplace was sure to be dwarfed if the mergers unfolded as planned. BNS would be left with only 17.1% of total Canadian bank assets, compared with the 38.7% for the merged RBC-BMO bank, and 37.4% for the merged CIBC-TD bank.

The threat of the mergers prompted BNS to embark on a communications initiative in late 1998, including public relations and advertising. In an effort to capture the positioning gap that would seemingly be left behind by its now-larger, internationally focused Canadian counterparts, BNS launched its first major advertising campaign in nearly ten years. While continuing with its traditional conservative marketing approach (avoiding direct mention of the mergers), the campaign was clearly attempting to build on the bank's hometown corporate culture, its emphasis on local relationships with customers, and its straightforward approach to business. A report in a Canadian marketing trade magazine explained, "While Scotiabank continues to fight against bank mergers on the public relations front, it saw the controversy surrounding the mergers as an opportunity to distinguish itself from competitors."[26] The television and newspaper campaign concept involved simple testimonials from customers and employees with the tagline "Putting People First." BNS apparently saw the uncertainty and public hostility surrounding the proposed mergers as a prime opportunity to reassure its Canadian customers about its hometown commitment, and to reach out to any of its competitors' now-discontented customers who might prefer to deal with a bank with small-town, people-oriented values.

BNS's advertising budget was small relative to its competitors in the preceding years. It spent approximately $12.1 million for advertising in 1997, less than half of what was spent by RBC during the same period.[27]

Credit Unions

While credit unions had traditionally experienced a number of obstacles to growth in Canada, including a public perception of inferiority to banks, and a customer reluctance to changing banking arrangements, the opportunity for them to deal with the increasing niche of disaffected bank customers became evident in the early 1990s. In particular, powerful credit union movements in western Canada and Quebec began to threaten the banks' customer base. Credit unions were beginning to be viewed as a viable alternative to banks. This was fuelled by a proliferation of advertising initiatives by credit unions that positioned themselves directly against the Big Six. For example, one advertising campaign developed by a credit union in British Columbia took aim at the Bank of Montreal's well-known advertising message that asked, "Can a Bank Change?" Its spot ads included "The banks will change when ..." followed by visuals of yodelling rabbits and flying hippos. The campaign was also licensed for use in other provinces including Ontario, Manitoba, and New Brunswick.[28]

Another well-known anti-bank campaign was developed by Canada's third-largest credit union, Richmond Savings. It first appeared in 1992, and was still running in an evolved format in 1998 because of overwhelming consumer response. The award-winning parody advertising campaign was built around a fictional bank called "Humungous Bank" (satirizing the "Big Six"), and included the tagline "We're Not a Bank, We're Better."[29] Public resistance to the proposed bank mergers made such ad messages more relevant to and accepted by consumers.

International Competitors

As a result of advances in technology that were becoming more widely accepted by customers, foreign competitors were already beginning to penetrate the Canadian marketplace in an effort to capture market share. Some of these banks operated primarily on a "virtual" or electronic basis.

Netherlands-based ING Direct was one such "branchless" bank. It entered the Canadian market in 1997 and was reported to have spent $25–$50 million on its marketing efforts.[30] It tried to differentiate itself by using a very unique marketing communications plan and creative. ING made a deliberate effort to ensure its creative looked entirely different from those of the Big Six. It used a strategy that playfully flaunted its Dutch heritage through a series of tactics, such as using orange, the traditional colour for Dutch people, in all its marketing materials. As one example, orange Tic Tacs and promotional postcards were distributed to potential urban customers by a bike patrol. Dutch-style cafés in Toronto and Vancouver sold branded coffees to customers, along with banking services. When asked about the impetus behind this seemingly quirky strategy, ING's vice-president of marketing, Jim Kelly, said, "They do things differently in Europe than they do in Canada. The approach we took highlighted that we're different and we would like to treat people differently."[31]

ING claimed that consumer response to the campaign was so overwhelming it had to cut back 25% of its print media executions to ensure it could maintain the level of promised service to Canadian customers. When its advertising agency was asked about the reasons for ING's initial success, a representative explained, "I think people see ING as being a rebellious consumer-advocate alternative to banking. And that's exactly what we wanted to accomplish."[32]

THE ROYAL BANK OF CANADA: COMMUNICATIONS STRATEGY

The Royal Bank of Canada was generally considered the largest domestic banking institution in 1997. It had the largest market share, number of employees, and assets under management (see Exhibits 1, 2, and 3). Originally named the Merchants' Bank of Halifax in the late 1800s, the bank changed its name to The Royal Bank of Canada in the early 1900s (and eventually to just Royal Bank of Canada) to reflect its growing national stature.

To reinforce its new name, the bank designed a logo using the arms of the British Royal family, borrowing a sense of tradition, strength, and stability. This logo soon became a symbol recognized in many countries as the bank rapidly expanded its international operations. In 1962, the bank created a more modern version of this well-known symbol. Two important design elements were retained from the original: a lion, as a symbol of dominance, strength, and authority; and a crown, to maintain the "royal" symbolism. To demonstrate RBC's global presence, a globe was added to the new logo.[33] By the late 1990s, a more modernized version of the "lion and globe" logo was being used, as the bank continued to position itself upon the traditional symbolism seen by Canadians for over 35 years. The distinctive RBC logo became one of the most recognizable symbols in corporate Canada.

RBC was responsible for many consumer-oriented technological milestones in Canadian banking. In 1995, RBC became the first Canadian bank to offer information through the Internet. By 1996, it was receiving more than a million hits per month throughout the world, and was named the "Best Canadian Web Site of 1996" by *Net Innovations* magazine. In late 1996, the first national personal computer banking service, PC Banking, was rolled out across Canada. Also in 1996, after two years in operation, RBC's Royal Direct Telephone Banking service was considered the fastest-growing telephone banking service in the world.[34]

While RBC had attempted several brand-building advertising efforts (e.g., the 1994 campaign with the tagline "We Got to Be Canada's Largest Bank One Customer at a Time"[35]), a large proportion of its advertising focused on communicating sponsorships and launching new products and initiatives. For example, RBC acted as a long-standing sponsor of amateur sport, especially Canadian figure skating. It was title sponsor of Canada's National Figure Skating Championships since 1989. Figure skating demographics indicated that the majority of figure skating enthusiasts had above-average household incomes and held a university degree. Additionally, the market was skewed female, with an increasingly male audience.[36] The RBC vice-president of advertising was quoted as saying, "It's a good reputational fit. ... Skating is classy. It also delivers a good audience with a wide age range, which is a little more upscale. You'd be surprised at the number of male executives who watch it."[37]

In 1996, RBC used advertising to promote its sponsorship of the Canadian rowing team. Four 30-second spot ads ran during the Olympics and focused on RBC's support of fundraising for the Canadian Olympic Association to assist athletes of the future. Television advertising also helped launch the Royal Bank Financial Group, a gathering of five RBC services.[38] The "Classic II" Visa card was also introduced with television spot ads, newspaper advertisements, and other promotional materials. They used the theme line "More Power II You."[39]

In mid-1998, the RBC announced its intention to purchase U.S.-based Security First Network Bank. RBC hoped to provide both Internet and telephone banking services to three target groups of interest: (1) two million "snowbirds" (typically retirees) who vacation or reside in Florida each year; (2) small and medium-sized Canadian businesses with branches or offices in the United States; and (3) U.S. consumers. Although it still required Canadian and U.S. approval, this initiative was considered the first step in RBC's bid to establish a retail banking presence in the United States.[40]

THE BANK OF MONTREAL: COMMUNICATIONS STRATEGY

The Bank of Montreal, opened in 1817, was Canada's first chartered bank. It served as Canada's central bank until 1935. BMO was also the first Canadian bank to open branches abroad, and in 1998 it was still active in Europe, Latin America, and East Asia, as well as in the United States.

Similar to its proposed merger partner, RBC, BMO was also a very-well-known brand in the Canadian marketplace. The BMO logo, made up of a blue underlined "m," was a widely recognized symbol by customers and by the broader Canadian public. While the marketing efforts of Canada's Big Six had generally resulted in a static, undifferentiated category, BMO could be considered the one bank that, in the years leading up to 1998, attempted to differentiate its brand image from the crowd through a more radical, cutting-edge approach.

In the early 1990s, BMO launched an advertising campaign with the tagline "We're Paying Attention."[41] This initial step in developing its brand distinctiveness was followed by a provocative and successful campaign entitled, "It Is Possible." The television campaign featured naysaying authority figures such as teachers, parents, and even bankers, who stood between people and their goals. Photographed through a wide-angle lens to grossly exaggerate the characters, these authority figures belittled those who dared to hope for the future by asking, "Do you really think this faith in the future is the sign of a sane individual?" or "Take it from me, this is as good as it gets."[42] According to the vice-president of corporate marketing, research showed that the "It Is Possible" campaign helped BMO to improve its ranking among competing financial institutions in terms of consumer aided and unaided awareness. Additionally, consumers who saw the advertising told BMO that they looked upon it more favourably as a company with which to do business.[43]

In 1995, BMO leveraged this success through another provocative advertising campaign. The "Sign of the Times" campaign, considered controversial by some, included a television component that showed gritty black-and-white pictures of real people holding up poignant signs that asked questions about their financial security. This was the first time a Canadian bank explicitly acknowledged consumers' concerns with banks. The question asked by BMO in the campaign was, "Can a Bank Change?"[44]

BMO launched "mbanx" in 1996, its virtual, branchless bank. BMO had conducted research that again indicated consumer ambivalence toward the banking industry in Canada, and a strong dislike for the paternalistic ways banks did business. BMO acknowledged consumers' dissatisfaction with the status quo by delivering the message that mbanx was able and willing to create something new to address consumer concerns. The mbanx brand identity was based on beliefs such as "Change is good" and "Everyone is important." The advertising campaign was fuelled by television ads based on the Bob Dylan song, "The Times They Are A-Changing." The TV campaign used children in the spot ads to represent hopefulness and innocence—emphasizing that mbanx was starting with a clean slate.[45]

THE CHALLENGE: A MARKETING STRATEGY FOR THE BMO-RBC BANK

By late 1998, the trade media were beginning to speculate about the new marketing strategy for the merged RBC-BMO bank. A number of trade publications provided an overview on the obstacles faced by the two companies in developing a unified brand identity:

- "From a pure marketing perspective, they're polar opposites," said Bruce Philip of Garneau Wurstlin Philip, the agency that did work for ING Direct. "BMO, through initiatives like its Mbanx electronic banking services, positions itself as 'the advocate of the common-man—the peoples' banker.' By contrast, the Royal [Bank] is the ultimate, paternalistic banking institution."[46]

- "The key to finding a suitable name, according to the experts, will involve tapping into Canadian consumers' values while presenting a globally palatable market image."[47]

- "They have to consider globalization, making sure they are the bank of the future, as well as conveying a sense of Canada, so that it doesn't sound like a Japanese or other foreign bank," says Naseem Javed, president of ABC Namebank International.[48]

- "It will be important to leverage the equity of each brand—the underlined blue M of the Bank of Montreal and Royal Bank's stately lion, crown, and globe. ... Even if the name or identity is completely new, it's going to have to be rooted in where it came from, otherwise they might be deepening the sense of betrayal that their customers could be feeling now," sayid Bruce Philip of Garneau Wurstlin Philip.[49]

The communications teams for both RBC and BMO had to decide on how to tackle these obstacles. In the light of all the changes occurring in Canada's banking industry, they needed to determine the most appropriate long-term marketing strategy for the merged bank. Specifically, they had to address the following:

- How to meet the needs of both domestic and international markets

- The positioning platform for both markets

- The branding strategy to build a strong brand identity in both markets

- How to maintain customer loyalty after the merger

- How to gain new customers in international markets

- An effective communications plan that would support all of the things that they were hoping to accomplish in both markets

The communications team had to move quickly to address these issues, as the federal government's decision regarding the bank mergers was expected very soon. If the mergers were permitted, it would be important for the banks to immediately implement an effective communications strategy.

Notes

1. Eric Heinrich, "How to Keep a Secret," *Marketing Magazine*, February 23, 1998.

2. Richard Blackwell, "Royal Bank, Bank of Montreal Propose $39B Merger," accessed July 14, 1998.

3. Remarks by Matthew W. Barrett, Chairman and CEO, Bank of Montreal Group of Companies, and John Cleghorn, Chairman and CEO, Royal Bank of Canada, at the announcement of the agreement to a merger of equals with Royal Bank of Canada, January 23, 1998. See also <www.tv.cbc.ca/national/pgminfo/banks/mergerchair2.html>, accessed November 9, 2002.

4. Richard Blackwell, "Royal Bank, B of M Propose $39B Merger," accessed July 14, 1998.

5. Chris Daniels, "Bank Campaign Touts Merger," *Marketing Magazine*, November 23, 1998.

6. John Gray, "Royal Bank, BMO Launch National Pre-merger Blitz," *Strategy*, November 23, 1998.

7. Canadian Bankers Association, *Canadian Bank Facts*, 1997/98 edition, available <www.cba.ca/eng/Tools/Brochures/tools_bankfacts_1998.htm>.

8. Ibid.

9. Ibid.

10. Canadian Bankers Association, "Banks Respond to Canadians' Need for Better Economic and Financial Information," press release, January 13, 1998, available <www.cba.ca/en/viewdocument.asp?fl=5&sl=13&tl=71&docid=156&pg=1>, accessed November 9, 2002.

11. Ibid.

12. Erik Heinrich, "The Big Six Take On Their Big Image Problem," *Marketing Magazine*, February 2, 1998.

13. Ibid.

14. Canadian Bankers Association, *Canadian Bank Facts*, 1997/98 edition, available <www.cba.ca/eng/Tools/Brochures/tools_bankfacts_1998.htm>.

15. Royal Bank of Canada, "Enhancing the Bank's Image: The Evolution of Bank Advertising," rbc.com, April 30, 2002 <www.rbc.com/history/quicktofrontier/posters.html>, accessed November 9, 2002.

16. Astrid Van den Broek, "Banking on Marketing," *Marketing Magazine*, March 29, 1999.

17. James Pollack, "Banks Up Advertising to Counter BMO," *Marketing Magazine*, 1998.

18. Van den Broek, ibid.

19. Toronto-Dominion Bank, "CIBC and TD Bank Announce Merger," press release, April 17, 1998, available <www.tdcanadatrust.com/tdbank/PressSearch/199804171.html>, accessed August 16, 1999.

20. Linda Leatherdale, "Battle of the Bankers," *Toronto Sun*, July 12, 1998.

21. Toronto-Dominion Bank, "CIBC and TD Bank Announce Merger," press release, April 17, 1998, available <www.tdcanadatrust.com/tdbank/PressSearch/199804171.html>, accessed August 16, 1999.

22. Bank of Montreal, "Bank of Montreal and Royal Bank Statement on Proposed Merger of CIBC and TD Bank," press release, April 17, 1998.

23. "CIBC Campaign Gets Back to the Future," *Marketing Magazine*, February 10, 1997.

24. Lara Mills, "Customers at Centre of CIBC Strategy," *Marketing Magazine*, November 9, 1998.

25. Lara Mills, "CIBC Promotes E-banking," *Marketing Magazine*, October 19, 1998.

26. John Gray, "Mergers Prompt Scotia Campaign," *Strategy*, October 26, 1998.

27. Ibid.

28. Eve Lazarus, "Credit Unions Keep Up Bank Bashing Ads," *Marketing Magazine*, May 18, 1998.

29. Eve Lazarus, "Big Bank Follies Are Fodder for Richmond," *Marketing Magazine*, February 16, 1998.

30. James Pollack, "ING to Spend $50 Million on Launch of Virtual Bank," *Marketing Magazine*, 1997.

31. Shawna Cohen, "Canadian Banking Goes Dutch," *Marketing Magazine*, June 21, 1999.

32. David Menzies, "How to Launch a Bank," *Marketing Magazine*, December 1, 1997.

33. Royal Bank of Canada, "Enhancing the Bank's Image: The Evolution of Bank Advertising," rbc.com, April 30, 2002 <www.rbc.com/history/quicktofrontier/posters.html>, accessed November 9, 2002.

34. Ibid.

35. "New Campaigns: Royal Bank Gets Personal," *Strategy*, May 30, 1994.

36. Michael Lang, "Royal Bank Hits the Ice in Edmonton," *Strategy*, January 10, 1993.

37. "Royal Bank / CBC Skating 'A Good Reputational Fit,'" *Strategy*, April 4, 1994.

38. David Chilton, "Olympic Sales Boom: Advertisers Paying Full Fare," *Strategy*, July 22, 1996.

39. Patti Summerfield, "New Royal Bank Visa Prompts Loyalty," *Strategy*, May 13, 1996.

40. Leo Rice-Barker, "Royal Bank Acquisition Targets Snowbirds: US Internet Bank Expected to Appeal to Canadian Customers," *Strategy*, March 16, 1998.

41. Barbara Smith, "Special Report: Brand Building Through TV: Bank of Montreal Shows 'It Is Possible,'" *Strategy*, February 6, 1995.

42. Ibid.

43. Ibid.

44. James Pollack, "Is the Mbanx Service Lost Behind Its Ads?" *Marketing Magazine*, March 29, 1998.

45. Menzies, ibid.

46. Lara Mills, "Bank Deal Will Reshape Financial Marketing," *Marketing Magazine*, February 2, 1998.

47. Erica Zlomislic, "What to Name the New Bank," *Strategy*, February 2, 1998.

48. Ibid.

49. Ibid.

Industritech Inc.

H. F. (Herb) MacKenzie

Keith Thomas was excited as he walked into Industritech's head office in early 2002. It was Monday morning and he was about to begin his first two days with the company before flying to Calgary on Tuesday night. On Wednesday morning, Keith would begin work at the Calgary branch as sales manager for western Canada. For his first day, he was scheduled to meet with Tim Smith and Tony Appina, the company's two owners, and with Bill Stockley, the sales manager for eastern Canada. Keith would meet Adam Burden and Hank Matheson on Tuesday. Adam Burden was a senior salesperson who lived in Winnipeg and who was responsible for Industritech sales in western Ontario and Manitoba. Adam was in Toronto to make a sales visit to the head office of a national account that was headquartered there, but that had several operating locations in his territory. Adam was scheduled to fly to Calgary with Keith and would introduce him to the rest of the staff there on Wednesday morning. Hank Matheson was a consultant who had just been hired to provide sales training to Industritech, but who had also been asked to provide advice or assistance to Keith while he established himself in his new position. While Keith was recognized as a very competent salesperson, he had no sales management experience prior to joining Industritech.

This case was prepared by H. F. (Herb) MacKenzie, Memorial University of Newfoundland, Faculty of Business Administration. St. John's, NF A1B 3X5. It is intended as the basis for classroom discussion and is not meant to demonstrate either effective or ineffective management. Names and places in this case are disguised. © 2002 by H. F. (Herb) MacKenzie. Reprinted with permission.

KEITH THOMAS

Keith Thomas received his early education in Newfoundland, and moved to Cambridge, Ontario with his family in the mid-1980s when his father took a job in the automotive industry. Keith completed a sales program at a nearby community college in 1990 and was hired by a manufacturer of valves as an inside order desk salesperson. Within three years, Keith had demonstrated his ability to provide application assistance to customers and he was promoted to outside field salesperson, responsible for handling distributor accounts in Ontario and the Atlantic Provinces. Keith worked closely with his distributors and was largely responsible for their sales growth over the next several years. In 2000, when the sales manager retired, the position was given to Jay Trerice, the salesperson who managed distributor accounts in western Canada. Keith was not surprised, although he was a little disappointed. Jay worked out of his home in Calgary, but he had a very good relationship with Industritech's senior management. Although Keith felt he was a better salesperson, he recognized that Jay was also very competent. Keith felt, unfortunately, that there were unlikely to be any opportunities for advancement in the near future as Jay was only a few years older than himself.

Keith began to think about looking elsewhere for a sales management job, but he did not actively pursue it until one of his distributors, Industritech, indicated that it was look- ing for a sales manager for western Canada. At first, Keith was unsure he wanted to apply as he was comfortable in his present position. He knew the products that he sold very well and one issue he had with working for a distributor was that he would have to learn about many different product lines. Industritech represented more than 300 manufacturers, and carried inventory for about one-third of them. The more he thought about it, however, the more he thought this might be just the challenge he needed. During the interview and hir- ing process, Keith was able to convince the owners of Industritech that he would be able to do the job. He knew a lot about valves and associated products, and he had enough techni- cal aptitude that he could learn enough about the other products quickly. He had good plan- ning skills, seemed to understand time and territory management issues, and he had a good understanding of the value of qualitative and quantitative sales performance analysis. He also recognized his weakness was likely to be his inexperience at handling "people issues," and knew that this would ultimately determine his success as a sales manager.

INDUSTRITECH

Industritech was a Canadian-owned industrial distributor with a head office and warehouse in Toronto, and offices and warehouses in Montreal and Calgary. The company had origi- nally sold maintenance, repair, and operating (MRO) supplies items such as hand tools, safety equipment, fasteners and fittings, and many items that were commonly bought by almost all types of businesses. It began operations in Toronto as Industrial Fasteners and Supplies Ltd. The company name was changed to Industritech in 1985 when more techni- cal product lines, such as pneumatic and hydraulic valves and cylinders, electric motor control equipment, vibration dampening equipment, power cable reels, and solid and liquid level control equipment, were added. It bought the Montreal and Calgary locations of another industrial distributor that went bankrupt in 1988. Gradually, salespeople were hired who worked from these branches but who resided in the territories where they sold.

In 2002, there were three of these salespeople: Adam Burden in Winnipeg, Bruce Stratton in Ottawa, and Rebecca MacIsaac in Halifax.

Tim Smith explained to Keith how the company's growth changed the way it managed sales. "At one time, things were very simple. We sold only MRO supplies. Everything came from our inventory and customers only bought from us when they needed supplies quickly for their operations. Now, however, things are more complicated. We assign all sales to one of three categories: warehouse (W), direct (D), or in-and-out (I&O). When we sell something that is normally an inventory item for us, the sale is coded as a warehouse sale. Those are usually the less technical, MRO supplies items, or sometimes things that we inventory because we have promised to do so for specific customers. A direct sale is one where we place an order with a manufacturer, and the manufacturer then ships the order direct to our customer so that we don't have to physically handle it. We simply get an invoice from the manufacturer, and we in turn invoice our customer. These are usually more complex items or items that we could not afford to carry in inventory because the turnover rate or gross margin for them would be too low. In-and-out sales are orders that we have the manufacturer ship to one of our warehouses and that we then immediately reship to our customer. We may do that for any of several reasons. Maybe we don't want the manufacturer to know who our customer is. Sometimes we may wish to consolidate items to save freight or brokerage fees. Sometimes we may need to make some product modifications before items are shipped to our customer. Or, in some instances, we need to consolidate shipments in our warehouse because customers request it to save them freight expenses or order processing costs. As we have added more and more technical products, the percentages of direct and in-and-out sales have increased."

"It's created other problems for us too," added Tony Appina. We have some salespeople who have adapted very well as the company has changed. One or two have resisted selling our newer product lines, maybe because they don't have the technical skills to be comfortable with them, or maybe because some people simply don't like change. We have one or two, like Adam Burden, who have focused almost exclusively on the newer product lines."

"Yes, that's true," Bill Stockley interjected. "But that's largely because salespeople such as Adam Burden who have territories more distant from our warehouses have to focus more on these types of products. Many customers buy MRO supplies items from local sources where they are assured of faster deliveries. A customer in Winnipeg doesn't want to wait one or two days to get nuts and bolts or safety clothing from Calgary. On the other hand, vibration dampening shock mounts will take anywhere from four to twelve weeks regardless of where they are ordered from, and there may not even be a distributor located in Winnipeg that sells them."

Keith was following the conversation until there was a brief pause. He felt they were expecting him to ask a question or make a comment, so he said, "I guess you are telling me that when I look at the sales figures, I need to consider many factors when evaluating performance."

"Yes," said Bill, "and it gets even more complicated." He looked at Tony. "Should I tell him now?" Tony shrugged and Bill took that as a sign to continue. "I have a very unhappy salesperson here in Toronto," said Bill. "Annie Cormier worked for several years to sign a contract to become the sole supplier for all MRO supplies for National Cement, headquartered here in Toronto. She finally got the contract effective January 2000. The account means nearly $3 million annually for our company. National Cement has manufacturing plants from New Brunswick to Alberta. With our accounting system we split the credit for many of these sales based equally on three factors: where the order originates, where the shipment is delivered, and where the invoice is mailed."

"I can see how that could create problems," Keith interrupted, sorry he did as soon as he spoke. The conversation stopped, waiting for him to continue. "I mean, in some instances, the salesperson who is responsible for the sale might get credit for only one-third of the sale and in other instances they might get credit for two-thirds of the sale. When a salesperson in my territory has to service a sale and only gets credit for one-third of the sale because it was ordered from a centralized purchasing department in Toronto and invoiced to that office, he might feel he deserves more credit."

"But in this case," Bill continued, "National Cement places local orders that are then shipped to their local operating locations with the invoice following to its head office in Toronto. Annie was a bit upset that she only got one-third credit, but she was prepared to live with it. About a month ago, however, she came into my office in a rage. Arthur Melchuk, your most senior salesperson, has two of National Cement's operating plants in his territory. In January 2001, he convinced them to request that all invoices go to the local plants to be matched with receiving reports before being sent to head office, and the head office agreed even though that policy has not been implemented anywhere else. In effect, that gave Arthur 100% credit, and Annie got none. She just found out that she lost credit for $125 000 in sales last year that she feels should have been credited to her. If we can't come to some agreement on this, she's going to make my life miserable, and I agree with her."

Keith thought about it for a moment. "I can certainly sympathize with Annie and I'm sure we can solve the situation. But I must request that you give me a few months so I can get to discuss it with Arthur. Can we talk about this later, once I get settled?"

"I'll stall Annie. She's easy to manage as long as she knows I'm working for her, and she trusts me to do that."

"Well, I haven't even met any of my sales staff yet, and already I got some people issues." At that point, Keith made a few notes in his folder and then the group decided it was time for lunch. They spent the rest of the day talking about where the company planned to go over the next few years and Keith quickly decided he was pleased to have taken his new position. He respected the two owners as he realized they knew their business well, and they were not simply putting in time until they decided to retire. They were committed to actively growing the company, but they seemed willing to delegate authority, at least where they felt it was warranted. Bill Stockley was an interesting person. In many ways, he seemed to be very much like Keith himself, and Keith thought they would get along very well.

When Keith arrived at the office on Tuesday morning, he was introduced to Adam Burden and Hank Matheson. Hank was preparing to make a sales call with one of the Toronto salespeople but had been scheduled to meet with Keith again later in the day. Adam was asked to spend the morning with Keith so they could talk about the Calgary operations. Keith had many questions he wanted very much to ask. He decided that he would ask some of them to Adam, but there were a few sensitive ones he thought best to save until he better understand his situation.

"Where do you want to start?" asked Adam.

"Well, I thought I'd like to know something about the man I'm replacing. What can you tell me about Tom Morgan? What was his management style? What would you consider to be his strengths and weaknesses?"

Adam looked directly at Keith. "Okay." There was a lengthy pause. "Tom was not a strong manager, but he did a reasonable job and I respected him a lot. Everyone liked him because Tom found it very easy to say yes, and very difficult to say no. He was smart enough to identify problems, but then never really wanted to solve them. He was a good man with numbers and he used them a lot for planning. He shared all his analysis with everyone on a regular basis, but he was never willing to push people when they needed it. He knew most of the older products very well, but as I'm sure you know, the company has changed considerably in the past few years. Tom never kept up with the newer products, so he was always uncomfortable visiting customers with me because that's where I focus most of my attention. Consequently, I think he made one trip to Winnipeg in the last three or four years. I didn't really need him, but sometimes I felt very isolated from everything. If you ask some of the others in Calgary, you might get a different perspective."

"One thing I do promise you, Adam, is that you will see me more regularly. You may not see me as often as the other salespeople do, but you will see me regularly and for longer periods of time than the others do. Once I get organized, you'll get my plans and you'll see that once I make them I treat them seriously." Adam nodded, and Keith continued, "Can you tell me if I'm going to run into problems coming to the organization from outside?"

"What you really mean is whether someone else is going to be upset because they didn't get a promotion. Right? Another good question, Keith. But you're lucky in that regard. Arthur Melchuk is the oldest member of the sales force. I'm glad he didn't get the promotion although, again, I like Arthur a lot. I don't think he would like the responsibility. He's been around a long time and he's very comfortable in his territory. Besides, he'll be retiring in four or five years so it might not make sense to promote him now. I'm the second most senior salesperson but I'm certainly not interested. I don't plan to leave Winnipeg. I don't know about Frank Kennedy. He certainly is an excellent salesperson, but he's a very independent guy. He gets along well with his customers, but he sometimes causes friction internally. He's not disliked, mind you. But I don't think he would get any support as sales manager either."

They continued to talk over lunch when Keith asked directly what Adam expected of him. Keith decided they were going to get along well and he was glad to have someone with Adam's maturity on his sales force. As the lunch proceeded, Adam seemed to grow more hesitant until Keith finally noticed. "I think there is something else you want to tell me, but you're not sure how to say it. I know we have only just met but I hope you feel comfortable enough to trust me with any problems you have. I am committed to working with you and for you wherever I can, and I hope we can be open with each other."

"Yes … no … I mean, I don't have any problems right now. I'm very happy and I'm sure we'll get along well. But, yes, I do have something I want to mention because I think it's important and you should know. I am hesitant though because I don't want anyone to know I was the source of the information, and I don't want to tell you where I got the information."

"You have my word. I won't ask where you got your information, and I won't tell anyone that I heard it from you. If it concerns the company, I would appreciate knowing, but if you're very uncomfortable and prefer to not tell me, I can respect that too."

"Well, it concerns another salesperson. Sheldon Armstrong covers northern Alberta and Saskatchewan. He basically goes to Saskatchewan every four weeks. I heard that he submitted an expense report for a trip to Saskatchewan last month but that he never left home. I won't tell you my source and you said you wouldn't ask, but I'm sure that everyone in the Calgary office knows about this."

"Thanks for your trust," said Keith. "That is information I should have, and I'll be sure to watch the situation." With that, they returned to the office where they separated so that Keith could spend some time with Hank Matheson. Hank had been scheduled to do some work at the Calgary branch, but that was now postponed until Keith had an opportunity to evaluate the branch situation. Hank would spend his immediate time in Toronto, but was "on call" to help Keith if needed. Keith thought it would be a good idea to make his own sales calls with his sales staff so that he could make his own assessments before having any outside involvement. Hank had agreed as that would give Keith an opportunity to get to know his staff better, and to do some of his own sales coaching.

"I really only have one question," Keith looked at Hank. "What exactly should I do tomorrow morning?"

"Let me ask a few questions first," replied Hank. "I heard you were a pretty strong 'numbers guy' so I expect you'll do a careful analysis of the numbers before you decide anything. I've given them a scan, but I have been asked not to discuss them with you for a few weeks unless you have some specific questions. Tim and Tony want you to make your own assessment first. I must ask though whether you plan to make sales calls with your salespeople?"

"Regularly. I have seen many sales managers who let this responsibility slip and I am committed to not do that. I plan to spend at least one day every month with each salesperson except Adam, the guy in Winnipeg. Because he is farther away, I plan to visit him quarterly, but I'll spend several days with him during each visit."

"Tom Morgan didn't do that, so I'm sure you'll get some resistance as soon as you announce your intentions."

"All the more reason to announce them immediately and to follow through quickly. They need to see my commitment to that and that my main purpose is to help them. I also want them to see that I do it regularly and I do it with everyone. Otherwise, it might be taken as a sign there are problems with specific people. I also think that once they see my intentions are good, it can be motivating for them."

"All right. That's certainly a reasoned approach," Hank responded, impressed with the answer. "Then, if that's your approach, I would recommend you call a group meeting tomorrow morning to introduce yourself. Give them some of your philosophy as a sales manager and as a manager in general. Let them know that you will be making sales calls with them every month and that you are looking forward to helping them grow personally and professionally. Promise to meet with them all individually in the next few days, but ask for some time to properly evaluate the region before you do that. Then, spend a few days doing your analysis. You won't have to ask all of your salespeople to meet individually with you. My hunch is that you will get a visit or two before you even finish your sales analysis. Anyway, that's my advice."

Keith looked puzzled. "Are you saying I should do things differently, Hank?"

"No. Not at all. You asked for my advice. I took what you gave me and added a few points to it for you to consider. I think your approach is the right one but unless I miss my guess, you will get some resistance early. The sooner you get a feel for the sales figures, the sooner you'll be able to predict from where."

"Any other advice?" Keith asked.

"Yes. Once you have looked at the sales figures by salesperson, you should look at how they are allocating their time across accounts."

"The old 20/80 rule," Keith commented.

"Yes, but in this company, you might want to group customers into the old A-B-C classification scheme. Maybe include each salesperson's 10 largest customers as "A" accounts, their 20 smallest customers as "C" accounts, and classify all the rest as "B" accounts.

"Have you already done this?" Keith asked.

"No. Just experience. I do have a sense of account distribution in this industry, by size of account. I may be wrong, but if there is anything of interest, this data should let you find it."

With that, the two men parted company, promising to be in contact within the next two weeks.

THE FIRST FEW DAYS AT THE CALGARY BRANCH

On Wednesday morning, Keith and Adam arrived early and went immediately to Keith's office. When the sales secretary arrived, Adam motioned her into the office and closed the door so they could all talk. Keith was also hoping to wait until everyone else arrived before meeting them as a group. Keith mentioned that as the branch sales secretary, she would be working for him as well as the sales staff, and he trusted she would handle any sensitive material she might see as confidential within the office. They continued to make casual conversation and Keith realized he liked her a lot. Gillian Strong was the type of person who would make an excellent administrative assistant. She was quite serious but friendly, and she had a lot of confidence and poise.

Shortly after 9:00, Gillian invited everyone to the boardroom. Once they were inside and seated, Keith and Adam entered, and Adam made the introductions. He pointed out each person in the room and told Keith who they were before Keith made his own introduction. "Let me tell you first how pleased I am to be here. I have been an employee of Industritech for only two days but I am excited about this company. I know Tom Morgan managed this branch for nearly 20 years, and I am sorry he didn't live to see his scheduled retirement next year. I do hope to gain the same support that you gave him as we continue to grow this branch in the years ahead. I promise to all of you my full support. I am dedicated to helping each and every one of you to develop personally and professionally, whether you are in sales or in sales support positions. I plan to spend the next few days assessing sales data for this branch and then I will meet with you individually to see how I can help you. You won't see much of me for the next few days. After my tour of the office and warehouse, I want to analyze our performance for the last few years. I will, however, have my door open and you will always find it open to you if you wish to discuss anything with me. Once I get a better understanding of our operations, I will begin making regular sales calls with each of the salespeople on a monthly basis." Before he could continue, Arthur Melchuk interrupted.

"Not with me, you won't. I've been with this company for 20 years. I have the highest sales in this branch. I know my customers and my territory," Arthur challenged.

"We can discuss this when me meet in the next week or so, Arthur." Keith tried to change the subject.

"You can make calls with the others if you wish, but you won't be making any with me. I don't need any help or interference." Arthur had become more aggressive.

"I'm sorry, Arthur. This is not open for discussion. Once I understand more about your accounts, I'll be in a better position to select which customers we will visit together." This time, Keith was successful at changing the topic as he asked Rick Mansour, the office manager, to give him a tour of the office and warehouse. But, he noticed that Arthur had left the boardroom and didn't seem to be in the office while Rick showed him around.

For the rest of the week, Keith stayed mostly in his office reviewing sales figures. When he looked at recent expense reports from the sales force, he knew he had justification to speak to Sheldon Armstrong without having to acknowledge that he was suspicious because of a conversation with another employee. Keith asked Sheldon to come to his office for a minute and when he did, Keith closed the door behind him. After a few social comments, Keith looked directly at Sheldon and confronted him with the reason for wanting the meeting. "Sheldon, I don't know quite how to put this to you, so I'll be somewhat direct. I have reason to suspect that you submitted an expense report last month for a trip you did not take." Keith expected Sheldon to either show some embarrassment, or to become defensive and ask where the information originated, but he did not. "Yes. I did. In fact, I did it twice in the last year. Tom suggested that I do it because I get the lowest base salary on the sales force, and he had no way to get me up to what we both agreed would be appropriate. An alternative, he suggested, would be for me to submit a few expense reports and claim some expenses. It would be tax-free and would raise me to the same income level as some of my peers."

"Does anyone other than you or I know about this?" Keith asked.

"It was supposed to be a secret between Tom and me. But, if no one else knows, you now have me curious as to how you became suspicious."

"It was simple, really. All your expense reports for travel show hotel receipts, and credit card receipts for gas and meal expenses. This expense report shows handwritten receipts from a bed and breakfast, and cash receipts for meals and gasoline." Keith nodded toward an expense report on his desk.

"Yes, I know. But Tom knew too and he approved my expenses."

"Okay. I can accept that. Mind you, I'm not happy with it and I certainly won't be party to it in the future. I am pleased it was done with Tom's blessing. If there is a problem with your salary, I'll find some way to compensate you appropriately, but it won't be on your expense account. We can talk about this at a more appropriate time. I'd like to have breakfast with you on Monday morning if you can manage it. This is just a way to meet people outside the office so we can get to know each other better. I'm hoping to eventually have a breakfast meeting with everyone a few times each year." They agreed to meet first thing the next week, and Keith got back to analyzing his sales figures.

By the weekend, Keith had put together the information he thought he needed (see Exhibits 1, 2, and 3). His major problem was immediately apparent, but he wasn't sure what to do about it. He wished he had some advice, and he looked forward to discussing it with Hank Matheson. But he knew Hank's first response would be to ask what he found in the sales data, and what his own recommendations would be. Keith thought back to his job interview and his first few days at head office. He was certainly right that his biggest problems were likely to be people problems.

EXHIBIT 1	Salespeople			

	Active Accounts	Sales Calls	Direct Selling Expenses	Gross Margin
Terry O'Brien	87	843	$ 118 645	$ 201 613
Adam Burden	77	868	124 688	171 054
Sheldon Armstrong	103	930	108 227	236 873
Frank Kennedy	122	1240	94 566	311 052
Arthur Melchuk	130	1146	104 258	324 335
Total	519	5027	$550 384	$1 244 927

EXHIBIT 2	Sales by Salesperson, 1997–2001					

		Sales ($000)				
		2001	2000	1999	1998	1997
Terry O'Brien	W	464 661	454 214	433 824	424 071	388 699
	D	209 400	190 302	182 901	160 422	140 238
	I&O	191 230	186 745	173 209	151 265	145 256
	Total	865 291	831 261	789 934	735 758	674 193
Adam Burden	W	368 908	347 371	336 600	323 540	317 655
	D	187 607	173 206	151 390	140 243	125 751
	I&O	231 750	201 202	189 879	160 444	153 243
	Total	788 265	721 779	677 869	624 227	596 649
Sheldon Armstrong	W	608377	567 463	525 429	527 539	466 848
	D	152 346	142 302	130 917	115 231	118 918
	I&O	222 153	208 962	190 902	170 345	163 183
	Total	982 876	918 727	847 248	813 115	748 949
Frank Kennedy	W	833 214	771 494	694 414	638 836	587 165
	D	185 901	184 129	170 774	145 148	157 236
	I&O	266 222	254 562	232 938	191 452	204 376
	Total	1 285 337	1 210 185	1 098 126	975 436	948 777
Arthur Melchuk	W	995 341	888 342	654 449	634 529	645 287
	D	113 043	108 241	106 789	94 536	109 258
	I&O	271 766	263 998	238 756	242 873	232 388
	Total	1 380 150	1 260 581	999 994	971 938	986 933

EXHIBIT 3	Sales Force Sales Calls and Sales Revenue ($000) by Account Importance		
	Top 10 Accounts	Middle Accounts	Smallest 20 Accounts
Terry O'Brien	108—302 599	552—512 816	41—49 876
Adam Burden	112—357 256	578—382 253	32—48 756
Sheldon Armstrong	128—414 215	545—488 907	47—79 754
Frank Kennedy	188—523 336	807—690 801	90—71 200
Arthur Melchuk	133—913 662	889—489 500	99—51 988
Total	**669—2 511 068**	**3371—2 489 277**	**390—301 574**

Sue Jones

H. F. (Herb) MacKenzie

Sue Jones didn't notice the heat and humidity. She sat in her car with her hands on the steering wheel, the engine running, and the air conditioner operating. She didn't realize that she had been sitting in that position for nearly 20 minutes, and she was unaware that several people inside the coffee shop where she was parked had noticed and were beginning to wonder whether there was something wrong.

BACKGROUND

Sue Jones was one of those people everyone liked. She was cheerful and optimistic; she was smart, both in intellect and dress; she was gregarious and loved to talk to people. With these personal qualities, it was no surprise when she finally got a sales position with one of Canada's largest transportation companies.

Sue had always wanted to be a salesperson. Her father had been a manufacturer's agent and had spent most of his life travelling across western Canada. He represented eight manufacturers and had developed his business "from a briefcase to a million dollars in one year," and to over five times that amount ten years later. Sue loved her father, and while she was growing to womanhood, she and her father would frequently walk for hours while he told her his selling secrets and what made "super salesmen." Before Sue finished elementary school, she had already decided that she wanted to grow up to be "just like daddy." During high school, Sue helped her father, sending direct mail flyers to his accounts, calling customers to make appointments for him, typing correspondence to both customers and to the manufacturers that he represented, and occasionally, travelling with him to visit his accounts when she did not have to attend classes.

By the time she completed high school, Sue decided she wanted to work. She left home and got a job in Mississauga, Ontario as a receptionist in a small office that provided temporary personnel services in and around the Toronto area. Her pleasing telephone personality was appreciated by many of the firm's clients and Mrs. Thompson, the general manager, eventually encouraged Sue to visit some of the major clients when she was not too busy, to help develop closer relationships with them.

Sue was quickly hooked on selling. She decided that she needed some formal training. She first thought about attending some professional seminars, but her father convinced her to get a degree in business and he offered to finance her education. Sue declined his financial help; she liked her independence. Sue decided to take her program on a part-time basis while continuing to work. At the same time, she searched for and found a full-time job in sales, selling transportation services for a Toronto-based trucking company. She loved her job and she was very successful, doubling sales in her territory over her first two years.

The job gave her some flexibility to complete her degree. While she certainly worked more than 40 hours per week, she did not have to follow a strict nine-to-five schedule, and she frequently took a day or two off when exams approached. Just before her graduation, a major Canadian trucking company advertised for a salesperson to assume an established territory in Calgary. Sue applied for the job, and the national sales manager was impressed enough with her that he hired her in March, but kept her in the Toronto area until she completed her courses a few months later. In June, Sue transferred to the Calgary office where she was the junior salesperson among six others, all men.

During her first week there, which she was supposed to spend in the office learning about her territory and planning her account strategy, one of the more senior salespeople, Joe Kirwan, suffered a severe stroke and had to be hospitalized. None of the more senior salespeople wanted Joe's territory as they did not want to give up their current customers.

Alan Best, the sales manager, decided it would be better to reassign Sue to Joe's territory as he had already been covering what was originally to be Sue's territory for several months, and he had developed some close personal relationships there. He felt she could continue to cover it until another salesperson was hired.

Joe's territory was one of the better territories. Joe had serviced it very well and he had a lot of loyal customers. In fact, Calgary Structural Contractors (CSC) was in Joe's territory, and it was the largest and most profitable account they had in Alberta. Sue spent her second week in the office, this time studying a new territory and a new group of accounts. She decided that because CSC was her most important account, she should visit them as quickly as possible. On Friday morning, she called Bim Hadley, the traffic manager, and made an appointment to see him early Monday morning. She explained to Bim that she was new to the territory. Because his account was very important to her company and she would be responsible for servicing it, she wanted to spend some time understanding what CSC did, what their transportation needs were, and how she could best serve them. Bim told her he would give her a tour of the plant, and she could see the material they used, how it was unloaded, where it was stored, and the finished products that they manufactured so she could understand their transportation needs for both incoming and outgoing shipments.

THE INCIDENT

When Sue appeared on Monday morning, she was looking forward to meeting Bim and getting a tour of CSC. Over a coffee in Bim's office, the two discussed the history of the relationship between their two companies, and what was important to CSC when it came to selecting a transportation service. Bim finally offered to take Sue on the tour he had promised. First, they visited the shop where the manufacturing was done; then they went outside where the structural steel inventory was stored. There were thousands of tons of steel, in all shapes and configurations. She remarked, "I don't think I have ever seen so much steel in one place." Bim replied, "We are the largest structural steel fabricator in the province, and next year is going to be even better for us. We are planning a major expansion as we have just been awarded three new multimillion-dollar contracts."

As they returned to the building, Bim motioned to a side door. "Let's take that one, Sue. It's a shortcut to my office." He held the door open for her and followed her inside. Sue noticed that she was in a long narrow office with a doorway at the far end. She turned to Bim to verify that she should proceed to the doorway when she suddenly felt his hand under her skirt. For the first few seconds, Sue was stunned. She could not believe that this actually was happening, but then she realized that it was, and it was not an accident.

After she left CSC, Sue pulled into a nearby parking lot and parked in front of a coffee shop. She was still shaken. She still could not believe what had happened. She didn't know what she should do. As one of the employees from the coffee shop approached her car, Sue got out and headed for the entrance. She entered, ordered a coffee, and took a table away from the other customers so she could think. She didn't feel like talking to anyone. Sue needed to compose herself, and to decide what her next actions should be.

Some Ethical Dilemmas in Business-to-Business Sales

H. F. (Herb) MacKenzie

The following were actual situations experienced by the case writer during more than 15 years in business-to-business sales and sales management. The names of firms and individuals have been disguised due to the nature of the material in this case.

HALCO MANUFACTURING

Dave MacDonald was excited when he got the unexpected phone call from Nicki Steele, a senior buyer from Halco Manufacturing.

"I know its a year since we bought that prototype reel from you, but we just got a contract from the government to build ten more 'bear traps' and we desperately need to hold our price on these units. Could you possibly sell us ten new reels at the same price you charged last year?" Nicki inquired.

"I'll see what I can do and call you back today," Dave replied.

Dave immediately retrieved the file from the previous year and saw that they had supplied the reel for $6990 F.O.B. the customer's warehouse. There was a breakdown of the pricing on the file:

Manufacturer's list price	$4000.00
Special engineering charge (25%)	1000.00
Total list price	5000.00
Distributor discount (20%)	1000.00
Distributor net cost	4000.00
Estimated currency exchange (8%)	320.00
Estimated duty (22½%)	972.00
Estimated freight	245.00
Estimated brokerage	55.00
Estimated distributor cost, F.O.B. destination	5592.00
Markup (25%)	1398.00
Selling price, F.O.B. destination	$6990.00

There were some notes on the file that Dave reviewed. The reel was designed as part of a "bear trap" on Canadian navy ships. These bear traps would hook onto helicopters in rough weather and haul them safely onto landing pads on the ship decks. The reel was really a model SM heavy-duty steel mill reel, except some of the exposed parts were to be made of stainless steel to provide longer life in the salt water atmosphere. There was a special engineering charge on the reel as it was a non-standard item that had to be specially engineered. The manufacturer had suggested at the time they quoted that Dave could keep the full 20% discount as they thought there was only one other manufacturer capable of building this unit, and their price would likely be much higher.

When Dave got a price from the manufacturer on the ten new units, he was surprised they quoted a price of only $3200 each, less 40/10%. When he asked for the price to be verified, the order desk clarified the pricing. First, there had been a 20% reduction in all SM series reels. That made the manufacturer's list price only $3200. Then, because there was a large quantity, the distributor discount was increased to less 40/10% instead of the 20% that was given on the original reel.

As Dave estimated his cost, things got better. The original reel was imported from the United States at 22½% duty as "not otherwise provided for manufacturers of iron or steel, tariff item 44603-1." In the interim, the company Dave worked for got a duty remission on series SM steel mill reels as "machinery of a class or kind not manufactured in Canada, tariff item 42700-1" and the duty was remitted (and the savings supposedly passed on to the end customer). The currency exchange rate also improved in Dave's favour, and the estimated freight and brokerage charges per unit dropped considerably because of the increased shipment size. Dave estimated his new cost as follows:

Manufacturer's list price	$3200.00
Distributor discount (40/10%)	1472.00
Distributor net cost	1728.00
Estimated currency exchange (2%)	35.00
Estimated duty (remitted)	0.00
Estimated freight	85.00
Estimated brokerage	14.50
Estimated distributor cost, F.O.B. destination	$1862.50

Now that he had all the figures, Dave had to decide what the selling price should be to his customer.

CROWN PULP AND PAPER LTD.

Bill Siddall had been promoted to the position of salesperson, and he was pleased when he received an order for nearly $10 000 for stainless steel fittings from the new pulp mill being built in his territory. Unfortunately, he quoted a price that was 40% below his cost.

"We have to honour the price quoted," Bill insisted.

"I know if you let me talk to Rory, he'll let us raise the price," replied Dave MacDonald, the sales manager. "Rory used to be the purchasing agent at one of my best accounts before he came to the mill."

"No. You gave me responsibility for this account, and I want to build a good relationship with Rory myself. He gave us the order over two weeks ago. He can't change suppliers now because he needs the material next week, and I don't want to put him on the spot now because it would be unfair. Since this is our first order, I would like to supply it without any problems. We'll get back the money we lost on this order many times if we can get their future business. This material is needed for a small construction job, and they haven't even started to consider their stores inventory yet."

After much discussion, it was agreed that the order would stand, but Dave would call the fitting manufacturer's sales manager, Chuck Knowles, as the two men were good friends.

"We need some help on that last order we placed with you. Bill sold it at 40% below our cost," said Dave.

"How could that happen?" Chuck seemed amazed.

"Well," replied Dave, "you give us a 25% distributor discount and we gave 10% to the customer due to the size of the order. What we forgot was to double the list price because the customer wanted schedule-80 wall thickness on the fittings instead of standard schedule-40. This was Bill's first large inquiry and he made an honest mistake. He doesn't want me to get involved with the customer, and I don't want to force the issue with him, so I'm hoping you can help us on this one order. We expect to get a lot of business from this account over the next few years."

"I'll split the difference with you. What you're selling now for $0.90, you're paying $1.50 for, and if I give you an additional 20% discount, your cost will come down to $1.20. Can you live with that?" Chuck asked.

"It's a help. We appreciate it. We'll see you on your next trip to our territory, and I'll buy lunch."

"A deal. See you next month." The conversation ended.

When it was over, Dave was feeling reasonably satisfied with himself, but he still felt somewhat uneasy. He promised not to call Rory, and he promised not to interfere with the account, but he still thought something could be done.

On Saturday morning, Dave went to the Brae Shore Golf Club. He was confident Rory would be there. Sure enough, at 8 am, Rory was scheduled to tee off. Dave sat on the bench at the first tee and waited for Rory to appear. Promptly, Rory arrived with Bob Arnold, one of his senior buyers. The three men greeted each other pleasantly and Rory asked who Dave was waiting for.

"Just one of my neighbours. He was supposed to be here an hour ago but I guess he won't show."

"Join us. We don't mind. Besides we might need a donation this fall when we have our company golf tournament. We'll invite you of course, and we'll invite Bill if he plays golf."

"He doesn't play often, but he's pretty good. Beat me the last time we played. How is he doing at your mill? Is everything okay?" Dave asked.

"Checking up on him? Sure. He's fine. He made a mistake the other day when he went to see our millwright foreman without clearing it through my office first, but he'll learn. He'll do a lot of business with us because we want to buy locally where possible, and you have a lot of good product lines. I think he'll get along well with all of us as well. He seems a bit serious, but we'll break him in before long. We just gave him a big order for stainless fittings a few weeks ago, but we told him to visit at 10 o'clock next time and to bring the donuts."

"I know," replied Dave. "Unfortunately, we lost a lot of money on that order."

"Your price was very low. I couldn't understand it because I knew your material wasn't manufactured offshore. Did you quote the cheaper T304 grade of stainless instead of the T316 we use?"

"No. We quoted schedule-40 prices instead of schedule-80. The wall thickness for schedule-80 is twice as thick, and the price should have been double as well."

"Heck. Double the price. We'll pay it. I'll make a note on the file Monday. I know you're not trying to take us and I can appreciate an honest mistake. At double the price, you might be a bit high, but you know we want to place the order with you anyway because you're local. Eventually we'll want you to carry some inventory for us, so we might just as well make sure we're both happy with this business."

STRAIT STRUCTURAL STEEL LTD.

Dave MacDonald was sitting in the outer office waiting to see Stan Hope, the purchasing agent for Strait Structural Steel, a new account that had just begun operations in a remote, coastal location about 64 kilometres from the nearest city. Stan had telephoned Dave the previous week and had an urgent request for four large exhaust fans that were required to exhaust welding fumes from enclosed spaces where welders were at work. The union had threatened to stop the project unless working conditions were improved quickly, and although Dave didn't sell fans at the time, he found a line of fans and negotiated a discount from the manufacturer, along with an agreement to discuss the further possibility of representing the fan manufacturer on a national basis.

When Stan gave the order to Dave for the fans, the two men discussed other products that Dave sold. Dave sold products for a company that was both a general-line and specialty-line industrial distributor. Included in the general-line products were such items as hand and power tools, cutting tools (drills, taps, dies), safety equipment, wire rope and slings, fasteners (nuts, bolts), and fittings (stainless steel, bronze, and carbon steel flanges, elbows, tees). Included in the specialty-line products were such items as electric motors and generators, motor controls, hydraulic and pneumatic valves and cylinders, rubber dock fenders, and overhead cranes. When the men finally met, they were almost instantly friends, and it was obvious that the opportunities for them to do further business were great. "One item that really interests me," said Stan, "is PTFE tape. We need some and we will be using a lot of it."

"We have the largest stock of PTFE tape in the country," replied Dave. We import it directly from Italy, but it's high-quality and is the same standard size as all others on the market; ½" wide, .003" thick, and 480" long (1 inch = 2.54 centimetres). How much are you interested in?"

"Let's start with 400 rolls," Stan suggested.

PTFE tape was a white, non-adhesive tape used as a pipe thread sealant. It was wrapped around the threads of pipe or fittings before they were screwed together to make a leakproof seal. The tape first came on the market in the late 1960s at prices as high as $3.60 per roll, but since then prices had dropped considerably. North American manufacturers were still selling the tape for list prices near $1.80, and were offering dealer discounts between 25 and 50% depending on the quantities that dealers bought. Dave was importing the tape from Italy at a landed cost of $0.17 per roll.

"We have a standard price of $1 per roll as long as you buy 200 rolls," Dave offered.

"No question. You have an excellent price. How much would you charge M H Sales?"

"I don't know. Who is M H Sales?" asked Dave.

"A small industrial supply company located in my basement. The 'H' is for Hope. I share the company with Bruce Malcolm, the 'M,' and he's in purchasing at Central Power Corporation. M H Sales is a small company and we are looking for additional products to sell. Between Strait Structural and Central Power, we could sell several thousand rolls of PTFE tape each year."

MCCORMICK GLEASON LIMITED

Dave MacDonald telephoned Clarey Stanley, a senior buyer at McCormick Gleason Limited. "Clarey, I'm calling about that quote we made on Lufkin tapes. Can we have your order?"

"Sorry. Your price was high. I gave the order to Ken Stafford. You need a sharper pencil."

"How much sharper?" Dave asked.

"I can't tell you that. But you were close." Clarey replied. "By the way, Kenny called me from the stores department this morning and he has a large shipment of electric relays that was delivered yesterday. They weren't properly marked and he can't identify the ones with normally open contacts from the ones with normally closed contacts. Do you want them returned, or can someone see him and straighten it out here?"

"Tell him I'll see him immediately after lunch. I can tell them apart and I'll see they get properly identified."

When the conversation ended, Dave made a note to see Clarey about the tapes. There was a problem somewhere. Dave knew his cost on Lufkin tapes was the lowest available, and he quoted 12% on cost because he really wanted the order. The order was less than $1500, but it meant that Dave could place a multiple-case order on the manufacturer and get the lowest possible cost for all replacement inventory. That would increase the margin on sales to other customers who bought smaller quantities. There was no possibility that Stafford Industrial, a local, one-person, "out-of-the-basement" operation that bought Lufkin tapes as a jobber, not as a distributor, could match his price.

That afternoon, while waiting to see Ken MacKay, the stores manager, Dave noticed a carton from Stafford Industrial Sales being unloaded from a local delivery van. Although he knew that Stafford supplied quite a few maintenance, repair, and operating (MRO) supplies to this customer, Dave decided to play ignorant.

"What do you buy from Stafford Industrial?" he asked the young stores clerk who was handling the package.

Opening the carton, the clerk read the packing slip. "It says here we ordered 144 measuring tapes, ¾" wide by 25' long" (25 feet = 7.6 metres).

"Are those things expensive?" Dave asked.

"Don't know. There's no price on the packing slip. Clarey Stanley in purchasing ordered them. You could talk to him." The clerk continued to unpack the shipment. As he did, Dave noticed the tapes were manufactured offshore and were poor-quality compared to the Lufkin tapes that he sold, and that he quoted to Clarey Stanley the previous day.

"Aren't those supposed to be Lufkin tapes?" Dave asked.

"Not that I know. The packing slip just says tapes. Wait and I'll haul our copy of the purchase order." The clerk went to a filing cabinet next to his desk and returned with a carbon copy of the purchase order. "No, it just says tapes. It doesn't specify any brand."

There was something wrong, and Dave was determined to get an answer.

Health Care Corporation of St. John's: Meal Delivery System

H. F. (Herb) MacKenzie

This case is designed to provide some insight into the purchasing process for expensive items, and to provide students with an opportunity to actually be involved in the negotiating process through a practical simulation. There are few marketing cases that involve experiential learning within one or two classes.

BACKGROUND

On April 5, 1998, Health Care Corporation (HCC) of St. John's called for tenders for a meal delivery system to service six locations within the city: General Hospital, Grace General Hospital, Janeway Child Health Centre, Leonard A. Miller Centre, St. Clare's Mercy Hospital, and Waterford Hospital. HCC was building an off-site food production, assembly, and distribution centre that would be responsible for providing all the food meal requirements for the six hospitals. The meals would be delivered to the six locations by refrigerated truck three times every day, and would then be rethermalized (reheated) at each site.

Along with an advertisement in the local newspaper, the request for proposal (RFP) was sent to five companies. The bill of material included 48 retherm units and 144 transfer carts (99 carts holding 24 trays each, and 45 carts holding 30 trays each). The bill of material also included plastic trays with lids, 6 oz. China soup bowls with lids (1 ounce = 29.57 millilitres), and coffee mugs with lids, in sufficient quantities to fill all of the transfer carts.

When the RFP closed on April 24, 1998, three companies submitted bids; however, only two of them, Grande Cuisine Systems and Burlodge Canada, committed to making on-site presentations to demonstrate their systems. A copy of the Grande Cuisine Systems quotation is shown in Exhibit 1.

EXHIBIT 1	Grande Cuisine Price Quotation

For: Health Care Corporation of St. John's
　　　RFP #1998-0445
　　　Meal Delivery System

Description	Unit Price	Quantity	Total Cost
Double-Flow Retherm Cart–24	14 982.00	33	494 406.00
Double-Flow Retherm Cart–30	15 118.00	15	226 770.00
Ergosert Transfer Cart–24	6 890.00	99	682 110.00
Ergosert Transfer Cart–30	7 073.00	45	318 285.00
Ergoserv Insert–24	2 830.00	99	280 170.00
Ergoserv Insert–30	2 924.00	45	131 580.00
Trays	35.00	3726	130 410.00
8" high-heat lids	11.10	3726	41 358.60
6 oz. soup bowl (China)	4.95	3726	18 443.70
Lid for bowl	1.60	3726	5 961.60
Coffee mug and lid	3.00	3726	11 178.00
Grand total			$2 340 672.90

Options

48 Timers		360.00 ea.	17 280.00
48 Polycarbonate doors for the double-flow terminal		956.00 ea.	45 888.00
144 Lockable doors for the Ergoserv		120.00 ea.	17 280.00

Special Terms and Conditions

Buy-back for current RXCF system	185 000.00	
Estimated freight to St. John's	34 300.00	

Standard Terms and Conditions

Delivery	26 weeks from order date
Penalty for late delivery	$5000 per month
Cancellation charges (if client cancels order)	5% of total contract price
Warranty	3 years, parts and labour; 5 years on Double-Flow units
Terms of payment	50% with order; 50% on delivery
Inflation escalator	3% per year
F.O.B. point	Montreal, QC

A formal procedure was developed so that the two systems could be fairly compared. Each system was tested with delivery and rethermalizing of 14 different test menus including, for example, a breakfast of cheese omelette and grilled ham with whole wheat toast; a lunch of macaroni and cheese with garlic bread and salad; a dinner of roast turkey, dressing, peas, mashed potato, and gravy. Other evaluation criteria that HCC used included a maintenance assessment, an ergonomic evaluation, an evaluation of warranty and service, and a formal company presentation by each of the companies. Burlodge Canada made the first presentation, followed by Grande Cuisine Systems.

Ted Mussett, the Atlantic provinces salesperson for Grande Cuisine Systems, arranged to have one system shipped to St. John's for testing. After the test period, Nigel Myles, vice-president of operations for Grande Cuisine Systems, travelled from Montreal to make the presentation with Ted. The two men met with Bruce Gorman, director of materials management for the Health Care Corporation, and Jean Day, director of food services for Nova Services, a division of Beaver Foods Limited. Bruce's role was to ensure that the RFP was written so that several companies could compete. He also was responsible to ensure that the bidding and evaluation processes were fair to all companies that were hoping to be awarded the contract. Jean's role was to help evaluate the food delivery system as it would be employees of Nova Services that would have to use the system once it was purchased. Nova Services had the service contract from HCC to supply food services to all of its hospitals. Nova Services would manage the central food preparation facility, and be responsible for food delivery to and distribution of food within the off-site locations.

THE FOOD DELIVERY SYSTEM

The system Grande Cuisine decided to offer was a combination of the Ergoserv (see Exhibit 2) and the Double-Flow Terminal (see Exhibit 3). The Ergoserve is actually made up of two parts, the Ergosert, which is the outside shell, and a stainless steel insert that holds the trays. The Ergoserv is divided vertically in two sections and both sections are refrigerated when the unit is attached to the Double-Flow Terminal. Approximately 40 minutes before meals are to be served, one section of the Ergoserv is rethermalized. This heats the items on one side of the tray while keeping the items on the other side cold.

The Double-Flow Terminal is a stationary unit kept at the six off-site locations. One of the major advantages of the Grande Cuisine system is that the Ergosert can also be kept at the off-site

| EXHIBIT 2 | Ergoserv (made up of the Ergosert and stainless steel insert) |

locations, preventing damage that might occur if the unit had to travel to and from the central food preparation site. The only items that had to be transported were the stainless steel inserts and the trays of food. When these items arrive at the off-site locations, the insert is pushed into the Ergosert, and the Ergoserv is then connected to the Double-Flow Terminal (see Exhibit 4). When the food has been rethermalized, the Ergoserv is disconnected and taken to the location within the hospital where needed. The insert is removed from the Ergoserv and trays are taken from the insert and distributed to patients. At the same time, the Ergosert can be returned to the kitchen area. This prevents staff from reloading the insert back in the Ergosert with dirty food trays and utensils that could make the whole unit unsanitary, requiring additional cleaning effort. In this way, the inserts and food trays are returned directly to the loading dock area where they go back to the central food preparation area to be cleaned and reloaded with the next meals.

NEGOTIATION SIMULATION

Your instructor will normally divide you into groups of four and one person will play each of the roles identified in the case: Ted Mussett and Nigel Myles (Grande Cuisine Systems), Bruce Gorman (HCC), and Jean Day (Nova Services). Your instructor will also provide each person with additional details of each role, with instructions. Using this additional information, the two teams are to negotiate an agreement that both agree to accept. Exhibit 5 is a contract that is to be completed and signed to finalize the negotiations between the two companies (a copy of the contract will be provided to the person playing the role of Bruce Gorman).

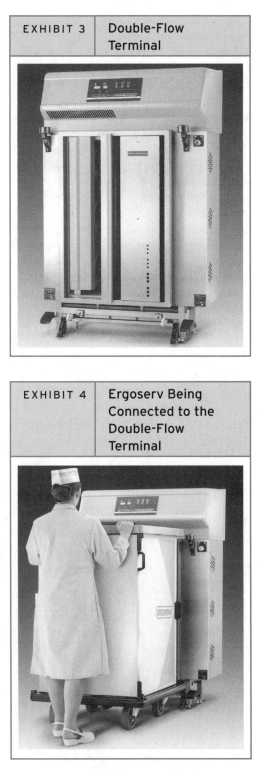

| EXHIBIT 3 | Double-Flow Terminal |

| EXHIBIT 4 | Ergoserv Being Connected to the Double-Flow Terminal |

CASE PURPOSE

Negotiations play an important part in the selling of many products in business and organizational marketing (and in consumer marketing too). One of the best ways to teach negotiating skills is through role-playing and similar experiential exercises. Hopefully, students will learn from the opportunity to participate in a realistic exercise such as this. Further, the exercise provides the basis to discuss various negotiation strategies and tactics appropriate for business and organizational buyers and sellers.

EXHIBIT 5	Final Contract

HCC Meal Delivery System

Description of final system if not completely as described in the Grande Cuisine Systems quotation:

_____

_____

_____

_____

System Price: _____

Options if taken:

    Timers: _____

    Polycarbonate doors for Double-Flow terminals   _____

    Locking Doors for the Ergoserve   _____

    Buy back for the RXCF system   _____

    Freight   _____

TOTAL: _____

Standard Terms and Conditions

Delivery	_____	weeks from order date
Penalty for late delivery	_____	per month
Cancellation charges (if client cancels order)	_____	% of total contract price
Warranty	_____	years, parts and labour
	_____	years on Double-Flow units
Terms of payment	_____	
Inflation escalator	_____	% per year
F.O.B. Point	_____	

Signatures: _____   _____

              Health Care Corporation of St. John's   Grande Cuisine Systems

Lucas Foods

John Fallows and
Walter S. Good

Bib Martin was marketing manager of Lucas Foods, a diversified food manufacturing and wholesaling company based in Edmonton. The company has recently had some success with a new product, Gold Medal Crumpettes. Jerry Lucas, the president of Lucas Foods, asked his marketing manager to recommend an appropriate strategy for the new product, which would best capture the available opportunity and support the mission of the company.

THE INDUSTRY

Lucas Foods was in the food manufacturing and wholesaling business, marketing a broad product line that included frozen egg products, shortening, flour, baking mixes, spices, and bulk ingredients. Its primary customers were the five major national food wholesalers, with smaller regional wholesalers and independent grocery stores accounting for a smaller portion of its sales.

Prepared by John Fallows under the direction of Walter S. Good of the University of Manitoba as a basis for classroom discussion rather than to illustrate either effective or ineffective handling of an administrative situation. © by the Case Development Program, Faculty of Management, University of Manitoba. Support for the development of this case was provided by the Canadian Studies Program, Secretary of State, Government of Canada. Reprinted with permission.

Gold Medal Crumpettes was a recent entry in Lucas Foods' bakery products group. The product fell into the product class commonly known as biscuits. Competitive products in this class included crumpets, scones, English muffins, and tea biscuits. Competition also came from a variety of substitute products such as toast, donuts, and muffins. Biscuit producers included such prominent names as Weston Bakeries and McGavin Foods Ltd., domestically, as well as the American firm of S. B. Thomas, which concentrated on English muffins and dominated the market for that product.

Lucas Foods estimated that the product life cycle for specialty bakery goods was from five to seven years. Generally, if a new product was going to be successful, it enjoyed quick acceptance in the marketplace. Introduced in 1984, Gold Medal Crumpettes had limited distribution. They had been sold in Alberta and Saskatchewan and were recently introduced in Manitoba, Montana, and Minnesota. Safeway was the only major chain to carry the product in Canada, but sales growth had been steady to date.

HISTORY OF LUCAS FOODS

The company was originally formed under another name over 50 years ago. It specialized in frozen egg products and later diversified into cabbage rolls and frozen meat products. The company was purchased by a major brewery in 1972, but the frozen egg portion of the business was sold back to the original owners six years later. They sold the business to Jerry Lucas in 1979. Since then, sales have doubled to their present annual level of $12 million.

The company followed a "portfolio approach" to its product line, regularly adding or deleting items according to established criteria with respect to the marketing cycle. With the single exception of frozen egg products, no specific product or product family dominated its overall product offering. (An exception was made for frozen egg products because of their unique life cycle and recession-proof qualities.)

In its statement of business mission, Lucas Foods indicated a desire to grow to an annual sales level of $50 million and to become a major national food manufacturer and wholesaler, as well as an exporter. Its major competitive weapons were believed to be its excellent reputation, product knowledge, marketing expertise, and level of customer service.

MARKETING GOLD MEDAL CRUMPETTES

Lucas Foods believed that the consumption of biscuit items was uniform across age groups, seasons, and geographic locations. It is a mature market. The merchandise itself was targeted toward the "upscale buyer." Package design, pricing policy, and product ingredients positioned Gold Medal as high-priced and high-quality relative to the competition. Therefore, the primary variables for segmenting the market were socioeconomic: Gold Medal Crumpettes were a luxury item.

The Crumpettes were designed to incorporate the taste and texture of scones, English muffins, and biscuits. They could be eaten with or without butter, either toasted or untoasted. They were available in four flavours: plain, raisin, cheese, and onion, and the company had plans to add three more flavours, including pizza. The product could be stored frozen. The name, Gold Medal Crumpettes, was specifically selected to imply quality.

Since wholesale food distribution in Canada was dominated by relatively few firms, management felt that it had little choice in the distribution of its products. Lucas Foods did not own a large warehouse to store its finished baked goods, but manufactured Gold Medal Crumpettes to order. The merchandise was then transported by common carrier to various customers under net-30-days credit terms.

The goal of the company's promotional efforts was to stimulate and encourage consumer trial of the product. There was some radio advertising when the product was first introduced. Although Lucas suggested the retail price, the distributor, especially in the case of Safeway, did most of the promotion. Typical promotions have been:

- Hostesses distributing free samples in supermarkets
- Crossover coupon promotions with jam companies
- Mail-out coupons to consumers
- Free products to stores
- Temporary price reductions for distributors

So far, $50 000 had been spent on the promotion of Gold Medal Crumpettes. To complement these promotional efforts, Lucas Foods had three salespeople who, along with the marketing manager, regularly called on all major accounts.

Gold Medal's high price was consistent with its positioning and was arrived at after evaluating consumer surveys and the company's production costs. The expected price-sensitivity of the market was also considered. A package of eight biscuits retailed for $1.89. The product was sold to supermarket chains in cases of 12 packages, with a factory price of' $12 per case. Manufacturing costs, including allocated overhead, were $8.40 per case. This provided a contribution margin of $3.60 per case, or 30%. Production capacity was available for up to 16 000 cases per month.

CAPTURING THE OPPORTUNITY

The estimated total potential market for Gold Medal Crumpettes is shown in Exhibit 1. Bib Martin guessed that Lucas Foods held a 16% share of the Alberta market.

EXHIBIT 1	Total Potential Market for Gold Medal Crumpettes (yearly sales)	
	Cases	Volume
Alberta	43 000	$ 520 000
Canada	960 000	$ 11 500 000
United States	9 660 000	$115 000 000

The Alberta consumer had been very receptive to the product, but outside Alberta, the company had only a limited reputation and was not well known as a wholesale food supplier. This lack of awareness made it more difficult for the product to obtain the acceptance of retailers. Also, the company faced an almost total lack of consumer awareness outside the province.

If Gold Medal succeeded in obtaining quick acceptance in new markets, competitors might view the development of a similar product as an attractive proposition. This could be particularly distressing if the competitor taking such an action was a major producer with an existing broad distribution system. Therefore, the speed with which Gold Medal Crumpettes could be introduced and developed into a dominant market position was very important to the long-term survival and profitability of the product. There was also the question of whether the degree of consumer acceptance the product had achieved in Alberta could be repeated in other areas.

Pricing research conducted by the company indicated that consumers were not prepared to cross the $2 price level at retail. If production costs were to rise and force an increase in selling price, sales might decline. Also, while the current exchange rate allowed Lucas to be quite competitive in the U.S. market, a strengthening of the Canadian dollar could damage the company's export position.

SELECTING A STRATEGY

Bib Martin had to propose a marketing strategy to Jerry Lucas that he felt would best take advantage of the opportunity available to Gold Medal Crumpettes. He was considering three alternatives:

1. *Maintain the product's existing market coverage and strategy.* This implied limiting distribution of the product and focusing the company's efforts on the Prairie provinces and the states of Montana and Minnesota.

2. *Phased expansion.* This would involve expanding across Canada, region by region, to become a major force in the Canadian biscuit market and begin selective entry into the U.S. market.

3. *Rapid expansion.* This approach would involve an attempt to expand rapidly in both countries, to precede and preferably preempt competitive products in all markets, and to seek a dominant position in the North American biscuit market.

During their early discussions, Jerry pointed out that the company had the financial capacity to undertake any of these options. It was a question of how best to focus the available resources.

Before evaluating his alternatives, Bib prepared a list of criteria to guide him in coming to an appropriate decision:

• The alternative should be feasible.

• The alternative should be profitable.

• The market opportunity should be exploited as far as possible while still meeting the first two criteria.

• The alternative should fit into the activities of the company.

• The alternative should be consistent with the mission of the company.

• The alternative should be consistent with Lucas Foods' portfolio management approach concerning return, risk, and diversity.

• There should be early evidence to support the alternative.

Artventure Children's Creative Art and Party Centre

Mark Haber and
Christopher A. Ross

INTRODUCTION

In May 1999, Eileen Walfish and Tina Diamant, the owners and only employees of Artventure, were reviewing the results of their first year of operation. While they were satisfied with the results, they were concerned about the years ahead. They expected significant challenges because of increased operating expenditures, especially wages, increased competition, and the introduction of new programming such as a proposed summer camp for 1999. Their challenge was to develop a long-term strategic plan for Artventure that would ensure the continued growth and profitability of the business.

Artventure is a creative and educational centre. Through a wide variety of activities and specialized programs, it provides artistic and educational stimulation to children between the ages of 8 months and 12 years. Artventure is not a daycare centre. Its mission is "to enhance the creativity and self-esteem of young children and pre-teens through various activities centring around the arts, as well as entertaining and coordinating children's birthday parties, catering to every parent and child's needs." The owners

This case was written by Mark Haber and Christopher A. Ross of Concordia University. It is to be used for discussion purposes only. It is not designed to illustrate either effective or ineffective handling of an administrative or commercial situation. Some of the information in this case has been disguised, but essential relationships have been retained. © 1999. Reprinted with permission.

aim to develop in children a love for the arts and sciences, in a pleasant, well-supervised environment. They also want to foster the child's intellectual growth, interpersonal and artistic skills, and self-esteem through a broad range of programs and activities. Artventure's services include photography, dance, animated music and cognitive games, and children's birthday parties. There are 100 party packages from which parents can choose.

BACKGROUND

Eileen and Tina had no previous business management experience, but both had training in early childhood education and practical experience working with children.

Eileen began working with children at the age of 12, at a day camp. She had experience putting on puppet shows and plays. She also organized activities for children between the ages of 2 and 8. In the summer of 1992, Eileen became the program director and counsellor-in-training, where she gained supervisory experience. Subsequently, she became involved in creating and teaching different activities such as swimming, dance, music, art, nature and science for children 2 to 8 years old. In addition she had organized graduation ceremonies, birthday and other children's parties, and holiday shows, and had conducted private art workshops in clients' homes. Eileen has a D.E.C. in Literature and Arts from Marie-Victorin College,[1] in Montreal, and a bachelor's degree in Education and Religion from Concordia University. During her educational years, she had received good citizenship, good sportsmanship, and achievement awards in physical education and drama.

Klimentina (Tina) has a degree in Education from the University of Sarajevo. Prior to her arrival in Canada in 1993 she had been director and coordinator of a youth theatre in the field of puppetry, and was experienced in the design and creation of marionettes. She was also responsible for scenery and costume design for various plays in which she had acted. That experience brought her new positions in children's television, in cartoon animation, and as a TV show host in Sarajevo.

In Canada, she maintained a strong interest in early childhood education and earned a D.E.C. in Education. She worked as an early childhood educator at a nursery, where she was responsible for planning, programming, and managing activities in creative art, dance, and shows. She also had experience coordinating special events for parents. In 1997, she became the art and jewellery specialist at a day camp, where she organized and conducted innovative and creative projects for children between the ages of 3 and 12.

In their past positions, the owners had developed strong relationships with clients—children as well as parents—which earned them an excellent reputation in the Jewish community in Côte-Saint-Luc, Hampstead, and Westmount (Exhibit 1).

THE CENTRE

Eileen and Tina believe that activity centres are needed to provide extended entertainment and education for children. The market, according to the owners of Artventure, needs centres that provide ongoing creative, innovative projects that challenge and enhance the child's creative talents and also cater to the needs of parents. Since parents have little time to spend with their families, these centres can act as "added parents," providing education, creative stimulation, and fun during the hours when it is difficult for parents to provide supervision.

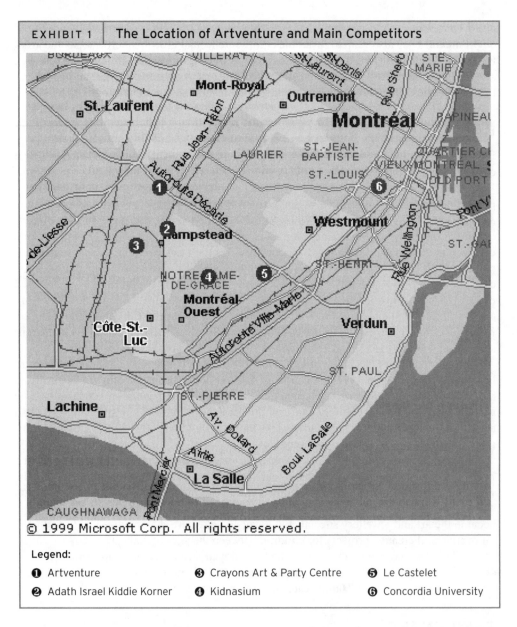

| EXHIBIT 1 | The Location of Artventure and Main Competitors |

Legend:

❶ Artventure   ❸ Crayons Art & Party Centre   ❺ Le Castelet

❷ Adath Israel Kiddie Korner   ❹ Kidnasium   ❻ Concordia University

Artventure commenced operations on May 3, 1998, and is located at 6900 Decarie Square, a shopping centre in Montreal. At this location, parking is plentiful and free of charge. Decarie Square lies next to Highway 15, a major north-south highway running through the city of Montreal (Exhibit 1). This location makes it very convenient to drop off and pick up children at the Centre. Artventure has 104 square metres of available space, which is more than enough to run its programs. Decarie Square, however, is not an upscale shopping centre. Much of the space is unoccupied and there is low customer traffic. While Artventure is nicely decorated, clearly indicating to mall traffic that it is a children's centre, one space next door is empty and the space on the other side is a clothing repair shop. Opposite to Artventure are a fruit shop and a home decoration store. Recently, some companies such as Aldo, Stokes, and Au Coton have established liquidation outlets at this shopping centre.

Eileen and Tina see Artventure as a provider of high-quality programs aimed at systematically developing the whole child. Artventure offers creative, stimulating, and entertaining activities such as original art activities, puppet shows, and drama plays for small children, enjoyable food and refreshments for children and parents, cognitive games, and animated music activities. Eileen and Tina believe that constant variation in activities allows for new and exciting experiences and that this variety is an effective method of capturing the attention of young children as they explore their creative spirits.

ARTVENTURE'S PROGRAMS

Artventure offers four programs:

- *Program 1, Creative Junior Tots*, is for children between the ages of 15 months and 4 years. This program is subdivided into two age categories, and both run for a period of four weeks. Mom and Tot, offered on Tuesday and Thursday, includes art, music, live animals, drama, stories, and creative movement. Junior Tots, offered on Monday, Wednesday, and Friday, includes science, music, and dance. For both programs, peanut-free kosher snacks are served. Exhibit 2 shows the two categories, their times, and prices. These two programs generate approximately 30% of Artventure's annual revenue.

EXHIBIT 2	**Creative Junior Tots**				
Age Category	Classes per Session	Duration of Classes	Classes per Week	Price per Session	Children per Group
15 to 24 months	8	9:30 am to 11 am	Tuesday and Thursday	$192.00	Min: 6 Max: 10
2 yrs to 4 yrs	12	9:00 am to noon	Monday, Wednesday and Friday	$288.00	Min: 6 Max: 10

- *Program 2, Photography Fun*, is intended for children 4 years and over. This program involves taking and developing pictures. More specifically, this program allows the children to see the results of their creativity. Artventure believes that Photography Fun is a great way for children to discover themselves and develop self-esteem. The children are also able to show family and friends the pictures that they have taken. The cost for a seven-class session is $112.

- *Program 3, Funky Dance*, is for children 5 years old and over. This program introduces the participants to modern dance techniques and fosters body coordination. It also incorporates costumes and props such as wigs, thereby enhancing the creative element. Upon completion of the program, Artventure invites parents to watch a dance recital performed by the participants. The cost for a seven-class session is $95. Funky Dance and Photography Fun together contribute 20% of Artventure's revenue.

- *Program 4, Children's Birthday Parties*, includes a creative and original atmosphere where children between the ages of 4 and 12 celebrate their birthday. Artventure offers theme parties or specialized parties. The theme parties focus, for example, on the child's favourite sports, TV shows, superheroes, or toys. Dramatic plays, puppet shows, treasure hunts, art activities, and many other cognitive activities capture the children's imagination while they participate in an original and zestful birthday party. The specialized parties focus on areas such as art, drama, jewellery, music, dance, photography, and video production.

Artventure provides juice, paper crafts and toys, specialized birthday cards, party surprises, art materials, decorations, animators, and coffee for the parents. Additionally, the parties have a unique style and emphasize an unlimited amount of fun. The parties last for two hours, from 4 pm to 6 pm from Monday to Friday and, by special appointment, any time during the day on weekends. The price is $200 for 20 children or fewer and $5 for each child thereafter. Artventure derives 50% of its revenue from birthday parties.

CUSTOMERS

Eileen and Tina feel that more young parents are seeking early educational development for infants and toddlers, thus creating a high demand for Parent and Tot programs. Furthermore, social interaction and a strong sense of the arts and culture for preschoolers and preteens make extracurricular activities a must during school hours and on weekends.

They also observed that parents increasingly hold their children's birthday parties outside the home. In the last six years, the popularity of this concept has grown as more mothers continue to join the workforce. In addition, many parties have up to 40 guests, so that all classmates, relatives, and friends outside school can be invited. In sum, they feel there is a strong demand for this service.

Artventure identifies their potential clientele as families with children aged 8 months to 12 years. These families are affluent. Many parents are university graduates and have careers in fields such as medicine, law, finance, and business ownership (e.g., jewellery, insurance, manufacturing, retail, import/export, and stockbrokerage). Although Artventure welcomes all religious, ethnic, and racial groups, the owners have built a strong reputation within the Jewish community and are trusted and known by many in that community. Ninety-five percent of the children attending Artventure are from Jewish families. The other 5% is made up of Italians, Greeks, and francophones. In fact, one of the owners' desires is to increase the number children from other ethnic groups.

Eileen and Tina describe the parents as having a strong interest in recreational activities, a high regard for the arts—dance, drama, creative arts—and a strong belief in education that enhances self-esteem and the intellectual growth of their children. The parents also want attractive, clean, spacious, and safe environments with innovative programming where their children can have fun. They believe that parents appreciate the involvement of the owners in the day-to-day activities of the Centre and the children. Price, available equipment, quality of the programming, and small classes are important considerations for parents. They look for style to keep up with other members of the community and the "latest trends." They are loyal to a service if it impresses them. The parents are also helpful and supportive, especially when they are more familiar with the business owners. They are potential promoters of the business when they are satisfied with the services offered.

Because of Eileen and Tina's experience and reputation in the Jewish community, this community was their major target. Until the 1970s, Montreal was the most important Jewish centre in Canada. Since the mid-1970s, however, a large percentage have moved to other areas in Canada, especially Ontario. By 1999, Toronto had replaced Montreal as the home of the largest Jewish community. There are, however, more than 100 000 members of the Jewish community in Montreal. In Montreal, 60% of Jewish children go to Jewish primary schools and 30% go to Jewish high schools. Artventure identified Côte-Saint-Luc, Hampstead, Town of Mount Royal, and Westmount as their principal markets. Exhibit 3 provides demographic data on these and neighbouring cities.

Eileen and Tina know that demand for their various offerings varies depending on the season. During the summer, for example, parents enroll their children in outdoor day camp programs. Therefore, afternoon art classes from June to August are quiet periods. Not all camps accept children under the age of 3, so Artventure is planning to design a day camp program for children between the ages of 2 and 5 years, while continuing to offer their Parents and Tots program for children between 15 months and 24 months. Many camps have half-day programs from 9 am to noon for children between 3 and 5 years old, so the owners want to offer special art classes to this age group from 1 to 3 pm. For birthday parties, June to August is slow, since many families are on vacation, or hold pool parties, or choose to wait for the school year so they can invite classmates. October to May is the busiest time for parties.

Eileen and Tina interviewed 50 families in the Hampstead and Côte-Saint-Luc areas and found that they had spent an average of $600 or more on birthday parties for their children. Given the income levels of their target market, the owners believe that these families, even in a recession, would continue to use these centres, especially for parties, since parents would find it difficult to deny their children a birthday party.

COMPETITION

Eileen and Tina believe that the industry of children's recreation and party centres is in a period of growth. In 1992, there was only one private play and party centre that catered to families with children between the ages of 1 and 6 years in areas such as Hampstead, Côte-Saint-Luc, Westmount, Town of Mount Royal, Saint-Laurent, and even the West Island. In 1999, however, similar centres can be seen in many areas. For example, there is Kidnasium Gym & Party Centre in Notre-Dame-de-Grâce (NDG); Neverland in the West Island; Crayons Art & Party Centre in Cavendish Mall; Artfolie in the Monkland area; and Adath Israel Kiddie Korner in Hampstead (Exhibit 1). Even the City of Westmount (at its Greene Avenue Centre) and Concordia University offer activities for children. Other centres, such as Bedrocks, Coconuts in the West Island, and Enfantastique Drop Off & Party Centre in Place Vertu and Carrefour Angrignon, which had sprung up to meet the demand, ceased operations in 1998.

Tina and Eileen identified three centres that they considered direct competitors:

1. *Le Castelet*, an artistic awakening centre, is a preschool located about three to four kilometres from Artventure, on Sherbrooke Street, one of the major arteries in Montreal. This centre is divided into three rooms, two of which are designated for artistic and intellectual usage. The third and larger room is used for dance and physical play. The centre is located directly across from a municipal park, which is easily accessible.

EXHIBIT 3	City Demographics				

	Côte-Saint-Luc	Hampstead	Westmount	Mtl.-West	Mt. Royal
Population:					
1991	30 126	7 219	20 239	5 180	18 212
1996	29 705	6 986	20 420	5 254	18 282
Total male:	13 280	3 310	9 200	2 565	8 610
0-4 years	640	225	435	210	475
5-9 years	710	205	520	220	570
10-14 years	710	220	590	235	615
Total female:	16 425	3 675	11 220	2 690	9 670
0-4 years	590	205	420	140	455
5-9 years	665	225	500	225	525
10-14 years	680	215	540	185	515
Mother tongue:					
English	15 205	4 615	12 035	3 655	5 305
French	3 300	835	4 065	465	7 215
Home language:					
English	20 265	5 520	14 245	4 370	7 190
French	2 920	735	3 745	330	7 400
Jewish population	19 395	4 935	4 345	825	2 625
Undergraduate or higher	6 190	2 520	8 850	1 715	6 640
Number of families	8 075	1 930	5 235	1 455	5 005
Median family income	$51 099	$93 855	$101 525	$81 156	$90 983
Family income:					
< $10 000	380	85	160	30	120
$10 000-19 999	680	85	240	60	220
$20 000-29 999	990	70	250	100	275
$30 000-39 999	995	95	305	95	370
$40 000-49 999	905	145	255	80	310
$50 000-59 999	760	105	240	95	400
$60 000-69 999	540	130	280	140	335
$70 000-79 999	460	110	270	105	180
$80 000-89 999	490	95	320	95	265
$90 000-99 999	325	80	240	65	205
$100,000+	1 555	920	2 670	590	2 320

Source: Statistics Canada, "Profiles of Census Divisions and Subdivisions," 1996 Census of Canada, Catalogue No. 95-186-XPB (Ottawa: Industry Canada, 1999).

The goal of Le Castelet is to provide an atmosphere of interaction that will prepare children for their entrance into primary education.

Le Castelet's programs centre on music, theatre, dance, and arts/crafts. Le Castelet designs these activities to encourage children to interact with other kids and to instill a sense of learning and openness. This centre specializes in the artistic environment and tries to implant a taste for the arts. The courses are conducted mostly in French. The instructors can communicate in English, but there is greater emphasis on communicating in French. The hours of operation and prices are as follows:

- Morning sessions: 8:30 am to 12 pm @ $16.75 per morning
- Full-day sessions: 8:30 am to 5:30 pm @ $24.50 per day

On a monthly basis the costs are as follows:

- 2 mornings/week = $134
- 3 mornings/week = $201
- 4 mornings/week = $268
- 5 mornings/week = $335

These programs follow the school calendar of the regular elementary schools. The year, therefore, is from September to June. There is also a summer day camp program that focuses more on outdoor activities like playing in the park. The price for the summer day camp is the same as the school-year program. The classes are divided into groups of eight per instructor. The age group for instruction is from 2 to 5 years old.

The school also has theme days every other week. These are used to teach the children about art, nature, and other subjects of interest. An example of a theme day would be Forest Day, whereby children learn about the different kinds of trees and animals in the forest. Parents supply all food, such as snacks and lunches. The school supplies fruit drinks. Birthday parties are celebrated for the children who attend Le Castelet; parents supply the cake.

2. *Kidnasium* is a 557 square metre facility that opened its doors approximately two years before Artventure. It enjoys fair success. The facility is divided into two parts: the indoor playground with a foam floor surface and playground equipment, and the gym. The goal of this centre is to provide children between the ages of 1 month and 6 years with noncompetitive programs in a group setting.

This centre is located at the corner of Somerled and Grand Blvd. in NDG and offers four programs. These are as follows:

- A gym program, which includes an instructor. The instructor teaches the children aerobic-type gym skills as well as tumbling and coordination. This program runs for fifteen 45-minute sessions at a cost of $225 per child, tax included. The maximum number of children per group is 12.
- The dance program, "Tooney Loonz," runs for fifteen 45-minute sessions at a cost of $215 per child, tax included. Two reputable instructors provide children with animated performances such as guitars and "singalongs."
- The open gym program does not include an instructor. The price is $6 per child, $10 for two children.

- The last type of program is birthday parties. Playground parties for 20 children cost $225 each. For 30 children or more, the cost is $285. A gym party costs $300 for 20 children or fewer and $385 for more than 20 children. Both parties last for two hours and include paper products, balloons, and fruit juice for the children; coffee for parents; and instructors for the gym activities.

Extra costs for the birthday party program, which can run up to an additional $400, include food for guests, cakes, loot bags, and entertainment such as music, clowns, and magicians. The location of this centre is not very central for the important market areas of Hampstead, Westmount, Town of Mount Royal, Côte-Saint-Luc, and the West Island or Saint-Laurent. Moreover, parents must also supervise their own children because of the high risk of injury in the gym area. The limited variety of programming for parties also forces parents to hire entertainment in order to please party-goers.

3. *Crayons Art and Party Centre*, situated in Cavendish Mall, Côte-Saint-Luc, has been in existence for about 18 months. It is a drop-off centre; this means that there are few scheduled activities. Anyone, at any time, can walk into the centre and participate in the art class of the day. The centre serves children older than 3 years old. It also offers art programs to senior citizens. The fee for drop-off is $10 per hour per person. A special six-week program is available at a cost of $90. This program concentrates on only one area of art, such as painting, drawing, and so on. Crayons offers these programs at hours that do not coincide with regular school hours, so this program is geared more to adults and senior citizens. Thus Eileen and Tina believe that this centre is not a significant threat to Artventure. Crayons is strictly an Arts and Crafts Centre and does not offer any programs in the other areas of the arts. The centre offers birthday parties. These parties cost between $140 and $210, with a choice of a party in jewellery or pottery. All materials are included as well as juice, paper products, and coffee for parents. The variety of parties is limited and does not capture the attention of partygoers for the full two hours. This centre is also physically small—about 74 square metres—and it gets very crowded when there are many children. Exhibit 4 is a comparison of Artventure's birthday party offerings with two competitors.

EXHIBIT 4	**Birthday Party Grid**			
Birthday Centre	Parties Offered	Services/Party Materials	Costs	Extra Costs
Artventure	Theme parties: Physical, cognitive and artistic activities. Parties in music, drama, jewellery, dance	Entertainment, specifically designed decorations, party animators, party favours, paper products, juice, coffee, birthday cards, balloons, birthday crowns	$200–$250	Food $40–$100
Crayons	Art and jewellery parties	Art materials, coffee, juice, paper products, monitors	$140–$210	Food, loot bags, entertainment Up to $400
Kidnasium	Gym and playground parties	Instructor, juice, paper products, balloons	$225–$385	Food, loot bags, entertainment Up to $400

In addition to the three competitors described so far, there are other potential competitors.

Adath Israel Kiddie Korner, for example, offers morning classes for 2-to-5-year-olds. It also offers specialty activities such as ballet, creative movement, and computers. Furthermore, there is a Mom and Tots group with programs for kids 18 to 24 months from 9:00 to 10:45 am, and for kids 12 to 17 months from 11 am to 12 pm. This centre also offers "Music with Toony Loonz" on Tuesday, Wednesday, and Friday. The City of Westmount at its Greene Avenue Centre offers children programs that include "Magical Fun" from 11:00 am to 12:30 pm, "Tumbling Tots Indoor Playground" from 9:30 to 11:30 am for preschoolers, and "After School Home Away from Home" from 3:30 to 6:00 pm for kindergarten to 6 years. Concordia University's Department of Education offers "Children and Parents Learning Together" for 3- and 4-year-olds on Tuesday, Wednesday, and Thursday, from 9:00 to 11:30 am. Parents and teachers discuss child-rearing on Thursday mornings.

Babysitters are also an ongoing competitive threat to any centre. Many parents prefer dealing with people they know and trust. Babysitters and domestics provide the service of "watching over" your children.

THE ENVIRONMENT

In spite of the growth in centres, the owners believe that the market is large enough for another centre to be successful. Their reasoning is that each centre focuses on different age groups and activities and they are situated in different locations. They estimate that some centres average $84 000 per year in birthday parties alone. They believe that in the Montreal region there is plenty of room for new players who cater to partygoers aged 6 to 12. The major centres do not offer services to this age group. They are also limited in their offering of different types of recreational activities other than art.

The owners of Artventure believe that as long as high-income families continue to cater to their children's desires and that mothers are in the workforce, party centres will have a strong and healthy place in the market. The industry is growing rapidly because of a new generation of parents who have healthy incomes yet no time or energy to be entertainers and creative specialists in their children's lives. These parents therefore seek outside assistance. With the increasing number of families where both parents are in the workforce, proper child care plays a critical role in the everyday lives of families. These trends, plus a genuine love of children, prompted the creation of Artventure.

Eileen and Tina are concerned, however, that at some point government regulations would make the business less appealing. For example, the government may enforce more rigorous safety requirements, or require that all centres carry high levels of insurance. They also feel that the ongoing political debate about the possible separation of Quebec from Canada makes conditions increasingly difficult for the business. They fear that many English-speaking families, Artventure's target market, will relocate outside of Quebec. Other possible administrative threats lie in the Quebec laws and regulations governing the use of language on all signs and mailings. Artventure may, in the future, face the prospect of bilingualization—both to comply with government regulations and to increase the pool of prospective clients.

PROMOTION AND STRATEGY

Artventure relies primarily on word-of-mouth and print advertising to generate awareness. Eileen and Tina believe that their attempts at advertising have been unsuccessful. In trying to increase growth in the number of clientele, Artventure advertised in a weekly newspaper, *The Suburban*; this publication, delivered at no cost to residents, has a circulation of 101 000, with approximately 41 000 distributed to homes on the West Island and the remainder in the other English sectors of Greater Montreal. Artventure feels, however, that the cost is relatively high compared to the results obtained. A one-quarter-page advertisement costs $600. They also advertised in the weekly *Canadian Jewish News*. The circulation of the Montreal edition of this newspaper is 18 735 households, and 96% are paid subscriptions. A quarter-page ad costs $320 for a maximum of four insertions. Beginning in November 1998 they placed advertisements in each issue of *Montreal Families* at a cost of $400 per insertion. *Montreal Families*, like *The Suburban*, is distributed free of charge at pickup points every other month in both the West Island and the English-speaking sectors of Greater Montreal. Circulation for *Montreal Families* is 25 000. Finally, Artventure uses a mailing list of about 300 families.

Artventure's strategy is to provide top-quality creative programs and parties at a price that "will not burn a hole in parents' pockets." The activities they offer—drama, art, dance, and music—do not require expensive apparatus. Expensive apparatus do not necessarily capture a child's attention, Eileen and Tina believe. In addition to their advertising in *The Suburban*, Artventure also offers discounts of up to 15% on the price of its programs to those parents who register their children early or who bring a friend. The service component of their strategy is to develop strong relationships with parents, subcontractors, suppliers, and with the children who participate in the activities. They take into consideration the different schedules and needs of the different age groups and design programs to suit clients. Services are unique and not repetitive, and entertainment services are included in party packages. Exhibit 5 shows Artventure's income statement, and Exhibit 6 is a copy of the balance sheet. (In the first year of operation, Eileen and Tina did not take a salary from the business. Their 1999 salary was paid by an agency of the provincial government in the context of a program designed to encourage small business and entrepreneurship.)

EXHIBIT 5	Artventure Income Statement, Year Ended April 30, 1999*		
Sales			$46 633
Less: Cost of sales			$ 23 841
Gross operating profit			$ 22 792
Less: Sales expenses		$ 5 014	
Less: Rent		$17 592	
Less: Administrative expenses		$ 4 200	$26 806
Net profit (loss)			($ 4 014)

*In their first year of operation, Eileen and Tina were paid an "off-balance sheet" salary by an agency of the provincial government. This subsidy was designed to promote entrepreneurship and small business in the province. This subsidy was available for only the first year of operation.

EXHIBIT 6	**Artventure Balance Sheet** as at April 30, 1999

Assets

Current Assets

Bank account	$ 5 000
Startup expenses	$ 0
Deposit−rent	$ 2 800
Total current assets	$ 7 800

Fixed Assets

Incorporation	$ 610
Betterment	$ 4 000
Art equipment and accessories	$ 9 028
Office equipment	$ 1 265
Party equipment	$ 3 180
Computer equipment	$ 4 000
Less: Accumulated depreciation	($ 2 000)
Total fixed assets	$ 20 083
Total assets	**$27 883**

Liabilities

Current Liabilities

Accounts payable	$ 0
Current portion of long-term debt	$ 3 000

Long-Term Liabilities

Long-term debt	$ 0
Total Liabilities	**$ 3 000**

Equity

Young promoters grant	$ 12 000
Capital investment	$ 16 897
Loss from operations	($ 4 014)
Total equity	**$24 883**
Total liabilities and equity	**$27 883**

At this point, Eileen and Tina have completed one year of operation and they are wondering whether they are on the right track. They had heard about the planned opening of Childzplay Party Centre in October, in their shopping centre. This venture, a 279 square metre entertainment haven, "will be replete with all number of attractions for kids under 10 including in-line skating, floor hockey, dance, jewellery making, magic, cartooning, animals, slides, a magic store, an earth ball, and a multitude of fun-filled activities. Childzplay will also be mommy-friendly with a cafe bistro where tired parents can sip on a cappuccino or nibble on a dessert while watching the kids explore the centre." They wondered about the possible effect on their business of this new arrival, and what else they should be doing to ensure the long-run survival of their business. Should they, for example, take their activity centre to schools and cruise ships? What they did not want to do was to develop their centre into a computer games arcade. A computer games strategy was not part of their vision. They also believed that these games did not stimulate the creativity and self-esteem that they wanted to develop in children. They believed that they had a winning formula with their services, but they wondered whether they had a sustainable strategy.

Notes

1. In Quebec, a student makes the following progression through the educational system: kindergarten, primary, secondary, CEGEP, and university. Marie-Victorin College is a CEGEP, and one normally attends for two years. CEGEP is an acronym for Collège d'enseignement général et professionnel.

Rocky Mountain House Co-op

Thomas Funk

Frank Gallagher, general manager of Rocky Mountain House Co-op (RMHC) was sitting in his office reviewing the performance of his organization when Milt Zirk, petroleum manager of the company, hurried into the room. "Frank, I'm afraid I've got some bad news," exclaimed Milt. "The word is out that United Farmers of Alberta is planning to open a new petroleum outlet in Rocky Mountain House. The petroleum end of our business has been going fairly well for us over the past couple of years. This could really mess things up! You know they are very aggressive marketers, and because they are a co-op like us, they could really eat into our market share. Frank, I'm worried! We're going to have to make sure we're ready for them. We've got to develop a plan to minimize their impact on our sales and profits."

ROCKY MOUNTAIN HOUSE CO-OP

Rocky Mountain House Co-op is a retail outlet located in Rocky Mountain House, Alberta, approximately 80 kilometres west of Red Deer, on Highway 11. Rocky

Mountain House is a community of approximately 6000 people with both an agricultural and commercial economic base. The area is characterized by mixed farming with most farms being relatively small and having at least some livestock. Industry in the area includes general business, trucking, construction, oil exploration, and logging.

The trading area served by RMHC is much larger than Rocky Mountain House itself and contains the following communities: Alder Flats, Alhambra, Caroline, Condor, Leslieville, Nordegg, Rocky Mountain House and Stauffer. The trading area has an approximate population of 16 000 people and a radius of 50 kilometres although the trading area on the west extends nearly 100 kilometres to the Rocky Mountains. Exhibit 1 shows the Rocky Mountain House trading area.

RMHC is a cooperative type business. Cooperatives are like regular businesses except they are owned by their users who purchase shares in the business. Instead of earning "profits" cooperatives earn "savings" which can be returned to members through "patronage dividends." RMHC is owned by 7332 active members. For the most part, these "owners" are people in the trading area who have become members by purchasing shares in the organization. Each share is valued at $1 and a minimum of five shares must be purchased to become a member. The main reason for being a member is to share in the savings of the business through patronage dividends. Patronage dividends are based on the amount of business a member does each year and have amounted to about 5% of purchases at RMHC over the past several years. In addition, members have a voice in the affairs of the co-op through their right to elect a board of directors to represent their views.

EXHIBIT 1	Rocky Mountain House Trading Area

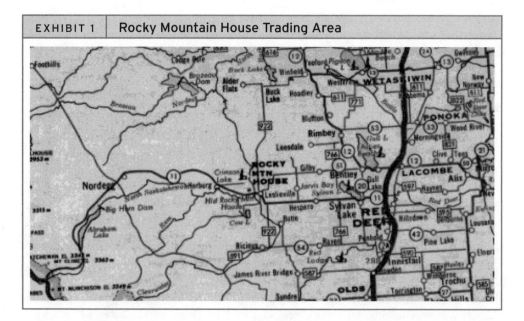

RMHC is involved in a number of retail businesses that they classify under three divisions: Home Centre, Shopping Centre, and Petroleum. The Home Centre consists of building materials, hardware, animal health products, livestock feed, livestock equipment, and twine; the Shopping Centre consists of food, hardware, clothing, and a cafeteria; and the

Petroleum Division consists of bulk fuels, propane, oil/lubes, cardlock, and a gas bar. Despite the fact that Rocky Mountain House is in a significant grain producing area of the province, RMHC has elected so far not to sell crop supplies. Sales, cost of goods sold, and gross margins for each division for 1995 are shown in Exhibit 2. Exhibit 3 shows the operating statement of RMHC for the same year.

EXHIBIT 2	Product Line Breakdown		
	Home Centre	Shopping Centre	Petroleum
Sales	$4 620 000	$11 044 000	$2 550 000
Less: Cost of goods sold	$3 536 000	$ 8 418 000	$2 294 000
Gross margin	$1 084 000	$ 2 626 000	$ 256 000
Less: Operating expenses	$ 931 000	$ 2106 000	$ 189 000
Contribution	$ 153 000	$ 520 000	$ 67 000

EXHIBIT 3	Operating Statement
Sales	$ 18 214 000
Less: Cost of goods sold	$14 248 000
Gross margin	$ 3 966 000
Less: Operating expenses	$ 3 226 000
Contribution	$ 740 000
Less: Indirect interest expense	($ 96 000)
Less: General overhead	$ 432 000
Savings	$ 404 000
Patronage dividends from federated co-ops	$ 683 000
Retained savings	$ 1 087 000

In 1995, RMHC received patronage dividends of $683 000 from Federated Co-operatives Limited in Saskatoon, the large wholesaling cooperative owned by several hundred local co-ops like RMHC across Western Canada. Like most other local co-ops, RMHC used Federated Co-op as their main source of supply for all products they sold. The patronage dividend they received from Federated was based on a percentage of purchases. In the same year, RMHC allocated $614 000 in patronage dividends to local owners. This, together with current savings, left RHHC with retained savings of slightly more than $1 million. This represented funds the organization could use for future expansion.

PETROLEUM DIVISION

The petroleum division of RMHC has always been a tough business. Margins in the petroleum division are much lower than in other areas of the company largely due to intense competition and the commodity-type products being sold. In the Rocky Mountain House trading area alone there are six major oil companies competing for a total fuel market of approximately 26.9 million litres. Exhibit 4 lists the major petroleum companies with facilities in Rocky Mountain House and their approximate fuel sales.

EXHIBIT 4	Competitive Petroleum Suppliers
	Estimated Litres
Co-op	5 900 000
Esso	7 500 000
Shell	4 000 000
Petro-Canada	3 500 000
Turbo	3 500 000
Husky	2 500 000
Total	26 900 000

Most of the 26.9 million litres of petroleum sold in the Rocky Mountain House trading area went to commercial accounts. Commercial accounts purchased 18.3 million litres in 1995 in contrast to 6.1 million litres to farm accounts and 2.5 million litres to consumers. Although precise market shares were not known, Milt estimated that Co-op and Esso were the major petroleum suppliers in the area followed by Shell, Petro-Canada, Turbo, and Husky. Exhibit 5 shows approximate market shares for each company by type of account.

EXHIBIT 5	Approximate Market Shares by Type of Account			
	Farm	Commercial	Consumer	Total
Co-op	34%	17%	30%	23%
Esso	31%	27%	27%	28%
Shell	13%	15%	16%	15%
Petro-Canada	6%	17%	4%	13%
Turbo	12%	13%	13%	13%
Husky	4%	11%	10%	9%
	100%	100%	100%	100%

RMHC currently sells four product lines in petroleum: bulk fuels, propane, oil/lubes, and gas bar (self-service pumps at the Shopping Centre). Sales, cost of goods sold, and gross margins for these products in 1995 are shown in Exhibit 6. Exhibit 7 shows the petroleum department expenses for the same year.

EXHIBIT 6	Financial Summary for Petroleum Products				
	Fuels	Propane	Oil/Lubes	Gas Bar	Total
Sales	$2 016 000	$ 41 000	$126 000	$367 000	$2 550 000
Cost of goods	$1 829 000	$34 000	$106 000	$325 000	$2 294 000
Gross margin	$ 187 000	$ 7 000	$ 20 000	$ 42 000	$ 256 000

EXHIBIT 7	Petroleum Department Expenses
Depreciation	$ 5 600
Utilities	$ 500
Insurance	$ 4 900
Repairs and maintenance	$ 9 000
Taxes and licences	$ 4 600
Total standby costs	**$ 24 600**
Employee benefits	$ 18 000
Staff discounts	$ 1 600
Training	$ 1 800
Salaries and wages	$ 99 000
Uniforms	$ 1 500
Total staff costs	**$ 121 900**
Advertising and promotion	$ 5 600
Delivery trucks	$ 29 000
Other expenses	$ 7 900
Total operating costs	**$189 000**
Contribution	**$ 67 000**

Like most petroleum suppliers in the area, RMHC sells five types of petroleum products: premium gasoline, regular gasoline, clear diesel, marked gasoline, and marked diesel. Exhibit 8 shows 1995 sales of the five products in each of the major markets while Exhibit 9 shows current pricing for each product in each major market. Marked gasoline and marked diesel are dyed purple to identify them as-tax exempt because they are used for off-road purposes and not subject to normal fuel taxes. At the moment, this means marked fuels sell for approximately $0.09 per litre less than clear fuels which are intended for on-road use and subject to a road tax. The prices established by RMHC are very similar to other petroleum suppliers in the area. Only Turbo and Husky sell petroleum at lower prices than other companies in the area and, in both cases the differences are very small.

| EXHIBIT 8 | Petroleum Sales by Market (in Litres) | | | |

	Farm	Commercial	Consumer	Total
Premium gasoline			16 500	16 500
Regular gasoline	200 000	1 173 000	666 500	2 039 500
Clear diesel		1 154 000	63 000	1 217 000
Marked gasoline	949 000	50 000		999 000
Marked diesel	937 000	736 000		1 673 000
Total	**2 086 000**	**3 113 000**	**746 000**	**5 945 000**

| EXHIBIT 9 | Petroleum Prices by Market | | |

	Farm	Commercial	Consumer
Premium gasoline			$0.540
Regular gasoline	$0.495	$0.480	$0.500
Clear diesel		$0.390	$0.420
Marked gasoline	$0.403	$0.390	
Marked diesel	$0.300	$0.300	

Margins on petroleum products do not vary by type of product, but do vary by type of customer. Current margins in the farm market are $0.049 per litre; in the commercial market $0.034 per litre; and in the consumer market $0.063 per litre.

In the petroleum end of the business, RMHC deals with three main types of customers: farms accounts, commercial accounts, and consumers.

At the moment, RMHC has about 350 farm accounts which purchase 2 086 000 litres of fuel. Although the average farm account purchases about 6000 litres of fuel each year, some purchase much larger amounts and many purchase much smaller amounts. The largest RMHC farm account purchases nearly 20 000 litres of fuel a year. Farms in the RMHC trading area are somewhat smaller than typical Alberta farms. A very high proportion of these farms have livestock as their principle operation.

Commercial accounts represent the major proportion of RMHC petroleum business. At the moment, RMHC has 175 commercial accounts which together purchase approximately 3 113 000 litres of fuel and range in size from 5000 litres per year to as much as 300 000 litres per year. The average commercial account buys 18 000 litres. Exhibit 10 provides a breakdown of commercial accounts into various types of businesses.

EXHIBIT 10	Types of Commercial Accounts	
Type of Account		**Percentage**
General business		29%
Loggers		11%
Truckers		18%
Construction		17%
Oil company contractors		22%
Institutional		3%

The final category of customer is individual consumers which currently purchase 746 000 litres of fuel. About 80% of consumer sales are through the gas bar at the Shopping Centre and the remaining 20% are through the cardlock system, described below.

Although all three type of accounts (farm, commercial, and consumer) can use the cardlock system, it is very popular among commercial accounts. The cardlock system allows approved buyers to have 24-hour access to bulk fuels at the main RMHC petroleum outlet. To obtain fuel, the buyer inserts a card into a metering device which then pumps the requested amount of a certain type of fuel into the user's tank. The user's name and the amount of the purchase are recorded electronically for future billing. Use of this system is growing very rapidly among farm and commercial accounts because of convenience and cost savings. The price of fuel purchased through the cardlock is generally $0.008 per litre less than bulk delivery. Although RMHC has a good, very clean cardlock operation, there are two problems that make it less than ideal. One problem is the fact that currently it does not sell marked gasoline and does not have the capability of adding this product into the existing system. This undoubtedly prevents some potential customers from using the RMHC cardlock. Another problem with the cardlock is that access to the facility is a little more difficult than some customers would like.

At the moment, the marketing program used by RMHC is fairly similar to that used by other petroleum suppliers in the area. In 1995, less than $6000 per year was being spent on advertising petroleum products. Most of this was for ads placed in local papers highlighting special deals on oils and lubricants (see Appendix A for a sample ad). In addition to advertising, a substantial amount of selling is done by Milt on farms, at the offices of commercial accounts, and on the phone. Milt maintains contact at least four times a year with most customers, and more often with larger customers. Some very large customers are contacted on a weekly basis. In addition, he spends a considerable amount of time calling on prospective customers. Milt's philosophy is that regular contact with prospects will put him in contention for their business if there is ever a reason for a customer to switch. History shows this to be a good strategy, as RMHC has picked up a number of new customers each year when they became dissatisfied with their present supplier. Customer loyalty in petroleum, however, is very high. Milt figures that less than 10% of customers change suppliers each year. Milt also follows the practice of driving the delivery truck himself on occasion so he can have more contact with customers.

Frank and Milt have long thought that the success of RMHC in the petroleum business was due to a number of factors:

- The company provides excellent service. All people working for RMHC are topnotch individuals committed to providing good service. In addition, the company prides itself on clean, modern facilities and prompt attention to detail. Any customer who needs fuel can expect to receive it the same day an order is placed. RMHC currently spends more than its competitors on staff training.

- Co-op products are quality products produced under strict quality control measures.

- Patronage refunds provide customers with "cash back" at the end of the year based on their volume of business. For many customers this is a real incentive to do business with a co-op.

- The company has an excellent highway location in Rocky Mountain House. This provides excellent visibility in the community.

- RMHC offers a very wide range of products making "one stop shopping" possible for customers.

UNITED FARMERS OF ALBERTA

United Farmers of Alberta (UFA), like RMHC, is a member-owned cooperative. UFA has approximately 30 outlets in Alberta in which they sell petroleum and a complete line of farm supplies. In addition, they operate approximately 90 outlets in which only petroleum products are sold through bulk plants, cardlocks, and gas bars. UFA has shown considerable growth in recent years through very aggressive marketing. This growth has come both from an increase in the number of retail distribution points as well as an increase in the volume sold through existing outlets.

Recently, UFA was granted a development permit to build a farm supply facility in Rocky Mountain House. The permit allows UFA to construct a facility that contains: a 204 square metre building, bulk petroleum plant, gas bar, cardlock, and farm supply distribution facility. It is expected that UFA will sell a complete line of both crop and livestock farm supplies through this facility. It is also expected that UFA will construct a cardlock facility that is larger than any other in the area and will sell a compete line of fuels.

The entry of UFA into this market has the potential of causing significant problems for RMHC for a number of reasons:

- UFA is a co-op like RMHC and therefore very similar in structure and philosophy. As a result, they might be considered a good alternative for many current RMHC customers.

- The fact that they are building a complete farm supply outlet might be attractive to many current RMHC customers who would like to purchase crop supplies where they buy petroleum.

- UFA's facility will be much newer than that of RMHC. This is of particular concern for the cardlock.

- UFA currently has a number of commercial accounts on the fringes of the RMHC trading area. This gives them a foothold into the market.

- UFA has demonstrated a willingness in similar situations to enter new markets in a very aggressive manner. Often this entails aggressive pricing, introductory advertising in local media, a direct mail campaign targeted to larger potential customers, and special introductory deals.

- UFA traditionally supports its marketing efforts with a high level of excellent service. This includes the availability of skilled technical experts who can answer questions and help customers make informed buying decisions, attention to detail in all aspects of the business, and frequent sales calls (either by phone or in person) with key customers.

DECISION

Although at first Frank was not overly concerned about the situation, as he considered it in more detail, he began to worry about the effects it might have. RMHC had worked hard over the last ten years to build a strong customer base and some of this investment in time and marketing dollars appeared to be at risk. To determine the seriousness of the situation, and to develop some plans to counteract it, Frank called a meeting with Milt for early the next week.

The meeting began by Frank raising the issue of what impact the entry of UFA might have on RMHC. After some discussion, the two men agreed that if RMHC did nothing to soften the impact, it was conceivable they could lose a significant portion of both their farm and commercial business, especially the larger accounts that were more price-sensitive. Although it was hard to come up with specific numbers, they felt that up to a quarter of their present volume might be at risk. What was even more alarming was the fact that RMHC had three very large commercial customers who each purchased 300 000 litres of fuel a year. Losing these people alone would result in a very large sales decline. Although these large commercial accounts had been with RMHC for a number of years, and Milt provided a high level of personal service through almost weekly contact, it was conceivable they could switch allegiance if they perceived greater value in an alternative supplier.

Given the seriousness of the situation, they then began to discuss alternative courses of action they might pursue to counteract the problem. A number of possibilities were identified and briefly discussed.

1. The first idea that came to mind was to pursue a preemptive pricing strategy. Under this strategy, RMHC would begin immediately cutting prices and margins to existing customers. The idea behind this strategy, of course, was to solidify business relationships with customers to the point that it would make it very difficult for UFA to be successful in taking customers from RMHC.

2. A second strategy they discussed was to match UFA's promotional programs dollar for dollar and engage in a substantial amount of local advertising and direct marketing themselves. Although neither Frank nor Milt had a precise idea of what UFA would spend entering the Rocky Mountain House market, they felt $30 000 was not an unrealistic amount. They considered stressing two main points in the promotion: their excellent staff and their outstanding record of providing patronage dividends. Frank envisioned ads and direct mail pieces with pictures and human interest stories about the staff as well as charts showing the steady growth in patronage dividends over the past few years.

3. Another idea they considered was to develop a program in which the rate of patronage dividends would vary by department. Under such a scheme it would be possible for the petroleum division, for example, to announce a patronage dividend of 8% where some other division's dividend might decline to 3%. They felt this might be particularly effective in the short run to meet a competitive challenge.

4. Yet another alternative they were considering was to get into the fertilizer and ag chemical business. On the assumption that some RMHC customers might be attracted to UFA because they had a complete line of crop and livestock supplies, this might provide existing customers with enough reason to stay with RMHC. It would, however, be a major investment for RMHC in a business they knew little about. Frank estimated it would require an investment of approximately $600 000 in facilities and working capital. In addition, two new full-time people would be required to run the business and work with farm customers. An additional five seasonal employees would be needed for a couple of months each year to help during peak sales seasons. Total additional labour costs would amount to approximately $150 000 plus another $50 000 in administrative costs. Margins on fertilizer were typically in the 15 to 20% range on product which sold for an average price of $250 per ton (1 ton = 0.9 tonne). Although an average farmer in the Rocky Mountain House trading area currently used only 25 to 30 tons of fertilizer a year, use appeared to be growing fairly rapidly as more farmers started using fertilizer and those already using fertilizer were increasing application rates. Ag chemicals were not widely used in the Rocky Mountain House trading area, so this would be considered a breakeven business which simply provided a complementary service to farmers who purchased fertilizer. Presently there are three fertilizer suppliers serving the 1200 farmers in the Rocky Mountain House trading area. One of these suppliers is a large independent farm supply outlet specializing in crop inputs while the other two are smaller operations, one of which is the local Esso dealer.

5. The final alternative Frank identified was to move up construction of a new bulk petroleum facility. The current facility was old and starting to show its age. Of particular concern was the fact that the cardlock system had reached its capacity and could not add a tank and pumping system for marked gasoline. Frank knew that the new UFA facility would be "state of the art" and have ample capacity for the present and for future expansion. Although Frank hoped to get another five years out of the present facility, he felt one option was to invest immediately in new facilities so they would be ready at least by the time the UFA facility was built. A new facility, which would include a new bulk plant, an expanded sales area, and a new and expanded cardlock, would cost $300 000 to construct.

Frank and Milt concluded the meeting wondering what to do. They agreed to consider the options more fully and do some real thinking about the consequences of each option and then meet again in a week to make a decision.

Appendix A

ROCKY MOUNTAIN HOUSE CO-OP AD

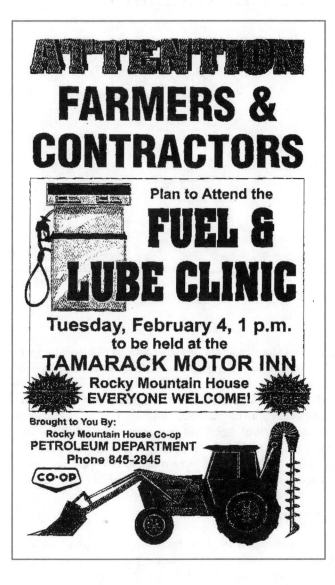

Steinhouse Knitting Mills (Canada) Ltd.

*Mark Haber and
Christopher A. Ross*

In the fall of 1999, Abraham (Abe) Steinhouse and his son Mark were wondering what action they should take regarding their knitting business. Steinhouse Knitting specialized in the manufacture and sale of men's sweaters. In 1998, annual sales were $2.7 million. In 1999, with overheads at about $100 000 per month, excluding management salaries, estimated annual sales were approximately $2.4 million (U.S. sales excluded). This latter figure was approximately 30% of their 1988 peak sales of $7.5 million. Since 1988, sales had been declining steadily. In 1993, for example, annual sales were $3.5 million. Both Abe and Mark felt that changes had to be made to the operations of the business in order to reverse this downward trend and ensure the survival of the business.

HISTORY OF THE COMPANY

Abe's father founded Steinhouse Knitting in 1929. He had been trained as a knitter. He began operations making babies' wear—romper sets—in the back of a store, with 12 square metres of space. He had a great sense of quality, though, according to Abe, he did not have a great sense of fashion. He manufactured babies' wear because he liked it. He also felt that the babies' wear industry was not as competitive as the ladies' or men's wear industries. While he made the outfits at the back, his wife sold at the front.

Abe was still in high school when he started the business in 1952. He took care of invoicing, the payroll, and some of the bookkeeping. As he became familiar with the business he realized that there was a low upper limit to price in the children's sweater business. For example, while price points for children's sweaters were $3.95 to $4.95 at retail, the price points for men's sweaters were $10.95 to $12.95. As a result, he started making more and more men's sweaters.

By the time Abe was 17, the company had a staff of 20 employees working in 279 square metres of space. At this time too, Abe began working as a salesperson selling to independent stores. In 1957, Abe graduated from university. By 1958, the physical space for the business had grown to 1115 square metres and it was located on St. Lawrence Street, Montreal. In 1960, annual sales were $500 000. By 1967, Abe had started visiting Europe looking for new styles and had also started to buy sophisticated computerized knitting machines.

By 1986, the business was well established, profitable, and successful. There was enough money for the family to live comfortably. In August of that year, Mark Steinhouse, Abe's son, joined the business. Mark had graduated in industrial psychology from McGill University in Montreal. He entered the business immediately after graduating and has never worked in any other business. His cousin was in charge of production and Mark worked in shipping, cutting, and sewing. After gaining experience and knowledge of the inner workings of the business, Mark went out to sell. He sold to independent men's wear stores for three years, a total of six selling seasons in all. Mark is 36 years old and Abe is 64 years old.

In 1988, with sales at $7.5 million, including imports, and approximately 50 employees, the owners made the decision to move from St. Lawrence Street to an owned location. The company had been on St. Lawrence Street for 30 years. They built their own plant and moved, in May 1989, to Chabanel Street, in Montreal. In that same year, the company made a brief and unsuccessful foray into the U.S. market. The company hired two sales representatives, one in New York and the other in New Jersey. These two salespeople were successful in bringing in new business but one of them was caught in fraudulent activities. Steinhouse Knitting lost about US$65 000. After this event, the company exited the U.S. market in 1991.

In 1990 Abe bought his sister's share of the business. She and her son left the company. Steinhouse Knitting continued as usual with Abe's father, Abe, and Mark as the management team. Steinhouse Knitting reentered the U.S. market in 1996, and by 1998 sales in that market was US$250 000.

In December 1997, the management of Steinhouse Knitting invited a family friend, Jacob Lieberman, to use part of their facilities as the head office of his sport-shirt manufacturing business, Styles JMD. The motivation behind this move was symbiotic: Styles JMD would benefit from economies of scale and Steinhouse Knitting would have a modern brand name, which also generated financial benefits. Steinhouse's executives owned 50% of JMD and financed the complete operation. The two businesses operated separately, although the owners shared ideas and overheads such as secretarial help, sales people, and computing facilities. Styles JMD paid Steinhouse 5% of sales in lieu of rent and overhead. All manufacturing for the shirt business, however, was subcontracted. In 1998, the year that Abe's father passed away, annual Canadian sales for Steinhouse Knitting were $2.7

million. By 1999, the sales of JMD shirts were about equal to the sales of Steinhouse's sweaters. Styles JMD also imported a small quantity of sweaters from Asia. Like Steinhouse Knitting, the customers of Styles JMD were also independent men's clothing stores in Canada and in the United States.

PRODUCT

Steinhouse Knitting manufactures and sells high-quality men's sweaters. The company produces three different brands: Steinhouse, Etcetera and España. Customers perceive España as having the highest quality and price. However, for the three brands, the company does not differentiate on the basis of style, price, or fabrication.

Currently 80% of the yarn used in making the sweaters is sourced from one supplier in Toronto. All the yarn is NAFTA-approved. Consequently, Steinhouse Knitting does not pay any duties on sweaters shipped to the United States. When the yarn arrives at the factory door, it is knitted, washed, and finished. Fabric softener is then added. It is also pressed flat, even, and smooth. Employees cut the sweaters one at a time. They are then sewn, cleaned, and tagged prior to shipping. In total there are 27 operations involved in making a sweater. Mark commented on the process, "[Our sweaters are] cut piece by piece as opposed to cutting in piles. That is one of the differences between a quality sweater and a so-so sweater. There are lots of differences among brands apart from the yarn. For example, an inexpensive manufacturer will not finish the sweater properly, and then when you buy the sweater it will shrink 10 to 15%. We take out the shrinkage; we tumble it with softener, so it is treated. We cut them one by one, so that each line will fall where it is supposed to fall. An inexpensive manufacturer will pile the material to cut and then when the sweaters are cut, the top one and the bottom one are off-centre."

Steinhouse Knitting has not changed its raw material inputs for the sweaters in the last ten years. All sweaters for the fall line are 70% acrylic and 30% wool. The fall line contributes 85% to annual sales. In the spring, the sweaters are 50% cotton and 50% acrylic. Management believed that their product quality was very good. There was a problem, however, in people's perception of acrylic. Most people cannot tell the difference between acrylic and wool, but when they read the manufacturer's label on a sweater and see "acrylic," they perceive a cheaper garment. However, the sweaters of Steinhouse Knitting are in the upper price ranges. There appears, therefore, to be an inconsistency between what customers perceive and the price points at which the sweaters are sold. Adding more wool is a possible solution to this problem. Even 5% angora, alpaca, or linen may make a difference, according to Mark. Abe pointed out, however, that European manufacturers used the same type of yarn as Steinhouse Knitting and that in the United States the image of acrylic was improving.

Steinhouse Knitting produces most of its sweaters to order. During the selling season, the salespeople visit the customers and book orders. All the orders are then entered into a computer, yarn is bought, and the orders are produced. Sometimes the company may have yarn in inventory ahead of time because, from experience, they may know what is popular. For example, there may be black sweaters in 20 different styles, so they may order 10 000 pounds (4536 kilograms) of black yarn. However, when the salesperson deposits the order with the company, Steinhouse begins production with inventoried raw material and does not wait until the yarn arrives. Thus, the company may purchase yarns ahead of time when they believe that the risk is minimal. It takes six to eight weeks to receive the yarn once the company places the order.

Steinhouse Knitting normally finishes the fall line at the beginning of January. From January to March, the factory is practically at a standstill. Only the principal employees are retained. The company may knit a few styles that they are confident will sell in the next period. Consequently, they will have some styles in stock, ahead of time. In past years, 10 to 15% of sweaters were knitted in advance.

The company makes about 30 different styles per season. Each style might be made in a polo, a cardigan, a crewneck, and a V-neck, and each might have four different colours, in four sizes. If the style is sized in "bigs and talls," these add eight more sizes. As a consequence, the company has many stock-keeping units (SKUs). The large number of SKUs sometimes results in inefficiencies, especially if the demand is only for a small quantity. About 10% of the SKUs are responsible for 50% of annual sales. In a few cases, only 100 sweaters may be made of a style. The company makes to order, but the order is rounded up to the nearest dozen. Thus, if an order is for 7.5 dozen, the company will make 8 dozen. If, subsequently, a retailer calls and requests additional sweaters and they are in stock, Steinhouse will ship them, but they will not make only one or two sweaters for a retailer. Retailers are therefore taking a chance that their order might not be able to be filled if they call for just one or two sweaters.

Like many other manufacturers in this industry, Steinhouse Knitting does not have an in-house designer. Prior to 1967, the company borrowed ideas for different styles of sweaters from competitors, from store displays, or from magazines. After a while, Steinhouse management began making annual trips to Europe to look at fashions and to examine different styles of sweaters. All the fashion in sweaters originates in Europe, according to Abe and Mark. Abe and Mark usually visit different European countries, shop at different stores, meet at some agreed point, and compare purchases. For the fall season of 1999, for example, they purchased upwards of 50 sweaters in Europe. Upon returning to Canada, they incorporate the best fashion ideas and colours into their own products while keeping their customers in mind. Because the equipment and machinery in Steinhouse Knitting is different from what is available in Europe, the products they make do not look exactly like the samples purchased.

Abe believes that the fashion business is like no other and that many factors determine the different trends. Men's sweaters are not as fashionable as they were, even five years ago. The fact that yarn is still at the same price it was 15 years ago indicates the market. The weather also determines the level of sweater sales. For the last three years in western Canada, for example, the winters were unseasonably warm. On the upside, in Europe, men's sweaters are becoming popular. It also seems that the name-brand concept may be weakening. This may benefit Steinhouse.

CUSTOMERS

Steinhouse customers are largely independent clothing stores. Steinhouse also sells to some stores with four or five outlets, and to Ernest with 34 stores and to Bovet with 22 stores. Ernest and Bovet are private-brand sales and account for 20% of Steinhouse's annual sales. Quebec and Ontario account for 30% of sales each, 5% of sales goes to the Maritimes, 10% goes to Alberta, and the rest goes to Manitoba, Saskatchewan, and British

Columbia. The typical order size is $1500. A few larger customers may buy $10 000, and a few smaller customers may buy only $800. Retailers will sometimes call for one or two sweaters if a client is asking for a special size or colour and they are out of stock.

Management believes that the independent stores are quickly disappearing (Exhibit 1). In Mark's experience there is almost a constant stream of bankruptcies among these stores. Mark believes that their customers are disappearing because of competition from category killers such as Wal-Mart and Price-Costco, and strong, established brand names such as Hilfiger, Polo, Nautica, and Point Zero. Very little effort has been made to sell to other types of customers. Steinhouse Knitting did try to win Simons as a customer, but was not successful. Simons imports most of its sweaters from low-wage countries. "We cannot compete against Chinese and Bangladeshi prices, and these and similar countries are the major source for stores such as Simons. We are the supplier of last resort," Abe said.

EXHIBIT 1	Men's Clothing Store Sales
Year	**Sales (000 000)**
1999	1536.4
1998	1581.7
1997	1569.5
1996	1516.0
1995	1623.0
1994	1848.1
1993	1756.3
1992	1622.5
1991	1703.2
1990	2202.0

Note: In 1999, department stores generated 27.1% of men's clothing store sales, discount stores generated 16.5%, apparel specialty chain stores generated 31%, independent apparel stores generated 14.1%, and all other outlets generated 11.3%.

Source: Statistics Canada CANSIM database, Matrix 2400, 1999.

Steinhouse Knitting does not do any market studies. Customers, for example, are not consulted before Steinhouse management makes their annual trip to Europe. From experience, the company believes that a major influence on the purchasing behaviour of their retail customers is the previous year's sales. Retailers examine what was popular last year and tend to buy similar styles. Another influence on purchasing behaviour is the business climate at the time the sales representative makes a sales call. The company believes that, in general, the sales representative who calls on the retailer first gets most of the business. The company has some sense of the kind of consumers who purchase sweaters from the independent retailers. Again, because of long experience in the industry and good communication with their retailers, the management of Steinhouse Knitting believes that women purchase most of the men's sweaters, for their husbands or boyfriends. Women probably purchase 75% of all men's sweaters. "We believe that most of the women are over 40 years old because at our retail prices, they must have income levels that are moderate to better," Abe said.

A recent trend among customers is the growing popularity of the "big and tall" sizes. About 20% of Steinhouse sales in 1999 was "big and tall" sizes. The cause of this popularity is not known for sure—customers may be getting bigger. Another problem is the trend to "dressing down" or what is sometimes called "casual days." Because of increasing informality at work, customers are buying fewer suits, and suits are what brought many customers into the store. For many stores, suits accounted for 40 or 50% of sales. Accessories like sweaters, shirts, ties, handkerchiefs, and socks accounted for the other 50%. Because men buy fewer suits, they visit men's wear stores less frequently and therefore they also buy fewer accessories such as sweaters. Furthermore, casual days also result in men buying fewer dressy sweaters. The weather over the last few years has also hurt business.

Both Abe and Mark also observed that customers were increasingly demanding higher-gauge, lighter sweaters made of natural fibres such as wool and cotton. Sweaters can be made in different gauges such as eight-, ten-, or twelve-gauge, for example. The higher the gauge, the finer the knitting and the lighter the sweater. This move to higher-gauge sweaters by customers is believed to be suitable for today. Fashion dictates change and thus other-gauge sweaters eventually appear. While their current machinery can knit natural fibres, the machines cannot produce higher gauges of knit. Thus, substantial retooling would be necessary and new machinery would be required if Steinhouse Knitting were to take advantage of this new demand. To convert all their machinery is a major investment. One of the biggest changes taking place in the industry is in the area of technology. Steinhouse's machinery can be programmed in a matter of hours, not a week as in the past, for example. New machines can be programmed to make the whole garment. They can also put the V-neck and button-holes in sweaters. These machines are, however, very slow and costly. The yarn has to be perfect. The price of this kind of yarn is high and it is not always available in North America. Abe believes that at the present time none of these machines are running in North America. The last time the company put money into machinery was about six years ago when they bought two new knitting machines. The capital cost for modern knitting machines is about $250 000 to $300 000 each. Steinhouse needs about 20 machines but is hesitant to purchase these in this market. Compounding the problem is Steinhouse's large inventory of acrylic/wool fibres that cannot just be disposed of, although they expect to reduce it to a reasonable level.

PROMOTION

Steinhouse Knitting depends largely on commission salespeople to promote its products. Salespeople in Montreal are provided with an office, and paid a straight commission. In Canada, the company has salespeople all across the country: one in the Maritime provinces, three in Quebec, three in Ontario, one in the Prairie provinces, one in Alberta, and one in British Columbia. They pay their own expenses and the company pays them commissions upon delivery of goods to the customer. The average commission rate is 7.5%, which is standard in the men's wear industry. If the salespeople discount prices to a customer, their commission is reduced. The company uses a sliding scale. For example, a discount of 10% reduces a salesperson's commission to 3%.

The salespeople visit customers twice a year—once for the fall line and once for the spring line. They do not do any servicing of customers between those two selling seasons. In the opinion of the salespeople it does not pay to visit customers at any other time. A sales booking season lasts from about four to six weeks, so the salespeople work for about three months of the year. For the rest of the year they are free to do whatever they wish.

Mark concluded, "I don't believe that our declining sales is because of our sales force. I believe that we have very good salespeople. In general, I am happy with our sales reps. I can't really blame it on them. They are pretty much stuck with the stores they have. Our reps sell to independent stores. Each one of those guys is losing market share—whether it is in British Columbia, northern Ontario, Toronto, Alberta, the Prairie provinces, or wherever. It is no secret that they are getting hurt by the same people we are getting hurt by."

The principal salesperson in Montreal recruited the salespeople in the United States. He called the U.S. accounts where Steinhouse Knitting was doing business and he obtained references about possible candidates for the job. As in Canada, commission salespeople are standard in the United States, except that a national sales manager might be hired. According to Mark, the hardest part about selling in the United States is finding good sales representatives. Current sales for the company in the U.S. are $250 000 and one person is responsible for about 85% of that. This sales representative covers the New Jersey / New York area. Because Steinhouse's customers in the United States are also independent men's wear stores, the company entered the U.S. market with more or less the same marketing mix—aiming at the higher end of the market with products exported from the Montreal plant. In the U.S., while the compensation system is the same as in Canada, straight commission at 7.5% of sales, the salespeople may also receive "draws" of approximately $1000 to $2000 per month.

The company has never spent money on advertising except for 1998 when it created a colour catalogue, at a cost of $25 000, and mailed it to its existing customers. The company participates in a number of trade shows. Steinhouse supported its reentry into the United States in 1996, for example, by participating in trade shows. At the trade shows, it often succeeded in winning some accounts. They participated for five years, two seasons per year. Each year cost about $60 000, which is expensive in Mark's opinion, but the government subsidized each year by about $20 000.

PRICING

Retailers pay anywhere from $22 to $70 for Steinhouse sweaters. However the average price is approximately $40. Steinhouse's average gross margin is approximately 40% of sales and its receivable-days is about 95. Customers of the retail stores pay an average of $80 to $100 for a Steinhouse sweater. In contrast, the average retail price for an imported sweater is $40 or lower. In 1998, 67% of all sweaters sold in Canada were imported. These were mostly women's and children's. The major source of imports in 1996 was Hong Kong (transhipped from China), the United States, China, Italy, and Taiwan. Today in Canada, retailers have difficulty if they merely sell the sweater at double the price they paid for it. A typical retail store must have a gross profit of 50% after markdowns.

COMPETITION

In Canada, the major sweater manufacturers are located in Ontario, Quebec, and Manitoba. In 1996, the total sales of sweaters in Canada—domestic production and imports— equalled $0.5 billion dollars. According to Steinhouse Knitting management, a number of plants that specialized in men's sweaters have closed in recent years (Exhibit 2). Current competition includes Cooper Knitting and San Remo Knitting in Montreal. Cooper

Knitting has approximately 50 employees and San Remo Knitting has over 100 employees. In Toronto, Straton Knitting has over 100 employees and Standard Knitting, in Winnipeg, Manitoba, has over 100 employees. Competitive profiles are shown in Exhibit 2.

In the view of Steinhouse management, competition is surviving because they are concentrating on the U.S. market. Others survive by reorienting their production to suit the demands of Wal-Mart and Zellers. Consequently, they operate more downmarket than Steinhouse Knitting does. They sell 100% acrylic or 100% cotton sweaters to these discount stores at $12 to $13 per sweater. While the material and the machinery might be the same, the sewing and cutting of lower-quality sweaters is inferior to Steinhouse sweaters. Furthermore, these downmarket competitors do not finish their sweaters the same way Steinhouse does.

In fact, there has been a polarization in the marketplace. Steinhouse products are too expensive for Price-Costco, Wal-Mart, and Zellers. These stores buy directly from Asian manufacturers, who require letters of credit. Steinhouse is at a big disadvantage in terms of financing as well as labour. Steinhouse sells in the fall for delivery in March and is paid an

EXHIBIT 2	**Competitive Profiles**					
Name	Location	Age in Years	Employees	Sales ($000 000)	Exporting	Main Product
Boutique Knitting Mills[a]	Montreal	24	175	<$25	Yes–U.S., Europe, Aus. <$500 000	Ladies' sweaters
Grace Knitting[b]	Montreal	15	39	>$25	Yes–U.S. <$100 000	Ladies' sweaters
Niagara Knitting[c]	St. Catherine's	8	45	<$5	No	Uniforms and school sweaters
Standard Knitting Ltd.[d]	Winnipeg	23	100	<$25	Yes–U.S., Europe, Latin Amer.	Men's sweaters
Straton Knitting Mills Ltd.[e]	Toronto	57	175	<$25	Yes–U.S., Japan, Asia <$1 000 000	Men's sweaters
San Remo[f]	Montreal	–	100	<$10	–	Men's sweaters
Cooper Knitting[g]	Montreal	70	50	<$10	Yes–U.S.	Men's sweaters

a. This company produces sweaters for men, boys, women, and girls in acrylic, wool, nylon, polyester and cotton.
b. This company produces sweaters for men and women, boys and girls, in wool, acrylic, and cotton.
c. This company produces primarily sweaters. Occupational clothing is secondary. They use standard materials and produce for the RCMP, Canada Customs, Correctional Services, and different police forces. It specializes in wind proof, lined sweaters.
d. This company produces primarily sweaters but also operates in the sporting goods industry. It uses cotton, wool, cashmere, silk, linen, and various blends. Its brand is Tundra.
e. This company mostly manufactures sweaters; it also produces some shirts. It uses the standard materials.
f. This company was owned by Dylex. Over 86% of its sales was to Tip Top, also owned by Dylex. Dylex sold Tip Top to Graft & Fraser, and San Remo is now for sale.
g. This company manufactures sweaters, with some private branding. It uses standard materials.

average of 95 days after that. The high end of the market, on the other hand, sells the Italian brands—sweaters that sell for $200 or more. The large department stores focus on the name brands such as Nautica, Polo, Tommy Hilfiger, and Point Zero at slightly lower prices. So with their customers, the independent boutiques and small chains disappearing, Steinhouse Knitting is in a precarious position.

THE COMPANY: CURRENT PERSPECTIVES

Management believes that they have a company that is financially sound. The firm has no long-term debt. Finance is therefore not a constraint on decision-making. If they had to, they could buy new technology or different kinds of raw materials. They also believe that they have tremendous experience in manufacturing and selling men's sweaters.

THE FUTURE

Both Abe and Mark feel that producing ladies' sweaters is not a viable option. The ladies business is very competitive and they would have to compete against extremely competent businesses. In any event, it is a very different business—in management's view, as different from their current business as marketing is to finance.

Abe and Mark also feel that getting into department stores is not feasible. Department stores in Canada have, in fact, almost disappeared. Only The Bay and Sears remain, and they sell mostly imported sweaters or name brands. The discounters such as Wal-Mart and Price-Costco buy in such large quantities that they do not need wholesalers and purchase directly from manufacturers in low-wage countries. Both Abe and Mark believe that Steinhouse cannot match the prices of the imported sweaters.

One possibility is changing the mix of yarn in the sweaters. Some customers, particularly in the United States, have made such demands. By adding a bit of cashmere to the sweaters, for example, it is possible that the established brands of Steinhouse may be perceived differently. But they cannot compete with the Chinese who produce cashmere. Cashmere yarn costs $50 per pound and it takes 1.5 pounds to make a sweater.

Another possible route for survival and prosperity is to make a bigger push into the U.S. market, since Steinhouse can export to the United States virtually duty-free. The independents are also disappearing in the United States, but it is such a big market that it is still possible to get 100 or 150 stores as customers—enough to be profitable. In addition, the low value of the Canadian dollar relative to the U.S. dollar is a big advantage. But the United States is a difficult market. Abe and Mark believe that to succeed they will have to modify their product, but in a way that it is different from American styles. Continuing to focus on the European styles is the answer, they believe. Right now they are crawling along but the goal is to double U.S. sales in the next two years. That target will depend on producing a lot more "big and tall" sizes.

A final alternative is to continue supplying customers who would like to have traditional Steinhouse products in their stores. At the same time, they could also import the type of sweaters that Steinhouse does not produce, from low-wage countries, and sell these to a different market segment. Sweaters imported from Asia, Italy, or Turkey would also yield a 35 to 40% gross margin. One consequence obviously is that the plant will continue to operate below capacity.

EXHIBIT 3	Some Salient Characteristics of the Clothing Industry

The clothing industry is labour intensive and can function with a limited number of special skills; it is therefore manufactured in almost every country of the world. Low-wage developing countries with an abundant supply of labour provide tough competition to countries such as Canada.

Statistics Canada classifies Clothing (SIC 24) into four sub-groups: Men's and Boy's Clothing (SIC 243), Women's Clothing (SIC 244), Children's Clothing (245), and Other Clothing (SIC 249) which includes sweaters, hosiery, fur, and occupational clothing.

In 1997, men's and women's clothing accounted for 68.1% of manufacturing output of this industry. Other clothing accounted for 25.8%, and children's clothing for 6.1%.

Clothing is manufactured in all regions of Canada except the territories. Fully 62% of establishments were located in Quebec in 1997, accounting for an equal% of the industry's shipments and 57.1% of employment. Ontario was home to 22.5% of establishments and produced 25.2% of the shipments.

Shipments originating in Quebec rose by 5.4% over the past decade, despite a decline of 42.5% in the number of establishments, indicating that there has some consolidation of apparel production and efficiency gains.

The industry as a whole has been slow to adopt advanced manufacturing technology, although some sub-sectors such as knitting (which is more capital intensive than other sub-sectors) and men's wear (which is less susceptible to style changes) have been quicker to embrace technological advancement.

The clothing industry consists of many small establishments. Of the 1665 establishments in 1997, 74.5% employed less than 50 people and contributed only 28.1% to the value of total shipments.

Canadian households in 1988 spent 6% of their personal disposable income on clothing and footwear. That was reduced to 4.7% in 1998. The demand for apparel has been affected by other competing priorities, such as the purchase of computers and electronics, by a trend towards shopping in discount stores, and by consumers' increased insistence on good value for the price paid.

Since 1989, domestic shipments of clothing have decreased persistently, except for 1995. Manufacturers have only been able to maintain the present level of production as a result of phenomenal growth in exports. While imports doubled, exports in 1998 were five times the value of 1988.

Source: Yasmin Sheikh, "Has the Clothing Industry Adapted to the Changing Economic Environment?" Statistics Canada site, December 1999 <www.statcan.ca/english/freepub/34-252-XIE/1999/34-252.htm>, accessed November 9, 2002. Yasmin Sheikh is a Statistics Canada economist in the Manufacturing, Construction and Energy Division of Statistics Canada.

Both Abe and Mark were wondering what they should do. They are very comfortable and can afford to close the business. They want to stay in business, however. They also know that cycles change. Sweaters will be in fashion again and Abe is committed to be more demanding on his customers when it becomes a seller's market. The biggest fear is that as the market changes, there will be nobody to sell to. Exhibit 3 provides some salient characteristics of the clothing industry in general, of which the sweater industry is a part.

Agri Train Inc.

Thomas Funk

Although his firm had been successful for a number of years providing marketing and sales training for agricultural companies, Tom Jackson, president of Agri Train, was wondering if the time was right to introduce a major new product line. Since the company's inception in 1982, all training programs had been conducted in face-to-face, classroom-type settings. Agri Train was very good at this traditional method of delivery, having a number of long-term, highly satisfied clients. Tom was not thinking of dropping this service, but was contemplating the introduction of a new service using online delivery of training programs. Given the rapid expansion of Internet use, Tom thought it might be time to move in this direction. He was unsure, however, of whether the market was really ready for this approach, and how he should proceed with the idea.

AGRI TRAIN INC.

Tom Jackson established Agri Train Inc., located in Milton, Ontario, in 1982 to provide marketing and sales training programs for agribusiness. Over the 17 years the company

This case was prepared by Thomas Funk of the Ontario Agricultural College at the University of Guelph. Much of the data in the case was developed by a group of undergraduate students at the University of Guelph as part of a project undertaken for an international marketing competition hosted by the National Agri Marketing Association in Kansas City, Missouri. The case is designed for classroom discussion and is not designed to illustrate either effective or ineffective handling of administrative problems. © 2000 by Thomas Funk. Reprinted with permission.

had been in business, revenues grew from just under $100 000 in the first year to $1 200 000 in 1999. In addition to Tom, Agri Train employed three full-time trainers and one full-time administrative assistant.

Agri Train's product line consisted of programs in marketing and sales. All of the company's programs were custom-designed and offered for clients in all parts of North America. Current clients consisted of both large and small companies in the seed, chemical, machinery, animal health, and feed industries.

A typical Agri Train program was three days in duration and normally held at a central location such as a hotel or a company's training centre. Although participants included middle and senior management, most were sales representatives. The usual number of participants at a program varied from 15 to 25.

Although Agri Train programs were custom-designed for individual clients, they were built around standard course modules. The customization usually consisted of changing the mix of course modules used, and some cosmetic changes such as use of the client's logo on visual materials.

Two Agri Train programs were very popular and accounted for nearly 75% of the company's revenue. The first of these was called Principles of Agri Marketing (PAM). This program was targeted at sales reps and designed to provide basic marketing skills. As in all Agri Train programs, the method of instruction consisted of lecture/discussions and case studies. PAM topics normally included:

- Marketing Strategy Planning
- Financial Analysis for Marketing Decisions
- Marketing Products and Services
- Building a Marketing Mix
- Customer Buying Behaviour

A second Agri Train program was called Strategic Agri Selling (SAS). This program was also targeted at sales representatives and designed to develop basic selling skills. In addition to lecture/discussions and case studies, this program involved role-playing sales situations. SAS topics normally included:

- Preparing for a Sales Call
- Opening a Sales Call
- Probing for Information
- Presenting Features and Benefits
- Handling Objections
- Closing the Sale
- Followup Service

THE ONLINE OPPORTUNITY

Agri Train had always relied heavily on computer technology in developing and presenting programs. It was one of the first training companies to adopt computer-generated graphics in the late 1980s when this technology was first developed. More recently, Tom experimented with digital video in presentations. For years the company used analog video in taping role-plays for subsequent analysis and discussion.

In July 1999, Tom attended an American Marketing Association conference on the use of online educational programs. Although the conference was designed mainly for university people who might want to start teaching online, Tom immediately recognized that this approach might be appropriate for the type of training programs his company conducted.

Online educational programs utilized the Internet as a delivery mechanism. Instead of face-to-face lectures, narrated PowerPoint presentations were used to deliver conceptual material. Various conferences were designed in chat rooms to allow participants to discuss cases or exercises. Assignments were completed using word processing programs and sent to the instructor as attachments. Tom was absolutely amazed at the versatility of this approach and began to think about how he might use this approach in his own company.

In October 1999, Tom signed up for a four-week online training program offered by the Ontario Agricultural Training Institute (OATI) entitled "Achieving Exceptional Customer Satisfaction." It was during this course that Tom really began to appreciate the power of online delivery. Although the course only attracted eight participants, that was a sufficient number for Tom to see the ability of online delivery to facilitate participant interaction. Each week the participants were given case studies to read and discuss and it was not uncommon for there to be a hundred or more interactions among the eight people. Not only were there numerous interactions but, in Tom's opinion, the quality of the interactions was superb. Tom was also very impressed with the quality and quantity of individual feedback provided by the instructor. On the basis of this experience, Tom became convinced that the online method of delivery was a viable alternative to more traditional methods.

After completing the OATI course, Tom began to investigate the feasibility of adopting this approach for Agri Train. He started to assemble information on the costs associated with online delivery as well as the potential market for this product.

Because online training was a new concept, cost information was difficult to estimate. Based on information gleaned from a number of sources, Tom developed the following cost estimates:

- Course development costs could range anywhere from $30 000 to $50 000 for a single course. This included the development of teaching material, software development, and programming. Once a course was developed it would cost at least $10 000 each year to update material and technology.

- Getting involved in online training would require more administrative support than the company currently had available. Tom felt this would cost an additional $50 000 each year.

- Because of the method of delivery, instructors for online courses could be retained on a per-course basis. Hiring the type of people required would probably cost Agri Train $150 per hour of instruction time. Tom estimated that it would take approximately 30 minutes per student per week of an instructor's time to provide basic instruction and feedback. Higher levels of individual feedback would require much greater instructor involvement, perhaps as much as one hour per student per week. Although the three people on staff at the present time were excellent in delivery of face-to-face training programs, Tom was not sure they were the proper people to deliver an online program. In addition, they were all fully occupied with current duties.

- Several Internet providers were willing to support online training. Their fees for hosting a course were in the vicinity of $15 per week per participant. This included Internet access as well as some technical support for participants.

- The cost of teaching materials varied a great deal depending upon the subject matter. Tom felt that $15 per participant per week would be a high estimate.

Although Tom had been involved in the training business for a number of years, online training was so new that he did not have a feel for this market. Consequently, he decided to do some marketing research prior to making decisions about this new venture. He retained the services of Kelso Marketing Research to conduct a telephone survey of 50 randomly selected agribusiness organizations in Canada and the United States. There were several main objectives of this research:

- To determine the size of the market for training in general
- To determine the type of training currently undertaken
- To determine the likely demand for online training

Summary results of this study are presented in Appendix A.

TOM'S DECISION

Armed with the cost and market data, Tom started to think about how he might expand his business to include online training. It was fairly apparent that the major short-run opportunity would be in sales training. Most agribusiness companies used sales training for their employees, and there appeared to be some dissatisfaction with existing programs.

Tom thought his first product would be a six-week introductory sales training course targeted at new sales reps. He thought this course could be offered on both a public and private basis. The public offering would be available to anyone who might want to take it. The course would be scheduled to run eight times a year and people from any company could sign up. This would result in a group of participants from different companies. The private courses would be sold to individual companies and customized to some extent to meet their specific training needs.

Both the public and private courses would contain essentially the same content as the current three-day sales training courses offered by Agri Train. Lectures would be in the form of narrated PowerPoint presentations. Agri Train would develop a number of video clips showing parts of sales calls that could be critiqued and discussed by participants in online conferences. An instructor who would monitor the discussion in the conferences would provide feedback. Participants would be expected to devote five hours each week to the sales training course. This made one week of online experience more or less equal to one-half day of face-to-face training.

Marketing the courses was a major consideration. Agri Train had not done much marketing in the past because there was a lot of repeat buying by satisfied clients. Moreover, word of mouth was an effective method in getting new clients. Tom knew he would have to develop an effective marketing program in order to be successful with the new online venture. Ideally, the online courses would be sold to new clients so as to not cannibalize existing face-to-face courses.

There appeared to be a number of ways he could develop a marketing program for the online product. One method was to hire one or more full-time sales reps for the company. Reps would use a combination of telephone and personal contact with prospects. A full time sales rep would cost Agri Train approximately $100 000 annually including all benefits and expenses.

A second method was direct mail. A nice direct mail piece could be designed and mailed to prospects for approximately $20 a contact. This included all the design work as well as the costs of distribution. Tom noticed that many companies were using CDs in direct mail. The advantage of a CD was its ability to demonstrate how the online learning system actually worked. Adding a CD to the direct mail would increase costs to approximately $25 a contact and would result in a one-time production cost of $30 000.

A third method was to use media advertising. The most logical publication to use was *Agri Marketing Magazine*. Sales and marketing executives in virtually all agribusiness companies received this magazine. One full-page colour ad in this publication costs $6000. *Agri Marketing Magazine* was published monthly throughout the year.

Regardless of the communication media used, a key issue was how to position the new product. Tom was not sure how to deal with this issue, but felt the marketing research would provide some insight.

In addition to developing a communication program for the online product, Tom also had to establish a price. This was a key issue. Normal industry practice was to establish prices on a per-participant-per-day basis. This, of course, was not appropriate for online training, so Tom had to think of other alternatives.

With all this in mind, Tom wondered if this was the right move for Agri Train at the present time. Online training seemed like the wave of the future, and if he could get established in the area before competition, he would have a real advantage. On the other hand, was the time really right for this move? Was the market ready to accept a fairly radical departure from current practice? If Tom invested in both marketing and course development and sales did not materialize, he could lose a substantial amount of money.

Appendix A

Market Research Summary

The objectives of this research were to determine the size of the market for training in general, the type of training currently undertaken, and the likely demand for online training. In total, 50 companies representing different sectors of agribusiness were interviewed in Canada and the United States. Company names were randomly selected from a listing of 2500 agribusiness firms found in the annual Marketing Services Guide published by *Agri Marketing Magazine*. It was felt that the 2500 companies encompassed virtually all agribusiness organizations in North America. The survey consisted of three sections. Section A focused on characteristics of the individual companies. Section B identified the various training programs currently used by these companies. Section C was designed to gain information on how people perceived online training and whether they saw this as a viable alternative to more traditional methods.

Section A

The first section focused on the companies themselves in terms of what they did, how large they were, and the number of employees participating in training programs. The purpose of this section was to get some idea of market composition and size.

How many employees does your company have?

Each company was asked to provide data on the number of people they employed. The responses from the sample companies varied greatly with the smallest having 10 employees and the largest having 85 000. The average company in the sample employed 410 people with 10% being involved in sales and marketing. All sales and marketing employees receive some training over the course of a year.

What business is your company involved in?

Respondents were then asked to list the type of business they were involved in. Possible responses were feed, seed, fertilizer, agricultural chemicals, farm equipment, financial services, and grain handling. Tabulation of the results revealed a good distribution among all of these sectors.

Approximately how many sales and marketing employees have access to computers and the Internet at home and at work?

Respondents were asked to provide the number of sales and marketing employees that had computer access at home or at work. Results showed that 64% provide computer access to all of their sales and marketing employees, another 12% provide computer access to more than 50% of their sales and marketing employees, while the remaining 24% provide computer access to less than 50% of their sales and marketing employees. These statistics decreased slightly when respondents were asked to give the number of employees who also had access to the Internet at home or at work.

Section B

The purpose of this section was to identify the different training programs currently in use. Information such as the styles of teaching, length, and frequency of the course, cost, amount of feedback provided, and level of satisfaction were explored.

What are some internal and external training programs that you have provided to your sales and marketing employees on either an individual or group basis over the last two years? What are some of the characteristics of these programs?

The main types of training programs used by companies were, in order of popularity:

- Sales training
- Product training
- Marketing training
- Time management

The majority of programs appeared to be customized to the needs of the individual companies. Only a small percentage of the programs were generic. Almost all of the programs were purchased from external suppliers as opposed to being provided in-house. The sample companies listed a large number of external suppliers.

Respondents were also asked to state the methods of instruction used in training courses. The most common methods were:

- Lecture
- Video
- Case

Most of the training programs were either one, two, or three days in length. The remaining programs were all less than one week in duration. Most of the courses were held either annually or biannually.

The range in the costs of these programs was from $3000 to nearly $30 000. The cost per participant per day varied from a low of $250 to a high of $600. The average cost was $500 per participant per day. These costs included:

- Fees and expenses paid to the training supplier
- Travel, food, and accommodations for participants
- Facilities for the program

The costs do not include the value of time away from work for program participants.

Not surprisingly, the number of participants in each course varied greatly. In most companies all sales and marketing people took some training each year. As a result, the number of potential participants can be directly linked to the number of people employed in sales and marketing.

Most respondents confirmed that their training courses provided some feedback. This feedback took many forms, including individual followup by the trainer, tests, and role-play sessions. All respondents stated that feedback was something they valued a great deal and was an area that needed considerable improvement.

The data showed that while most respondents felt that training programs were effective, many stated that there was definitely room for improvement.

Are there other programs that you would like to see? How would they be structured?

When asked to list any training programs they would like to see, most people responded by saying that they would like to see more customized programs related to their company, products, and people. Virtually all respondents stressed the fact that sales training programs were the highest-priority training activities in their companies.

In your company, what are the biggest problems you have faced with the training of employees?

This question was asked to determine limitations of traditional methods of training. The most frequently cited responses to this question were:

- Time required to do training and have people away from their work
- Costs associated with travel, lost production, and the training program itself
- Finding training programs that meet the needs of the individual
- Identifying the skills that require improvement
- Finding time to complete the training and getting everyone into one central location
- Lack of ability to measure the impact of training on an individual or group basis
- Lack of individual feedback to participants during and after a training program

Section C

The last section of the questionnaire was designed to gain information on people's perceptions of online training. This information included awareness, benefits, concerns, and price.

Prior to this interview, have you ever heard of or have you used online training?

Two-thirds of the respondents confirmed they had heard of online training. Twenty percent stated they had heard of and actually investigated online training. Only 8% of the respondents stated they were using online training at the present time.

Where did you hear about online training?

The most common ways people had become aware of online training were:

- The Internet
- Magazines and newspapers
- Universities
- Training suppliers
- Colleagues
- Other companies

List the benefits you think online training might provide your company.

The most significant benefits identified were:

- Lower costs
- Increased convenience
- Can learn at own pace
- Flexible to needs and schedule
- Superior feedback and interaction

List any concerns you think you might have with online training.

The most significant concerns identified were:

- Not enough interaction with other participants or the instructor
- Motivating trainees to actually do the program
- Participants may not have the required technology or feel comfortable with this technology
- Difficulties in monitoring performance
- May be hard to provide good feedback

Assuming that online training in sales and marketing were available at a reasonable price, would your company be interested in trying this method of delivery?

In responding to this question:

- 12% stated that they definitely would try online training.
- 20% stated that they probably would try online training.
- 36% stated that they may or may not try online training.
- 28% felt the probably would not use online training.
- 4% said they definitely would not use online training.

Would you expect this type of training to be, on a per-student basis, less expensive than, as expensive as, or more expensive than traditional training?

Nearly 72% of the respondents felt online training would be less expensive than traditional training; another 20% felt that online training would cost the same as traditional training; while the remaining 8% felt online training would be more expensive.